Last Steps

Last Steps

Maurice Blanchot's Exilic Writing

Christopher Fynsk

FORDHAM UNIVERSITY PRESS

NEW YORK 2013

Copyright © 2013 Fordham University Press

All rights reserved. No part of this publication may be reproduced, stored in a retrieval system, or transmitted in any form or by any means—electronic, mechanical, photocopy, recording, or any other—except for brief quotations in printed reviews, without the prior permission of the publisher.

Fordham University Press has no responsibility for the persistence or accuracy of URLs for external or third-party Internet websites referred to in this publication and does not guarantee that any content on such websites is, or will remain, accurate or appropriate.

Fordham University Press also publishes its books in a variety of electronic formats. Some content that appears in print may not be available in electronic books.

Library of Congress Cataloging-in-Publication Data

Fynsk, Christopher, 1952–
  Last steps : Maurice Blanchot's exilic writing / Christopher Fynsk. — 1st ed.
    pages cm
  Includes bibliographical references and index.
  ISBN 978-0-8232-5102-5
  ISBN 978-0-8232-5103-2
  1. Blanchot, Maurice. I. Title.
  B2430.B574F96 2013
  848'.91207—dc23

                                   2012046487

15 14 13   5 4 3 2 1
First edition

CONTENTS

List of Abbreviations vii
Acknowledgments ix

Introduction 1

PART ONE: SABBATICAL ACQUIESCENCE

1. Toward the Question of Peace 17
2. "The Indestructible" 34

PART TWO: REFUSAL/AFFIRMATION

3. Beyond Refusal: *The Madness of the Day* 57
4. A Simple Change in the Play of Words: *The Infinite Conversation* 76
5. Compassion for Suffering Humanity: *The Instant of My Death* 109

PART THREE: THE EXILIC STEP

6. The Step Not Beyond 125

Final Note: Through the Double Imperative 225

Appendix: Blanchot in *The International Review*   235

Notes   249
Index   299

ABBREVIATIONS

IC	Maurice Blanchot, *The Infinite Conversation*, trans. Susan Hanson (Minneapolis: University of Minnesota Press, 1993); *L'entretien infini* (Paris: Gallimard, 1969)
IMD	Maurice Blanchot, *The Instant of My Death/Demeure*, trans. Elizabeth Rottenberg (Stanford, Calif.: Stanford University Press, 2000)
MD	Maurice Blanchot, *The Madness of the Day*, trans. Lydia Davis (Barrytown, N.Y.: Station Hill Press, 1981)
NTR	Emmanuel Levinas, *Nine Talmudic Readings*, trans. Annette Aronowicz (Bloomington: Indiana University Press, 1990); *Quatre lectures talmudiques* (Paris: Les Éditions de Minuit, 1968)
OB	Emmanuel Levinas, *Otherwise Than Being, or, Beyond Essence*, trans. Alphonso Lingis (Pittsburgh: Duquesne University Press, 1998); *Autrement qu'être ou au-delà de l'essence* (Dordrecht: Martinus Nijhoff, 1974)
PW	Maurice Blanchot, *Maurice Blanchot: Political Writings, 1953–1993*, trans. Zakir Paul (New York: Fordham University Press, 2010); *Maurice Blanchot: Écrits politiques, 1953–1993*, ed. Eric Hoppenot (Paris: Gallimard, 2008)
SHBR	Maurice Blanchot, *The Station Hill Blanchot Reader*, ed. George Quasha (Barrytown, N.Y.: Station Hill Press, 1999)
SL	Maurice Blanchot, *The Space of Literature*, trans. Ann Smock (Lincoln: University of Nebraska Press, 1982); *L'espace littéraire* (Paris: Gallimard, 1955)
SNB	Maurice Blanchot, *The Step Not Beyond*, trans. Lycette Nelson (Albany: SUNY Press, 1986); *Le pas au-delà* (Paris: Gallimard, 1973)

TI Emmanuel Levinas, *Totality and Infinity: An Essay on Exteriority*, trans. Alphonso Lingis (Pittsburgh: Duquesne University Press, 1969); *Totalité et infini: Essai sur l'exteriorité* (The Hague: Martinus Nijhoff, 1961)

UC Maurice Blanchot, *The Unavowable Community*, trans. Pierre Joris (Barrytown, N.Y.: Station Hill Press, 1985); *La communauté inavouable* (Paris: Les Éditions de Minuit, 1983)

WD Maurice Blanchot, *The Writing of the Disaster*, trans. Ann Smock (Lincoln: University of Nebraska Press, 1986); *L'écriture du désastre* (Paris: Gallimard, 1980)

Note: Citations appear with the pagination for the English translation preceding the reference to the French edition. Changes have been introduced in the English translations where required for consistency within the context of this volume or for accuracy, but always in cognizance of the immense contributions of the translators.

ACKNOWLEDGMENTS

The cover design and the drafted image, *The Dust Devil* (based on a still from the work of Leslie Thornton), are by Thomas Zummer; for this gift, I want to express my deep gratitude.

Chapter 1, on the thought of Emmanuel Levinas, was originally published under the title "Sabbatical Acquiescence" in *Poiesis*, ed. Stephen K. Levine, Vol. 8, 2006, 18–39. Chapter 2, "The Indestructible," was originally published in *After Blanchot*, an issue of *Monash Romance Studies* edited by Leslie Hill, Brian Nelson, and Dimitris Vardoulakis (Newark: University of Delaware Press, 2005), 100–122. The appendix, "Blanchot in *The International Review*," was first published in *Blanchot's Epoch*, a special issue of *Paragraph*, Vol. 30, No. 3, Nov. 2007, ed. Leslie Hill and Michael Holland (Edinburgh: Edinburgh University Press), 104–120. My thanks to the editors of the respective volumes for their encouragement and to the respective presses for their permission to reprint these essays.

Introduction

"An engaged literature"? One cannot easily assign such a phrase to Maurice Blanchot's writings. But in 1981, Blanchot offered a rather surprising answer to a questionnaire from Catherine David on the theme.[1] "I'm sent back thirty years," he said, adding that this was a period when almost every writer on the left found this an irritating imperative for literature. Even Sartre himself, Blanchot observed, was obliged to reconsider this simplistic formula under the pressure of a call to answer the appeal that Blanchot had played an important role in drafting, the "Declaration of the 121."

Yes, he continued, the writer brings a cultural influence into play. But this power is ambiguous, and it always risks falling into the service of other powers. At its limit, he added, writing is not something that is in one's power; it is rather a search for a nonpower that refuses mastery, order, and all established authority. It is a search that requires endless contestation of every usurping authority.

He then risks an entirely different figure of engagement, pointing to texts "in the ancient period, when literature did not exist":

> The first, the one closest to us, is the Biblical story of Exodus. Everything can be found there: liberation from slavery, wandering in the desert, waiting for writing, that is, for legislative writing, of which one always falls short, so that the only tablets received are the broken ones that cannot make up a complete response except in their breaking, their very fragmentation; finally the necessity of dying without completing the work, without attaining the Promised Land, which is inaccessible as such, though still always hoped for and thereby already given. If, in the Jewish ceremony of Passover, it is traditional to set aside a cup of wine for the one who will precede and announce the messianic coming of the just world, it is understandable that the vocation of the (committed) writer is

not to consider himself a prophet or a messiah but to save the place of the one who will come, to preserve their absence from all usurpation, and also to maintain the immemorial memory that reminds us that we were slaves, that even liberated we remain and will remain slaves as long as others remain so, that there is thus no freedom (to put it too simply) except for others and through others: certainly, an infinite task that risks condemning the writer to a didactic, teaching role and, in so doing, of excluding the demand he carries within him and that constrains him to having no place, no name, no role, and no identity, that is, to being never yet a writer.[2]

For the trajectory of reading attempted in the present volume (and particularly in the case of the reading of *The Step Not Beyond*), a vital part of the essential is indeed there. The points of resonance cannot be enumerated in advance of the reading, but I will offer a few brief notes with the hope of offering this paragraph to its echo in the subsequent chapters of this book and advancing the passage to which they are devoted: those last steps to which Blanchot was impelled in the post-war period.

What would engagement (the translator has preferred "commitment" in accordance with established usage) be for the writer? Blanchot's paragraph suggests that it is to remain faithful to the imperatives of justice and freedom, despite the *double* burden implied by this infinite task. For, if the writer is drawn insistently and inevitably into a didactic stance, this is because justice requires, even if its ground is infinite, a constant sociopolitical vigilance. For the responsible intellectual, there is no escaping the imperative of the public role. But the latter imperative insistently draws the writer away from the more uncertain and difficult responsibility that is inextricably tied to the first and that requires him or her to be forever less than a writer, to assume an anonymous function that consists in *engaging and holding open* the infinite relation from which a community of freedom might be announced—even if this is never by the one writing and never for them. This is an unending task that requires an uncompromising stance: the contestation of any appropriating instance, be this some myth, or some other discursive authority (including the discourse of reason itself). It requires, at the same time, an ever more resolute undertaking with language. Thus, an unending critical vigil as well as another waiting in despair and hope that takes form *from an experience of fragmentation* (hence with language) and in the temporality of "return": always from the knowledge that one cannot expect to see the fulfillment of a promise that is nonetheless already obscurely given together with the exigency of writing.

Opening and holding open the place for another in a becoming anonymous, refusing the seductions of the name and any order that would claim or occlude this space. Engagement, for Blanchot, was thus to engage *the exigency of a different relation* from which the imperatives of justice and what Blanchot too rapidly evokes in the preceding passage under the name of freedom (the word is normally too philosophically charged for him) became ever more insistent. We hear the call to such an engagement from the very first line of *The Step Not Beyond*: "Let us enter this relation."[3] For the Blanchot who endeavored, after the war, never to forget (his reference was to oppression and the Shoah, of course, but the imperative also extended, we may presume, to his own slavery[4]), writing had to hold to its infinite commitment to justice and *therefore* had to become an act of going out to the other; it had to assume the imperatives of exile and hospitality. Blanchot's writing thus became *ever more* hospitable and *ever more* exilic, I want to suggest, as he proceeded in what I am calling his last steps. "Peace, peace far and near." The task of honoring justice was not just double for Blanchot in the sense that it might involve two equally demanding but perhaps ultimately irreconcilable exigencies, one oriented to social justice, the other addressing its ethical nonground. Rather, it involved the infinite undertaking of making the exigency of the one (bringing peace to those "near" in history) resound in and from the other.[5]

"Last steps." These have begun perhaps already (I cite *The Instant of My Death* with this phrase) during the period of the Second World War—perhaps in the conversations with Bataille. They appear in greater relief against the backdrop of a decisive refusal of the postwar technopolitical order (as we see already in *The Madness of the Day* and then more powerfully in the political writings of the late 1950s and thereafter). But they are not easily followed to the extent that they engage that crossing of a wasteland that Heidegger, in his meditation on nihilism, claimed would necessitate a change of language.[6] There, in that desert, they appear furtively with the imprint of "*le pas au-delà*"—the step not beyond.[7] But this figure conceals as much as it indicates, because the exilic movement in question carries beyond the order of representation, beyond the figural, as long as this latter remains ordered to some visual reference. Thus, terms like "disappearance" or "effacement" (which Blanchot links to the thought of a dying) are no less pertinent for this movement. They point to last steps (and beyond) because they indicate a passage for which barely a trace of another language is given—or that is given in sparse fragments and subtle alterations in the play of words, but which we must learn to read. They are steps into anonymity from a relation to *le neutre*[8] for which Blanchot's text gives a kind of posthumous testimony. ("*How had he come to will the interruption of the discourse? . . . And at once this had happened, the heart ceasing to beat, the eternal speaking drive stopping.*")[9] And they are no less difficult to hear for the fact that they are steps *into* an affirmation of community that acquiesces *without ressentiment* (in the sense of the term developed by Nietzsche) to becoming, separation and loss. "*And when this day fades, I will fade along with it. A thought, a certainty that transports me.*"[10] How do we receive the joyful acquiescence of such an affirmation; where does it take us? And where do we begin?

Let me emphasize again that we could take our departure from almost any point in Blanchot's literary experimentations in an effort to follow his exilic turn. The opening to the outside was always there (as soon as Thomas faced the sea . . .). But the passage evoked in Blanchot's statement to Catherine David directs us more specifically to the movement of thinking and writing that gathered in the decades following Blanchot's return to national politics in 1958. The reference to Jewish thought (and thus the influence of a renewal of a thinking companionship with Emmanuel Levinas) is obviously crucial. But, more broadly, Blanchot's attention to the writer's ethico-political task (which includes becoming something less than a "writer" in a search for a nonpower) reflects his experience of the preceding twenty-five years and is indicative of the degree to which he had carried a singular path of thinking and writing into an open engagement with the societal and intellectual convulsions of its time.

The broad lineaments of this later work, and numerous themes from it (friendship, fragmentation, disaster), are widely known. But if I am correct in describing Blanchot's response to David as surprising for most readers, it is because this work has received relatively little sustained attention. Blanchot's earlier, momentous contributions to modern French literature (starting with the two versions of *Thomas the Obscure*) and critical thought (in volumes such as *The Space of Literature* and *The Book to Come*) still hold a predominant place in the understanding of his achievements.[11] Literary scholars and philosophers, though, seem almost to hesitate before the works in which Blanchot submitted manifestly to the imperative of fragmentation.

Awaiting Oblivion, *The Infinite Conversation*, *The Step Not Beyond*, and *The Writing of the Disaster* have been available for some time, with sections of the second and fourth volumes receiving considerable mention. The latter attention, however, has not coalesced into a broad understanding of the thinking that unfolded in these works or the shape of their role in modern French thought. Few readers—though these few have made notable contributions to which I will return—have sought to confront them in a sustained manner. *The Step Not Beyond* itself has gone almost without commentary, despite the fact that Jacques Derrida devoted one of his most imposing essays to the "step" (*pas*) of its title.[12]

This situation is more than a little curious in light of the immense tribute paid to Blanchot's work by Derrida and by figures such as Barthes, Foucault, Lacan, and Deleuze (or Paul de Man in North America) and the part he played in opening the space that came to be called poststructuralism. Blanchot had helped deliver to modern French thought the most radical dimensions of Heidegger's challenge to the metaphysics of subjectivity. With Heidegger (in an often discreet accompaniment that stretched from the 1930s to the 1970s), he breached the horizons of phenomenology and ontology, all the while subjecting Heidegger's own thought to a disruptive repetition and finally a severe critical assessment. This rigorous but subversive repetition entailed drawing out the abyss in the experience of finitude that Heidegger had recognized but had left largely unexplored in his failed effort to found a fundamental ontology in the 1920s (Blanchot's long meditation on death may be read along these lines, but so may the thought of the *il y a* and some dimensions of *le neutre*). It also involved carrying the thought of language that surfaced in Heidegger's text in the 1930s to its extreme in what Blanchot was given to identify, with Derrida, as a thought of writing. Also with Heidegger (but one would also have to point to figures such as Kojève), but more immediately after Bataille and in the midst of sociopolitical struggles for which he did not hesitate to name dialectical materialism as the intellectual horizon,[13] Blanchot undertook to move beyond dialectic and the thought of the negative. He thus explored an affirmative thought of relation under the name of friendship and brought a singular articulation of Nietzschean affirmation into play even as he spoke (sometimes anonymously) for a practice of dissidence and helped bring the problem of the political relation as such into view. Much of this, of course, was pursued in literary experimentation and through a singularly literary thought that helped make the *question of literature* a guiding thread in some of the most revolutionary thinking of the twentieth century.

There is an immensely complicated history of reception to be written here, for which the preceding sketch offers barely a hint of the difficulties involved (even for the concept of such a history). Did the powerful gestures of the French intellectual figures to which I have alluded somehow eclipse Blanchot's ongoing contributions, despite the recognition paid to him? Obviously, one cannot underestimate the sheer force of these gestures for the generations of readers that took to them, and surely some generational effect compounded factors such as Blanchot's reclusion and the shadow of his prewar commitments. But it is clear that the texts of the authors I have cited lent themselves to "theory" (I refer both to a market and a mode of discourse) in a way that Blanchot's did not. Their difficulty was (and remains) notorious; these were *written* texts with distinctive signatures whose adoption in the marketplace of theory was never without betrayal. But they offered themselves to repetition and exchange (as discursive statements identifying a theoretical approach) far more than did Blanchot's writings. In short, Blanchot's thought remained *recalcitrant*. For many French writers and critical voices of the postwar period, these writings were even intimidating.

There was perhaps something more than difficulty involved here—difficulty and that strange effect produced by a Gallic lucidity and a no less singularly limpid prose at grips with an irreducible ambiguity. I have written elsewhere of the resistance in contemporary philosophy and theory to the thought of language brought into the twentieth century by figures such as Heidegger and Benjamin. I need not rehearse again my suggestions about the way the "linguistic turn" in modern theory turned past this form of exploration and what it enabled: for example, Derrida's thought of the trace, Foucault's elaboration of the thought of the *énoncé*, and Lacan's meditation on "the human that suffers the signifier." Blanchot not only pushed such thinking to new extremes, but he also pushed forward relentlessly on a path of literary thinking that never ceded to the discursive laws of conceptual articulation, even when its interrupted, fragmentary emergence (as "literary") appeared in juxtaposition with passages of critical or theoretical reflection. The juxtaposition—the fragmentation—only augmented the obscurity. Can we be surprised if this vital reference for the most advanced theoretical work of our time, this reference and this *interlocutor*, could appear in the space of public intellectual exchange as little more than a shadowy presence and pass unread in many important respects?

Clearly, there are substantial grounds for seeking to redress this situation. But it is not clear that it is best addressed at this point by seeking to provide a *better representation* of Blanchot's postwar contributions in relation to those of other figures in the broader intellectual and sociohistorical context. Any study that remains at the level of comparative critical and theoretical exposition runs the substantial risk of further occluding Blanchot's real interventions in contemporary thought. A greater understanding of the very nature of these interventions is required before any attempt to situate them in an intellectual history. Thus, the present study does not attempt a standard critical appreciation of Blanchot's thinking or achievements. It seeks, rather, to engage the movement of his thinking and to follow this movement through a textual topography for which even the word "complex" (to use a metaphor taken from the sciences) does not quite suffice. It attempts to follow, in particular, the affirmative dimension of that exilic step that defined for Blanchot the meaning of *engagement* and the strange impetus Blanchot attributes to the "nonpower" to which he alludes in his statement to Catherine David.

It is perhaps worth noting, here, that the attention given in this volume to the affirmative dimension of Blanchot's thinking counters a firmly established tendency to stress a negative or even morose turn in Blanchot's writing (a tendency most noticeable in Anglo-American criticism, but not restricted to it). Maurice Blanchot, I want to emphasize, cannot be understood as *dwelling* with the negative in his writings, however far he took his meditation on "the death that is the impossibility of dying," or on affects like anxiety or affliction, and however strong his tendency to turn to human suffering and a topic (not among others for Blanchot) such as the Shoah. There is the writing of a long agony, to be sure.[14] But his later writing is carried by a turn of thought, a passage in thought, that is indissociable from a yes. It can be challenging to draw this forth at times (consider, for example, the weight of the theme of fatigue in "The Infinite Conversation," over against the furtive signs of a form of releasement, to which I will return), but it is always to be found in the kind of attentive reading I have sought to practice. *On the way* in this reading, the question of language appears in a manner that has been frequently neglected in commentary on Blanchot, and the ethico-political import of his writing, both literary and theoretical, emerges to view. I have sought to bring the questions of being-with and community to the fore while moving toward the most enigmatic, but also overwhelming textual events—for example, the "Come . . ." with which *The Step Not Beyond* closes.

This is a reading that seeks to follow Blanchot's *thought* of an exilic passage at the limits of discursive possibility, and thus it is not inappropriate to describe it as philosophically oriented. But the reference to "philosophy" here can be doubly misleading, for the passage in question, as Heidegger intimated, leads beyond what could still take the name of philosophy in our time. Blanchot presents the enigma and challenge of a "recalcitrant" literary thinker who understands his practice to join with other usages of his time ("in correlation with certain possibilities offered by knowledge, by discourse, and by political struggle") in the questioning elaboration of an epochal turn that leaves nothing of the values bound up in the Book, or the founding concepts of onto-theology, untouched.[15] His writing (and the textual practice for which it calls) attempts to engage language in a way that is transformative for language itself. To follow such a movement, recourse to the concept is obviously inevitable. Blanchot himself was not above conceptual elaboration in long efforts of inquiry and examination. But his literary thinking and practice drew upon language in ways that ultimately require a different hearing and exploration. I thus reiterate a core point by expressing my hope that if the present study has distinguished itself in any way, it is by the form of textual engagement it attempts in an effort to draw out the traces of a speech ("of writing," Blanchot would say) that exceed the boundaries of meaning and open that *other* relation that Blanchot called "the fragmentary the neutral." I have thus held conceptual elaboration in abeyance even while reopening to reflection, wherever possible, questions such as that of community or the experience of finitude. The effort has implied an attempt to negotiate passages between literary and more theoretical or expository writing that are no less uncertain (no more *given*) than the relation between a writer's experience with language and an understanding of the grounds of the ethico-political relation in general.

"Last steps." The phrase echoes a Blanchotian motif that leads us back to the conversations with Bataille even as it evokes the later developments in Blanchot's text regarding the passage that is *le pas au-delà*. But its hint of a finality should be tempered, and for this purpose I might suggest that the analyses contained in this book remain, as far as the author's experience is concerned, in the domain of first steps, a phrase that is all the more suitable for the fact that it is Blanchot who guided me as I took up, with Jean-François Lyotard, the theme of infancy.[16] Indeed, an immediate link may be made between the last pages of the dialogue of *Infant Figures* and the attempt, here, to pursue an affirmative thought of passage or effacement. But I should specify that the actual genesis of this volume lies in an effort to approach a thought of ethico-political engagement that would not be forever caught in a stance of negation (even in the form of engaged deconstructive critique offered, for example, by Gérard Granel). This was not an effort to escape critique and contestation, but rather to find a ground (or nonground) for ethico-political engagement not beholden solely to the negative for the preparation of a transition in our change of epoch.[17] Reading Levinas on the motif of peace and something he named "a sabbatical existence," I believed I glimpsed the opening of the path I was seeking. This engagement with Levinas, which is presented in the first chapter of this volume, also carried me again to Blanchot.

I thus attempted to read Blanchot after Levinas with the motif of "sabbatical acquiescence" in mind. Because I was following a motif with a source in Jewish thought, I turned first to Blanchot's enigmatic pairing of two essays in *The Infinite Conversation*, one of which contains his most sustained statement on Judaism and the imperative of "going out." This initial step, which addresses many of the issues involved in the question of justice and the relation to the other (*autrui*, in the usage Blanchot takes over from Levinas), constitutes the first section of this book.

The results of this reading, however, were modest as regards my goal. The first of Blanchot's paired essays evoked a promise linked to the notion of peace (foregrounding the motif of exodus that I have taken in this introduction as my starting point). But the second, on Robert Antelme's *L'espèce humaine*, appeared to suspend it indefinitely. I was thus prompted to move on to the texts that had, in fact, first inspired my search in Blanchot for figures of acquiescence or affirmation comparable to the "yes" in Levinas's thought: *The Madness of the Day* (a narrative from 1949 in which we read the sentence on effacement cited earlier) and "The Infinite Conversation" (a narrated "conversation" from 1966, where we read the decision to leave the space of discourse). Of course, these are texts with very different structures and with concerns that reflect their respective dates. But both link forms of refusal, a notion that is fundamental to Blanchot's political thought, with an assumed passage into effacement. *The Madness of the Day* does this by pairing a resounding "no" ("A story? No. No stories, never again")[18] with a no less astonishing "yes." "The Infinite Conversation" enacts the same passage as a movement in and through language (become writing).

Readings of these two last texts made it feasible and imperative to take up, in turn, *The Step Not Beyond* and its opening invitation: "Let us enter this relation." But the step in question, as I have noted, is of a singular order of difficulty, and to prepare it I paused briefly over a third narrative, Blanchot's last: *The Instant of My Death*. The reason for this detour is that Blanchot explicitly links the motif of *le pas au-delà* in this text to the theme of human finitude and "being-with" via what he names "compassion with suffering humanity." Thus, a reading of *The Instant of My Death* allowed me to introduce questions relating to the topic of community and thereby approach a motif that is central to my reading of *The Step Not Beyond*. The thought of *le pas au-delà*, as I try to demonstrate in this reading, involves a singular thought of being-(and dying-) with. It moves at the limits of the ethico-political relation.

The analyses presented in the second section of this volume, then, prepare my reading of *The Step Not Beyond*, which stands alone in the third section. I attempt in this long engagement with the text (interrupted by a significant excursion into *The Unavowable Community*), the construction of a trajectory of thought and writing that spans a forbidding assemblage of theoretical, meditative and narrative fragments. This sketch of a textual movement that traverses the volume as a whole must be recognized as a risky and problematic undertaking, since the volume is fundamentally fragmentary in character. It inherently resists any gathering design—perhaps even in a schema like the one Blanchot offers for Exodus (but does such a schema gather?). As Blanchot writes firmly in one of its fragments, focusing on the "ex-" of "exteriority" and "exile": "*Seule* demeure *l'affirmation* nomade" ("There *remains* only the *nomadic* affirmation").[19] But the traversal of the desert it brings to figure in its principle narrative line also involves what Blanchot names in *The Unavowable Community* a "search" for the "final words" of a certain kind of writing: "*Come, come . . .*" and appears to embody at least one important stage of what Blanchot names at the outset of his volume, "a long course." *The Step Not Beyond* gives us the trajectory of this search in both reflective and narrative modes and effectively performs that invitation. It writes the conditions of a community whose claim still requires our thought.

I want to emphasize that the reading of *The Step Not Beyond* offered here does not pretend to saturate this text's space by any means. Even to attempt such a reading would be to neglect some of this volume's most explicit indications. Nor is it secured by sure conceptual reference points. In this respect, it moves as much by question and supposition as it does by argument, frequently entertaining irreducible ambiguity or a peculiar form of neutral writing. It seeks essentially to trace a path that branches multiply, to follow trajectories of thought and experience across the full volume. It does not focus on any particular theme (not even *le pas au-delà*, for reasons that will become clear in the course of this analysis). Instead, it tries an approach (in the manner of climbing); it attempts an experience with the text through close and sustained commentary. It is to be hoped, once again, that such a form of engagement will shed light on a range of critical Blanchotian motifs, and open fundamental questions regarding topics such as language, the relation of being-with, the ethico-political relation, and the task of writing. I hope, in particular, that this book will offer a new figure of Blanchot's becoming-anonymous.

Given my emphasis on the ethico-political dimension of Blanchot's later writings, I should perhaps add a note on this fraught topic in Blanchot scholarship and account for my decision to concentrate on the exilic movement that took shape from the grounds of what he called his "conversion" in a document from the early 1980s referring to his early political involvements.[20] Can one proceed so easily toward the question of effacement without renewed consideration of some of the pre-war and wartime history that precedes this turn in Blanchot's writing (that is, without the fear of participating in a different form of effacement)? The questions here are immense, but I believe that the excellent contributions of scholars such as Christophe Bident, Leslie Hill and Michael Holland (among a growing number of others) will justify my formulaic—necessarily reductive—statement that the turn in Blanchot's political stance whose aftermath I follow was both long prepared by literary experimentation and fundamental. A profound but inadequately thought disjunction in literary practice and ideological affiliations and commitments in the 1930s allowed the dramatic passage to a new thought of contestation once those commitments showed their emptiness and then, in the catastrophe, their complicity with oppressive, murderous forces.[21] The experiential and intellectual dimensions of this passage (the friendship with Bataille, for example) resist summary and require further documentation and study. I am convinced that the period between the onset of the war and the return to public politics in the late 1950s must have been a terrible one for Blanchot in many respects. But the statements made at the time of that return are clear; they are statements of unqualified refusal vis-à-vis political and ideological formations that Blanchot considered dead (and perpetuating a death he had known all too intimately). This refusal was grounded in deep reflection on the grounds and possibility of dissidence, and it was accompanied by an absolute commitment to social justice and concrete steps devoted to fostering political transformation on an international level. The commitment to social justice was also increasingly inflected by a reading of Levinas as the thought of the "outside" became inseparable from the thought of encounter with *autrui*. It is not easy to define or date the early impact of Blanchot's opening to Judaism (or to gauge what was offered to him in this respect by his friendship with Levinas), but his statements on the fact of this opening are firm. Whatever the remorse regarding past involvements and past errors (surely, it was there), I see no ground for understanding Blanchot's engagement with Jewish thought as finally anything other than affirmative.[22] I accept the powerful evidence of Blanchot's efforts in the period of the war and thereafter to answer for the "change" that occurred in him.

I hope that this summary statement will explain my inclination to move quickly toward the opening in Blanchot's thinking that introduced the question of an anonymous community. There remain, as I have noted, many important questions regarding the turn in Blanchot's political thought. But I understand the turn to be irreversible and to have issued in an effort to rethink the political relation as such. Of course, Blanchot intervened precisely and with great vigor in political circumstances in the late 1950s and for the decade that followed, as has been well documented; he did not retreat from political activism, even if his refusal of compromise was unqualified. But his political engagements were carried by an ethico-political impetus that exceeded any determinate political cause and still-current assumptions about political identification and affiliation. On this basis, I believe that Blanchot's participation in the events of 1968 was of capital importance. We know that important aspects of his experience of that year left him disappointed. But the thought of community that informed his participation in that revolutionary moment (and also took shape there) was at the heart of the political relation he was seeking in the postwar period. There was a direct link between this thought and the "messianic" hope to which "Peace, peace far and near" and *The Step Not Beyond* point. To the extent that the present study can claim an ethico-political orientation, it is insofar as it seeks the time and space of that hope.

In some respects, the statement I am making here might itself be considered a bit radical, a bit too fixed on a utopian moment in his text (the "impossible" opening of the promise of peace). Did Blanchot not always call for a *double* stance once he reentered politics in the late 1950s, one that would honor the imperatives of the dialectic for the cause of social justice? Blanchot was not above lending his name, as I have noted, to a precise articulation of positions. But the movement he was seeking, I believe, finally superseded the reference he maintained to the imperative of a dialectically defined struggle, and even the maintenance of a double practice. Indeed, it is not finally clear to me that the "double" imperative could be anything more than a provisional articulation that had to be upheld in painful acknowledgement of its inadequacy. He was ultimately seeking, I want to argue, a transformation of this double articulation whereby the political stance would be thought from the one he sought with his meditation on friendship and community. This is where the thought of *le pas au-delà* was leading. It is from here that we are to hear the redoubling of the word "peace."²³

With that assertion made, however, I do not want to urge a view that ends up excluding important elements of Blanchot's postwar political thinking and activism, or that forces his endeavors in a misleading manner. Blanchot himself was often quick to phrase political issues in a rather absolute way, to be sure. But he was also prepared to devote immense efforts to working through the painful theoretical difficulties to which I have referred in quite deliberate terms. For this reason, I have appended to the three sections of this book an essay composed some years ago on Blanchot's involvement in *The International Review*. I document there an articulation of the double stance and an emergent thought of literary "responsibility" that would assume the exigency of fragmentary writing. I have refrained from inserting this essay in the principal sections of the volume because its focus is not ultimately the passage involved in *"le pas au-delà."*

The question, "Why this Blanchot, why now?" has a final dimension which I want to touch upon briefly. As it happens, I have waited to read *The Step Not Beyond* for quite some time; in fact, it has constituted something like a distant goal for me. But the imperative of approaching it on this occasion in the course of addressing the issues I have discussed in this introduction presented itself with an unexpected urgency. And the pleasure of doing so via a return to texts as moving as *The Madness of the Day* or "The Infinite Conversation" has been of a special order.

There is, perhaps, a significant question to be addressed on "the times of reading." What do age and experience, literary and otherwise, enable and what do they take away? In the first version of my essay on "The Infinite Conversation," I described the stations in my reading of Blanchot. There is an intellectual trajectory involved that can be recounted with perhaps some degree of accuracy (involving a movement between levels of analysis), to which could easily be appended notes on existential and external factors. I can certainly recognize the sociopolitical and intellectual circumstances that prompted my return to the question of community, after thirty years, and topics such as peace. These determinations and the claims of a problematic (which have allowed me, at the same time, to limit my choice of texts) are relatively clear to me. But ultimately, I believe, there is no accounting for what makes one prepared to write—for the need and the sudden capacity, without capacity, to address a work such as *The Step Not Beyond*. I am inclined to recognize in this a kind of gift with a very complex temporal structure and multiple sources. This is why I have written this book with a sense of gratitude. Gratitude to Maurice Blanchot first of all, whose grace and integrity I had the pleasure of experiencing from afar, and then gratitude to those who have helped sustain my relation to his text, too many to name appropriately: colleagues, friends, and students to whom I have sought to offer it over these many years.

PART ONE

Sabbatical Acquiescence

ONE

Toward the Question of Peace

Almost midway through *Totality and Infinity*, Emmanuel Levinas makes passing reference to something he calls a "sabbatical existence." The phrase does not recur and is not significantly defined. But I think we may understand by it a form of life that would honor in its acts a relation to the infinite Good, and thus subordinate all work founded in need to the ethical relation.[1]

What are the conditions of this form of relation to the other and to the world? Is it possible to give this notion of sabbatical existence (introduced in largely theological terms with a reference to a notion of creation *ex nihilo*) an existential meaning that is philosophically grounded? By starting from Levinas's commentary on a portion of the Talmudic tractate "Shabbath" in his essay, "The Temptation of Temptation," I may seem to undermine any effort to seek in the phrase a worldly experience rather than a religious one. But I will implicitly follow Levinas along the difficult path of seeking the philosophical grounds of something he would finally understand as a religious meaning,² and attempt to grasp the structure of this "sabbatical" way of being from the basis of his understanding of an originary assent or acquiescence that would lie at the heart of the ethical relation and human subjectivity itself. By then linking this notion of assent to the structure of "saying" as it is developed in *Otherwise Than Being*, I hope to provide the means for understanding a worldly practice of the ethical relation.

Levinas's commentary on the Talmudic tractate takes its title, "The Temptation of Temptation," from Levinas's effort to characterize in the essay's opening pages a defining inclination in Western knowledge. It is a curious choice of title for the essay—though decidedly arresting—since it summarizes the essay's prefatory remarks rather than the body of its argument, which consists of an effort to describe an alternative path. It would seem that Levinas felt the need, on this occasion, to address a kind of remonstrance to his predominantly Jewish audience.³ But the message of these initial remarks is not without its pertinence for the contemporary theoretical and philosophical world, so I will take them for my own point of departure.

Levinas wants to describe with his notion of temptation something he calls the "condition" of Western man (NTR 32/71). It is the temptation of worldly experience: the lure of a life rich with possibility and guided by the assumption that all wisdom is drawn from the trials of history. Westerners, and this includes many Western Jews, Levinas says, oppose the severely defined existence offered by societies regulated by law and ritual. Sympathetic with the Christian vision of a "dramatic life" of struggle with the tempter, they want to explore the universe and know both evil and good. At the same time, however, they also want to preserve their security and independence. They want to hear the song of the sirens without succumbing to it. What is tempting for the Westerner, Levinas argues, is to be simultaneously outside everything and to participate in everything. In short, what is tempting is knowledge, or at least that form of knowledge that comforts an ego's need for both pleasure and independence. It is an infinite temptation, Levinas emphasizes, and his words here suggest that he might have taken considerable interest in Walter Benjamin's analyses of the structure of subjectivity and signification in the German *Trauerspiel*.⁴ But while Levinas shares with Benjamin a sense that we must rethink subjectivity and signification to find a way past the abyss, he does not share the temptation to the same degree, and quickly turns from this introductory theme in his essay. He dwells on it only long enough to emphasize that the privilege accorded to the form of knowledge he has described is evidenced in a morality that values an informed, reflective judgment over naive spontaneity and the "congenital narrowness" of the pure act. Western society demands that naiveté be raised to philosophy, which Levinas defines here as "the subordination of any act to the knowledge one may have of that act" (NTR 35/76). The act must be theorized, subordinated to a careful reasoning, so that "it will no longer leave the other in its otherness, but will always include it in the whole, approaching it, as they say today, in a historical perspective, on the horizon of the All" (NTR 35/76). Today, we would tend to speak rather of a "political perspective," I believe, affirming that the horizon is the political. But the argument would be the same for Levinas. "From this," he writes, "stems the inability to recognize the other person [*autrui*] as other person, as outside all calculation, as neighbor, as first come" (NTR 35/77).

Let us pass over the seeming anachronism here. After all, the essay is from 1964, and we can hardly fault Levinas for failing to anticipate the immense progress we Westerners would make in learning to theorize difference as we approached the millennium! How could he imagine this would become the order of the day? (Or did he in fact anticipate this potential progress and realize it would have little to do with a genuine step in ethical thinking and practice, in his sense of these terms?) However this may be, our concern with these pages must lie in grasping how Levinas proposes to think a form of action that does not issue from a crude reversal of the theory/practice hierarchy, or worse, from the childlike innocence of faith. How does he propose to think a different order of knowing?

The answer will come via commentary, that is to say, commentary on commentary addressed to the phrase from Exodus that the rabbinical tradition has used to characterize the Jewish response to revelation: "We will do and we will hear" [*na'aseh ve'nishma* (Exodus 24:7)]. Levinas will try to show us that this is not the simple reverse of the Western ordering of understanding and action.

The tractate to which Levinas turns in his commentary approaches the phrase by asking, first, whether revelation is not inherently a violent imposition of a message that can only be received in submissive acceptance. How could revelation be received freely if freedom is only consequent upon its event? How could the people of Israel have had any choice at Sinai, and how, therefore, are we to understand the character of their adherence? Is the possibility of responsibility something one can choose responsibly, and if not, what is the nature of the assumed responsibility? The Talmudic tractate goes right to the point by offering a literal translation of the sentence from *Exodus* (19:17) whereby "and they stopped at the foot of the mountain" becomes: "and they stopped under the mountain."

> Reb. Abdimi bar Hama bar Hasa has said: This teaches us that the Holy One, Blessed be He, inclined the mountain over them like a tilted tub and that He said: If you accept the Torah, all is well, if not here will be your grave. (NTR 37/82)

So there we are right from the start, Levinas exclaims: "*eyn b'rira*" (NTR 37/82)—no choice. The "difficult freedom" of being Jewish is a choice between the Torah or death, and thus not much of a freedom at all. For again, the teaching, which the Torah is, cannot be accepted after deliberation: "the recipient of the message cannot yet benefit from the discernment this message is to bring him" (NTR 36/79–80). So the beginning must be violent. Unless, Levinas says, we are dealing with a different form of consent from the one given after inspection: "Perhaps death threatens a betrayal." He continues:

> Reason would rest either on violence or on a mode of consent that cannot be reduced to the alternative liberty/violence and whose betrayal would be threatened by violence. Wouldn't Revelation be precisely a reminder of this consent prior to freedom and non-freedom? (NTR 37/82)

Folding revelation back upon a prior form of relation, Levinas urges that we consider it a "reminder" of a consent given before any exercise of a freedom of thought. The content of the Torah's teaching would confirm a prior form of adherence that precedes any possibility of temptation and that allows us to conceive of an exercise of reason that includes its prehistory when it comes into being (NTR 38/84). I will return to the temporality of this structure, but for the moment I want to continue to follow Levinas who notes and puts aside momentarily the question of an originary assent, an originary "yes."

He puts this motif aside to follow the tractate and to explore the nature of the alternative expressed in the phrase, "the Torah or death." The tractate, as Levinas reads it, insinuates that death is to be understood as historical existence without the Torah and it suggests, further, that even the

Torah itself is menaced since the Law says "no" to the violence of history and is preserved only in the frail human conscience. But being receives a challenge from the Torah, Levinas affirms:

> In challenging the absurd "that's the way it is" claimed by the Power of the powerful, the man of the Torah transforms being into human history. Meaningful movement jolts the Real. If you do not accept the Torah, you will not leave this place of desolation and death. . . . You will not be able to begin history, to break the block of being stupidly sufficient unto itself, like Haman drinking with King Ahasuerus. You will not be able to exorcise fatality, the coherence of determined events. Only the Torah, a seemingly utopian knowledge, assures man of a place. (NTR 39/85–86)

One might recall Benjamin, once again, for illumination of what Levinas is claiming here: specifically his protest against passive acceptance of the given order that is always underwritten by the history of the victorious and the assertion that this is how it had to be. One might recognize, further, that the history unredeemed by the conscience that embraces Torah is nothing other than the history faced by Benjamin's disconcerted angel who is driven backwards by an avalanche of catastrophic events. Of course, Benjamin's appeal to something he calls a *"weak* Messianic power" in the past's claim upon the present diverges considerably from Levinas's prophetic eschatology since it is embedded in Benjamin's own vision of dialectical materialism. Levinas does not think in such historicizing terms as he seeks the messianic conditions for peace. But when Benjamin writes that the dialectician who undertakes a redemptive critical practice (and that would be the dialectical materialist who accepts the hidden but critical role of theology, to which Benjamin points in his first thesis on history) "can't see history as anything other than a constellation of dangers," he is giving voice to a sense of responsibility not foreign to Levinas.[5] The dangers, for Benjamin, are formed by the narratives of the reigning ideologies that suppress revolutionary potential at any given moment. But the moment is also dangerous for the fact that both past and present hinge in the balance of the critical response. Messianism or death, we might say, and the response, no less for Benjamin than for Levinas, requires a philosophy of language that is not afraid of what theology has offered in its thought of revelation.

Let us now return to Levinas's commentary. He adds to what we have seen regarding the redemption of history the Talmudic assertion that creation itself hinged on the response of the Israelites at Sinai. The structure of response he is exploring has ontological import. In the tractate we read:

> And why did the earth become afraid? The answer is provided by the doctrine of Resh Lakish: For Resh Lakish taught: What does the verse [Genesis 1:31] mean: "Evening came, then morning, it was *the* sixth day"? The definite article is not necessary. Answer: God had established a covenant with the works of the Beginning. If Israel accepts the Torah, you will continue to exist; if not I will bring you back to chaos. (NTR 41/90)

Remaining in the language of the tractate (and thus a form of theology), Levinas continues with the following: "God, therefore, did not create without concerning himself with the meaning of creation. Being has a meaning. The meaning of being, the meaning of creation is to realize the Torah. The world is here so that the ethical order has the possibility of being fulfilled" (NTR 41/90). And then in conclusion: "The problem of ontology finds its answer in the description of the way Israel receives the Torah."

So the very meaning of ontology hinges upon the structure of acceptance we are considering, the "we will do and we will hear." Every inspired act, even artistic, Levinas suggests (NTR 42/91), follows this order of acquiescent engagement wherein commitment precedes articulation of that to which one has committed oneself—acquiescent engagement being the condition of any interpretation and understanding. Martin Buber attempted to restore this order to logic by offering a perfectly valid translation of the Hebrew, which gives: "We will do *in order* to understand."[6] But Levinas sees in the phrase a different mode of knowing altogether and argues thereby for the fundamental character of its apparent inversion of logic. It is a "sovereign" mode of knowing, he says, a way of knowing that is indifferent to the temptation of temptation since it effects a relation to the good that precedes any balancing of good and evil. It is a *"way of actualizing without beginning with the possible*, of knowing without examining, placing oneself outside violence without this being the privilege of a 'free choice'" (NTR 43/95). And following the tractate's reference to it as a secret "used by angels," he stresses that is a sovereign, but also utterly lucid assumption of responsibility. The theme will be familiar to Levinas's readers: Judaism is an adult religion; it is a form of knowing embodied in the alert integrity of Jacob, the virtue named "Temimut" (NTR 42/93).

So "Temimut" is the name for the ethically inspired mode of relation Levinas seeks to define. It is an integrity determined not by norms of conduct (since it precedes any articulation of such norms) but by the structure of a subjectivity that *gives itself* originally to the other. Temimut is the assumption of an originary exposure to the Good, the fulfillment of the Torah. To which Levinas adds:

> But here is where the logical integrity of subjectivity leads: the direct relation with the true, excluding the prior examination of its terms ... that is, the reception of Revelation—can only be the relation with a person, with another. The Torah is given in the Light of a face.... Integral knowledge or Revelation (the receiving of the Torah) is ethical behavior. (NTR 47/103–104)

The invocation of the relation to *autrui* is striking at this point and may even appear forced or dogmatic (at least for the reader who is not familiar with Levinas). But if we read carefully, we recognize that it has, in fact, been prepared from the very beginning of Levinas's commentary, from his first words regarding his reticence in using the word "God" and his insistence that comprehension of the Divine emerges only at the "crossroads of human journeyings" (NTR 32/71). The consent from which revelation unfolds *as a reminder*, derives, as Levinas quietly urges throughout the essay, from the very structure of human subjectivity.

The ego is allowed one more protest in this text. If assent to an alliance, or a "being-with," is originary, then are we to accept that the bonds of community are not the result of a free choice? Levinas's reply is lapidary. One reasons here as though one had witnessed the creation of the world, as though the world were the product of man's will, or as though there were some place to hide from creation itself. Scripture, he notes, reproaches Job with this presumptuousness of the philosopher (NTR 49/107). No, the finitude of the subject is such that we must think the emergence of the ego *from obligation* instead of positing an ego that is free to undertake obligation from some place outside the world. If the ego is to achieve real separation, it is only in and by responsibility, by the weight of the world that comes upon an ego that takes on responsibility for the suffering of the creature. The ego only truly separates in responsibility.

"We will do and we will understand." In *Otherwise Than Being*, Levinas will pursue such a sovereign form of action under the name of "prophetic witnessing." And here we meet a severe articulation of the temporal inversion to which Levinas alluded in speaking of revelation as a "reminder" of a prior consent. The subjective relation Levinas finds in "Temimut," the movement toward the other human being, is thought here from the basis of a radical diachrony of which consciousness knows only a trace: the traumatic provocation of an exposure that is both painfully fresh (like a wound) and already almost lost to oblivion, so faint is its scar. Human subjectivity is born, he says, in the response to a claim whose absolute urgency exceeds any conscious schematization or representation, any thematization. Indeed, the infinite obligation known in exposure to this always prior passing only reaches formulation in the response. Only in the consenting signification of obligation does the command take form.

> The order that orders me to the other does not show itself to me, save through the trace of its reclusion, as a face of a neighbor: through the trace of a retreat preceded by no actuality and that is present only in my own voice, already obedient—the hard present of the offering and the gift. (OB 140/220)

The command is articulated in the mouth of the one who receives it, and prior to any hearing:

> Witnessed, and not thematized, in the sign given to the other, the Infinite signifies out of responsibility for the other, out of the-one-for-the-other, from a subject supporting everything—subject to everything—that is, suffering for everyone, but charged with everything, without having had to decide on this taking charge that amplifies gloriously as it imposes itself. An obedience preceding any listening to the command. The possibility of finding the order, anachronously, in obedience itself and of receiving the order out of oneself. This turning about of heteronomy into autonomy is the very way in which the infinite happens. (OB 138/232)

The infinite passes through the assent of the obeying subject; it happens (*se passe*) in the linguistic event wherein the subject assents in an originary manner to the burden placed upon it. This is a linguistic "event" because the "yes" of voiced assent (OB 121/194), or in the passage we are reading, the "Here I am" of the subject's self-offering, is not in any way a representation of the relation contracted between the finite and the Infinite, the same and the other. The saying, rather, is the happening of the event itself, its diachrony. I referred earlier to the necessity of a philosophy of language; we see this necessity clearly in Levinas's assertion that the diachrony of transcendence can only be thought in and as saying.[7] Only in language, Levinas says, can a relation be drawn that absolves the other of relation and preserves its transcendence. Only in language could there be an exposure of and to the other that does not reduce the other, in advance, to the same. There is no experience of the Infinite or its glory, no epiphany of a face prior to or outside its receptive saying. Thus the saying of responsibility is a saying *of* the relation to the Infinite and as such it is *witness—prophetic* witness since obedience precedes hearing.

"There is witness . . . only of the Infinite," Levinas writes (OB 146/229)—an immense statement if one tries to link to it an understanding of *Otherwise Than Being* as a testament to those who died in the Shoah. It suggests, from this point of view, that witness to the events of the Shoah cannot possibly be reduced to speculation on what Auschwitz reveals of an inhuman, which Giorgio Agamben claims to give us in the figure of the Muselmann.[8] The inhuman, to the extent such a state can be identified (and it certainly cannot be heard, as Agamben pretends when he gives voice to this figure), offers no command. Witness to the dead of the Shoah or of the other holocausts of our history (to the "closest" amongst whom Levinas dedicates *Otherwise Than Being*) must evoke our *responsibility* to the dead in their human vulnerability and thus be comparable, in some way, to Levinas's effort to give voice to the command that comes in the encounter with the other's mortality. The face, Levinas writes, "is a trace of itself given over to my responsibility, but to which I am wanting and faulty, as though I were responsible for its mortality and guilty of surviving" (OB 91/145). The obsessive character of the writing in *Otherwise Than Being* is itself the saying of a kind of survivor's guilt, but we must understand this act of witnessing as the affirmative assumption of a command, a witness to the Infinite.

In *Otherwise Than Being*, this last phrase is underscored firmly, almost awkwardly. "There is witness, a unique structure, an exception to the rule of being, irreducible to representation, only of the Infinite. The Infinite does not appear to the one who bears witness to it. On the contrary, it is witness that belongs to the glory of the Infinite" (OB 146/229). Two points are conveyed here. On one hand, Levinas means to emphasize that the saying in which relation to the Infinite is both contracted and offered is an exception to the order of discourse in that it speaks without representation, without thematization or evidence. The trace of the Infinite brought to language in the saying of the witness is not a representation of a past presence. To grasp this modality of presentation in all its difficulty, and to give it its philosophical weight, we might perhaps start from what Heidegger sought in the phrase *es gibt* (arguing that the saying of essence that occurs in language could never be the object of conceptual grasp). But only Blanchot's and Derrida's thought of writing will bring us to what Levinas seeks to think with his notion of the trace. The difficulty of this latter thought and the problems it introduces for Levinas himself should not be underestimated, as Derrida powerfully demonstrated. But the general point to be made here is that the notion of the ethical relation requires a thought of language that exceeds the order of representation.

The second point Levinas means to convey in insisting that there is witness only of the Infinite is that witness is indeed *of* the Infinite in the sense that it is provoked by it, even required by it. The Infinite comes to language as a kind of exigency. Thus witness "belongs" to it as we heard a moment ago; it brings the Infinite to language in an originary manner, but in so doing, it *answers*. The subject's "Here I am" is implicitly "Here I am in the name of God," though witness so humbles itself that it cannot claim the grounds of its authority and will not risk reducing that to which it testifies to a theme. Again, it is without representation, else it is not witness (hence Levinas's extreme reserve in pronouncing the name of God). Of itself, and of the subject born in this saying ("Here I am"), there is no more than the expression of an inability to hide, converted positively into a repeated self-offering that recurrently strips itself of all reserve in an everpurer response, an ever more "sincere" expression of answerability and responsibility. This is not the recurrent exposure or offering of a subsisting being that would choose this engagement or even suffer it passively; the subjectivity of exposure gives over its own passivity in an exposure of exposure itself, a communication of its self-communication.[9] *Otherwise Than Being* reiterates this incessantly; the exposure of subjectivity is a giving sign of its own signifying. The testimony "Here I am" exceeds itself to say its own saying. Thus we could well describe witness as *giving language to the other*. The Infinite passes only in this offering to the other of saying itself.

This last formulation captures something of the essential poverty and extremity of witness—at its limit, it offers its own saying (or just its voice, as Levinas says at one point[10]) to glorify the Infinite, and nothing more. But saying, as Levinas emphasizes in *Otherwise Than Being*, is inherently a temporal occurrence; as we have seen, it is the saying *of* the event, *of* the passing of the Infinite. It says the time in which it is given to speak (still "nothing more," but already the possibility of every redemptive act). We might thus presume that an essential part of its glorification of the Infinite inheres in the way it signifies for the other (the fact of) its temporalization of the absolute urgency of the command that has provoked and directed it. How do we understand the structure of this temporalization?

Levinas asserts that every form of saying temporalizes in its manner of anticipating its own possibility. He mentions particularly, in this respect, gratitude and prayer (OB 10/24). To the extent that such forms of address are forms of saying, they fold to mark the relation to the transcendence that makes them possible. They all partake, in this sense, of the "intrigue of temporality" we considered in the phrase, "We will do and we will understand." But the self-testimony of prophetic witness would seem to offer its time most immediately inasmuch as it testifies to the emergence of subjectivity itself in the experience of the diachrony of transcendence. "Here I am" must implicitly say, "Here I am in my mortality," or "Here I am in my finitude" as it offers to the other witness of a passing that this responding subject has known only as a temporal lapse that refuses itself to any schematization or temporal synthesis. It says the time given it in giving its own time, which is originally the time of a traumatism, the time of a radical dispossession. The glorifying trace is thus borne in the evidence of the subject's finitude; it limns its finitude in marking the interruption and the immeasure that has exceeded the subject's capacity to appropriate this experience for itself.[11] This is why, appearing *as face* (and one will recall that the face is to be thought as trace), it appears with traits proper to the subject's own senescence or mortality. It is the trace of the other in the same, as Levinas puts it, and the subject cannot but offer to the experience of the other metaphors of its own finitude as it gives itself in substitution or conversion for the other.[12] But in limning the subject's finitude, its very exposure (and exposure must be understood here as *exposure to*), the trace is also trace of the absolute other. It is a trace of the opening of time that occurs in the relation without relation that is exposure to the beneficence of the Good. The saying of this relation glorifies the Infinite in giving evidence of the diachrony of transcendence. Levinas will thus say that the trace of this passing (without any present) *shines* as the face of the neighbor, and I do not believe we would betray the spirit of Levinas's argument by understanding the illumination of this face in relation to Celan's famous figure of the burning down of a candle on the seventh day.[13]

Indeed, I think we could very appropriately speak of the given time of testimony as a "sabbatical" time because Levinas does everything he can to separate the saying of the diachrony of transcendence from the schematizing production of past, present, and future in consciousness. Despite Levinas's own recourse to a notion of production at certain points, we should hear in the term a key link to the modern metaphysics of subjectivity and the role played there by the notion of labor, or work. When Levinas contrasts a "sabbatical existence" (informed by the positivity of desire in relation to the other) with one that is shaped by need and the work it informs, he opens the possibility of thinking the rest and peace proper to the Jewish Sabbath (celebrated in and through the release from work) from the ground of his understanding of the ethical relation. Likewise, he invites us to think the ethical relation in terms that might be informed by a speculative meditation on the meaning of the Sabbath. Thus, we might well say that the time of saying becomes "sabbatical" (and even, from a theological point of view, "sanctified," like the time of the Sabbath) to the very degree that the elected subjectivity assents to its own dispossession and "unworking" ("*désoeuvrement*") in exposure to the Infinite. Assenting to the orientation of the Good, once again, it draws forth the diachrony of transcendence as a kind of deferral or fold in the schematization of time produced in consciousness, an interruption or suspension of the temporalizing "work" of consciousness. It opens a sabbatical time—the very time celebrated each Sabbath.

But this conclusion still falls short of what I believe must be implied in a notion of "sabbatical existence" because the ethical relation, like the celebration of the Sabbath itself, is not separable from a yes to the world.[14] We have been following the notion of an originary assent that unfolds in prophetic witness. But responsible saying must also contain another form of acquiescence. Its offering of itself is inseparable from an assent to the world it offers for redemption; this is assent to a kind of burden (the burden of being itself), but it is also acquiescence to what in this burden exceeds the subject's power. In this latter respect, as I will attempt to show, the assent of responsible saying takes on another "sabbatical" trait.

It is Levinas's concern for justice, that is to say, for equity in the relations between the other and all others including the subject itself, that leads Levinas to argue that there is a kind of bridge between the ethical relation and the time produced in consciousness. Saying, as Levinas suggests in a marvelous phrase that may evoke for us Derrida's notion of "*différance*," "hesitates" between its saying of diachrony and the temporalization of essence; it preserves or reserves that opening even as it renders possible the order of commensurable relations required by justice.[15] But nothing is harder to think than this bridge between the ethical relation and the possibility of justice, as Derrida has himself shown,[16] and probably nothing was harder for Levinas given the strange way in which this crucial motif is reiterated but also held at bay in *Otherwise Than Being*, and then given only the briefest development in its concluding pages. Levinas is insistent on the place of justice, however, and the integrity of his thinking requires that the bridge be articulated.

One could argue that it simply could not be otherwise for Levinas. How could fulfillment of the command that is only given by the obedient voice have a redemptive value for all of being if the ethical subject were not directed by this command to just action? Only ethical saying glorifies the Infinite, but this responsible saying is never divorced from a concern for justice. Thus Levinas asserts that saying "calls for justice,"[17] and renders this justice possible by its reference to being (OB 7/18). It calls for justice, he says, because the neighbor to whom saying is directed is always in the presence of a third party; it is always also a face for a third that stirs consciousness to move in the realm of phenomenality and obliges it to raise the question of equity and thus define an order of intelligibility. Ethics is always already philosophy. But how can Levinas maintain the priority of the ethical relation while allowing this mediation in saying, this "contradiction" by which saying turns to the sphere of representation even as it gives itself to the other?

I do not believe Levinas ever explores the structure of saying enough (from the viewpoint of a philosophy of language) to enable us to find firm answers to these questions,[18] though he does make it clear that we must think the order of derivation in the relation of ethics and justice from the basis of his notion of temporalization. The opening of time in the saying of the diachrony of transcendence *orients* the constitution of meaning in the concern for justice, gives it its sense (*sens*). Justice, we might say, must be conceived as being always *with reference to the other* in the substitutive movement of responsible saying.[19] And for whom is justice to be conceived, first of all, if not for *autrui*—that other who is absolutely exposed in his or her powerlessness and vulnerability? Do not the figures by which Levinas identifies this other (widow, orphan, etc.) bear evidence of this first demand for justice? At the same time, however, the articulation of justice and equity would have no ethical basis were the face of *autrui* not also appearing phenomenally in relation to that of third parties on a horizon of commensurable relations.[20] And how would this horizon have been constituted if not in the subject's act of assenting to the burden of being for the other? Justice could only emerge as an exigency for a subject that is *with autrui* in allegiance or solidarity, giving itself unreservedly to the other and *for* the other to the point of assuming the world in which both exist in relations with others. If the demand for justice is truly more than empirical contingency, as Levinas insists, it can only take form in the subject's manner of assuming all being for the other.[21]

Thus we are led back to a recurrent motif from *Totality and Infinity* that is offered to account for the generation of a common ground of meaning in the ethical relation (the problem of justice as it is described in *Otherwise Than Being*), and in full cognizance of the radicalization of Levinas's thinking from one volume to the other, I believe we can retrieve the earlier motif to say that the responsible subject *says the world to autrui*. In the earlier volume, saying was described as both "apology," in which the self gives itself to the other (we see virtually the same thing in the theme of witness in *Otherwise Than Being*), and a giving of the world, to and for *autrui*.[22] The subject of this giving is conceived differently in *Otherwise Than Being* from the way it is in *Totality and Infinity*, but the act must be of a comparable nature.[23] Indeed, in *Otherwise Than Being*, we read at one point that saying "thematizes" being to enunciate it to *autrui* (18/35). Would not the very possibility of justice take form in this saying of the world wherein the subject necessarily situates itself in relation to *autrui* and thus in relation to the rest of its world, including every third party?

Heidegger argued in his works of the late twenties (including *Being and Time*) that the fundamental act of the Dasein would inhere in the manner in which it gives or announces to itself a world, understood as an order of signifiability where all meaning is ordered to the Dasein's concern for its own being. The very hermeneutics of the Dasein were to take their possibility from the way the Dasein gives itself to understand its being in the world and the facticity of its existence.[24] When Levinas writes that "Being is a world in which one speaks and of which one speaks" (TI 181/198), and that "to see the face is to speak of the world" (TI 174/190), he would appear to invoke a comparable notion, though here, of course, the saying of the world in which I cannot but situate myself is *for the other*. Whether or not this reference to Heidegger would sit well with Levinas himself, it is clear that if I perform the act of taking all being upon myself for the other, if I *convert* my existence that way, then I must articulate in that orientation the commensurable relations that are the ground of any justice. At the heart of responsible saying, there is an offering of peace without conditions, but it must also bring with it the means for representing that peace if it is truly ethical, truly an act of conversion for the other.[25] Justice can only be served in that manner; though, at the same time, proximity must continue to orient the concern for justice.

Would the concern for justice still belong to what we have called a "sabbatical existence"? Does the saying of the world (and the assumption of the burden of justice) not mark already a form of departure from the sabbatical relation? It would be hard to avoid this conclusion did Levinas not add a further, and immensely difficult, point regarding the nature of the subject's worldly being and what its act of saying must signify. He notes that the order of essence or being is inevitably experienced by the subject as entrapping or engulfing. He evokes here the "horror" of the *il y a* in its incessant murmur and rustle. The subject of representation represents itself as free and sovereign, but it inevitably finds itself subject to an anonymity and monotony in being itself that comes to grip it. In *Totality and Infinity*, this noise or undertow that afflicts being is attributed to the strangeness of the earth, to the material being on which the subject's *jouissance* depends. In *Otherwise Than Being*, we find a comparable linkage of the *il y a* and sensibility,[26] though the ambiguity of the *il y a* manifests itself here in the subject's entrapment in immanence and an endless resurgence of a horizonless inauthenticity, a hollowing out and crumbling of substantial being and a fading of essence. The theme requires long treatment, and it must be pursued via Levinas's dialogue with Blanchot. But I think it is possible to glimpse the implications of Levinas' assertion that even this experience of a meaninglessness that saps all determinations of being (and hence justice itself) is somehow given over to the other in the saying of the responsibility the subject takes *for all*. The subject, in substitution, bears all for the other, Levinas tells us, even its capture in the abyssal inauthenticity of the *il y a*. Indeed, he insists that the expiation of substitution is even made possible by acquiescence to the *il y a*, a susceptive or acquiescent taking-upon that in its "bottomless passivity" is prior to any act of reception:

> The self is a substitution for the other, subjectivity as a subjection to everything, as a supporting everything and supporting the whole. The incessant murmur of the *there is* strikes with absurdity the active transcendental ego, beginning and present.
>
> But the absurdity of the *there is*, as a modality of the-one-for-the-other, *signifies*. The insignificance of its objective insistence, recommencing behind every negation, crushing me like the fate of a subjection to all the other to which I am subject, is the surplus of nonsense over sense, through which expiation for the self is possible, an expiation which the oneself indeed signifies. The *there is*—this is all the weight that alterity weighs supported by a subjectivity that does not found it. (OB 164/255)

If the saying of responsibility were merely a giving of meaning, a significant world, to the other, the representing self would claim its rights; the identity of the elected or assigned self would take foot and affirm itself in the determinations of being. To achieve expiation in the ethical relation to the other, the subject must acquiesce to meaninglessness itself. "To *bear* without compensation, the excessive or disheartening hubbub and encumberment of the *there is* is needed" (OB 164/255). Thus, beyond apology, and beyond any gift of the possibility of justice to the other, though together with these and as the condition of their possibility as gifts, the subject must say yes, *for the other*, to the most abyssal dimension of factical existence. The responsible subject must acquiesce to the seemingly irredeemable dimensions of existence for the ethical relation to be fulfilled. Even the *il y a* signifies, Levinas asserts. But he does not mean that it is made meaningful. Rather, the subject lets its powerlessness over this dimension of existence be (instead of recoiling from it in work), and bears this very powerlessness for and to the other. It says yes even to the *il y a*; it gives this exposure to *autrui*.

Thus the "sabbatical existence" Levinas evokes in *Totality and Infinity* would entail more than an affirmation of a desiring relation that exceeds the subject's powers as they are expressed in the structures of production. Or rather, we might say that the condition of the peculiar peace known and celebrated on the Sabbath is indeed an affirmation of a relation that exceeds the subject's productive power, but not just on the transcendent side, so to speak. A full ethical existence is only possible when the subject acquiesces to its immersion in earthly existence. Only by acquiescing to its own material finitude can it find the possibility of affirming the limits of its power in relation to *autrui* and affirm this very exposure to the other as the giving of a sign that gives itself as saying. An ethical existence is irreducibly *of the world*, and existence becomes truly sabbatical when its saying entails the gift of finitude.

TWO

"The Indestructible"

In the reading of Levinas that Blanchot pursues in *The Infinite Conversation*, there is little response to what might be termed the first word of *Totality and Infinity*. Later, at the very end of *The Step Not Beyond*, and then in subsequent statements, we will hear an evocation of peace.[1] But in the long introduction of the question of *autrui* in *The Infinite Conversation*, the reference is essentially to a staying of violence and something Blanchot terms later in the volume "the exigency of a different relation" (IC 192/287). The form and ground of this other relation, however, does not come easily to definition, and it does not appear to be thinkable apart from what threatens to foreclose it, as Blanchot suggests in his disconcerting formulation of the impossibility of destroying its exigency as it comes to us obliquely in the presence of *autrui*: "Man is the indestructible, and this means that there is no limit to the destruction of man" (IC 135/200).[2]

Especially striking is the fact that this latter formulation (punctuating several dialogues in *The Infinite Conversation* in different phrasings) is pursued most directly and at greatest length in a brief essay, "Humankind" ("*L'espèce humaine*"—the title is taken over from Robert Antelme's volume by that name[3]), coupled to another bearing the subheading "Being Jewish" ("Etre juif")—the latter constituting what is one of Blanchot's most significant statements on Judaism. The essays are joined with the chapter title, "The Indestructible." Since "Being Jewish" may be construed as the description of a *form of existence* that bears witness to the exigency to which I have referred, the meaning of Blanchot's gesture of coupling the essays should give us pause. Is Blanchot proposing a question to Levinas that obliges us to address more severely (from a philosophical perspective, at least) what it means to go out toward the other and to receive the promise that opens in this relation? Blanchot's indications are muted, and my own answer to this question at this point can be only tentative, since it will require for its proper articulation the reading of *The Step Not Beyond* to come. But even if the texts immediately at hand do not offer the means of developing the theme of peace at any length, I want to take my departure from it, acknowledging by this means some of the circumstances that have made this problematic seem urgent, today. In a time when acts of torture and other forms of barbarism are normalized in our societies, the meaning of Blanchot's discreet response to Levinas via the motif of "the indestructible" seems critically important.

I will not review the beautiful pages from the beginning of *Totality and Infinity* that set Levinas's notion of peace against the privilege accorded to war in philosophical thought. I will retain only his critical assertion that peace comes about when human beings are able to answer for themselves, rather than lend their voices to the anonymous words of history and their totalizing demands. Peace, he tells us, is nothing other than "an aptitude for speech."[4] By the latter, Levinas refers to the promptness of responsive and responsible saying in what he will later term the diachrony of transcendence. As a giving over of language itself, and with it, the time, the world, even the finitude of the responding subject, it is a kind of unconditional surrender. But it is a surrender to no power, and thus it is more like an unconditional offer. And even though Levinas claims that the visage requiring this response communicates a commandment ("thou shalt not kill"), the offering to the other cannot be predicated on some obedience (the prohibition can only be articulated in the relation), or take form against the horizon of possible hostilities. The offering, in this ethical relation, is absolute, and the gift of peace must have a positive dimension. Though Levinas does not dwell long on this motif of peace in *Totality and Infinity*, it is clear that it cannot denote simply a nonviolent approach and find its place simply as the absence of violence or its withholding. What, then, might we learn from Blanchot's meditation on the encounter with *autrui* and the possibility of learning an "aptitude for speech"?

We find the latter scene of encounter staged at numerous points in *The Infinite Conversation*, though Blanchot draws out the alternative of speaking or killing in a distinctive way. The dialogue, "Keeping to Words," for example, introduces the encounter as "something terrible" by reason of its radical character inasmuch as *nothing* stands between the individual and the naked presence of *autrui*. We speak to the other or we kill because nothing upholds the relation prior to our act. In worldly affairs, what Heidegger named *Mitdasein*, relations are always mediated, be they of rivalry or cooperation. But in the moment of encounter, the mediating barriers fall:

> The walls have fallen: those that separate us, those too that permit us to communicate, and those, finally, that protect us by keeping us at a distance. Now, man is in some sense the inaccessible, but the inaccessible is in a sense the immediate; what exceeds me absolutely is absolutely at my mercy. Here is man come forth in his presence, that is to say, reduced to the poverty of presence. . . . My intervention—that of the self—will not be limited to the partial violence of work, to the limited and veiled negation of refusal; there, if I assert myself still as a power, my power will extend to death, and this is not a partial but a radical death. (IC 60/86)

In the encounter, once again, I speak or I kill. My choice is radical in character. But either act, Blanchot tells us, proceeds from an initial exposure of the presence of the other that is already a kind of speech. To the extent that my receptive speaking has occurred in the space of the alternative, its possibility has already opened (as has that of its alternative); it opens from a speaking that has offered the other in their fragility, or what he thematizes as "human weakness."[5] Deferring a lengthier consideration of this prior opening, this tracing of a difference from which speech opens, Blanchot gives the following to one of the voices in his dialogue:

> This isn't the moment for us to give an account of it. But I will say two things: first, if this speech is weighty, it is because, being bare presence, it is what lays

presence bare, what thus exposes it to radical violence in reducing it to the fragility of what is without power. To speak at the level of weakness and of destitution—at the level of affliction—is perhaps to challenge force, but also to attract force by refusing it. And second: in this situation, either to speak or to kill, speech does not consist in speaking, but first of all in maintaining the movement of this either . . . or; it is what founds the alternative. To speak is always to speak from out of this interval between speech and radical violence, separating them, but maintaining each of them in a relation of vicissitude. (IC 62/88)

The speech to which Blanchot refers, again, is a kind of speech before speech, opening the space for a responsive speaking, or violence. "What is that speech?" Blanchot's interlocutors ask at various moments about this always prior opening. How do we understand the saying that occurs in the encounter with *autrui*, and how might we understand a speech that responds to the exigency it carries?

Blanchot offers multiple approaches to the site of this exposing speech in *The Infinite Conversation*, and multiple accounts of what it means to draw out its saying in speech and in writing. But he also attends insistently to a critical difficulty for any meditation on peace. The essential point might be summarized in Blanchot's Hegelian-inflected vocabulary of this period by noting that no exposure of and to the other can ever ultimately be held apart (that is, for more than the instant of a time outside time) from the mortal power of the negative at work in language. This thought of the work of negation is offered in eloquent and inexhaustible terms in Blanchot's monumental essay, "Literature and the Right to Death." Blanchot's reflections on Orpheus and Eurydice also tell the same story. At the scene of encounter, where before *autrui* we speak or we kill, death is surreptitiously entering the scene. It is present if only in the saying of its own suspension before what escapes its power. There is an interruption here, but the deferral is like a fold in what seems an almost inevitable violence. Here, once again, is Blanchot's unforgettable meditation on Kaliayev's "*I cannot*" from Camus's *Les justes*:

> What we sense is that the recoil of violence—its arrest in front of the children's weakness, Kaliayev's "*I cannot*"—coincides with the moment at which violence lays bare the visage and makes man this extreme destitution before which death draws back because it cannot reach it, because this weakness is this arrest, this drawing back itself. . . . There is *the time* of the word, there is the moment at

which speech begins, lays bare the visage, says the encounter that is this nakedness and says man as the encounter with the extreme and irreducible limit.... "*I cannot*" is the secret of language where, outside all power to represent and to signify, speech would come about as what always differs from itself, and thus holds itself back as difference. It does not merge with the moral interdiction against killing, nor with the fact that one cannot really kill. "*I cannot*" is the speech of death in person, an allusion that it formulates when, in the act of killing, it comes up against the evidence of the visage as though it were its own impossibility; a moment that is death's own drawing back before itself, the *delay* where speech can take place, and that is its place. (IC 186–187/279)

This is indeed terrifying, as the next paragraph underscores in the strongest manner.[6] Can one even entertain the question of peace from here? But the passage also affirms that the instant of encounter, the time of speech at its origin somehow remains. It forms what Blanchot names earlier in the volume a "reserve" in thought that is not a point of dissipation or seizure, but rather the point of a possible turn: "The impossible is not there in order to make thought capitulate, but to let it announce itself according to a measure other than that of power" (IC 43/62). Thus in the instant shadowed by "radical violence"—a violence deriving from the power of the negative proper to language itself—there would subsist or survive the ground of a different, perhaps affirmative opening to alterity, and thus perhaps the possibility of a hosting (the grace of hospitality), or perhaps an approach that offers peace.[7] But how do we think the maintenance and affirmative assumption of that instant relation to the "impossible," a form of being not founded in the exercise of the power of the negative, or being, thought as possibility? How do we think an affirmative reception of *autrui*?

Blanchot's essay, "Being Jewish," provides an approach to this question that is astonishing in its force. Moreover, Blanchot's gesture of linking it to his meditation on Robert Antelme's *L'espèce humaine* under the title, "The Indestructible," suggests strongly that the mode of existence he calls "being Jewish" would exceed any relation of power and be *other* than a relation of power (and any "being possible," in Heidegger's sense). But can "being Jewish" fully testify to the experience Blanchot finds evoked in Antelme's volume, or does this latter experience somehow oblige us to rethink the forceful claims made in Blanchot's essay on Judaism? What happens when

Blanchot links these two stunning essays? I will approach these questions by reading each of the essays in turn, and by then considering, albeit briefly, how Blanchot's last words from the second essay fold back upon the first.

Being Jewish

"Being Jewish" offers itself quite demonstratively as a philosophical statement, even while asserting that the questions it seeks to address require a long meditation that is "more personal than erudite" (IC 125/182). It is, in any case, far more avowedly philosophical than many of the sections of *The Infinite Conversation*. Answering the "denegations" of anti-Semitism (the effort to reduce Judaism to some negative essence, and to move from this negation to active annihilation), and countering a Sartrean effort that Blanchot describes respectfully as "rigorous" to make any Jewish "difference" a mere reflection of the anti-Semitic gaze, Blanchot affirms in Judaism a ground of "historical reality and authenticity" that derives from the manner in which Judaism engages "the relation of every man to himself" (IC 124/182). Being Jewish is an historical event with an import of universal character; it designates a "grave truth" that must be brought forth in an always personal engagement.

> There is a Jewish thought and a Jewish truth; that is, for each of us, there is an obligation to try to find whether in and through this thought and this truth there is at stake a certain relation of man with man that we can sidestep only by refusing a necessary inquiry. (IC 125/183)

A Jewish thought and truth, and an obligation to undertake them in order to determine whether the relation to the other, the human relation as such, is at stake there for us. This strong, almost redundant statement ("an obligation . . . a necessary inquiry"—one is historically based, the other ethico-philosophical) appears to condense three assumptions that Blanchot will develop in the course of his essay and which can only be summarized here as we move toward their meaning. It affirms, first, a "truth" in the revelation that is assumed as Judaism, and the founded character of the tradition of reflection devoted to it. It does this, however, in such a way as to evoke the philosophical essence of Judaism (as opposed to any religious commitment or some cultural significance). Second, it interprets the thought and truth of Judaism along the lines of something Blanchot will name a "Jewish humanism," suggesting that "being Jewish" may offer the means to address a responsibility that is general in nature. This second step does not suggest that all humanism—if so we may name a thought of a just relation to the human other (which carries us past established humanisms)—must be Jewish or that the "authentic" human relation must be a "being Jewish," but it does suggest that Judaism points to the truth of what we might term "humanism." Third, it links the thought and truth of Judaism to a history of oppression that gives the affliction suffered by the Jewish people, throughout history and throughout the world, a *general* significance; it thus implicates every individual in a relation of responsibility to what Blanchot terms "being Jewish." Thus, to an exigency that speaks already in the Jewish "truth" (and thus calls upon each of us in the manner described by Levinas), there is a moral and societal imperative that is historically founded to face that to which being Jewish testifies.

These claims are challenging enough, and we will need to return to them. But another step, also triply articulated, follows immediately as Blanchot asserts that everything he would want to convey is held in that dense expression, "being Jewish" and the factical meaning to which it testifies. Answering Pasternak's questions "What does being Jewish mean? Why does it exist?" Blanchot writes:

> I believe that among all the responses there is one in three parts that we cannot avoid choosing, and it is this: [being Jewish] exists so that the idea of exodus and the idea of exile should exist as a just movement; it exists, through exile and through the initiative that is exodus, so that the experience of strangeness should affirm itself close at hand as an irreducible relation; it exists so that, by the authority of this experience, we should learn to speak. (IC 125/183)

"Being Jewish" testifies, it seems, *from the beginning*. It stands witness to the just character of the act of exodus (as a movement of response) in and by this movement's manner of offering itself or going out to an event whose occurrence both founds this justice, and takes on, through this founding, the authority of a teaching. In its testimony, we might say, being Jewish *institutes*—from the beginning. It stands witness to its own possibility. In this, it is a "quasi-transcendental" of sorts (and thus, "Etre Juif" is also aptly translated as "Jewish Being"), a way of being that is a structure of relation.

It does not institute a relation between two terms or some teaching (in the sense of a doctrine); rather, it institutes the way of a relation that may become a teaching.

Blanchot remarks in one of the earlier dialogues from *The Infinite Conversation* that prepare the argument of "The Indestructible" that only the recognition of the privilege and distance of *autrui* can teach me both what humankind is, and the infinite that comes to me from the other human being. I must accept the other as other (exalted or abject) if I am to begin to learn what the human is and the nature of the alterity its presence brings. This statement implies that the question of the human opens only in an *event* (this is a crucial point to which we must return), and it suggests that this event must be prepared. How am I to recognize the other before knowing who or what the other is? Levinas urges that teaching occurs in the sheer presence of *autrui* (the Torah is given in the light of a face to which acquiescence must inevitably be accorded, if only to be refused). He also tells us that the path of this teaching is a form of prophetic witness: "We will do and we will hear." Fully historical in its instantiation, but of the same temporal order, "being Jewish" would name the ground of that latter act. Bearing witness to that possibility from the start (thus anticipating itself as a discipline of witness), it would found an ethical praxis.

These formulations may not fully capture Blanchot's manner of displacing Western ontology with this account of a self-founding praxis of truth. But they point to a question that is difficult to avoid: Can the practice of Judaism be so subsumed philosophically and not surrender its specificity? The question is not a simple one, as we will continue to see, but it is vital to underscore here Blanchot's understanding of the historical ground of this form of relation. For, while Blanchot describes it as a *form* of being (of life?), he emphasizes that it is revealed only in the course of a history and through the exigency of response. Justifying the first of the three points addressed to Pasternak's question, Blanchot points to the painful evidence offered by history: "If Judaism is destined to take on meaning for us, it is indeed by showing that, at whatever time, one must be ready to set out, because to leave (to go to the outside) is the exigency from which one cannot escape if one wants to maintain the possibility of a just relation" (IC 125/183). Here, the *nomadic* essence of Jewish being is asserted against those forms of paganism (both Levinas and Blanchot situate Heideggerian ontology here) that link truth to a rooted dwelling and permanence. And in this nomadism, in the dispersion it implies, there emerges a form of truth: "Just as it calls for a sojourn without place, just as it ruins every fixed relation of force with *one* individual, *one* group, or *one* state, it brings forth, before the exigency of totality, a different exigency and finally prohibits the temptation of Unity-identity" (IC 126/184). Needless to say, this is an exigency difficult to reconcile with the directions taken in the contemporary state of Israel.[8]

Two points in Jewish history define this form of being: Abraham's act of separating from his Sumerian world and his passage to a "not yet world," his act of beginning (an act that "founds the human right to beginning, the sole veritable creation"; IC 126/185), and then Jacob's "enigmatic contact" whereby he takes the sign of election. Here, the response to the Foreign becomes a form of solitary responsibility. Israel's solitude, Blanchot writes, derives not only from its relation to surrounding peoples, but from "this particular relation with itself that placed this extreme, infinite distance, the presence that is other, in its proximity" (IC 126/185). That self-relation, once again, is the assumed responsibility of exodus, of going out. This is a positive relation to truth, Blanchot emphasizes, that diverges radically from that of philosophy in its Greek provenance:

> Exodus and exile indicate a positive relation with exteriority, whose exigency invites us not to be content with what is proper to us (that is, with our power to assimilate everything, to identify everything, to bring everything back to our I). Exodus and exile express simply the same reference to the Outside that the word existence bears. . . . Facing the visible-invisible horizon Greek truth proposes to us (truth as light, light as measure), there is another dimension disclosed to man where, beyond every horizon, he must relate to what is beyond his reach. (IC 127/186)

Again, we see described a form of relation that becomes, in its historical unfolding, a form of life.

Yet it is with regard to the revelation of Judaism that Blanchot's philosophical gesture is most dramatic (his own word here is "brutal"). What we owe to Jewish monotheism, he asserts, "is not the revelation of the one God, [but] the revelation of speech as the site where men hold themselves in relation with what excludes all relation: the infinitely Distant, the absolutely Foreign" (IC 127/187). Jewish thought, he tells us, countering Hegel's infamous words about the "insurmountable abyss" in the Jewish spirit, honors the separation that language preserves as it gives relation to the infinite without reducing it to the same. It teaches us, he says, that speech inaugurates an "original relation." It teaches us what it means to speak:

> To speak to someone is to accept not introducing him into the system of things or of beings to be known; it is to recognize him as unknown and to receive him as foreign without obliging him to break with his difference. (IC 128/187)

Earlier in *The Infinite Conversation*, in the dialogues that prepare the thought of "The Indestructible," Blanchot asserts that such an understanding of language constitutes the "unique dignity" (IC 51/73) of the relation philosophy invites us to entertain with the unknown. The "philosophy" Blanchot is reading in Judaism has an "existential" cast, in a certain sense, but it is essentially a philosophy of language which holds that language takes its meaning (meaning itself) from the "absolute" relation it measures, without any form of reduction or mediation of that radical alterity. As such a philosophy, it is essentially ethical in the sense of the term proposed by Levinas. Only shortly after the statement about the "unique dignity" of the philosophical relation, Blanchot introduces Levinas's name and asserts that his thought constitutes a new beginning for philosophy: "We are called upon to become responsible for what philosophy essentially is, by receiving, in all its brilliance and in the infinite exigency that are proper to it, precisely the idea of the other, that is to say, the relation with *autrui*" (IC 51–52/73–74).

We would appear to be moving in a circle. Blanchot reads the history of Judaism from philosophy, but he does so with an understanding of philosophy he has drawn from Levinas. Still, Blanchot breaks the circle when he refuses the religious commitment of Levinas's thinking and brackets the name of God. We have read this gesture in "Being Jewish," and we may find its expression elsewhere in *The Infinite Conversation* when Blanchot asserts that only the other human being brings me before an in-finite, only the presence of *autrui* communicates an absolute difference. If the revelation of language at stake in Jewish monotheism is a revelation about the manner in which language *maintains* difference, it is also a revelation about the relation to the other human being, since difference comes to us only by the other, by *autrui*.

Accordingly, there follows in Blanchot's essay a brief meditation on what he calls "Jewish humanism," which is astonishing, in relation to Greek humanism, by reason of a concern for human relations that is so constant and so preponderant that, even where God is nominally present, it is still a matter of man, of what lies between human beings when nothing stands between them. The marvel, as Blanchot comments in relation to Jacob's remark to Esau, "I have seen your face as one sees the face of Elohim" (IC 129/188), is human presence, that Other presence that is *autrui*— a presence that is terrible, he reminds us, for the fact that the issue of such an encounter can only be either speech or violence. Does a philosophical humanism of a radical kind, finally shorn of the name of God, gain the final word here?[9] We recall that Blanchot began by affirming a thought and a truth in Judaism that obliges each of us to confront a certain relation of humankind with itself ("a certain relation of man with man") at stake there. The thought and the truth, as we have seen, are borne in, and *occur* in a "being Jewish" that is inseparable from a recognition of the privilege of *autrui* and an opening, an exposure, to the question of the human via a teaching that is a "learning to speak." But Blanchot does not claim in conclusion that humanism is the truth of Judaism. Sensing that he has ventured a bit far, perhaps, in letting the name of God dissipate, and perhaps stopping short of Judaism for this very reason (this point appears to be marked by his citation of Rosenzweig; IC 128/188), he concludes with the statement that the "truth" of what he has sought to convey in speaking of the affirmation of separation at the heart of "being Jewish" is that whoever seeks to read the history of the Jews *through Judaism* must reflect on the way the Jews bear witness to the difference brought to us by the presence of the other human being. They recall to us, he says, "the exigency of strangeness . . . designating as pure separation and pure relation what from man to man exceeds human power, which is capable of everything" (IC 129/189). This manner of bearing witness to the indestructible character of an "infinite distance" is itself indestructible: "no form of force can have done with [it] because no force is able to meet up with it" (IC 129/189). Hence the furor of anti-Semitism, he suggests, which is fueled by an anxious need to submit to the all-power of death what cannot be measured in terms of power and to efface the responsibility to which it testifies.

Humankind

> ["I cannot"] coincides with the moment at which violence lays bare the visage and makes man this extreme destitution before which death draws back

because it cannot reach it, because this weakness is this arrest, this drawing back itself.... What we are left with is this second. There is the *time* of the word, there is the moment at which speech begins, lays bare the visage, says the encounter with the extreme and irreducible limit.

I propose that we read "the indestructible" in relation to what Blanchot says here of these words, "*I cannot.*" It names what exceeds power, as we have seen, but also an exposure that *remains*, and the burden of this remainder, which is an ineffaceable ethical responsibility. When enunciated in the presence of the human, "the indestructible" does not name an essential trait of some kind, any more than do "simplicity," "poverty," or "innocence." When Blanchot states in "Humankind" that "man affirms himself at that limit where possibility ceases: in the poverty, the simplicity of a presence that is the infinite of human presence" (IC 132/194), he is describing the irreducible trace of an exposure. This relational structure, occurring in language, as language, does not give us a substance to which could be attributed the term "indestructible"; rather, "the indestructible" would first name something of the manner of this giving. It is salutary to recall here Blanchot's words regarding the designation "*autrui*":

> When we ask ourselves, "who is *autrui*?" we question in such a way that the question necessarily distorts what it pretends to call into question. *Autrui* cannot designate a nature, it cannot characterize a being or an essential trait. To express oneself crudely, *autrui* is not a certain type of man whose task it is to occupy this role—in the manner of the saints and prophets, delegates of the Most High—opposite the clan of the "I's." This must be recalled, even if this precaution is a bit ridiculous, because our language substantifies everything. (IC 70/100)

What cannot fail to strike the reader of "Humankind," the second section of "The Indestructible," is Blanchot's articulation of the way the human relation will remain a burden for those who seek to rise above it and a responsibility for those who are called to bear witness to it. Blanchot's assertion, early in *The Infinite Conversation*, that only the presence of the human other brings us before an infinite and confronts us with a radical difference, is here joined by a complementary ethical assertion as Blanchot insists that one cannot be rid of this presence. The torturer, for example, cannot become a god and assume the objective powers of a fate or nature—they remain human, subject to the indestructible that emerges at the limits of their power. And the tortured, who become bearers of this unattained infinite, will hold to the indestructible in the knowledge that only human power can torture in this way, that violence is an irreducibly human choice in the scene of the encounter where one speaks or kills. "Indestructible" says that for the human being, there is no escaping the human. Where Levinas would ultimately assert, after the Psalmist, that there is no escaping the presence of God, Blanchot insists that there is no escaping the human. Both, in turn, seek to convert this powerlessness into an affirmation. The indestructible to which "I cannot" bears witness is the ground of an irreducible ethical affirmation that must be brought to language. This is what it would mean to learn to speak.

It is crucial to underscore that it is in and from such responsibility that Blanchot attempts to approach the question, "who is *autrui*?" in *The Infinite Conversation* (a question, he says at the start of "Humankind," that leads him back to Antelme's volume every time it is articulated; IC 130/191). This is why his thinking diverges so dramatically from an argument like that proposed by Giorgio Agamben in *Remnants of Auschwitz*, who fails to think the remnants of human relation.[10] And this is why he considers Robert Antelme's testimony in *L'espèce humaine* so essential, for the question *happens* there as a question. The book thus "teaches" as it introduces us to the understanding "that man is the indestructible, and that nevertheless he can be destroyed." It leads us to the indestructible via its account of affliction.

It is also vital for a reading of this essay to see what Blanchot means by "destruction," for it is through this destruction that humankind emerges as the indestructible. Destruction is not immediately annihilation; it is the reduction of the human being to an affliction wherein the human subject is stripped of its power to posit itself as subject and say "I." The human being who afflicts in this manner is capable of everything in the sense that he or she can strip another of their relation to the world, denying this other (by any number of means, including torture), the whole of relations of power and meaning, thereby unmooring the hold of the self.

> In affliction—and in our society affliction is always first the loss of social status—the one who suffers at the hands of men is radically altered. Having fallen not only below the individual person, but also below every class and every real collective relation, the person no longer exists in his or her personal identity. In this sense, the one afflicted is already outside the world, a being without horizon. (IC 131/193)

In a sense, there is no limit to destruction, since affliction is a kind of abyss, and there is no end to the fall (IC 133/197). But a limit to power appears in that the act of destruction cannot alter the inexorable affirmation that emerges as the human being slips from the world (of being):

> That man can be destroyed is certainly not reassuring; but that despite this and because of this, in this very movement, man should remain the indestructible—this fact is what is truly overwhelming, *for we no longer have any chance of ever seeing ourselves relieved of ourselves or of our responsibility.*
> (IC 131/192, my emphasis)

There is the meaning of "the indestructible" to which I pointed above; it emerges in and as the presence of the human, which the oppressor cannot reach. Antelme: "*But there is no ambiguity; we remain men and will end only as men. . . . It is because we are men as they are that the SS will finally be powerless before us. . . . [The executioner] can kill a man, but he cannot change him into something else*" (IC 131/192).

In this self-identification, as Antelme understands it (for Blanchot, as we will see, it cannot be the act of a self, and certainly not a self-identification), the afflicted retains the capacity to know that his or her affliction is of human doing. This is the last recourse for the afflicted: "to know that he has been struck not by the elements but by men, and to give the name man to everything that assails him" (IC 131/194). Affliction is abyssal, and inasmuch as the afflicted loses all sense of self, this last recourse is like a handhold that must give way. Here, we glimpse that Blanchot actually diverges from Antelme, who holds firmly to the prisoner's consciousness of the oppressor. But Blanchot retains the latter relation in his own way, and does not allow the dissolution of self in affliction (which he describes quite radically) to eliminate a relation to one's own presence, which is not a presence to self, but relation to the other in oneself: the presence of *autrui*. Here, a speech occurs that *reserves* itself from the language of power, not just by the fact that it escapes that language essentially, but by a kind of refusal. Thus, the tortured, Blanchot asserts, will refuse to cede to the language of the torturer (except in an extreme passivity that cannot give satisfaction to the latter and only reiterates the refusal) in order to preserve the "true speech" that they know is confounded in this instant with their silent presence, which is that of *autrui* in them:

> A presence no power, even the most formidable, will be able to reach, except by doing away with it. It is this presence that bears in itself and as the last

affirmation what Robert Antelme calls *"the ultimate feeling of belonging to the species."* (IC 132/195)

These are astonishing words for Blanchot to take over. But let us translate "species," here, as "kind" (following Hanson's translation) and ask: what is this feeling of belonging? Is this an affect? And does it entail a sense of community? Blanchot's answer, which he claims to find in Antelme as "the book's most forceful truth" (IC 133/195), is that affliction reveals a radical *need*. When man is reduced to the extremity of need, "we see [*l'on s'aperçoit*] that he is reduced to himself, and reveals himself [*se découvre*] as one who has need of nothing other than need in order to maintain the human relation in its primacy, negating what negates him" (IC 133/195). Blanchot, as we see, sidesteps the question of the subject of this "self-discovery" in this phrase (even while he maintains relation to the oppressor with a problematic evocation of a dialectical "negation of negation"). But he insists that a relationality endures. The afflicted being who knows radical need maintains "the human relation in its primacy" (the phrase is repeated at IC 135/199)—a kind of pure exposure "where all relation is lacking" (IC 135/199). This is not a relation to the other human being, then, but the "impossible experience" of becoming *"autrui"* for oneself (IC 135/199), not a self-possession (or a sense of belonging), but a dis-possession. Or, as Blanchot puts it in an even more stunning formulation: "It is as though I received the Other [*l'Autre*], host not to myself but to the unknown and the foreign" (IC 133/196).

This is a terrifying account of the (non)ground of human community, and Blanchot does not attenuate it in the least. He argues that need, the "most terrible kind of egoism" must be distinguished from *jouissance*, as Levinas describes it, inasmuch as the latter relation always maintains and affirms a relation to *self*. For Blanchot, on the contrary, need in its radical form is nothing more than a "naked relation to naked life" that is not some bare life in a corporeal sense, but "human existence pure and simple," and as such, a relation to the other. I quote once again to underscore the "primacy" of the relation:

> One can therefore say that when, through oppression and affliction, my relation with myself is altered and lost—making of me this foreigner, this unknown from whom I am separated by an infinite distance, and making of me this infinite separation itself—need becomes radical: a need without

satisfaction, without value, that is, a naked relation to naked existence; but this need also becomes the impersonal exigency that alone bears the future and the meaning of every value, or, more precisely, of every human relation. (IC 133/196)

I touch, in affliction, the (non)ground of all community and all hospitality. I live (I eat) not *for myself*, but *for the other*, and what affirms itself in my place is the strangeness of *autrui*, the affirmation of an infinite exigency (IC 132/195). This, once again, is Blanchot's interpretation of that "last affirmation" that is "the ultimate feeling of belonging to the species." "I" incarnate a kind of pure ethical exigency in relation to which no sufficient answer or act of solidarity will ever be possible.

I noted earlier that Blanchot takes something of a distance from Antelme when he defines the structure of self-relation in affliction. We see this distance open in the light of admirable words by Sarah Kofman, when she interprets the notion of belonging to humankind in relation to a notion of community that is based not on a common ground of any kind, but rather upon "a shared power to choose, to make incompatible though correlative choices, the power to kill and the power to respect and safeguard the incommensurable distance, the relation without relation."[11] She draws here on Blanchot's notion of community, but she also emphasizes a power of choice that is foreign to Blanchot's account of the experience in the camps and she justifies this, appropriately in the terms of her argument, with a remarkable assertion by Antelme. Following a remark on the offense constituted by forms of intimacy (such as music or sport) with the oppressors, and a citation of Blanchot's devastating sentence ("There is a limit at which the practice of any art becomes an affront to affliction"), she continues:

> The camps also taught a lesson about the abyss that can separate one detainee's judgment from another's, one choice from another choice, for the necessity of choice was greater there than it has been anywhere else: "Here is where we'll have known both the greatest esteem and the most definitive contempt, both love of mankind and loathing for it, with a more total certainty than anywhere else, ever.... The more transformed we become, the farther we retreat from back home, the more the SS believe us reduced to the indistinctness and irresponsibility of which we certainly present the appearance—the more distinctions our community does in fact contain, and the stricter those distinctions are. The inhabitant of the camps is not the abolition of those distances; on the contrary, he is their effective realization."[12]

Blanchot's account does not follow this claim of differentiation. He acknowledges that a sporadic society could appear among the deported that would afford them a sense of self-relation in relation to others and against the powerful. But the *truth* of the situation, he says, speaking in strongly dialectical terms of a structure that is not dialectical, and thus willfully seeking a relation to the language of political action, is that the death camps housed a sea of others who had become *autrui* for a murderous Subject:

> Between those men who are Other and the Self of Force, no language is possible; but neither is there any possibility of expression between them. What is then said is essential, but *in truth* heard by no one; there is no one to receive as speech (save through the momentary exchanges in which, through camaraderie, a self is revived) the infinite and infinitely silent presence of *autrui*. Now each has no relation with words other than the reserve of speech that he must live in solitude. (IC 135/199)

Blanchot argues here that an external subjectivity must emerge to receive the silent word of *autrui* and to bring its truth to speech. He then adds, in a step that recalls Levinas's struggle with the notion of justice, but seems almost to despair of it, that a collective subject must emerge that recognizes in the affliction of the other an injustice committed against all and thereby finds the point of departure for a "*common demand [revendication commune]*" (IC 134). For a just political response, he suggests, must be totalizing (IC 448 n. 7/197).

The step Blanchot makes here is a disconcerting one in that it seems to short-circuit possible developments of the argument of "Being Jewish," or even suggest that the form of existence described in that essay is incommensurable with political imperatives (a possible conclusion to which Blanchot's long footnote hesitantly pointed, but also skirted). Moreover, it is hard to see the justification for passing so imperatively from the need for the singular act of testimony (Antelme's, for example), or a conceivably communitary form that might be latent in the thought of "being Jewish" and the task it enjoins of "learning to speak," to the totalizing terms of traditional political action that Blanchot evokes with his reference to "class consciousness" (IC 134/197). However, the dialectical turn in his argument appears to serve more than a political statement; it seems also designed to expose in absolute terms what Blanchot names for a second time, "the human relation in its primacy" (IC 135/199). This does not make it less problematic, to be sure, but the effect would be to draw forth the ethical exigency that speaks in the event of the Shoah by drawing forth the silence of the word, the saying of the presence of *autrui*—to draw it forth to such a point that an abyss opens between this silence and the just speech that would bring it to expression. This is a wound, Blanchot infers, that language itself would have to bear, without ever saying it (or closing it). It is a pain that would afflict every event of speech.

Blanchot makes this last statement by commenting on Antelme's expression of his inability to bridge the distance between the silence of the camps and a just speech that would represent its truth. "Hardly had we begun to recount and we were choking" (IC 135/199). Blanchot's interlocutors take this up as follows:

> —Why this wrenching? Why this pain always present, and not only here in this extreme movement, but already, as I believe it is, in the simplest words?
> —Perhaps because, as soon as two individuals approach one another, there is between them some painful formulation, of the sort we expressed in beginning. They speak, perhaps, in order to forget it, to deny it, or to represent it.
> —That man is the indestructible who can be destroyed? (IC 135/200)

Our leitmotif, we see now, is something like the saying of a pain that can never be fully articulated, of that "terrible responsibility" that is the presence of the other—a responsibility to which I cannot respond sufficiently and cannot escape. It is a "saying," as I have suggested, of a very particular order since it would be haunting every instance of speech addressed to the other; the "simplest words" would bear it as the latent expression of an abyssal origin of meaning they cannot fully speak. In this sense, though it is given by Blanchot's interlocutors as an attempted "formulation," a necessarily inadequate rendering whose opacity is the only "adequate" sign of its weakness, its status would be comparable to that of the "I cannot" Blanchot isolates in the passage I have cited again as an epigraph to this section—words (also figural or "formulaic," in their way) that bear "the secret of language." It would be comparable even to the phrase "a child is being killed" from *The Writing of the Disaster* (WD 71–72/116). All of these are phrases that speak in some sense "before" signifying language, sayings of the rending from which language opens.

To read Blanchot, I believe, we must learn to read in the instant of the appearance of such phrases, or simply *from* such linguistic events. I will want to say a brief word on what this might mean for the texts at hand before concluding. But we should first pause to consider what is communicated in the formula offered in "Humankind." For what haunts in it is not merely the difficulty of the too-patent antinomy it offers (the juxtaposition of an "impossible" that is infinite—the indestructible—with the finite order of the "possible": "man is the indestructible who *can* be destroyed") and what it tells us of humankind. What is devastating in the phrase is what it communicates of an exposure to violence, or a vulnerability: the fact that the presence of the indestructible *delivers man to infinite destruction*. The final phrasing of what it teaches us, strongly underscored by one of the interlocutors ("Yes, I believe we must say this, hold onto it for an instant," IC 135/200), brings home this dimension of the phrase. A reader could have expected the interlocutor to turn from the terrible testimony it gives as the dialogue reaches its conclusion; that is to say, they might well have anticipated after "man is the indestructible," something on the order of: "and therefore cannot be touched even as he is subject to endless destruction." Instead, we have an assertion that reinforces the vulnerability that is given each time in encounter: man is the indestructible and *this means* ("*cela signifie*"—and how *literally* may we read the reference to signification here?) there is no limit to the destruction of man. To be sure, this is a kind of descriptive statement that honors Antelme's staggering account of his experience. But the furor of the Nazis testified to something more.[13] Humankind is open to limitless destruction, it seems, inasmuch as every act of violence—every effort to impose a term to human finitude—makes the horizonless character of its presence both surge and recede; the latter presence provokes to further violence, *delivers humankind up* to further violence, without term. Thus, the human is, from the first opening of its presence, delivered to violence, and the phrase seems almost to say: because man is the indestructible, *there will be* a violence without term. Again, "this means . . ." seems to hint at the *provocation* of presence and the violence that inevitably follows.

But a further step must be taken, for we must also recall Blanchot's words regarding the phrase, "*I cannot*," words that would seem to pertain to every formulation of its kind. We must recall, in other words, that in the exposure of *autrui*, violence always waits; indeed, the argument of "Reflections on Hell" suggests that the exposure of presence is nothing other than a violence deferring itself.[14] As Blanchot's explication of the phrase suggests, the imminence of violence is inherent to the instant of exposure as it is given in speech. Violence necessarily haunts the indestructible, almost as its aura; it is already gathering. We may *learn to speak* in such a way as to defer and perhaps turn from the destruction (*The Step Not Beyond* will entertain the thought of an *exceptional* saying, in this respect). But in every encounter with the other, "as soon as two individuals approach one another," there is the rending that is the exposure of the infinite offering of human presence to violence. In "The Infinite Conversation," we will read of a plaint, a lamentation that is proper to what speaks in interruption. There must be such a plaint attending all "true" speech.

Does the meditation on "being Jewish" accommodate this thought? Or do the words in "Humankind" require us to examine further the ethical praxis Blanchot describes in the essay to which it is coupled? At first appearance, "Being Jewish" and "Humankind" stand almost as complementary statements, counterparts (this impression is underscored by the concluding paragraph of the former essay in that it seems to establish a firm bridge between them). The former describes a mode of self-relation that is a relation to the other. The latter describes the exigency of the other to which the former responds. But can "being Jewish," as it is described, become the path of a relation that escapes the violence that haunts this encounter as it is evoked in "Humankind"?[15] Returning to the discussion of the Jewish revelation in "Being Jewish," we note that language is thought as the site of a nonviolent encounter with alterity, an encounter where an absolute distance is preserved in its purity and the other is received as other. From here, Blanchot can evoke a form of promise: "In this sense, speech is the promised land in which exile is accomplished as sojourn, since it is no longer a matter of being at home, but always Outside, in a movement in which the Foreign offers itself without renouncing itself" (IC 128/187). Can this promise be sustained from the ground of what is said in "Humankind," or could it be sustained? If so, and perhaps as an "instantaneous," impossible opening (we will return to this motif in considering Blanchot's brief narrative, *The Instant of My Death*), how do we think this form of "being outside"?

I do not know whether it would be appropriate to say that the meditation in "Humankind" is meant to subject the statements of "Being Jewish" to some kind of trial. Blanchot affirms in that former essay that it is precisely the imperative of facing history that requires the reflection it proposes. But I believe we have to ask whether the experience of the Shoah, as Blanchot encounters it through the testimony of Antelme, among others, forces us to go farther in thinking a "practice of peace" than does the "Jewish humanism" Blanchot takes over from Levinas in the first essay. For, while it does not undermine the previous description of the revelation of language, it does oblige us to entertain dimensions of this revelation (and the terrible responsibility it opens) to which the first essay can at best allude when it briefly evokes the dying that belongs to the encounter with *autrui*.[16] I do not doubt that the notion of a "sabbatical existence" can be affirmatively articulated, but it requires the searching thought for an ethical practice that belongs to the inspiring impetus of *The Step Not Beyond*.

PART TWO

Refusal/Affirmation

THREE

Beyond Refusal: The Madness of the Day

ce jour s'effaçant, je m'effacerai avec lui . . .

The enigmatic phrase that has impelled this study offers itself innocently and openly in the first paragraphs of *The Madness of the Day*:

> I am not learned; I am not ignorant. I have known joys. That is saying too little: I am alive, and this life gives me the greatest pleasure. And what about death? When I die (perhaps any minute now), I will feel immense pleasure. I am not talking about the foretaste of death, which is stale and often disagreeable. Suffering dulls the senses. But this is the remarkable truth, and I am sure of it; I experience boundless pleasure in living, and I will take boundless satisfaction in dying.
>
> I have wandered; I have gone from place to place. Settled, I lived in a single room. I was poor, then richer, then poorer than many people. As a child I had great passions, and everything I wanted I obtained. My childhood has disappeared, my youth is behind me. It doesn't matter. I am happy

about what has been, I am pleased by what is, and what is to come suits me well enough.

Is my life better than other people's lives? Perhaps. I have a roof over my head and many do not. I do not have leprosy, I am not blind, I see the world—what extraordinary happiness! I see this day, and outside it there is nothing. Who could take that away from me? And when this day fades, I will fade along with it—a thought, a certainty, that enraptures me. (MD 6)

The affirmation is modulated but not lost as the narrator continues with allusions to an interrupting madness occasioned by the loss of loved ones, and a no less catastrophic interruption of an almost unlimited scale—an unleashing of madness on the level of the *world* (here we will find reference to the event that will form the object of a subsequent chapter: "I was made to stand against the wall like many others. . . . The guns did not go off"; MD 6). The affirmation resurfaces with the narrator's account of a persisting, and thereby disconcerting, happiness:

As reason returned to me, memory came with it, and I saw that even on the worst days, when I thought I was utterly and completely miserable, I was nevertheless, and nearly all the time, extremely happy. That gave me something to think about. The discovery was not a pleasant one. It seemed to me that I was losing a great deal. I asked myself, wasn't I sad, hadn't I felt my life breaking up? Yes, that had been true; but each minute, when I stayed without moving in a corner of the room, the cool of the night and the stability of the ground made me breathe and rest on gladness.

Men want to escape from death, strange beings that they are. And some of them cry out "Die, die" because they want to escape from life. "What a life. I'll kill myself. I'll give in." This is lamentable and strange; it is a mistake.

Yet I have met people who have never said to life, "Quiet!", who have never said to death, "Go away!" Almost always women, beautiful creatures. Men are assaulted by terror, the night breaks through them, they see their plans annihilated, their work turned to dust. They who were so important, who wanted to create the world, are dumfounded; everything crumbles. (MD 6–7)

Other interruptions will follow as the narrator turns to his "trials" and the disaster of his near-blinding. But intense fatigue and a lapse of will, even the affront of invasive surveillance and interrogation, do not overturn an acquiescent, often generous bearing carried by the yes to life, the yes to death. The passion, the passions of this narrative, devolving into a playful, if sometimes weary passivity, will never take a negative turn. There is objection ("Where were these talents that were made to speak like gowned judges sitting on benches, ready to condemn me day and night?" MD 14), but no aggressive contestation and no *ressentiment*. Even the narrator's evasion of his doctors' prying concerns remains playful.

Until, of course, the affirmation *falls* from the apparent present of its enunciation to reveal itself, and the account whose tone it sets, as *having been recounted* in what is given, textually, as an infinite return. How do we locate the end that revealed itself as "a surprise to all of us" (MD 18)? Only the final statement of refusal diverges in such a manner as to split off definitively from the narrative that otherwise folds into itself. Standing in an indefinite present, the statement begins with the same words as those with which the narrator had acquiesced to the doctor's request: "A story?" (MD 18). Separating in this manner with its redoubled "no," its present closes the door to a narrative that now refuses itself in an infinite retreat. "*Un récit, non, pas de récit, plus jamais*" (MD 31). No, no story. This is not a story, you will not have a story, no more stories.

What, then, of the acquiescence, the offering of this acquiescence and the affirmation with which it opened? Are these sealed in a textual tomb (together with the narrator's silence, which as we learn near the end will have resonated throughout the whole), or are we to entertain some other relation between the sovereign yes and the sovereign no?

We take a woefully abstract tack by isolating from this brief, but magnificent, narrative the question of the relation between the yes and no. But only recitation and long, patient analysis—the work of an entire volume—could ever honor the exquisite balance of the writing in this text, its rare humor and the infinitely haunting hints (almost nothing in the text is without its echo across the divide that comes with the "discovery" of the madness of the day). What analysis is up to the measure of sentences as insistently perfect as Kafka's "He was looking out the window"? Where does analysis come up more insistently against a writing this literary (in the senses of this term given to us first of all by Blanchot)?[1]

We have, already with the question of the yes and the no, a daunting task. For, we have in the yes already *le pas au-delà*, and with the no a refusal that is fundamental to Blanchot's political thought. Our aim reaching toward Blanchot's last steps, the analytic constraint is vital. So let us start, once again, with the yes.

The account offered from the outset by the narrator is a strange one, to be sure. It goes immediately to something like the "essence" of a life-story from the basis of a joyful assumption of the being of this life, in what it has been and in what it will become. It will become all the stranger once it reveals itself to have been given under interrogation. For we recognize then that it has reserved a silence that those for whom it is destined are unprepared to entertain (or all too prepared—for somewhere in this silence they perceive a threat). Moreover, this recognition entails our discovery of some level of implication in the demand for which this fragmentary account is offered in response (for have we not, as readers, joined the learned doctors at some point in seeking to secure the meaning of what has been offered?). In short, the ecstatic, unreserved opening will come to echo with a silence as this narrative, without the demanded cause, gives itself as response.

In the apparent commencement, in any case, the narrator affirms pleasure and he affirms a form of knowledge, both the substance of a "remarkable truth." Asked for the facts of how things happened—"*au juste*"—he gives the authorities the essence of what he knows and thus says yes both to what has been and what is to come. "Is my life better than other people's lives?" he asks (MD 6). A modest response gives way to an assertion of a supreme good. It is not without ironic reference to its situation, since the narrative required concerns a near-blinding. And to be sure, the narrator is grateful for his sight. It is not clear, however, that the seeing that brings him "extraordinary happiness" is wholly a matter of sight, for what he sees is the world—the world as such. This impossible phenomenon—the object of no sensible faculty—is given to him, he claims, as an inalienable gift; it cannot be taken from him (it is indestructible). Or so he declares under an interrogation that has demanded all, and to which he has given all and more (which turned out to be less than demanded). Not even death, it seems, can touch the joy relating to this transcending knowledge of immanent being: the day and nothing beyond. From the limit of the day and this opening onto a nothing *not beyond* (*pas au-delà*), the only death that matters to the narrator is one of his own act. When this day fades (*ce jour s'effaçant*), I will go with it (*je m'effacerai avec lui*) . . .

Is the certain passage envisioned here to be understood as properly an act? The reflexive construction in French hints, in its second occurrence (and in contrast with the first, which it mirrors), at something that is perhaps *more an act* than an event that is to be suffered. The supplemental trace of agency would almost be a mark of freedom where this not so insistently an affirmation of finitude. Still, this subversive echo of the Cartesian assertion (where truth is grounded in the certain capacity of representation) does not entirely undermine the prerogative of the subject of enunciation. The prerogative is given otherwise, in an enigmatic capacity of self-effacement that takes its impetus from a *thought*.

Let us move slowly to try to begin to capture the distance (and the question) that opens here. We must emphasize, first, the ontological turn of the statement. The narrator anticipates a fading of the day that is not a function of the fading of consciousness, the consequence of a dying. He is envisioning the eclipse of the day and *with* it (perhaps in some con-sequence, but no causal relation is asserted) a self-effacement. The vision is aptly termed apocalyptic, for the day revealed to him is that in which unfold the days and the nights; it is their opening and what holds them in being. And with its unconcealment comes knowledge of the passing of this day. The gentle, but leading, "and" ("*Et ce jour s'effaçant* . . .") indicates that to enjoy the revelation is also to know the imminence of an end. Hence the phrase, "When I die (perhaps any minute now)"—though no worldly measure is possible for this coming time of an end of time, this waiting instant.

Who could enjoy such a knowledge and such *satisfaction*—a contentment, a joy without measure, that is apparently inseparable from some form of acquittal? (As always, one cannot read Blanchot without hearing the Latin, in this case, *satisfacere*, or even *satisfactio*.) The narrator of *The Madness of the Day* will find the insistent concern with justice brought to him by the doctors and other representatives of the social order they serve (it is perhaps a policeman who asks if he wants to bring charges at his awakening after the near-blinding) "bizarre" and somewhat trivial. Obviously, an *other* satisfaction—sovereign, unlimited—is to be thought in relation to the cause of this affair (*casus*). But again, who is the subject of this satisfaction? The question will persist through the very last lines of *The Step Not Beyond*.

The epithet "apocalyptic," should not arrest our questioning. For what is meant by an end in this passing he terms "*effacement*"? Surely, the two experiences of interruption, the two deaths he has known, have something to do with this ecstatic relation. The first death, cited above (it is apparently the first), remains the object of no more than an allusion: "the guns did not go off." But it will be recounted in another narrative, as we have just noted, as "the instant of my death." Its enduring trait, as we will see, will be a feeling of elation. The second dying, the second mortal exposure, is of course the near-blinding that constitutes a kind of fault line for the narrative ("this discovery"—here again, an unconcealment—"bit straight through my life"; MD 12). It follows almost immediately after a "brief vision" that is powerfully *desiring* in character and that one would be tempted to describe without much qualification as a "primal fantasy" were the narrator not so insistent about its "real" character.[2] When the blinding interruption intervenes, therefore, it comes almost as a castrating incursion that again confronts the narrator with a figure of the law—here in the form of a final judgment:

> "You were asleep," the doctor told me later. I was asleep! I had to hold my own against the light of seven days—a fine conflagration! Yes, seven days at once, the seven deadly lights, become the spark of a single moment, were calling me to account. Who would have imagined that? At times I said to myself, "This is death. In spite of everything, it's really worth it, it's impressive." But often I lay dying without saying anything. In the end, I grew convinced that I was face to face with the madness of the day. That was the truth: the light was going mad, the brightness had lost all reason; it assailed me irrationally, without control, without purpose. (MD 11)

One cannot but recall a sentence to which Blanchot repeatedly turns: "Whoever sees God dies."[3] From this immediate confrontation with the highest Law, which devolves into an experience of a day gone mad, there is, it would seem, no possible acquittal, no escape in conscious life. And yet the narrator presents us, as we have seen, with a kind of deliverance whose enduring trait is acquiescence and a waiting carried by a form of affirmation. The catastrophe of near-blinding (lived as a sublime spectacle at moments, a silent passion at others) appears to have left the narrator in anticipation of a repetition, in "effacement," of something like the interrupted affect, the joyful, "immense" transport of his desiring vision. And even if we presume too much in linking the interdicted joy released by the apparent suspension of the "paternal no" with the satisfaction in the projected passing of effacement, we are surely invited to understand that the narrator has undergone through this catastrophe—or *both* catastrophes—some conversion whereby his relation to the negative (as instantiated in the law with which he once identified; MD 9) has been transmuted. The breach in the day that the narrator experiences as exposure to its inner "madness" (a movement at once within and without) gives a relation to the day as such and leaves the narrator with not only an affirmative relation to life and death (which renders any temptation of suicide a "strange error"), but a capacity for repetition—if only in the form of a capacity to affirm repetition. In *The Step Not Beyond*, a transmuting passage of this kind is described as an affirmation of the neutral that effaces its trait of negation.

What are we to make of the effacement, then, if it is not to be confused in any manner with suicide and represents, perhaps, no end? *The Madness of the Day* gives little hint, but the term is insistent in Blanchot's thought of the experience of writing and the neutral. For this immediate context, an especially important appeal to the term occurs in *The Writing of the Disaster* in pages that precede the scene Blanchot hesitantly calls "primal" and that shares important traits with the catastrophic experience of glass shattering in the eyes, including an "unexpected" feeling of joy and a vertiginous knowledge that "nothing is what there is, and first of all, nothing beyond." A markedly theoretical statement appearing just before the primal scene gives the following:

> "A child is being killed." Let us make no mistake about this present: it signifies that the deed cannot be done once and for all, that the operation is completed at no privileged moment in time—that, inoperable, it operates and that thus it tends to be none but the very time which destroys (effaces) time. This is the effacement or destruction, or gift, which has always already been exposed in the precession of Speaking—Speaking separate from and outside of anything spoken, the sheer saying of writing—whereby this effacement, far from effacing itself in its turn, perpetuates itself without end, even in the interruption that is its mark.[4]

Is not such an effacement what the narrator awaits, ecstatically, in *The Madness of the Day*? Twice he has known the day's interruption, and in this repetition he has come to await not what we might immediately link to the term "apocalypse," but an end of the day that will come again as a gift, already said, already written. The relation of waiting is named "survival" in *The Writing of the Disaster* (WD 179/116): "living by acquiescence to the refusal" (wherein what has come without coming about in any present will remain forever imminent). Earlier in the volume, and of the *writing* relation, Blanchot offers a statement that reiterates what we read in *The Madness of the Day* of a kind of ethical stance:

> Dying means you are dead already, in an immemorial past, of a death which was not yours, which you have thus neither known nor lived, but under the threat of which you believe you are called upon to live; you await it henceforth in the future, constructing a future to make it possible at last—possible as something that will take place and will belong to the realm of experience.
>
> To write is no longer to situate death in the future—the death which is always already past; to write is to accept that one has to die without making death present and without making oneself present to it. To write is to know that death has taken place even though it has not been experienced, and to recognize it in the forgetfulness that it leaves—in the traces which, effacing themselves, call upon one to *exclude oneself from the cosmic order* and to abide where the disaster makes the real impossible and desire undesirable. (WD 65–66)

To accept suffering what will have never taken place in any present (of lived experience, *Erlebnis*), to know it in forgetting, and to recognize the exigency of self-exception from the cosmic order—to except oneself and to wait *there* ("where the disaster . . ."). There again is an appeal to an enigmatic (non) agency, doubly envisioned in a passivity (that Blanchot will describe in *The Step Not Beyond* and *The Writing of the Disaster* as self-transgressive, beyond any passivity) and an act of sovereign exception.

Is the one who says yes in *The Madness of the Day* a writer? Of course, he is designated so explicitly by the authorities. We could almost conclude (following the narrator's insistence on this point and leaving aside some other apparent reasons for his institutionalization) that he is incarcerated *because* he is a writer, and thus presumed capable of an answer to the demand for a reasoned account. The affirmed self-effacement is perhaps not necessarily the preserve of the writer, but its self-reserving enunciation in this text is given to us as *written* in a sense the authorities could never recognize, and written perhaps from the same space as that of the excepting "no."

But there is our question: how does the "no" of refusal communicate with the "yes" (both the acquiescence in which the retreating narrative is carried and the affirmation that sounds in it)? Is there a relation? The importance of the motif of refusal in texts from throughout the postwar period obliges us to move again outside *The Madness of the Day* in search of an answer. Let us begin from its emergence in this text.

The "no," as we have seen, takes exception to the request to which the narrator originally acceded. The initial acquiescence, it must be acknowledged, was not simple; the relation to the doctors was playfully deceptive to the extent that he offered everything (even the day) as well as nothing. Thus, a silence was preserved even as it was offered. The "no," however, receives the request as an arraigning demand. One could argue (depending on how one situates the actual end of the narrative and in maintaining a certain narrative order) that it follows a kind of realization on the part of the narrator, something like a gaining of focus. When the narrator offers his acknowledgment that he was now incapable of forming a narrative, the demand only becomes more exigent:

> Then I noticed for the first time that there were two of them and that this distortion of the traditional method, even though it was explained by the fact that one of them was an eye doctor, the other a specialist in mental illness, constantly gave our conversation the character of an authoritarian interrogation, overseen and controlled by a strict set of rules. Of course, neither of them was the chief of police. But because there were two of them, there were three, and this third remained firmly convinced, I am sure, that a writer, a man who speaks and who reasons with distinction, is always capable of recounting facts that he remembers. (WD 18)

Having playfully described the doctors as "kings" demanding their due of the patient, the narrator now recognizes the coalescence of an epistemic and juridical order in this arraigning call, this *Geheiss* of modern technical reason. He has already glimpsed the limits of the rational and legal authority that speaks in this demand for a reasoned account. Those limits were explored with the figure of the law who appears behind the backs of the technicians in silhouette (MD 28–30). The narrator's marvelous descriptions of the erotic activities to which he lends himself with this feminized figure (here again we glimpse his passivity) give us another version of sovereignty—let us call it Bataillian—that Blanchot seeks, perhaps, to delimit in relation to both the sovereign yes and the sovereign no.[5] But the demand of reason that requires total compliance, however "incomplete" this arraigning order might actually be in relation to its presumption of a completely secularized and complete authority, provokes an *absolute* refusal.

The text closes with a trenchant denial that appears to convert the previous acknowledgment of incapacity (an inability to form a narrative by reason of a loss of a sense of history: "it happens in a good many illnesses"; MD 18) into a resolute stance. In its decision, it bears an entirely different edge; if it speaks to an incapacity, it does so from a knowledge of interruption that was not previously evident in the narrator's statements (as though the refusing subject—and nothing guarantees that this is the same subject— has taken the meaning of what is recounted in the retreating narrative). Indeed, the no seems to issue from a space or time other than that of the incarceration described in the lines that precede it. It speaks to the law and the sovereignty of reason, to be sure, but it now draws a line in relation to the latter's demand. The line marks what is perhaps the end of a history (the closure of a symbolic order that will be echoed in Adorno's statement to the effect that no poetry could be possible after Auschwitz), but its rhetorical force is resolutely ethical and political.

A refusal of this form can be traced back quite far in Blanchot's political writings,[6] but its reemergence in the postwar period is most dramatically visible in two sets of texts that mark the opening, and, to some degree, the closing of Blanchot's return to political activity in the decade between 1958, when Blanchot joined Dionys Mascolo in the project of *Le 14 juillet*,[7] and 1968, when Blanchot gave unqualified support to the Comité. An ethico-political exigency continues to resound in his work, as we will see in *The Step Not Beyond* and *The Unavowable Community*, but by the time of the former publication (1973), his political activism had receded.

The first group of texts includes "The Declaration of the 121," which Blanchot principally drafted, and the accompanying statements to Madeleine Chapsal in "The Right to Insubordination."[8] The political context for these texts is precise, and the response (involving a definition of right as opposed to duty) is precisely drawn. The manifesto is a statement on the part of intellectuals, many of whom, as Blanchot later noted, would not describe themselves as political or "engaged" in the Sartrean sense (its origin was thus not determined by a preexisting political stance) that is meant to support and justify a refusal on the part of young French soldiers to bear arms against the Algerian people. Insubordination, as Blanchot underlines, is "a solemn word of utmost refusal" (BR 196). The force with which this word is underscored leads us back, in turn, to the brief text published in 1958 in the second issue of *14 juillet*, and collected in *Friendship*,

"Refusal," which Blanchot dates "exceptionally" in the latter volume with the additional mention that it was written "just a few days after General de Gaulle returned to power, borne this time, not by the Resistance, but by the mercenaries."[9]

The justification of insubordination appealed to a notion of freedom; it was a "right," Blanchot argued, precisely because it was not dictated by some established moral imperative or some duty (indeed, the "Declaration of the 121," as he asserts, had argued that "traditional civic duties had ceased to exist as obligations"; BR 197). The right of insubordination called upon a "sovereign decision" on the part of each individual: "Right is a free power for which each person, for his part and in relation to himself, is responsible, and which binds him completely and freely; nothing is stronger, nothing is more solemn" (BR 197). It could be argued that Blanchot will never fully abandon the language of responsibility, even as he moves from a notion of *being responsible for* to a notion of "*answering for*" that is no longer a bearing of responsibility. It will be maintained at least as long as he maintains the necessity of a double response to affliction (to which I return below). But already in the text of 1958, individual or "solitary" refusal, in its absolute or categorical character (thus refusing all conciliation, even when what is refused is "not without value or importance") draws from an anonymous source that constitutes the "friendship" of a "certain No" (PW 7/130)—a bond that remains when "the time of common affirmation" has been suspended. When this movement of refusal takes form, a rupture has occurred, Blanchot declares, and this movement proceeds from the most modest of sources:

> When we refuse, we refuse in a movement without scorn, without exaltation, a movement that is as anonymous as it can be, for the power of refusing is not brought about from the basis of ourselves, nor in our sole name, but from a very poor beginning that belongs first to those who cannot speak. (PW 7/130)

In this respect, it already communicates with that powerless refusal that Blanchot locates in that final resistance to torture or oppression to which Antelme bore witness.[10]

In his text from the third issue of 14 *juillet*, "The Essential Perversion" (MD 8–14), Blanchot suggests that this refusal has taken form in relation to a regime that represents political death—indeed, the neutralization of any politics. In this respect, the "no" that he articulates multiply in relation to de Gaulle confronts not just a political order but also an essential perversion wherein political existence (in a democratic form) surrenders to a power of salvation that emanates from a man who assumes the role of a destiny. The "no" is thus not political (in the sense that it would emerge from a determinate political position); or, rather, it is fundamentally political in that it seeks to preserve the opening for the political as such. It is thus of the same "absolute" order as the "no" of *The Madness of the Day*, which draws a line in relation to an epistemic and juridical order that has roots as ancient as those of Western reason,[11] but whose modern accomplishment is the sociopolitical apparatus that has emerged with that "destiny" Heidegger termed *Technik*.

The "no" proceeds from rupture, as Blanchot states in "Refusal." In 1968, Blanchot will affirm that "the revolution is behind us" as he calls upon a (non)power of refusal to *affirm the break* (BR 200). The language bears the inflections of the *extrême gauche*, and thus what is sometimes the fatal ambiguity of such revolutionary language.[12] But much of it is also, in important respects, *pure Blanchot* (which is to say, Blanchot becoming-anonymous), and one can recognize the intense anticipation from which Blanchot greeted and affirmed the rupture that had already occurred when it showed itself in the real possibility of revolution.[13]

"To affirm the break": to draw out ("make it more and more real, more and more radical"), in writing and theory, a rupture with all extant formations of power, wherever they manifest themselves—all alienating forms for which the "proper" to be reaffirmed is not some vital force or identity, but a relation to "the non-structurable" of the break itself, and for which Blanchot appeals to the language of "disaster" (BR 200–201). The refusal that answers the "communist exigency," as Blanchot articulates it—at once rupture and a call *to go out*[14]—must exceed its moment and exceed its negative thrust, even as it maintains its refusal vis-à-vis any accommodation. Thinking this refusal *as affirmation*, Blanchot declares, "is one of the theoretical tasks of the new political thinking" (BR 201).

How is it to be affirmed? How is this theoretical project to be pursued? The writing in which this last statement is made constitutes one answer; another, of course, will be delivered in the multiple forms of theoretical writing that belong to *The Step Not Beyond*. And other writers will deliver other answers.[15] Blanchot is categorical in declaring that it must not be pursued in commentary, analysis, or any form of "epitaph." It cannot be a matter of writing *about* May 1968 since the event is "destined, precisely, (along with others) to prevent us from ever again writing *about*" (BR 204). To objectify in some historicizing, thematizing, or theorizing gesture is to paper over the break (but the metaphor is too coy: it is to *foreclose* the break) and resuscitate the very form of "History" as a gathering, unifying, and totalizing continuity, the Book:

> We shall therefore never write about what took place or did not take place in May; not out of respect, nor even a concern not to place restrictions on the event by circumscribing it. We admit that this refusal is one of the points where writing and the decision to break coincide: each of them always imminent and always unpredictable. (BR 204)

The break may come at any time, writing may come at any time (*ce jour s'effaçant...*)—the break will have always already occurred, and the exigency is to actively wait from the ground of this disaster, already in writing.

Hence the imperative of "tracts, posters, bulletins" (BR 204). In a very real sense, *The Madness of the Day* will have already anticipated, already prepared this upheaval. Its refusal to answer the arraigning demand for an account, its fragmented, quasi-mythopoeic narrative of a "hero" who is neither quite human nor divine (something of a blinded Oedipus, something of a fallen deity, a miserable library worker treated as an "insect," and so forth)—these are already a coupling of the decision to break and the writing that bears witness to the rupture for which Blanchot now seeks fragmentary forms. In "Tracts, Posters, Bulletins," there is even an unmistakable echo of *The Madness of the Day*: "No more books, never again" (BR 205). The thought that important parts of his own "oeuvre" would be swept away in the winds that destine all bulletins to the street (the soaked streets of Paris that will become the desiccated streets of the city of *The Step Not Beyond*) would not dissatisfy its author. This is part of what the "yes" was to: effacement.

It would be facile to declare that *The Madness of the Day* was properly *of* 1968, or *for* 1968, even if we draw to mind the odd way in which other narratives by Blanchot have appeared as strangely premonitory.[16] But it might be appropriate to say that a vital part of its truth emerged in that event, and particularly if we underscore to what degree that "truth" sheds its light on the writing for which Blanchot was calling. Let us recall again Blanchot's response to Catherine David in *La Nouvelle Observateur* under the title "To refuse the established order." Having addressed the topic of engagement, Blanchot adds:

> There is, perhaps, a cultural power [enjoyed by writers]. But it is ambiguous and always risks losing this ambiguity by placing itself in the service of another power that subjects it. To write is, at the limit, what of itself cannot (be done), therefore always in search of a non-power, refusing mastery, order, and first of all the established order, preferring silence to a word of absolute truth, thus contesting and contesting ceaselessly.

This is not just contestation, obviously, and it is not just silent resistance. It is a search for a nonpower, and in this it is greeted in advance by the passivity we have seen in the words and acts of the narrative voice in much of *The Madness of the Day*, even in its most fatigued form. Here, we glimpse a dimension of refusal to which Blanchot returns in a later statement (in a text initially published in 1975 in *Le Nouveau Commerce* and subsequently collected in *The Writing of the Disaster*):

> Refusal is said to be the first degree of passivity. But if refusal is deliberate and voluntary, if it expresses a decision—though this be a negative one—it does not yet allow us to separate it from the power of consciousness, remaining at best of a self that refuses. It is true that refusal tends toward the absolute, toward a sort of unconditional. This is the core of refusal which Bartleby the scrivener's inexorable "*I would prefer not to* (do it)" brings to us: an abstention which has never had to be decided upon, which precedes every decision and which is more than a denial [*dénégation*], something more like an abdication, the renunciation (never pronounced, never clarified) of ever saying anything, of the authority of speaking, or else an abnegation understood as the abandonment of the self, a relinquishment of identity, a refusal of self that does not cleave to refusal but opens to failure, to the loss of being, to thought. "I will not do it" would still have signified an energetic determination, calling forth an equally energetic contradiction. "*I would prefer not to* . . ." belongs to the infinite of patience, offering no hold to dialectical intervention. We have fallen out of being, in the field of the outside where, immobile, walking with a slow and even step, the destroyed men come and go. (WD 17/33–34)

A trace of such inexorable refusal is perhaps audible in "A story? No, no stories, never again," particularly inasmuch as the statement follows an expression of incapacity. It is clearly a far more radical renunciation than anything envisioned by Heidegger or even Benjamin (in the poet's *Absagen* or the translator's *Aufgeben*). Here, the opening of thought is also a fall outside being and into the errancy of "the field of the outside"—the deserted space of the concluding pages of *The Step Not Beyond*. This is a passage into effacement, as a subsequent fragment from *The Writing of the Disaster* clearly indicates, echoing, almost as its "negative" obverse, the affirmative sentence from which we began:

> In "Bartleby," the enigma comes from "pure" writing, which can only be that of a copying (re-writing), from the passivity into which this activity disappears, and which *passes* imperceptibly and suddenly from ordinary passivity (re-production), to the beyond of everything passive: to a life so passive— for it has the hidden decency of dying—that it does not issue in death, never makes death an escape. Bartleby copies: he writes incessantly, and cannot stop long enough to submit to anything resembling control. *I would prefer not to* (do it). This sentence speaks in the intimacy of our nights: negative preference, *the negation that effaces preference and is effaced therein* [my emphasis]: the neuter of that which is not among the things there are to do—the restraint, the gentleness that cannot be called obstinate, and that frustrates obstinacy with those few words. . . . Language goes silent in perpetuating itself. (WD 145/219)

Do we have in this self-effacing negative, a negative without the motivating power to sustain any preference (in the sense of a putting or carrying forward) or its own self-negation, a failing negative that as such is an opening to thought, already the trace of an affirmation? Or are we, perhaps, at the neutral border of the yes and the no, in the incipient passing of *le pas au-delà*, where acquiescence has not yet become affirmation, or invitation? Where a no veers into a yes without accomplishing the turn of return?

These are questions that remain abstract at this point and must await further development of the question of relation to the neutral. Let us therefore draw to a conclusion by returning to the question from which we began: what is the relation between the sovereign yes and the sovereign no? Does the concluding refusal of *The Madness of the Day* communicate somehow with the infinite act described at the start? Does the same impetus sound in its concluding decision as the one that carries the ecstatic engagement of the narrator that is pronounced in the phrase on which we have focused: *ce jour s'effaçant, je m'effacerai avec lui?*

The "no," of course, has a trenchant, adversary character (even as it follows the expression of incapacity). It draws the line of a rupture in relation to any complicity with the arraigning demand for an account (which is perforce a self-accounting) even as it draws a line in relation to the reigning juridical and epistemic order. As such, it is a political act that remarks the political order as such. To the extent that it is read as concluding from interruption (the "discovery" of the madness of the day), it points toward an end in History itself, declaring the disruption of any foundation for narrated "histories."

The step (not) beyond of which the narrator describes himself capable in the opening of the text (again: is this necessarily the *same* narrator?) points to a *passage* in exception—a crossing of the line, so to speak. It announces a "freedom" (but the word is surely risky here), that would seem to be of a very different order from the distance claimed in the refusal—a rarer, and ultimately more enigmatic transcendence. But does the concluding "no" deny or suspend this affirmed passage? Does its perhaps preserve or safeguard it somehow?

In conceptual terms, and from the sole basis of this text, there would appear to be no way to establish the relation between the sovereign act of exception (which takes exception from the demand for an ordered account) and the sovereign will to self-effacement. *Both proceed from an experience (or experiences) of interruption*; they appear to have the same origin. The bridge between them, though, if it exists, escapes conceptual articulation. Nothing assures us that the "no" is carried or inspired by the "yes" (in the sense that refusal would find its force in a different relation), or that it could ever carry beyond the knowledge of interruption—it carries, in effect, no further than the engagement embedded in its statement. It does not apparently negate the preceding, infinitely receding yes (what preceded it was hardly a story and the no is only to the demand—it does not renounce anything said and only refuses the form of the required saying), any more than it actively guards or prepares its advent in a rigorous commitment to waiting. It refuses surrender, but it does not look explicitly beyond the demand from which it turns.

Must we then satisfy ourselves with saying that it is a neutral or interrupted relation? The conclusion is not insignificant in itself, but it demands development, and for this it is tempting to seek clues in other texts. For the question we confront here is in fact reproduced in every one of Blanchot's appeals to a double movement or double exigency, every instance in which Blanchot affirms the imperative of holding to a political response even as he evokes a relation that exceeds the political order. We saw a version of this dilemma in Blanchot's reading of Antelme, and we find it again in the preparatory writings for *The International Journal*, where Blanchot articulates the dual imperative of answering a political responsibility that is "at once global and concrete" while pursuing a literary responsibility, all the while confronting the "discordance" between these exigencies. A letter to Bataille of January 1962 offers it once again in terms of the exigencies of thought and poetry, and once again affirms the necessity of "uniting the incompatible."[17]

An immense question lies here that requires a careful analysis of the inherent ambiguities of both the affirmative and the negative as they are encountered in activism and/or explored by "literary" writing (this is the topic already explored at considerable length in "Literature and the Right to Death"). Not only must we think the articulation between what we might call orders of discourse (the "silent refusal of true speech," for example, and the concerted no of political struggle), and this within a "single" subject, or in moving from the individual to the collective, we must also entertain multiple versions of the relation between the yes and the no. The events of May 1968 pointed to a coexistence of refusal and affirmation as participants sought a razing of the ground in ceaseless reference to a destructuring rupture. Can refusal be thought *from* affirmation or some form of "yes" that does not reproduce a now abstract radicalism?

Blanchot will never abandon the question of political responsibility, but a movement to the limit of politics will take the preponderant place in his writing. The path of the "yes" will assume priority as Blanchot thinks the affirmation of fragmentary writing, or what he calls in *The Unavowable Community* "a certain kind of writing" (UC 12/26). The "yes" to effacement will accordingly become the focus of the succeeding chapters as we move toward *The Step Not Beyond*. But I would like to close this one by drawing out a kind of loose end (or loose beginning). For, in following the narrator's ecstatic affirmation in *The Madness of the Day*, we left behind one of the instances of affirmation from which we started and over which we paused for only the briefest remark, as a pleasure in living was coupled to an enigmatic satisfaction in dying. What of that pleasure that resurfaces as the world (and God, perhaps our narrator: "I said to myself: God, what are you doing?") regains its equilibrium and reason returns to the narrator with memory? The losses of the ego cannot override a strangely "grounded"—but grounded in the earth: "the cool of the night and the stability of the ground"—elation (*allegresse*). *Breath* and *repose*, gathered in reason and memory: the thanking thought of the day given in its proximity to the night. This receptive opening onto the day as to a kind of environing element gives the possibility of thinking a relation to being that is without defense or refusal in the sense of that "great refusal" described in *The Infinite Conversation*, where resistance is directed to "the universal corruption that reigns over what is"—the death or the nothingness that is inseparable from "the earth, where everything disappears" (IC 33/46). In describing what this refusal closes out or loses in this later essay, Blanchot will pass from the most delicate poetic statement evoking the "real presence" of earthly being to an evocation of chaos and the sacred, focusing at length on relation to an impossible "immediate" (we will return to these pages). In the opening section of the text, though, he offers a rather gentle evocation of a relation to life and to death that affirms their commingling, and where the *other* night is not foreclosed. Something like this relation is affirmed by Blanchot's narrator in *The Madness of the Day*. It is not the relation of life and death Hölderlin ascribed to the vision of "poor Oedipus" (what Oedipus knows with his "eye too many": "life is death, and death is a kind of life"). Rather, Blanchot's "Oedipus" is affirming—or at least admiring the capacity for—the most elemental, hospitable assumption of the presence of death in life, and a yes to the insistence of life (natality, to begin, and then every interruptive upsurgence in being) that no "no" can ever silence. A yes to the real of the gift of natality/mortality.

Thus, in the ecstatic "yes" of "*je m'effacerai*," there is enfolded another yes to effacement—a yes to finitude that does not need to sublate the real given in the exposure of mortal being in some project, or some name; a yes that can face the confusion of death (the other, the "impossible" death) and death (corruption) to which Blanchot recalls us in the solemn phrase from his famous essay on friendship: "*tout s'efface*."[18] At "every minute," and thus in a present without ecstatic temporalization (as in the first yes to effacement), the narrator is capable of something that makes him evoke the receptiveness of those whom he calls "beautiful creatures." It is of course intriguing that Blanchot appends to this capacity the sign of sexual difference, even while acknowledging that the "capacity," the thinking "usage" in question, is not exclusive to women. (Men are a "bizarre species," though some—"almost always women"—are capable of not erecting defensive borders of the proper, masking becoming in the form of a world that would exclude everything *immonde*.)

On this occasion, I will take the latter question no further than to ask, in anticipation, whether the young girl of *The Step Not Beyond* deserves the epithet "beautiful" for her gesture of receiving the one in fear who seeks her aid. Her gesture of unreserved hospitality is one that the narrating, reflecting voice, *cannot qualify* in political or moral terms, even though it may well be the ground of any sharing, any "communism" in the sense Blanchot seeks for this term. I will try to suggest, in any case, that the almost unthinkable possibility of this hospitable yes motivates in an essential manner the writing of *The Step Not Beyond*.

Let us close this reading of *The Madness of the Day*, then, with the very simplest question, and thus the most alluring enigma: Could the relation between the yes and the yes hold the key to a transmuted relation between the yes and the no? Could the yes that passes, in this text, by way of sexual difference couple with the yes of writing to allow that *other* relation to the political order (thinking refusal from affirmation) that Blanchot sought under a name such as "community"?

FOUR

A Simple Change in the Play of Words: The Infinite Conversation

From the Backdrop of Echoing Conversations

In the last lines of the narrated conversation ("*l'entretien*") that opens *The Infinite Conversation*, we read of a refusal that is perhaps a willing of effacement, perhaps a step. The fragment in which these lines appear should be cited in its entirety, if only for the sheer poise with which it evokes the enigma of a willed departure from the apparent peace of a forever offered present.

> ±± He listened to the speech of the everyday, grave, idle, saying everything, holding up to each one what he would have liked to say, a speech unique, distant and always close, everyone's speech, always already expressed and yet infinitely sweet to say, infinitely precious to hear—the speech of temporal eternity saying: now, now, now.
> How had he come to will the interruption of discourse? And not the legitimate pause, the one permitting the give and take of conversation, the

benevolent, intelligent pause, nor that beautifully poised waiting with which two interlocutors, from one shore to another, measure their right to communicate. No, not that, and no more so the austere silence, the tacit speech of visible things, the reserve of those invisible. What he had wanted was entirely different, a cold interruption, the rupture of the circle. And at once this had happened: the heart ceasing to beat, the eternal drive to speak stopping. (IC xxiii/xxvi)

The one who chooses interruption refuses a *near perfect* comfort: not the grounding of the earthly elements, but that of another form of element, the speech of the everyday, whose forever renewed promise finds what is perhaps its sublation in the promise of the end of history, held out by a logos reflecting its accomplishment in the silence of a library (IC xiv/xi). There has been simply the intervention of an almost negligible (*"infime"* [IC 207/307]) interruption; a breach in the horizon of the forever-reiterated *now*, and with it the insistence of an enigmatic exigency to which at least one of the interlocutors has been driven to bear witness in the conversation that takes form in relation to it.

Since this last interdicting exigency has for the most part been *suffered* in the time and space it has opened (fatigue, pain, solitude, the pressure of a form of unremitting inquiry), the act of willing the interruption gives itself as a stunning step. From where would the impetus come? The answer, a partial answer at least, appears to lie in the conversation itself, in an *experience* of conversation (hearing in this the Latin *experire*, a passage involving danger) that "The Infinite Conversation" will have sought to narrate. For, as we are told in a fragment near the end of its trajectory (a fragment not easily assimilated before we read the end), interruption communicates a "cold force" that proves impelling for this dialogue that now becomes "infinite."

> Interruption: a pain, a weariness.
> While speaking to someone, he comes to feel the cold force of interruption assert itself [*s'affirmer*]. And strangely, the dialogue does not stop; on the contrary, it becomes more resolute, more decisive, yet so hazardous that their relation to the common space disappears between them forever. (IC xxii/xxiv)

To will the interruption of the discourse, in other words, is not only to "affirm the break"; it is to will something that communicates or affirms itself in that break. It is to open to the fragmenting force of an infinite conversation and to will disappearance, in friendship, from the common space of achieved understanding (be this in its everyday form or in that of a dialectical completion).

We thus glimpse how the last lines of "The Infinite Conversation" open upon the volume to which this conversation has lent its title.[1] They effectively indicate the opening its essays will explore in what Blanchot names (provocatively for our time) a "research."[2] This is a field of resonance that will not fail to produce internal references so strong that one is tempted to ask whether a significant portion of the theoretical reflections presented in the volume (which can themselves sometimes take a conversational form) are somehow the theory *of* what has occurred in the overture, or whether the conversation itself is the "fictive" recitation or repetition of those concepts (though repetition here must take a very particular sense, particularly as the concepts themselves will have already been caught in a play of repetition).[3] A question we will encounter again appears here as we are invited to consider the relation between "theory" and the writing Blanchot cautiously calls "literary."[4] But because our question is more restricted—we are following the steps of effacement—let us concentrate, to begin, on only one of these points of internal reference, one of perhaps special resonance in that it evokes a lived precedent for the conversation we seek to read here. This reference should help open to our hearing—but *by relief*—an often-enigmatic conversation.

The precedent is the conversation Blanchot pursued with Bataille in the early forties, and then beyond.[5] This exchange is clearly informing pages devoted in *The Infinite Conversation* to Bataille—particularly those paragraphs in "The Limit-Experience" concerning Bataille's startling presence in speech. These paragraphs take up after an indication of the point from which Blanchot believes we might hear "what reading alone" will draw forth from Bataille's work,[6] a point that is marked in a response to a question concerning the very possibility of a desire of/for an experience that affords no return for the subject that abandons itself to it (and thus the possibility of some relation to its communication). The response is unexpected, Blanchot suggests, but Bataille's own books, and with them, "the surprise of his language," allow us to suppose it.

> Speech entertains what no existent being in the primacy of their own name can attain; what existence itself, in the seduction of its fortuitous particularity, in the play of its slipping universality, could never hold within itself. And not only

does speech retain what decidedly escapes in this manner, but it is on the basis of this always foreign and always furtive affirmation—the impossible and incommunicable—that it speaks, finding there its origin, just as it is in this speech that thought thinks more than it can. And no doubt this is not just any speech. It does not contribute to discourse, it does not add anything to what has already been formulated; it would wish only to lead to what, outside all community, would come to "communicate" itself if, finally, when "everything" was consummated, there was nothing more to say: saying then the ultimate exigency. (IC 210–211/312)

The Infinite Conversation returns repeatedly to the thesis that it is in language, in a certain speech (where speaking, as Blanchot notes elliptically, becomes writing; IC 77/109) that relation with the immeasurable other—and first of all, the alterity, the neutral presence of *autrui*—is given. The task of *The Infinite Conversation*, to put things in the simplest terms possible, is to bring that speech (and the exigency it communicates) to the fore—multiply. When Blanchot draws that exigency forth from Bataille's speech in the essay under consideration here, he gives us the means to link his account of conversation with Bataille to the long dialogical presentation pursued in reference to Levinas in the first part of *The Infinite Conversation*, his meditation on the infinite set of relations that open between "the two men there in a room" (IC 73/104). Bataille's thought of "the inner experience" and the affirmation at stake there is thus firmly brought into communication with that presence of the neutral/the neutre that Blanchot attributes to the relation with *autrui*.

Thus it would be quite misleading to suggest that exchanges with Bataille brought to theoretical exposition in "The Limit-Experience" give us the key to the conversation that opens *The Infinite Conversation*. They allow an invaluable perspective on its conditions and its site, however. Regarding its site, Blanchot underscores that its possibility opens at that limit where the project of meaning has consummated itself, where all making and doing have produced or at least projected their end (with the production of "man" himself). This prospect of an end of history is where there appears the strange surplus of an *"infime interstice"* [IC 207/307] that creates the exigency of another speaking. Accordingly, the host in the conversation we are approaching feels he has something he must try to bring to speech (*il lui faut parler*). The exigency itself, however, cannot be produced as such, and the task cannot be fulfilled by any work or project. Requiring a fidelity of an impossible kind, it will be known in a debilitating fatigue.

The "conditions" include a commitment and a decision that Blanchot recognized in the singular character of Bataille's approach to conversation. Blanchot points, in this respect, to Bataille's unique power of speaking; his power of bringing his own presence into speech, and by this presence prompting the attention of thought. Such power, Blanchot writes, alerted his interlocutors to the gravity of the fact that "as soon as one speaks, and even in the simplest manner of the simplest facts, immediately something inordinate is at stake, something that waits in the reserve of familiar discourse" (IC 211–212/314). It called attention to what is afforded to thought by language, the chance of a relation "'immediately' without measure." It allowed Bataille to assume the inescapable lightness of speech (its infidelity in communicating the important, its misuse when spent in insignificant matters) in such a way as to answer the "frankness" of another's presence. In all of this, a *precaution* in speaking guided by the awareness that in every word "everything is already at stake" (IC 212/315): we speak or we kill. But this was not a form of prudence; it was rather a form of attention that opened onto a "presence between" that transforms the meaning of "*entretien*," making conversation a holding open, in speech, of relation to an "impossible":

> What is present in this presence of speech, as soon as it affirms itself, is precisely what never lets itself be seen or attained: something is there that is beyond reach (of the one who says it as much as of the one who hears it). It is between us, it holds itself between, and conversation is approach on the basis of this between-two: an irreducible distance that must be preserved if one wishes to maintain a relation with the unknown that is the unique gift of speech. (IC 212/315)

Conversation with Bataille was a shared approach to the other, the sharing of a friendship *for the other* that ultimately exceeds the relation between the one interlocutor and the other. The conversation that opens *The Infinite Conversation* stages this point of egression quite dramatically, as we will see, and opens the question of what it might mean to sustain, in solitude, this relation of friendship.

The condition, then, was a peculiar form of care and an enigmatic assumption of the non-familiar that comes in thought when it *becomes* thought by sustaining the intention of this nonfamiliar. Thought can know, in the intimacy of the speaking that occurs in conversation, in the space of its "between," a kind of conduit to a thinking that opens beyond what it can think. Blanchot names the opening of this intimate other in thinking an *attention* that forms the true site of the conversation:

> What solicits thought is always the non-familiar. There is no recognition of what it aims for; each time there is a new beginning and a decision to offer itself up to the non-known whose intention thought sustains. And yet this non-familiarity that the strangeness in speech preserves is also the intimacy of thought; it passes by way of this abrupt and silent, I mean implicit, intimacy that is destined to open within the known and frequentable space between two interlocutors another space where habitual possibilities steal away. This other space opened by the non-familiar intimacy of thought is the space of attention. But let us specify immediately that it is not simply an attentive listener of whom the one speaking would have need. This attention is between the one and the other: center of the encounter, sign of the between-two that brings close as it separates. Attention empties the site of all that encumbers it and renders it visible. This is a profound and at times painfully hollowed out absence on the basis of which, and in coinciding with it, the presence of speech is able to affirm itself. In the sense that this attention is the attention of no one, it is impersonal; but it is also, through speech and beyond those who are there, the waiting [*l'attente*] for what is in play, through speech, between those who are there. (IC 213/316)

There is a most arresting evocation here of the emptying (and exposure) of space pursued in Blanchot's narratives, and an intriguing allusion to the presentation of speech: the affirmation that awaits in language is inseparable from this "affirmation" of language itself (though Blanchot will insist that we hear this in the neutral). We also encounter again the conditions for an "infinite" conversation. For the "waiting" of the attention Blanchot has named is said to *respond* to an understanding between the interlocutors that is founded in an ever-renewed commitment:

> Yet this attention also responds to an accord between two beings, each one carried by the decision to sustain the same movement of research and thus to be faithful (without faith and without guarantee) to this same rigorous movement. Here a mutual promise is made that commits the play of thought to a common openness in this game in which the players are two speaking beings and through which thought is each time asked to affirm its relation to the unknown. (IC 213/316–317)

Thus, in the answer to the "understanding" between two interlocutors, we glimpse the possibility of an *other* conversation, a conversation in which the

82   *Refusal/Affirmation*

communication of an infinite is at stake: "Let us understand that what is at stake in this game is the essential: the arrival [*l'atteinte*] at an infinite affirmation" (IC 213/317).

We thus meet again the vital Blanchotian motif of *une attente*: a waiting, an awakening that opens beyond any subjective capacity. We have met it as a trait of survival.[7] In *The Infinite Conversation*, (in another, very strong instance of the kind of resonance between conversation and volume to which I referred), it appears as the "measure," in language, of the immeasurable. Evoking the forms of interruption that can be at work in conversation, Blanchot points, beyond those pauses that allow a give and take, or the articulation of opposing positions (interruption in these cases is the very breath of discourse, the hinge of dialectic), to a more enigmatic rupture that bears witness to the strangeness between two beings, that alterity that Blanchot designates as *neutre*:

> To simplify, let us say that through the presence of the other understood in the neutral there is in the field of relations a distortion preventing any direct communication and any relation of unity; or again, there is a fundamental anomaly that it falls to speech not to reduce but to convey, even if it does so without saying it or signifying it. Now it is to this hiatus—to the strangeness, to the infinity between us—that the interruption in language itself responds, the interruption that introduces waiting. (IC 77/109)

We will have occasion to return to this passage, which goes on to evoke the "simple change" of our title. But let us note merely that such a waiting forms the ex-centric orientation of the first stages of the conversation we seek to approach. Something or someone ("*il*": "someone else, the event" IC xvi/xv) attends and awaits response in the conversation to which the interlocutors commit themselves: some other for which a place is kept and "who would be their true interlocutor . . . were they (it) addressed" (IC xiv/x). As the conversation becomes "infinite," this place will itself disperse.

But the site of waiting is also a site of forgetting. The ultimate exigency of the inner experience, Blanchot tells us, remains latent: "For no recollection could confirm it, as it goes beyond all memory and only forgetting is of its measure, the immense forgetting borne by speech." He continues: "For this affirmation, the most transparent, the most opaque (the obscure as transparency), which man does not remember, but which waits in the attention of language, Georges Bataille was called to be the respondent" (IC 211/313). Committing themselves to the conversation, therefore, the interlocutors also commit themselves to forgetting, as well as to the peculiar form of effacement that lies in the destiny of the spoken word. The effacement communicates with the one affirmed in *The Madness of the Day* (which we can now read as also profoundly Bataillian), to be sure. But as we saw in that text, the effacement proper to the passage beyond is not ultimately separable from the passing that is part of the experience of finitude, even though it opens an infinite excess in relation to the "banal" perishing that affirmation cannot deny. Such a passing is marked in a distinctive way in speech, Blanchot affirms, in that commitment to conversation is commitment to chance and becoming, a special assumption of the contingencies of life that communicates with a more profound assumption of the finitude of language itself.

> Let us understand, then, why it can happen that speaking does not bow to writing. Speech bears in it the fortuitous trait that links thought in the game to chance. Speech depends immediately upon life, on the humors and fatigues of life, and it opens to them as its secret truth: a weary player may be closer to the game's attention than the brilliant player who is master of himself and of his attention. Above all, speech is perishable. Scarcely said, it is effaced, lost without recourse. It forgets itself. In the intimacy of this speech forgetting speaks—not only a forgetting that is partial and limited, but the profound forgetting out of which all memory arises. Whoever is speaking is already forgotten. (IC 214/317)

L'attente, l'oubli. And thus, in this "resolute" conversation, a yes to life (conceived as "the inner heart of thought") and a yes to death and dying in the sense of becoming. These are not a subject's prerogative; they are offered by an affirmation given in the conversation.

Can we read such an affirmative movement in the written conversation we seek to approach here? If so, how do we do it? Having noted the fragmentary character of the conversation that opens *The Infinite Conversation*, we cannot avoid the question as to whether it is in fact possible or permissible to follow the "decisive step" (IC 208/310) whose possibility we have just described. Does the narrated conversation, as we have qualified it, in fact lend itself to some narrative account that is not brutally reductive? Can we fail to recall the refusal of narrative order that closes *The Madness of the*

Day, particularly in light of its echo in the willed interruption of discourse at the end of "The Infinite Conversation"? There is no simple answer to this question, and we will see it recur dramatically as we read *The Step Not Beyond*. But we also find in *The Step Not Beyond*, near its outset, reference to a "*long cheminement*"—a long passage undertaken by the one who writes. If our brief characterization of *The Infinite Conversation* as the bringing to language of a speaking that engages the neutral/the neuter has any purchase, might we then read the course of the conversation that opens it, and particularly its approach to the *entre-dire* from which it proceeds, as something like a "being underway to language (or writing)"? Might this give us the grounds for establishing a form of narrative line (albeit interrupted)?

This question introduces us to a third reference, a third "interlocution" that is not summoned quite as immediately as those involving Bataille and Levinas, but has implications at least as far-reaching. The reference is in fact so indirect as to be without clear textual evidence. Yet the force of the resonances involved opens a set of compelling questions that should not be ignored. Would Blanchot have read Heidegger's *Gelassenheit* at the time of its publication (1959), or at least before the composition of "The Infinite Conversation"? Could a reading of *Was Heisst Denken* (1954), or its French translation by Gérard Granel in 1959, together with *Unterwegs zur Sprache* and Heidegger's *Nietzsche* have sufficed for the connection that suggests itself with these resonances? It seems most probable, in fact, that Blanchot was in fact familiar with all of these texts in some capacity. Whatever the precise history of Blanchot's reading of Heidegger, we may observe something quite stronger than textual echoes of Heidegger's late thinking in "The Infinite Conversation." Indeed, we find something we might be tempted to term textual *homologies*, with all due caution regarding the allusion to a shared logic or a common logos. With a strong dose of irony, we could even be tempted to evoke a form of accompaniment (though the profound divergence in the paths of thinking with all their political and ethical implications will not let such a figure pass, whatever the dose). There is, in any case, something more than the shared problematic to which I alluded in my introduction with the motif of crossing the line and the writing of a new language for what Heidegger termed a "new beginning." The parallel engagements with language undertaken for the purpose of producing a saying of language, or a speech of writing (at a certain level, the phrases work for both writers), produces comparable forms of *cheminement*, as we will see in the opening sequence of "The Infinite Conversation."

It might be added that "The Infinite Conversation" also pushes further along this course by following Heidegger in a disruption of the metaphysics of the will and the transcendental horizon of representation via what may well be an exploration of dimensions of the Heideggerian problematic of usage, *der Brauch*. The theme of fatigue or weariness in "The Infinite Conversation" echoes powerfully Heidegger's evocation of truth's need, in the event of *Ereignis*, for a human essence that Heidegger describes as "powerless" with regard to truth. The independence of truth's advent in relation to any human doing or acting by this use of the human is further echoed in the motif of the "non-concerning" neutral that is brought to language in the conversation, and the motif of usage is echoed by the displacements experienced by the subject who undergoes the experience of writing in the conversation. The echoes can even become a bit dizzying if we look more broadly in Blanchot's text. In the closing lines of "Conversation on a Country Path," the second part of *Gelassenheit*, we encounter a reference to "the child in man" that observes the nearing of stellar distances by a gathering night.

The broader question of the relations between the texts of Heidegger and Blanchot, including the topic of Heidegger's own "step back," must be kept for another occasion. Our aim, here, is to follow Blanchot's steps toward effacement (because it is *from those steps* that a comparative exposition must take its departure) and to draw forth some dimensions of this movement, using the Heideggerian motif of "being underway to language" as a kind of guiding thread. We will have occasion to explore points of contact with Heidegger a bit farther as we proceed, and it has been perhaps salutary, to this point, to counterbalance the reference to Bataille's singular power of speaking with Heidegger's thought of a powerlessness "proper" to the essence of humankind. But the intertextual references we have adduced are meant to highlight or backlight the narrated conversation in such a way as to alert the reader to forms of reflection that the text actually inhibits, for essential reasons.[8] They are meant to awaken attention to questions traversing the powerfully literary language of the text that can remain otherwise latent or unapproachable.

The multiplication of conceptual or referential "filters" in these opening remarks may perhaps also serve in another manner altogether, by helping to release in the language the insistence of its latent neutrality. For the text quietly resists interpretive capture, and intertextual reference, or even reference to possible lived precedents, cannot remotely exhaust its play. Thus we might say that the conversation's astounding poise (comparable to what we find in *The Madness of the Day*), together with its "natural" ease, actually obscures in two ways: it deflects conceptual grasp, as we have noted, while also veiling (hiding in plain hearing, we might say) what it nevertheless presents *immediately*. The reader must therefore find a way to breach the lulling elegance of the text. Its "benevolent" portrayal of friendship ceding to friendship, and its gentle evocation of an inexorable separation and the experience of writing, must be interrupted in order to release a thinking awareness of its resolute fragmentation and its presentation of a neutral language. The brief sounding of thematic notes pursued in this introduction through its chain of references (to which many more could certainly be added) should finally serve to prepare attention for an exilic passage by way of *le neutre*.

"L'entretien infini"

> ±± *His feeling, each time he enters and when he studies the robust and courteous, already aged man who tells him to enter, rising and opening the door for him, is that the conversation began long ago.*
>
> *A little later, he becomes aware that this conversation will be the last. Hence the kind of benevolence that emerges in their talk.* (IC xiii/ix)

We enter the relation between waiting and understanding in the very first fragment of the conversation, where the "wait" informs what is termed "benevolence." "*Bienveillance*," of course, points immediately to a beneficent willing (via the root *vouloir*). However, "*veillance*" also evokes a "*veiller*"—the attention of a watching over that may persist through the night. The conversation, as we will see, maintains its own *veille*. Here, at the outset, benevolence is a trait of the interlocutors who know that they are taking their last steps together. But the benevolent words bear the trace of something that waits beyond their meaning or their doing. How, in fact, do they know that the conversation will be the last? Is the fatigue (of which they have not yet spoken) so advanced that they know the limits of what they can bear of it together? And how do they know the imminent exigency of a benevolence that is not their own (neither the exigency, "still unknown to us and of which we are to be required to bring proof," nor the benevolence itself that must extend beyond their persons or human reference, are properly their own). This is to be a benevolence that maintains itself "before the event" that refuses any ground to its good intention, a benevolence, to draw on an archaic English, that must remain *unmeet*. Does the understanding between the two men, the *entente*, extend that far?

It reaches at least as far as the promise that they have made to "evoke" the event in this last "*séance*." A pregiven accord with respect to this promise is the very condition of this conversation, even if this accord is itself unevenly shared, leaving one waiting for what the other has always already given, if not to the other, then to the conversation.

The promise, however, appears impossible to uphold this time, and though the conversation is understood to be the last, talk will quickly turn to rescheduling. The problem is fatigue. The host, who has invited the other to speak with him ("*I had something to say to you*," IC xiv/x) cannot surmount a fatigue that inhibits his capacity to speak and sustain the conversation. Fatigue, he had thought, might facilitate the speaking (perhaps allowing a passage beneath the barriers of propriety, precision, caution, inhibition, or even fear). Yet it has complicated even the flow that comes with surrender. Further, it is not a simple matter of an impediment; what the host needs to say is inseparable from the fatigue that prevents his speaking. The latter fact is expressed with a kind of sardonic amusement (conveyed in a "gaiety"; IC xiv/x), but this quickly gives way to an apparent oppression that is indistinguishable from a drowsiness. The guest's presence only adds to the other's burden.

The guest, it must be emphasized, is no less fatigued than the host. They share the fatigue, and thus there are grounds for asking whether their roles are not exchangeable (a point that is also suggested by the strange formality of the conversation's beginning)—as though one simply assumes a role that the other could equally assume. True, one (the one designated here as the host) seems in advance of the other in this movement that increasingly calls to mind a kind of dying. Thus it falls to the other to come in assistance, to bring a human solicitude, an amicable hand. But the course of the conversation—or rather an interruption in the dialogue—creates the conditions for a possible substitution. Nothing confirms that such an event of substitution actually occurs, but one cannot avoid the interpretive possibility that the guest comes to occupy the place of the other in a repetitive movement and a kind of permutation in the relation of friendship.

They propose to adjourn, then, but a sudden gesture on the part of one opens to the expression of a difficulty that perhaps reflects what the two share of what the host needed to say. The one turns brusquely toward shelves of volumes so ordered and peaceful in their number that they pass unnoticed, as though he is confronting their silence, and it is apparently this one who refuses the concordant answer (*"in a low, but distinct voice"*) of the reassuring other who appears to suggest that it would be possible for them to fade with the day.

> *He does not touch a single volume, he stays there, his back turned and utters in a low but distinct voice: "How will we manage to disappear?"*
>
> *In a low, but distinct voice, as if night, settling around them with its rumor—it is broad daylight, he could recognize this—obliged him to reply: "Well, it would suffice for us . . ."—"No, it would not suffice . . ."* (IC xiv/xi–xii)

In a passage succeeding the one that follows this exchange, there is another evocation of a "silent universe" in which the books have all been written (though it is notable that it is expressed, in this case, by one who appears to be writing the conversation, or attending it in writing; IC xv/xii). How does one announce the end when discourse has reached its completion, the condition that Blanchot repeatedly notes is necessary for the emergence of the imperative of fragmentation? Where does one find the strength to say it, or a place for this supplementary word, and what happens to this order when the supplementary word is uttered? *"One writes only what I have just written, finally that is not written either"* (IC xv/xii). No doubt the disappearance desired by the two interlocutors is linked to the end state evoked in this passage, and perhaps even the fading acknowledged by the writing "I." But the passage following immediately after the brusque exchange (*"It would suffice. . . . No, it would not suffice"*) suggests that the dilemma is ultimately more unsettling and has to do with a "breach" between them that already signals fragmentation. What is at issue is a speech that says the true "cause" of their need for this conversation and the true source of their mutual understanding (*entente*).

> ±± *From the instant that this word—a word, a phrase—slipped between them, something changed, a history ended; an interval should be placed between their existence and this word, but the word always comprises this very interval, whatever*

it may be, and also the distance that separates them and separates them from it. They are always very conscious of this; it sometimes happens, through guile or through neglect, that they remain far from one another—it is easy, life keeps them apart. And when they stop seeing each other completely, when the city assigns them rounds of life that do not risk bringing them back together, they would be satisfied, if contentment were not also the manner in which the understanding of the word imposes itself upon them. They are not satisfied therefore, and this is enough to render vain both distance and forgetting. (IC xv/xii)

Is the word, the "phrase" in question here, the one that has immediately preceded this passage: "*No, it would not suffice*"? Its refusing denial may well recall to us the "I cannot" that Blanchot comments in his reading of Camus's *Les justes*, a phrase that says, we recall, the secret limit of language in its powerlessness before the alterity of the other. The phrase could thus be read as saying the impossible character of the relation in which the two are held, remarking in its abruptness the interruption that has opened the conversation.

But we must observe the signs of fragmentation in this dialogue, starting with the graphic signs that introduce each passage: the redoubled configuration of what is apparently a plus and a minus.⁹ Thus, while the section describing the intercession of "a word, a phrase" seems to follow immediately after the phrase of refusal, we cannot ignore that it appears to recount in the past tense the event that breaks open the horizon of the present conversation (the French "*entamer*," favored by Derrida in this period, catches this breaching opening precisely). So, while the "*No, it would not suffice*" appears to say something of the relation that opens with the introduction of the phrase to which the following section refers, this "word," this "phrase," remains in waiting. The unsettling "origin" of the conversation will only come to be inscribed in speech after a second statement of the dilemma that prompted the "*No, it would not suffice.*" In the meantime, the waiting word will haunt even their efforts to escape it, recalling them to their fatigue and their absence from the conversation.

So we might assume in asking what has brought the visiting interlocutor back on this current occasion. What form did the call to him take? The host needs to speak, and for this speaking he needs the other.¹⁰ The relation between these two forms of needing/wanting, these two imperatives, is enigmatic, and, for the host at least, unavowable to some degree. His unease in this respect is such that he cannot proceed ("*I asked you to come . . . He stops an instant*" [IC xv/xiii]—the first are almost the same words he began with earlier in saying he had something to say) without reassuring himself with regard to the circumstances of the present meeting. Was he the one who had taken the initiative? What has brought the guest? The guest's reassuring responses do not resolve the unease, which is brought to expression shortly thereafter: "*I hold no secrets from you, you know this; it's just that I wasn't certain you would come*" (IC xvi/xiv). Whether or not the host has invited the other, something has not been said: something that could or should not be said, and could have prompted the guest, if said, to stay away. The guest, still in his mode of solicitude, offers to understand this unspoken as a fatigue (a suffering, a weakness) that he assumes the one might not want the other to see. Now, having seen him in this condition, he can say that indeed he might not have come had he known. But the unseemly is not entirely related to the host's physical condition, and the latter is not, alone, what brought the guest. Still in the mode of solicitude, he now acknowledges that he has come despite the wanting invitation or anything he might have surmised. He has come without "sufficient" reason or cause: "*But I came, nothing else matters*" (IC xvi/xiv). The return acknowledgement of this act of friendship (pronounced "*with benevolence, with honesty*"; IC xvi/xiv) seems to draw forth the benevolence of the conversation itself, obliging them gently to withdraw into it and making resound words that are the background for all of their words: "*weary or benevolent, we understand one another*" (IC xvi/xiv). But this sounding of their common "*entente*" opens, in turn, onto a new, but "expressionless," *neutral* enunciation of the difficulty already articulated between them. This almost unspeaking statement allows, in turn, a question about what is perhaps the event they had promised to evoke:

> "*I don't know what's to become of me.*" *This re-echoes softly. It does not let itself disturb. And softly too he asks:* "*But tell me, what has happened?*" *and in the same way receives the response:* "*What had to happen, something that does not concern me.*"
> (IC xvi/xiv)

What is coming to speech here may well be the waiting phrase that articulates the "cause" of this conversation—that speaking *between* the two that was remarked after the first statement of the problem of effacement ("How will we disappear?"). But the guest is not yet prepared to follow the other, and will not quite follow as a kind of *counterword* is spoken to the waiting, absent other of the conversation. At the outset, the interlocutors seated themselves in such a way as to leave a space at the table "*large enough that another person might consider himself their true interlocutor*" (IC xiv/x). Now, this place of the other is addressed directly and the conversation itself enters a new space with the introduction of an outside that does not concern either of the speakers. The conversation becomes an "absence" of conversation, and the benevolent interlocutor accedes to its forgetting:

> "*Do you want me to understand that this might concern me?*"—"*It concerns neither one of us* [ni l'un ni l'autre]*." The silence has a character to which he does not attend, given up entirely to the impression that a threshold has been crossed, a force of affirmation broken, a refusal thrust aside, but also a challenge issued—not to him, the benevolent interlocutor, but impersonally, or—yes, it is strange—to someone else, to the event in which precisely neither one is involved. He would like to be able to keep himself at a distance in order better to reflect on this, and it seems to him he will have the time for this, as though he had been forgotten, that is, as though he had to confront this forgetting in order to think of it.* (IC xvi/xiv–xv)

A threshold is crossed, an affirmation broken, a refusal thrust aside. Is this already *le pas au-delà*, this engagement of the other? We will return later to the figuration of "*il*" ("*quelqu'un d'autre*") in the place of this other, and we should perhaps reserve as well the question of the step taken, noting only that this step is still to be repeated, perhaps multiply, before it is assumed in the final steps of this conversation. The step (not) beyond, in any case, is here beyond the sustaining bounds of conversation, and possibly even beyond the *entente* of the conversation ("the silence has a character to which he does not attend")—though if the words that emerge here are indeed in some manner the first transcription of "the word, the phrase" that waits between the interlocutors, then we might perhaps have to speak of an *entente* that has become an absence of *entente*, an other *entente*. Most striking, however, is the transgressive, countering character of the address that comes after the interlocutor requires clarification (unable to free the words spoken from reference to his self). The sentence is in some respects *more neutral* than its previous articulation ("*ni l'un ni l'autre*" is a phrase Blanchot will use extensively to evoke "*le neutre*"), which was already "hardly soliciting" and did not change the morning light. But, at the same time, the formulation is somehow daring in relation to the other, the event. Hence, it seems, the immediately renewed, more urgent need for help.

> "This concerns neither one, this concerns no one."—"Is this what you wanted to tell me?" The other gives him a pained look: "I didn't want to, and still now I do not want to." After which he is silent in a way that can only mean: help me, you must help me.
> (IC xvi/xv)

Heidegger envisaged a daring counterword as the condition of bringing language to speech as language. The region to which such a saying would open, however, was conceived far differently, as we will see, and the need for the other took a profoundly different form. Indeed, while thought's "counterword" could not be written without the accompaniment of another saying (poetry), the countering relation to the other did not require the presence of the other human being. In Heidegger's account, the relation of need and use (of the human by language) does not require the intervening presence of the other—even if the exigency of conversation would seem to follow from the primordial fact of *being-with* for the constitution of *being-there*. In Blanchot, the human other is needed, even at the limits of friendship that we now approach in this conversation. This need takes a dual form; it is both in relation to the engagement with the event, and it is a quite "human" need for support.

Something of what complicated the host's invitation has now emerged. One might soften the dilemma by interpreting the host's words as suggesting that it has never been, nor did he ever want it to be, a matter of a *vouloir dire* in his relation to the other; in any case, never a function of a willing (which is one reason for thinking that fatigue might help). But the pain in his expression, and his subsequent words about fearing he might compromise the other, indicate that his need to say what has now been spoken had been held back. He had not wanted to bring this to the other despite his need for the other's presence. Here was the true risk of impropriety: if the event did not concern him, how could he appropriately invite the other to discuss it, risking the impropriety, at the same time, of making it the concern of the other or obliging him to live with it (with the brutal turn in fatigue this nonimplication has involved and a fatal suspension of their relations, which will now pass by way of what does not concern). To what impossible relation does he condemn the other? The impropriety would extend both toward the event and toward the other. Even the hint of such a design would constitute a fault. But how could he proceed (toward the inevitable separation) without the other? Having broken his silence now, with words that are like the first figuration of that circle in which neither of them are enclosed, it is as though he is falling.

The hand of the other comes with a question and then a renewed statement of the commitment that had been pregiven (and still awaited by one) at the start. There is no danger of compromise, he asserts, inasmuch as they had already pledged themselves to a form of mutual assistance in and before ("*as before the same arbiter*"; IC xvii/xv) a common discourse. Twice, we might emphasize, the reassuring interlocutor invokes a shared "engagement," and one might well wonder whether Blanchot is quietly but insistently situating an aspect of the *engagement* enjoined by Sartre with these words. Clearly, the guest has not taken the full immeasure of the interruption in discourse implied by the sentence his friend has uttered. We have observed throughout the dialogue the guest's humane concern for the other and what appears to be a tardiness in relation to the movement of the other toward effacement. The guest, despite his own fatigue (and certainly some form of knowledge of what he shares with the other in a relation to what does not concern), seeks to maintain the two in a common space. He is concerned with the other's well-being, and he is not yet able to shed a form of *self*-concern from which the other is now slipping, even if he still reaches to the other in distress. Though he has passed the bounds of the conversation with his partner (as he has understood them to this point), his trust remains in their common engagement in the "same discourse." The other, however, and as though alerted by the term "engagement," is prompted to mark a limit.

> "*Engaged together?*"—"*Engaged in the same discourse.*"—"*True, but because of this also we must take heed. I am aware of my responsibilities.*"—"*As I am also, in regard to you.*"—"*You are, it would be unfriendly not to recognize it, but up to a certain point.*" (IC xvii/xv–xvi)

By reason of this engagement, he seems to say,[11] there are responsibilities that go beyond our persons. Or to rephrase this more precisely following the host: it would not be unfriendly, at a certain point, not to recognize the other's conscientiousness. Are we to conclude that there is still friendship beyond the suspension of recognition, or that another form of friendship begins there? Are we approaching the benevolence evoked at the start of the conversation: that benevolence that could not be limited to their persons?

The guest, still apparently unprepared, hastens to locate this point at the limit of what he understands by "speaking"—a point the host then sharply delimits by suggesting that the other would not listen if he were in fact to speak.

> "You mean, inasmuch as we speak. That's right, speaking is the last chance remaining for us, speaking is our chance."—"You would not listen to me, if I spoke."—"But I listen."—"I too listen."—"Well, what do you hear?" (IC xvii/xvi)

There is a breach here, a scission from which the two will perhaps never quite return (at least in the same mode of shared understanding). The host claims knowledge of a form of speech to which the other does not yet have access, to which the other would not attend, he asserts, if it were proffered. And undoubtedly the host has already been speaking in this manner, despite his will, in his enunciation of the neutral phrase, for it is apparently a hearing *in the neutral* of which the guest does not yet show signs. This would be the hearing evoked in the sentence of the text taken as an epigraph for *The Infinite Conversation*: "The neuter, the neuter, how strangely this sounds for *me*."[12] To listen to the speech of the other in this manner would be to receive the word "too many" of that other to which the host had addressed his challenging phrase and to enter the space of that *other* conversation where any being-*together*, with oneself or with the other, is suspended. The guest is not at that point, as the host acknowledges regretfully in receiving the other's "I understand." Here, in this space, it is not a matter of comprehension. The *entente* in which they joined has now become a limit.

The conversation will continue, most immediately in a stilted manner, and then briefly in a more easy flow. But its discursive boundaries will grow imprecise as it unfolds alongside other developments and reflections in a space that that now announces itself with a narrative that concerns what we might term the onset of writing:

> ±± He recalls in what circumstances the circle was traced as though around him—a circle: rather, the absence of a circle, the rupture of that vast circumference from which come the days and nights.
>
> Of this other circle, he knows only that he is not enclosed within it, and, in any case, that he is not enclosed in it with himself. On the contrary, the circle being traced—he forgets to say that the line is only beginning—does not allow him to include himself within it. It is an uninterrupted line that inscribes itself while interrupting itself. (IC xviii/xvii)

What has happened? Whose experience is this, and who is recounting? We have followed the exchange of the two interlocutors to the point where their mutual understanding suffers a decisive interruption (the tearing "decision" coming with the challenge to the event by which the conversation breaches an outside), at which point the account of the advent of writing just cited gives what may be the true "subtext" of the event to which the host has referred, or some form of its repetition. It would be "repetition" if we entertain the possibility noted earlier that the guest is somehow assuming the other's position in relation to the event after the break in the conversation. The host's recession from the space of the conversation introduces the possibility that we are now reading an account of how the guest came to write this narrative (and, of course, references to "he" to this point in the text have primarily referred to the guest). But the way in which the continuation of the dialogue interlaces with the narrative of writing from this point forward (and even appears to prepare this passage of the recollection of its onset immediately before its appearance: "*there was the concern over not having attended to it earlier*"; IC xviii/xvii) lends strongly to the impression that this is in fact a new account of the experience of the host. Indeed, this would seem the most intuitively satisfying explanation (one should not say "probable" because there are no grounds for assuming that there is a single, correct answer). The text would thus now be doubling back to an origin that cannot be situated in a past present ("*Everything began for him, when everything seemed to have come to an end.... Everything begins for him—and at this moment everything seemed to have come to an end*"; IC xviii/xviii).

Who is offering the account? The guest, to be sure, has narrated most of the conversation, but how would he accede to the position of witness (giving all due weight to this term) to the other's experience? We will hear of a "guardian" in a sequence to follow (IC xxii/xxv), but the exchange occurs in this case in the second person, whereas the exchanges between the host and the guest employ the formal *vous*. Should we assume that the one recounting this advent of writing is someone other than the narrating guest? In which case, we should undoubtedly look to that other who has already appeared in the present of writing. Has this other always been the one writing (the guest's narrative), and has this other now shifted focus in such a way as to move between the perspective of the one previously identifiable as the guest and the other who has begun to write, or *had begun to write* (and this would be part of the "event")? But why would this displacement occur, unless the event of interruption (the rupture in the conversation) somehow implicated this other discursive instance? This point would suggest that the one writing (both the account of the breaking conversation narrated by the guest and the fragmented accounts that follow) could be either the host or the guest, but from a time of writing that makes it impossible to identify him, simply, with the figures in the conversation. As we will see in *The Instant of My Death*, Blanchot is perfectly capable of offering what appears to be an autobiographical testimony in such as way as to dissociate the narrator from the protagonist of the narrative—"himself"— through most of its unfolding, suggesting that their relation is an interrupted one.

A voice that emerges later in *The Infinite Conversation* will interrupt the dialogical meditation on the question of the relation between self and *autrui* at its most advanced point with the following words:

> *I listen in my turn to these two voices, being neither close to the one, nor close to the other; being, nevertheless, one of them and being the other only insofar as I am not me—and thus, from the one to the other, interrupting myself in a manner that dissimulates (simulates only) the decisive interruption. How can one pretend to receive the enigmatic force that comes from the interruption that becomes infinite relation in speech, and that we betray with our insufficient means?* (IC 72/103)

Needless to say, nothing tells us that this is the same voice as the one that identifies itself as writing in the opening conversation, or that the structure is the same as the one we are considering. The narrative construction of the opening conversation, with its fragmentation, renders it far more complex than what we encounter in the give and take of the more "theoretical" conversations that follow it. Indeed, the complications we have entertained regarding the identity of the one writing hardly cover the discursive field that opens with the rupture in the conversation. How, from the basis of the interpretive possibilities considered and with the purpose of offering a unified account, could we also explain the exchanges in the second person (again, the interlocutors, for their part, always use a formal *vous*) that tend to take an interrogative, sometimes inquisitorial form? (They appear to be "internal" exchanges, in some cases, external in others.) What roles are *the others* playing in the multiple discursive situations? (There are addresses in the second person singular to "the circle" [IC xviii/xviii] and to what is named a silence [IC xxii/xxv]; then there are references to other voices: "*someone says this close to me, someone I do not know*"; IC xxi/xxii). Could any account "saturate" this space for which even the term "complex" will prove insufficient if we accept that the text itself has inscribed in its course an interruption that alters continuous linguistic order? The complications in the narrated conversation are such, in fact, that one might be tempted to ask whether the rather modest reference to simulation in that later section of *The Infinite Conversation* is pertinent to it. What might "simulation" mean if we have entered a literary space where fragmentation is in play? The fragmentation in the dialogue, to put this perhaps naively, hardly feels "simulated" in any simple sense. And the text does not "simulate" fragmentation in quite the same way as the one under questioning near the end of the conversation claims to "simulate reflection," for there is manifestly *no ground* for assigning some of these juxtaposed passages to one another or to consistent enunciative positions.[13] There are unmistakable *reprises* and threads of narrative, but the relations that inhere between these apparent continuities remain irreducibly ambiguous. One might therefore be tempted to affirm, still in the naïve mode, that the text does not simulate fragmentation; that rather it *is* an instance of fragmented writing, with all the simulation proper to language that echoes repetitively in the space of fragmentation.[14] But this assertion cannot fail to provoke another voice that would note in protest that such a supposition implicitly presupposes the "decisive interruption" to which Blanchot refers. Can one legitimately call upon a notion of fragmentation (without metaphor, let us say) from the ground of an ambiguity in diegetic structure? And what signification or thematization of such an event of silencing interruption could language offer that would not be marked by "simulation" of some kind? The dilemma is not in any way lightened by the fact that the interruption Blanchot seeks to bring to language is only given to us by an experience with language itself.

An impossible linguistic situation is marked here (and remarked as I write by the temptation of dialogical form) that prompts an apparent despair on the part of the voice that interrupts the theoretical dialogues of *The Infinite Conversation*. The second sentence from the last passage quoted can be read as a simple question, but it bears another note which we can perhaps bring out in paraphrase: How could one undertake to *feign* the experience to which the speaker (with all due recognition of the complexity, let us identify this voice with Blanchot) seeks to testify? How could one pretend to do such a thing, even if all means are wanting, radically insufficient even in their insufficiency? The nature of the experience is such that a play of simulation is inevitably confronted with an awareness of its culpable wanting and vanity—again, how could one undertake such a thing? How could the fact of the exigency it brings be acceptably consigned to some simulation? The exigency demands some other form of witnessing, some form of account that honors the reality of its insistence. Blanchot appears to be evoking a *need* to testify to this event that is comparable to the host's need for speech, however impossible the task might be (simulation? No, it would not suffice).[15] Might this be part of what drives him to recount the onset of writing, sometimes in testimonial form, even as it drives him into multiple modes of answering the exigency? In considering the repeated figuration of the event of writing, we must acknowledge Blanchot's repeated insistence upon the writer's peculiar responsibilities. He needs to move to the limits of language, and something in language that it cannot say has driven him to do it.

And what of the "decisive interruption," with its enigmatic force? Let us continue this digression by returning to an essay subsequent to the opening conversation concerning the theme of an "interruption in being," attending again to the resonance between this theoretical statement and the conversation we are reading. Once again, the meditation concerns the manner in which *it falls to speech* to mark the interruption that delimits (infinitely illimits) the relation between two human beings:

> Now it is to this hiatus—to the strangeness, to the infinity between us—that the interruption in language itself responds, the interruption that *introduces* waiting. But let us understand that the arrest here is not necessarily or simply marked by silence, by a blank or a gap (this would be too crude), but by a change in the form or the structure of language (when speaking is first of all writing)—a change metaphorically comparable to that which made Euclid's geometry into that of Riemann. A change such that to speak (to write) is *to cease thinking solely with a view to unity*, and to make the relations of words an essentially dissymmetrical field governed by discontinuity; as though, having renounced the uninterrupted force of a coherent discourse, it were a matter of drawing out a level of language where one might gain the power not only to express oneself in an intermittent manner, but also to allow intermittence itself to speak: a speech that, non-unifying, is no longer content with being a passage or a bridge—a non-pontificating speech capable of clearing the two shores separated by the abyss, but without filling in the abyss or reuniting its shores: a speech without reference to unity. (IC 77–78/109–110)

The words appear to reflect the severe fragmentation to which "The Infinite Conversation" opens once the event of writing enters this account. It reaffirms that only in language can the exigency of the infinite relation be borne; only there does it wait. But with this exigency, there comes, *with and through the renunciation or refusal that receives it*, a *power*. This is a power of speaking (writing) assumed by *one who would express themselves intermittently* while giving speech to intermittence. And this speech, we learn, would be *capable* of reaching the other shore.

There is, to put it mildly, quite an affirmation here. And one can well imagine that from such an experience with language, one could write a sentence such as *"Ce jour s'effaçant, je m'effacerai avec lui . . ."* But can the passage to speech here be the function of a subject's willing? The passage we have just read appears to repeat a passage from "The Infinite Conversation" that appears in the course of the narrative of writing:

> ±± *The situation is like this: he has lost the power to express himself in a continuous manner, as one would properly, either by conforming to the coherence of a logical discourse through the succession of this intemporal time that belongs to a mind at work, to one seeking identity and unity, or by yielding to the uninterrupted movement of writing. This does not make him happy. Still, in compensation, he believes now and then that he has gained the power to express himself intermittently, and even the power to give expression to intermittence. Nor does this make him happy.* (IC xxi/xxii–xxiii)

If there is a willing here, it has a neutral or indifferent character; it is seemingly without transport. Or the transport comes from the other, as the fragment following the one we have just read suggests most beautifully:

> ±± *The non-concerning. Not only what does not concern him, but what for itself is of no concern. Something illegitimate insinuates itself that way. As once, in the sadness of a knowing night, he could have evoked the foreign spirit simply by modifying a few terms; now he is himself evoked by a simple change in the play of words.* (IC xxi/xxiii)

Perhaps what is acquired (the power to give speech to intermittence) is not appropriately termed a capacity at all. Or it is a capacity thought from a *usage* in which the "I" is used as much as using, and thus released to the power in question. Is this not how Blanchot repeatedly describes the experience of the writing subject, as in this statement, which appears immediately after the citation of the epigraph later in the volume?

Me: can one still speak of a self? We have to do, perhaps, with an I without a self, a non-personal punctuality oscillating between no one and someone, a semblance that only the exigency of the exorbitant relation invests silently and momentarily with this role, or establishes in the position of the Self-subject with which it can then be identified in order to simulate the identical—so that, on this basis, through writing, the mark of the absolutely nonidentical in the Other might announce itself. (IC 71/102)

To be sure, this puts quite a twist on the question of simulation. The question becomes, now, one of affirming simulation in and as the becoming-other of the writer in what Blanchot calls shortly after this passage "that place where there is a place for dying" (IC 72/103). We will return to a formation like this at much greater length in our reading of *The Step Not Beyond*.

But let us now return to the narrative of the event of writing and consider more carefully the new fold in the conversation. As it happens, this account stresses that the relation to the event—now inseparable from the event of writing—is not immediately a matter of will.

The event may be said to be *of* writing both in the sense that "writing" is itself the event and in the sense that it is written. We have already seen it described as a breach of the horizon of being ("that vast circumference from which come the days and nights," IC xviii/xvii) that occurs with the tracing of a "circle." But why the metaphor of a circle to evoke the disruption of any gathering design (any continuous topological order or any closure achieved through reflection and self-reflection)? The "circumstances" of the event that are recalled are nothing other than the disruption of this horizon of every *circum*stance, every delimitation of a sphere of *concern* (in French, we would hear "con*cerner*"), and any ground for self-*com*prehension. Is Blanchot distending the hermeneutic circle (which was never a circle) by inscribing in it the *circulus vitiosus deus*—offering thereby a spatiotemporal disorientation that cannot be circumscribed? The latter suggestion might well be confirmed by the emphasis Blanchot places on the temporal disruption involved in this event that the protagonist cannot place in the past for the fact of its never having come about, or having come about without gathering in any definite point. Or should we merely presume that it is named a circle for the fact that it inscribes the *hyperbolic* interruption to which Blanchot refers in his text, "Interruption," when he moves from a description of that interruption that is fatigue (or affliction) to the consideration of what might be its "savage" extraontological ground?[16]

The tracing of the circle is given at the same time, however, as the act of the protagonist (let us suppose that this is the host, with all the reservations already detailed), or someone "like him." Here, however, the act of entertaining the thought of the circle indicates the disruption of any possible reference to an exercise of will or capacity. Instead, we encounter a suspension and a veritable dispersal of any *supposing* engagement or any decision regarding urgency.

> *Of this other circle, he knows only that he is not enclosed within it, and, in any case, that he is not enclosed in it with himself. On the contrary, the circle being traced—he forgets to say that the line is only beginning—does not allow him to include himself within it. It is an uninterrupted line that inscribes itself while interrupting itself.*
>
> *Let him admit* [Qu'il admette] *for an instant this trace traced as though in chalk and certainly by himself—by whom otherwise?—or else by a man like him, he does not differentiate. Let him know that it disturbs nothing in the order of things. Let him sense, nevertheless, that it represents an event of a particular kind—of what kind he does not know, a game perhaps. Let him remain motionless, called upon by the game to be the partner of someone who is not playing . . .*
>
> *And sometimes addressing himself to the circle, saying to it: Try once, indifferent circle, if only for an instant, to close up again, so that I know where you begin, where you end.*
>
> *That this circle—the absence of a circle—should be traced* [Que ce cercle soit tracé] *by writing or by weariness; weariness will not permit him to decide, even if it is only through writing that he discovers himself weary, entering the circle of weariness— entering, as in a circle, into weariness.* (IC xviii/xviii)

In turning to *The Step Not Beyond*, we will consider a passage from *The Infinite Conversation* where the assumption of the exigency of writing is undertaken with gestures of supposition and acquiescence ("Do you accept . . . Then perhaps you will accept"; IC 458). But here (and at least to this point), such acquiescence, even where backed with knowledge and a presentiment, cannot quite take form, or leads nowhere when it is entertained. It is suspended in relation to the indifferent, neutral circle, leaving only a circle of fatigue.

The fatigue thematized in this section and those that follow is certainly not other than the fatigue that is the object of the opening exchange between the host and the guest. But what might have been taken initially in a fairly straightforward manner as an inhibiting powerlessness (or, more precisely, the result of its burden) has emerged as a more enigmatic and even culpable experience of relation to an impossible. And if host and guest somehow shared fatigue, it is now apparent that they did so in suffering their *entente* of the intervening word or phrase that absorbed any distance between them and illimited their conversation. We will now learn that it is in fact fatigue that brought the guest to the conversation despite the imprecision of the invitation. He came with no cause other than the friendship of fatigue. (*"The thought came to me that the reason for your friendship, perhaps its sole reason—and I could never say enough how constant, how disinterested it is— is what is most particular to me, my privileged part. But can one become attached to a weary man and only by reason of his weariness?"* IC xx/xx) But fatigue, at this point, is not something that can be assumed. And while it absorbs all, it is not even "real" fatigue, in the sense that it exceeds the order of the forces of life. Like the passions of dying we will consider in *The Step Not Beyond*, it does not stem from the burden of existence or relate to any living interests. If it belongs to the life of the spirit, if only as an affliction, it is not something spirit can appropriate for itself. Its truth (even as relation to alterity) cannot be produced. And because it cannot be intentionally grasped, it cannot be used or turned to advantage. It cannot even be adequately communicated in and by the imprecision it brings. Every appropriative act in relation to this experience of being disappropriated (implicated in "what does not concern") will prove faulty and even culpable. The passages devoted to this dilemma are stunning and have been well captured (if such a phrase is admissible) by Leslie Hill.[17] They also merit careful rhetorical consideration in that they bear witness to a kind of discursive fatigue, a suffering of fragmentation that is visible in a slippage of discursive positions. The fatigue is indeed shared without being shared, and this sharing is intolerable, as we learn in a fragment that passes from a reflection on the host's fatigue to a plaintive cry (*"Oh neutral . . ."*) which may or may not be from the host (the diegetic marks are missing) and then into a sequence of interrogation in a familiar second person which ends in a statement of dismissal: *"All of this is ridiculous* [dérisoire]. *You work, but at what is laughable. I leave you to work, then, since it is the only way for you to realize that you are incapable of working"* (IC xx/xxii). The ones suffering fatigue are profoundly *désoeuvrés*.

But there is a turn in the questioning of fatigue (the questioning of the interlocutor, but also that of another instance or instances, including fatigue "itself," who appear with each slippage of the one who is fatigued from the place or stance he should responsibly hold in relation to the ever-recurring demand for an account) whereby the expression of an incapacity to affirm anything of fatigue, including the possibility that it might give access through its neutral character to *le neutre* itself, gives way to another voice. We glimpsed this other—or one like it—in the description of the tracing of the circle. Here it appears in an inconsequential murmur:

> *Do you really believe you can approach the neutral through weariness, and through the neuter of weariness, better hear what occurs when to speak is not to see? I do not believe it, in fact; I do not affirm it either. I am too weary for that. Only, someone says this close to me, someone I do not know; I let them talk, it is an inconsequential murmur.* (IC xxi/xxii)

It is after this weary fragment (the marks of discursive exchange have disappeared), that the citation of the volume's epigraph occurs. And it is in the succeeding passage that the decisive phrase of the conversation comes to language, again via the voice of another (or himself as other) and as an expression of intermittence.

> *When he speaks, he speaks like everyone, or at least so it seems to him; when he writes, he does so by following the paths that he has opened for himself, and without encountering more obstacles than in the past. What has happened then? He asks himself this, and from time to time he hears the reply: something that does not concern him.* (IC xxi/xxiii)

The sentence that the host had not wanted to say to the other was indeed never a matter of a *vouloir-dire*. It comes from the other (from somewhere beyond himself and the other interlocutor). The simple change in the play of words, as we have seen, inheres most immediately in the fact that the one who once had summoned in the late hours of writing is now *evoked*. And when the sentence is retranscribed in the subsequent section (in the one sentence to appear in roman type in the text), it comes in fact as a kind of *sentence*, and thus again from the other, since no one can sentence themselves: "To live with something that does not concern him."

An examination of the phrase will not lessen its burden ("*It is a phrase easily received, but eventually it weighs upon him. He tries to test it,*" IC xxi/xxiii). It will persist, if somewhat reduced, in a stubborn neutrality, a matted insistence, neither affirming nor denying ("*To live (with) what does not concern,*" IC xxi/xxiii). This becoming-neuter of language is also part of the "simple change": still signifying as it must, it also signifies *otherwise* ("*He comes to understand that the sentence—which sentence is in question?—is there only to provoke intermittence, or through this intermittence to make itself signify, or give this intermittence some content; so that the sentence—is it a sentence?—besides its proper meaning, for it must surely have one, would have as its other meaning this intermittent interruption to which it invites him*" IC xxii/xxiv).

It seems, however, that as soon as the sentence is uttered (transcribed), the question of a relation to its saying emerges. It is as though the bringing to speech/writing of the phrase affords a new question of relation that allows the acknowledgment of a new set of potential interlocutors, a "community" of those who apparently have had to face a comparable experience of *le neutre*: "*There are diverse ways of answering to this situation, some say . . .*" (IC xxi/xxiv). Three groups of responses will be cited, the first two of which entail an imperative *il faut*: (1) one must live without regard for living; (2) one must live without changing anything in one's life. And then a declarative statement that is somewhere between a description and an imperative: (3) "*You change, you live the non-change as the trace and the mark of that which, not concerning, could not change you*" (IC xxi/xxiv). To bring to all existing the trace of alterity, therefore, to change by *living* nonchange as a writing of the relation to something that does not concern the interests of life in the world. Living a neutral relation: not to life, but to *le neutre*. Neither insouciant indifference, it seems, nor a pious observance of the given, for the phrase "you change" marks response to an exigency that is neither entirely active nor passive (thus comparable, perhaps, to what we hear in "*je m'efface*"); the initiative here involves a third path of living *en différance*.

One might seek to understand this paradoxical stance as a form of finite transcendence, with an accent on relation to the "beyond." But might this be, perhaps, the first step of a conversion that releases the possibility of an infinite, absolute relation to what concerns in life? A simple change in relation to all of being? It is true that the "engagement" in the neutral relation remains utterly suspensive in this articulation as regards living matters (though not as regards "life"). But in *The Step Not Beyond*, an acquiescent relation to dying that carries beyond any "living" concern will be described as issuing in an affirmative relation to existence that might be described as being *from* the neutre.[18] The latter formulation, in turn, points to a possible rethinking of the ethico-political relation. Here, there is hardly a hint of an acquiescent assumption of the non-concerning neutral (little ground for evoking the motif of a "sabbatical relation"). But the transcribed phrase is said to *invite*, in its peculiar manner of being there, to the transgressive interruption to which it calls. It invites to a transgression of the logos. The interruption, in its turn, and by its very discretion, as we will also see, generates an ambiguous interdiction. Thus the sentence is bringing to language and calling upon *le pas au-delà*. The one who wills the interruption of the discourse effectively accedes to this invitation in assuming the received sentence. They will take the invitation when the invitation itself takes. Again:

> *While speaking to someone, he comes to feel the cold force of interruption assert itself. And strangely, the dialogue does not stop; on the contrary, it becomes more resolute, more decisive, yet so hazardous that their relation to the common space disappears between them forever.* (IC xxii/xxiv)

To will the interruption of the discourse is thus inseparable from engaging the conversation at a new level. It is an exilic step ("*If* [these interruptions] *occurred in such a way that you should once have to be silent, you would never again be able to speak of them*," IC xxii/xxv) and even a mortal step (at least for life in/of discourse: "*the heart ceasing to beat, the eternal drive to speak stopping*"). But it is also an *accompanied* step, despite the irreversible separation it brings ("*While speaking to someone . . . their relation*").

How had he come to will this interruption? In some measure, one could say he was prompted to do so—that once what the host needed to say was brought to the speech of writing, the renunciation of the logos and the separation from the common space was a small step. The course was almost an inevitable one. And what more was involved but attention to a plaintive silence? ("*Of what do you complain, silence without origin?*" IC xxii/xxv)

But as the text approaches this end (this beginning), it gives voice to resistance—a defense of the law. The illegitimate fatigue *offends*, as we begin to hear in the voice that labels the writer's posture "*dérisoire*" ("*I'll let you work then . . .*"). The bringing into speech of interruption then provokes a veritable interrogation ("*You know very well that the only law*," IC xxiv/xxii). Thus, the situation in the closing portions of the conversation is comparable to the one we encountered in *The Madness of the Day*, and the will to interruption must accordingly be understood as a *refusal* of the all-embracing law of discourse. Behind the gently reassuring temptations of everyday speech, there is an implacable order, "*la règle d'airain.*"[19]

The apparent origin of the plaintive silence, the interruption from which it proceeds, is not without its own binding character. Some law speaks in it, however discreetly. We force this hint of another law by contrasting the *de facto* ("*it is not an incident of simple interruption*" [*une simple interruption de fait*]) with the *de jure*, but it seems that some forcing, or at least some dissimulation, some "travesty" is inevitable in relation to the unimposing, but obliging, character of this law of a discerning discontinuity (to draw on the etymology of "discreet") this "pure arrest":

> *This is not an incident of simple interruption, even if it offered itself at the start as accidental; it has, and, fundamentally, it has always had, a certain obligatory character; true, a very discreet obligation, one that does not impose itself. Still it demands respect on account of its very discretion. A kind of interdict is asserted this way, without one knowing whether the proscription of the interdiction does not already travesty, in decreeing it, the pure arrest.* (IC xxii–xxiii/xxv)

Was the host not obeying this obligation in his reluctance to speak, his uneasiness in giving voice to this prohibiting obligation that did not concern, but discerned?

The will to interruption, as we have seen now, is hardly arbitrary. Grasped in relation to the refusal it bears, it is perhaps well described as a will to releasement, where release is *from* the sovereign will of the discourse and apparently *for* another law, another exigency. It can be *for* this other law, however, only once the suffering of its exigency (which creates its own desire for release[20]) is transmuted through an experience of what impels and releases in its discerning, interdicting interruption. Might we call this other law "exilic," given that it is never received except as broken, and inasmuch as it appears to enjoin an exilic movement (*pas*) even as it interdicts (*pas*)? To what wandering is the one who wills interruption released?

Indeed, if we have aptly followed in this conversation the inscription of a kind of open-ended interregnum ("*The pure arrest, the sentence that interdicts, in such a way that there should intervene, by an unappointed decision, the time of the inter-dicting,*" IC xxiii/xxvi), then it is difficult to avoid asking how this time and space of a *saying-between* might be inhabited or traversed, presuming this could only ever be in a form of passage, and certainly no dwelling. Surely there is no need to belabor the point that the "region" of fragmentation onto which the infinite conversation opens does not gather a human community in relation to any "fourfold." The text offers little in relation to the physical site of such a disrupted spatiotemporal order—*The Step Not Beyond* will give us much more; but its "Riemannian" character clearly does not lend to the relational gathering Heidegger projects in his own account of "being underway to language." Indeed, discursive boundaries are consistently transgressed and even dispersed in this space between. A statement in *The Step Not Beyond* says this divergence from a Heideggerian order trenchantly: "Only the *nomadic* affirmation *remains*" (SNB 33/49). Of course, we thus venture to speculate on what follows the host's departure from the order of the reigning discourse, left only with a few threads for questioning left in the echoes of the conversation's own disruption of that order. But these should not be left unattended.

Who, to begin, would partake in the conversation of this "saying between," and what might such a conversation resemble, presuming that it must be plural? "*Les uns*" (then "*d'autres*") are pursuing discussion of what it means to live "what does not concern," and a relation to life itself is apparently at stake. Does this discussion belong to "the more resolute" conversation that disperses belonging to a common space ("*And strangely, the dialogue does not stop; on the contrary, it becomes more resolute, more decisive, yet so hazardous that their relation to the common space disappears between them forever,*" IC xxii/xxiv)? Are those who pursue such a conversation "friends," and perhaps by reason of the benevolence to which they must in some manner bear witness, even if it exceeds them?

And what might such a benevolence represent? Is it more than renewed commitment to this exilic movement—more than a renewed *will* to interruption, a renewed *waiting* in the "understanding" of the *entre-dire* (bienveillance), a renewed survival or watch? Is it not indeed more if it is impelled by some good, perhaps even some form of beauty (attending to the roots of the Latin *bene*), despite its forever unredeemed, "unmeet" character? Do we touch here on the ethical impetus of this extralegal community: a "good" beyond the order of the possible and any work or doing (benefaction)? Undoubtedly, the benevolence in question is responsive to the suffering brought by interruption, the plaint of its silence: some irreducible lamentation of which the text we have been reading gives only the briefest hint (we will turn in our next chapter to a striking reference to "suffering humanity" in *The Instant of My Death*). We might recall, here, Blanchot's concluding evocation of the relation to the indestructible in the essay by that name, which afflicts all language with the pain of what exceeds any speaking.

And even if the plaint is somehow not human, the text appears to indicate that it draws a human response (this too would be part of what drew the host).

But if "benevolence" must extend beyond *all*, and hold (*se maintenir*) before the event, might we glimpse its impetus in the dual "yes" we observed in *The Madness of the Day*, where an acceptance of life and death on the part of "beautiful creatures" was coupled with a yes to effacement? This joyful acquiescence would carry beyond lamentation (without cancelling it). Like friendship, and perhaps an essential part of friendship, the benevolence in question would be *for that other* that releases to a community it forever disrupts and discerns. It would be something on the order of a hospitality to the other that is never known outside the *needed* human relation (always needed by the one and the other, and for that instance that is located in neither one nor the other). A hospitality infinitely required and forever faulty, always welcoming its imminent effacement.

FIVE

Compassion for Suffering Humanity: The Instant of My Death

and perhaps already the step not beyond

These last words follow shortly after the description of an experience of *deliverance* in Blanchot's last publication, *The Instant of My Death*—the brief narrative in which Blanchot retells the story of being brought before a firing squad (the scene also figures, as we have seen, in *The Madness of the Day*). It is a startling phrase, and not only for the fact of the bridge made between the autobiographical and the conceptual.[1] What gives pause is the further alignment of this thought/experience with a declared joy in deliverance to human finitude. The link is striking not simply for the way the "not" and the passage of "*le pas au-delà*" help to define the finite character of the experienced transcendence.[2] What most surprises is the coupling of the phrase with the affect released in this deliverance, the "feeling of compassion" that accompanies the happiness in "not being immortal, or eternal"—in short, an affective knowledge of the ground of being-with that will be coupled with an enigmatic relation to death.

How is "*le pas au-delà*" linked to a thought of finitude and being-with? The question can be fully addressed only once we enter the space of the volume that bears that name, and specifically the pages devoted to the transgressive passions of being-with and dying-with. But Blanchot's narrative of his near execution offers a precious approach to this problematic, and I would like to use a brief consideration of this narrative as a kind of opening to my reading of *The Step Not Beyond*.[3] For this purpose, two passages from the narrative should be called to mind, and I will cite them here before undertaking a reading.

The first recounts the narrator's recollection of the experience of the young man who was made to stand before the firing squad. The narrator, who separates in this manner from "himself," will not analyze—he simply seeks to evoke:

> I know—do I know it—that the one at whom the Germans were already aiming, awaiting but the final order, experienced then a feeling of extraordinary lightness, a sort of beatitude (nothing happy, however)—sovereign elation? The encounter of death with death?
>
> In his place, I will not try to analyze. He was perhaps suddenly invincible. Dead—immortal. Perhaps ecstasy. Rather the feeling of compassion for suffering humanity, the happiness of not being immortal or eternal. Henceforth, he was bound to death by a surreptitious friendship. (ID 5)

The second links the "unanalyzable" feeling of lightness described in the text to what will become in Blanchot's later work the notion of *le pas au-delà*:

> There remained, however, at the moment when the shooting was only a matter of waiting, the feeling of lightness that I would not know how to translate: freed from life? the infinite opening up? Neither happiness nor unhappiness. Nor the absence of fear and perhaps already the step beyond. I know, I imagine, that this unanalyzable feeling changed what there remained for him of existence. As if the death outside of him could only henceforth collide with the death in him. "I am alive. No, you are dead." (ID 8–9)

Finally, the last sentence of the narrative: "All that remains is the feeling of lightness that is death itself or, to put it more precisely, the instant of my death henceforth always in abeyance" (ID 11).

Since I want to approach these sentences with the motif of "compassion for suffering humanity" in view, let me begin by underscoring in *L'instant de ma mort* the narrator's tortured attention to the question of social distinction and his sense that his survival was probably due, at least in part, to his association with the upper classes in the eyes of the occupying forces. He bore, by reason of his residence in "Le Chateau," a social privilege that saved him.[4] The narrator's experience of a feeling of compassion, the collapse of any conceptual or social walls between him and "suffering humanity," thus represents a suspension of the distinction that will return to him in a sense of an acute sense of injustice: the fact that he should have survived by reason of this distinction, while young peasants from his neighborhood, guilty only of their youth, did not. In this perspective, we see that *The Instant of My Death* attests, in small part, to the burden Blanchot carried in the postwar period.[5] More important, perhaps, it contributes to our understanding of what he would come to understand, in this period, by the word "communism." Indeed, I would suggest that the significance of the text in this perspective actually outweighs what it might offer in the way of testimony to Blanchot's affiliations in the period of Nazi occupation (and thus any motives, any "calculations" relating to the possible impact of its publication in the mid-1990s). Never losing sight of the respective weight of the "essential" and the "empirical," we must resist reducing this document to a piece of evidence relating to the crude trial to which Blanchot was subject in the years preceding its publication. The "truth" of the experience recounted here does not fully inhere in the accuracy of the facts alleged.[6] The very first sentence of the text obliges caution regarding any approach that seeks to reduce this narrative to an historical subtext.

"Prevented from dying by death itself—and perhaps the error of injustice." Already, in these words from the first sentence, the "historico-political" and the "transcendental" are conjoined. But how can the "error of injustice" (an enigmatic phrase suggesting that social injustice is coupled in this case with a tactical mistake in that young *innocent* peasants are killed instead of the *implicated* chatelain) be coupled in this manner with "death itself" in the prevention of the young man's dying? Or, simply to get started, in what sense would death prevent a dying?

Jacques Derrida understood the "prevention" in question to derive from a suspension in death "itself." To put this reading as succinctly as possible: as soon as the young man is confronted with the evidence of his involvement in the Resistance ("Look what you have come to"—again an allusion to his fallen station: he is being condemned as a common combatant; ID 5), the end has come. The cortège of women, the formal ceremony of taking his position before the assembled squad—all of this unfolds in the space of a death that has already announced itself, already come.

> The eschatology of the last man is marked in the phrase that states in the mode of fiction ("as if") that the end has already taken place, however unexperienced its experience may remain in the absolute acceleration of a time infinitely contracted into the point of an instant. The screenplay is so clear, and it describes the action so explicitly in two lines, that the program is exhausted in advance. We know everything with an absolute knowledge. Everything, all of it, has already happened because we know what is going to happen. "As if everything were already done," it already happened. The end of time . . .
> "The encounter of death with death?" With a question mark, this last question may appear tautological, redundant, or hollow, unless it is saying the essential, namely, death itself, for once at the tip of the instant of imminence, at gun point, *at the moment when* and *from the moment that* death was going to arrive—because he has not been shot yet. Perhaps it is the encounter of death, which is only ever an imminence, only ever an instance, only ever a suspension, an anticipation, the encounter of death as anticipation with death itself, with a death that has already arrived according to the inescapable: an encounter between what is going to arrive and what has already arrived. Between what is on the point of arriving and what has just arrived, between what is going to come and what has just finished coming. (*Demeure* 62, 64)

With the reference to absolute knowledge, there is a very nice evocation of Hegel to which we will have to return. The analysis is richly suggestive—as ever. But "dying," the abyss of dying as an "unexperienced experience" remains little explored and the interpretation admits almost nothing of that "other" death to which Blanchot gives so much attention throughout his work. Derrida's own citations from *The Writing of the Disaster* regarding the "impossible necessary death" (ID 47) remain strangely without bearing in this statement. Do we not better read this account, if it is indeed testimonial, or indicating, via its testimony, the experiential basis or matrix for the thought to come, by understanding the encounter in question as one between "the impossible death" and the one promised by the firing squad's bullets? In this perspective, the deliverance known by the young man would be something like a deliverance or release *to* a death that was already there without ever being there: a death that is now *drawn out* in face of the imminent command (all but spoken) that will bring his death. It is from the place of exposure to this other death that the young man would know "compassion with suffering humanity" and the joy in his mortality—two sentiments that are perhaps not identical, even if they are conjoined in the same instant.

Of course, such a thesis requires recourse to other texts by Blanchot, even if one risks overwhelming the narrative with such references (though its very brevity also calls for them), and even if they ultimately have no more weight as "evidence" than the letter cited by Derrida. But one must recognize at the same time that the text implicitly calls for such references with its own allusions to texts in Blanchot's oeuvre (through its mention of *le pas au-delà* and through the inevitable echo of *The Madness of the Day*, where the thought of exposure—effacement—brings transport*)*. Several texts from *The Infinite Conversation* that stage scenes of encounter between death (as a murderous, negating power) and what Blanchot will come to call "my death" are effectively drawn forward in this manner. Indeed, one will recall most immediately that other scene of an interrupted killing that Blanchot cites from Albert Camus's *Les justes*—most specifically, that passage concerning the encounter of death with its extreme limit in that moment when death confronts naked human being. The terrorist Kaliayev, we recall, is initially unable to fire the fatal shot when confronted with the visage of his victim, a presence Blanchot identifies with that of his wife and children. (The firm underscoring of a similar presence of women in *The Instant of My Death* must be observed here.) Kaliayev's "I cannot" says the confrontation of death, as the power to negate and destroy, with it limits. The passage is so rich with respect to our concerns here that it should be cited in full once more:

> We sense that the recoil of violence—its arrest in front of the children's weakness, Kaliayev's "*I cannot*" coincides with the moment at which violence lays bare the visage and makes man this extreme destitution before which death draws back because it cannot reach it, because this weakness is this arrest, this drawing back itself. The children and the wife, their innocence, are nothing other than the visage of the grand duke, the naked visage that Dora had made Kaliayev see in advance: nothing other than the nakedness that is man in proximity with death's revelation, nothing other than the "*moment at which you will look at him.*" What we are left with is this moment. This is the *time* of the

word, the moment at which speech begins, lays bare the human visage, says the encounter that is this nakedness and says man as the encounter with the extreme and irreducible limit. "*Understand, I could not, and now, too, I cannot.*" "*I cannot*" is the secret of language where, outside all power to represent and to signify, speech would come about as what always differs from itself, and, as difference, holds back. It does not merge with the moral interdiction against killing, nor with the fact that one cannot really kill. "*I cannot*" is death speaking in person, an allusion that death formulates when, in the act of killing, it comes up against the evidence of the visage as though it were its own impossibility; a moment that is death's own drawing back before itself, the *delay* that is the site of speech, and where speech can take place. (IC 187/279)

We have here, then, the original time of speech, and as Blanchot tells us in the last sentence, its site. Is this not the experience of *différance* that remains to the young man: "*l'instant de ma mort, toujours en instance*"? Here is the encounter of death with death; from here, in this site and time, the essential testimony of this text must be read.[7]

The passage I have cited concludes, in the paragraph following, with a reference to the tale of Orpheus and Eurydice, which was also evoked immediately before the discussion of Camus. In that prior discussion, the encounter (the word is emphasized by Blanchot) of death, as an absolute power, with its limit in the naked human presence is described more brutally and more enigmatically, for the exposed presence in question is that of Eurydice in Hell. Here, the exposure of the human in speech is inseparable from an exposure of dying. As Blanchot says earlier in *The Infinite Conversation* of the relation to *autrui*: "When I speak to the Other, the speech that relates me to him 'accomplishes' and 'measures' that inordinate distance (a distance beyond measure) that is the infinite movement of dying, where death puts impossibility into play. And, in speaking to him, I myself speak rather than die, which means also that I speak in the place where there is a place for dying" (IC 103/72). The "I" of the text speaks from a place that has been given—inscribed—for dying.

The passages that I have just cited from *The Infinite Conversation* give of an "unexperienced experience" only the relation provided by language at its limits. They do not take us to the other side, so to speak, where we find that experience that is the object of the hesitant memory of an affect known by the young man standing before a firing squad: that feeling of lightness, that beatitude which is not joyful, that elation. The young man, as we have heard, was as though relieved of the weight of existence that was still his as he left his dwelling in anticipatory resolution (which is perhaps a heavy-handed way of interpreting the "priestly manner" in which he obeys the Nazi lieutenant's commands, but the solemn step contrasts noticeably with the elation of the coming moment). Once he is before the firing squad and awaiting the final command, he is delivered to another relation to his mortality. This is a relation not to that "possible" death that would be his "right," according to Hölderlin's famous phrase, but rather to that "impossible" that he shares with suffering humanity. The young man is delivered, by this experience of the impossible, from every mortal menace, being now nothing but mortal.

But other texts, again, prepare us to read this movement, most notably the "primal scene" from *The Writing of the Disaster*, where the infant, in a kind of ecstasis, sees "the happy murder of himself that gives him the silence of speech" (WD 177/115). The child, we read (and here again, it appears that this was an event in the life—the deaths—of Blanchot), knows a feeling of unexpected joy, which becomes the "interminable trait" of this scene (just as in *The Instant of My Death*, where "there remains only the feeling of lightness"). It is a ravaging joy that the child will attest to only by tears, "an endless streaming of tears." These tears are referred to as "the tears of an entire life, of all lives," suggesting that we have to do here with something like a compassion for suffering humanity—the sharing of a passion that is virtually the passion of all.[8]

A comparable exposure (though in radically different circumstances) is described, we will recall, in Blanchot's reading of Antelme's *L'espèce humaine*, specifically in his account of the "indestructible" presence of the one who suffers a murderous oppression. That silent presence, Blanchot tells us, emerges at the limit and as the limit of destructive power when it seeks to reduce the human relation to the terms of this power. For the victim of this oppression who maintains this silence, it is the presence of the very (non) ground of human relation: "A presence no power, even the most formidable, will be able to reach, except by doing away with it. It is this presence that bears in itself and as the last affirmation what Robert Antelme calls *the ultimate feeling of belonging to humankind* (IC 132/195).

Let us recall here *The Instant of My Death* and the young man's sense (experienced in lightness) that he was "perhaps suddenly invincible" (ID 5). Already dead, yes, and thus untouchable for the death that awaits. But this step beyond death is not that of a self released from fear (the fear of an anticipated future). Blanchot is precise on this point. The self is rather dispossessed of its defining limits as it opens onto an otherness within itself, opening thereby to the presence of an affirmation (and an exigency that will mark the rest of his existence) in which is at stake "the human relation in its primacy" (IC 135/199). The young man of *The Instant of My Death* has known that "impossible experience of being *autrui* for oneself" (IC 135/199), and has known it as the joy of delivery from the eternity or immortality of a signification or representation (of the "self," or of "humanity") to the immediate knowledge of human finitude in "compassion for suffering humanity." That knowledge is "immediate," but it is also given to him through a surreptitious relation with death.

In evoking finitude, and in light of the subsequent statement regarding the bond with death, one might be tempted to conclude simply that the young man is delivered to his own mortality. But what is meant here by "mortality"? Is the "impossible" known in this experience of "our most human belonging to immediate human life" (IC 47/67) simply the fact of possible impossibility, as the Heideggerian formulation would have it? Let us assume that there must be something of this in the joy known by the young man; he is released to be simply human—a profound release for one perhaps already burdened by the injustice that will come to torture him by its "error" in his regard. But how are we to understand the turn by which the young man affirms being for, toward, or *with* the suffering other in compassion? What step occurs here?

We have to do here, as we will see in the next chapter, with a turn that belongs to *le pas au-delà* itself. But rather than go immediately to *The Step Not Beyond* to illustrate this movement, let us continue to attempt to approach it through *The Infinite Conversation*, focusing now on the motif of "suffering humanity" and a thought of the impossible. Pertinent pages here are found in Blanchot's essay "The Great Refusal," where Blanchot attempts to think the possibility of an experience of what exceeds human power, which is capable of all. He turns, for this purpose, to extreme suffering, by which he designates a suffering pushed to a point where it can no longer be suffered, In such extremity, Blanchot suggests, the "I" is dispossessed of its own capacity to suffer and thus slips into an empty, abyssal time without present and without future. This is an indifferent, a neutral suffering, where all proximity to self and other is lost to the stifling intrusion of the outside.

Suffering of this kind is rare, of course, but also, in another sense, commonplace, inasmuch as all suffering is essentially open to this immeasure.

> Thus we can begin to surmise that "impossibility"—that which escapes, without there being any means of escaping it—would not be the privilege of some exceptional experience, but behind each one and as though its other dimension. And we can surmise as well that if possibility has its source in our very end—which it brings to light as the power most proper to us, according to Hölderlin's demand: "For what I want is to die, and it is for man a right"—it is from this same source that "impossibility" originates, though now sealed originarily and refusing itself to all our resources: there were dying means losing the time in which one can still come to an end and entering into the infinite "present" of a death impossible to die; a present toward which the experience of suffering is manifestly oriented, the suffering that no longer allows us the time to put a limit to it—even by dying—since we will also have lost death as a limit. (IC 45/64)[9]

The experience of suffering opens immediately onto the experience of the death that is the impossibility of dying; it shares with all passions pushed to their limits the general trait of being an experience of the impossible[10]—a phrase that, in this meditation, is almost redundant:

> Impossibility is nothing other than the mark of what we so readily call experience, for there is experience in the strict sense only where something radically *other* is in play. And here is the unexpected response: radical non-empirical experience is not at all that of a transcendent Being; it is "immediate" presence or presence as Outside. . . . But we know, perhaps, how to name such a relation, which is the hold over which there is no longer any hold, since it is again what we have tried to designate (confusedly) by the term *passion*. So we shall be tempted to say provisionally: impossibility is the relation with the Outside; and since this relation without relation is the passion that does not allow itself to be mastered through patience, impossibility is the passion of the Outside itself. (IC 46/66)

Suffering that has become the passion of the Outside: this is what the young man knows with those caught in the affliction of the ongoing struggle, which in the neighbourhood is general ("Everywhere fires, a continuous succession of fires; all the farms were burning," ID 5) and measureless. Time is distended in this moment like the swollen cadavers of the horses: "In reality, how much time had elapsed?" (ID 7). Suddenly released to this affliction in the face of certain death, the young man knows what Blanchot terms in *The Infinite Conversation* "our most human belonging to immediate human life." This is what Blanchot designated in "The Indestructible" as the (non)ground of the human relation: "The life that it falls to us to sustain each time that, stripped through affliction of the clothed forms of power, we reach the nakedness of every relation: that is to say, the relation to naked presence, the presence of the other, in the infinite passion that comes from it" (IC 47/66).

But suffering-with, become compassion determined by a joy in finitude, thus brings something beyond the immediacy of co-belonging. The narrator testifies not to dispersion and loss of self in a community of affliction, but rather to the opening of another relation via a secret bond with death that he does not hesitate to name *friendship* and that allows him to affirm being *with*, and in some measure, *for* the other. The appearance of the term "friendship" is not surprising here, for reasons we will see in *The Step Not Beyond*, but as the name for a bond with death, it is strikingly direct and not without echoes of the sense of the term evoked by Sophocles in *Antigone*.[11] This engagement with death also belongs to what Blanchot will call *le pas au-delà* as he pursues the thought of a transgressive passion decades after the events recounted in *The Instant of My Death*. This passion will lead to the heart of his thought of community in *Le pas au-delà* as it exceeds itself in exposure to what Blanchot will name the neutral. The structure of this movement will form the focus of the next chapter.

The ecstasis known by the young man carries him "outside" the world, outside reality, we might say, and return will come only in stages. The gunfire that distracts the lieutenant marks an "abrupt return to the world," though the firing squad remains in place "in an immobility that arrested time" (ID 5). Is the gesture of the "German" who breaks formation by revealing himself with a kind of laugh to be in fact Russian itself an act of compassion? In any case, it allows the young man to "move off" in the enduring lightness which resists the "sudden" rediscovery of "a sense of the real" in the nearby woods and will not itself pass until he learns later of the peasant deaths and is exposed to "the torment of injustice" (ID 7). Strictly speaking, the sentiment of lightness, and its moment, will never pass ("There remained, however, at the moment when the shooting was no longer but to come, the feeling of lightness," ID 7). Only the ecstasis is brought to its end with the sentiment of complicity in "the error of injustice."

This long passage by which time and the world regain their hold (without fully covering over the exceptional moment the young man has known) is modulated in a curious way by Blanchot's reference to Hegel's own experience of suffering an invasion of his *demeure*. The link is made by a spurious connection with the date engraved on the facade of the Chateau, 1807, which Blanchot assigns to Hegel's experience of seeing Napoleon, "the spirit of the world" (ID 7), pass by his window on "his little gray horse" (the event occurred in October of 1806). Why is Hegel, who is elsewhere (in *The Writing of the Disaster*) credited with the recognition that one cannot distinguish the two deaths, the empirical and the one Blanchot describes as "impossible necessary," treated in such a mocking manner for the discrepancies in his account of this event? To one correspondent Hegel reports that his home had been pillaged; to another he described his feeling of excitement at seeing Napoleon, reporting that his home had been left intact. "Lie and truth," Blanchot remarks, indirectly recalling Goethe's *Dichtung and Wahrheit*, as Derrida appropriately observes. Blanchot then follows with the sardonic: "But Hegel knew how to distinguish the empirical and the essential" (ID 7).

Clearly, in the forever awaiting instant of his death, which Derrida describes as the lived matrix of his future thought, Blanchot could not have been farther from such a distinction of the empirical and the essential. This experience of finitude, which we have seen described as "radically non-empirical," forces a complete reordering of the terms and renders impossible any invocation of an embodied spirit of the world. Indeed, we can see that it forces such a reordering from the very outset of the narrative, when Blanchot writes that the young man of his story was "prevented from dying by death itself—and perhaps the error of injustice." We can recognize, now, just how unstable this sentence is. I have implicitly suggested already that we might hear Hölderlin in the first allusion to dying. Is the young man prevented from the dying Hölderlin claims as a human right by death itself once he is delivered to it (the impossible necessary death, that is) *by death itself*, or death "in person," whose figure he meets in the firing squad? And might he have been prevented from that same "right to death" by the error of injustice, in that dying could never be simply assumed thereafter as a "right" (a reading that allows us to honor both the historico-political and the quasi-transcendental)? Was the dying from which he was prevented simply the "empirical" one that only the error of injustice could have forestalled, and that no step could forestall beyond the eternity of its instant (though "dying" in this scenario would have all the import of the inconsequential passing that Blanchot sees in suicide)? Or might "death itself," in the person of the Russian soldiers, have momentarily known the exposure described in *Les justes*, in which case, "death itself" and "the error of injustice" might be seen to have fallen together? The sentence is radically unstable, *remarkably* unstable in its willful alignment of the "empirical" and the "essential."

Do we need to stabilize this ambiguity, settling, along the way, some of the more thorny issues relating to this testimony? Surely it is best to respect Blanchot's insistence throughout his oeuvre on leaving "death itself" to its radical ambiguity. It is worth noting, however, that a stabilization of sorts occurs as the narrative progresses beyond the hesitant avowals of the narrator's memory to that fictive exchange where the young man is addressed firmly by "his death" ("I am alive. No, you are dead") and then moves to an apparent identification of the speaking "I" and the young man. In the final coda, a reference to the young man in the third person ("Later, having returned to Paris, he met Malraux") is superseded by the narrator's reference to "the instant of my death." But how can the passion of dying to which he was delivered become "his"? Of course, we have recognized the tracing of a "surreptitious bond" with death in the course of these most singular circumstances. Is the assumption of this bond, which is firmly "in" him even as it exceeds him ("as if the death outside him could only henceforth collide with the death in him"), the condition of this appropriation? Who, then, is saying "my death"? Could such an enunciation be made by any other than an "I" that has assumed, in writing, its own dispossessed, "problematic," "fictive" character (IC 313/458—here we anticipate our discussion of *The Step Not Beyond*)? The reference to a lost manuscript in the concluding paragraphs—a haunting, while very "real" loss in the circumstances of the event—reminds us that it was one writing who contracted this friendship with death (while also telling us that the event could not have been the *original* matrix of his writing).

To prepare the passage to *The Step Not Beyond*, I note that in *The Infinite Conversation*, Blanchot ascribes to a certain commitment to writing the possibility of a joyful assumption of death. Entertaining the question of the relation between the neutral and the Other, then substituting death for this Other, Blanchot, or a voice, notes that only the self that would give itself over in such a way as to become the fictive partner of this Other could encounter the death that obsesses or preoccupies it. "Then inscribe your death" comes the response, which is developed in an invitation that is almost an investiture:

> *Will you, as a self, accept taking this self as problematic, as fictive, and nonetheless therefore more necessary than if you were able to close up around yourself like a circle sure of its centre? Then, perhaps, in writing, you will accept as the secret of writing this premature yet already belated conclusion that is in accord with forgetting*: that others write in *my* place, this place without occupant that is my sole identity; this is what makes death for an instant joyful, aleatory.

From this point, we will be able to approach the question of being-with and dying-with in *The Step Not Beyond*, where a dying "*toujours en instance*" is carried into a thought of the Return.

PART THREE

The Exilic Step

SIX

The Step Not Beyond

. . . nor the absence of fear and perhaps already le pas au-delà

Perhaps long before the publication of *The Step Not Beyond*, the anachronous step named in its title will already have been made. In relation, precisely, to what subsequent advent or occurrences, however? Will it have marked every text that follows the recounted event of 1944—every step in Blanchot's "existence," in Blanchot's oeuvre, up until the time of *The Step Not Beyond* (1973), when it formally receives the name that Blanchot apparently cites in his text of 1994?[1] Will it have always been in progress, or already prepared from the time of what Blanchot termed "the instant of my death" (*toujours en instance* . . .) until the time of that naming, or will it have been merely anticipated at each step, waiting to become itself in the language of the latter text or some event or events in Blanchot's life to which this text provides some form of testimony? Let us pass momentarily over the gaping question that opens here regarding the relation between existence and word, or oeuvre, and merely add the further question of the nature of the temporality implied in these various alternatives. For, clearly, any teleological account would prove misplaced in this text, and any narrative trajectory would have to be thought from a course of interruption, not to speak of suspension (already latent in the double meaning of "*pas*"). How might the step already made be thought in the time of the return?

On the second page of *The Step Not Beyond*, we read:

> ♦ Time, time: the step not beyond that is not accomplished in time would lead outside of time, without this outside being intemporal, but there where time would fall, fragile fall, according to this "outside of time in time" towards which writing would draw us, were we allowed, having disappeared from ourselves, to write under the secret of the ancient fear. (SNB 1/8)

Let us offer a provisional and simplifying "solution" by following the most evident path suggested by these words: it was *writing* that would have drawn Blanchot into the time from which he could say, sometime in the early 1990's, "perhaps already." We have to add immediately that this writing, intervening between 1944 and 1973, would also have retraced steps already well advanced when the young man knew the instant of his death. (The opening pages of *The Step Not Beyond* seem to allude to the writing of *Thomas the Obscure*, an "event" unfolding probably over a full decade preceding the end of the war, when they evoke the turns and detours of a "long course"—that is, *un cheminement très long*, for which Nelson gives "process" while Hill prefers "itinerary").[2] Perhaps, in the arrested, repeating time of writing, a step already advanced in the decade of the 1930s, and then recognizable in 1944, could come to "itself" in the thought of 1973, wherein the conditionals of the passage cited earlier ("would lead," "would draw us") could each name what is essentially the drawing of the same threshold, the chiasmic crossing of existence and writing from which it would be possible to say or write "*le pas au-delà*." And perhaps in the same space/time of writing, the deliverance that is *already* the step beyond in 1944 can become a lived anticipation like the one we have read in *The Madness of the Day*: "*ce jour s'effaçant, je m'effacerai avec lui, pensée, certitude qui me transporte.*" We might even hazard that this anticipated passage is repeated in an affirmation that will haunt *The Step Not Beyond* in the furtive promise of a form of peace.

Of course, the condition—the conditional—of the supposition risked here is the effacement named in the passage cited before: "were we allowed, having disappeared from ourselves, to write." Such a condition could appear to suspend indefinitely the hypothesis governing this study: that the notion of *"le pas au-delà"* could open onto the "sabbatical acquiescence" to which Levinas invited. The point is not made in order to withdraw what would be promised by some form of theoretical coyness. It is rather to remind us that the steps tentatively linked in the course of these chapters (from the "willed" interruption of discourse and disappearance to the sovereign act of affirmation in *The Madness of the Day*, and finally to the thought of *"le pas au-delà"*) cannot be articulated theoretically in the discursive form governed by the concept—or at least that such a theoretical articulation (which nevertheless remains required if we are to make any sense of this hypothesis) cannot suffice. Even the language of the thesis or the supposition is problematic here, because it cannot be a matter of positing in a traditional philosophical sense. The space of the linkages offered remains the space of writing, a space that by Blanchot's own careful account and any serious reader's experience, is broken or fragmented—irreducibly plural. As it happens, one of the several "plates" in the fissured, shifting space/time of *The Step Not Beyond* is a narrative of disappearance, an allegory of the writing that would perhaps make possible a thought of *"le pas au-delà"* that would be something more than its *theory*.

The methodological constraints governing any account of *The Step Not Beyond* and what it allows us to understand or formulate of steps perhaps already made (constraints we will not cease to obey and explore throughout these pages) are perfectly apparent from the sheer fact that the notion of *"le pas au-delà"* remains so little and so infrequently defined. The phrase appears explicitly or by allusion in perhaps no more than a dozen instances over two hundred pages.[3] The volume does not appear to be reserving its title; rather, it appears strangely indifferent or powerless in relation to it. There are a few theoretical formulations linked to the terms "passivity," "passion," "patience," and "transgression," and Blanchot stipulates at one point that we can perhaps *think*—"only think" (SNB 122/167; cf. 125/171)—in what he terms "affliction" such a movement. The subsequent paragraph, however, advances the name only in quotation marks and as a question, adding that this transgressive passivity can *come to the name* only in and by the abandonment of the dying of *autrui*, only in that relation.[4]

It is apparent, then, that we cannot simply ask what "*le pas au-delà*" is or would already have been (in some past present), even if we cannot quite avoid this step. Rather, we must seek to ask what happens when (if) it comes to language. We should ask, further, by what path it would be brought to language. What path in writing would *engage* it in such a way that it might be said? What form of saying would this entail and what notion of language would be presupposed by such a saying? If this phrase, "*le pas au-delà*," is to be something other than an inherently abstract concept for a movement exceeding that of the concept—a product of excessive speculation or a logical anomaly at best, at worst a literary frivolity—then a work *of* and *in* language is required. Or what Blanchot would call an *unworking* of language.⁵

Let us also acknowledge that Blanchot's unconcerned posture in relation to this name is a hint that it is perhaps not of special conceptual importance (its importance as a theoretical signifier, we might say, would not be of special importance to him).⁶ Its role would not be that of a key or master signifier. As a concept of relation (to borrow a notion from Benjamin: "*Relationsbegriff*"), the relation it would engage or *relay* would be of greater import than the hold it might allow us to gain on the topology it indicates. From the perspective of linguistic play and rhetorical reach, the motif is really little more than a conduit. Indeed, what is brought to language by the name far exceeds what it offers by connotation. This is not to belittle what we have drawn forth with the term, namely the movement of transcendence wherein "disappearance" (or "effacement" or "exception") folds in a movement of acquiescence. Clearly, the term offers all the linguistic resources Hegel or Freud loved in the speculative word or turns of phrase. But to everything associated with a notion of transcendence, we must add Blanchot's thought of the social relation (as we have seen already in *The Instant of My Death*, where what was perhaps already *le pas au-delà* is named in relation to a movement that involves "compassion with suffering humanity"). Thus, even when we give the phrase all the weight of its allusion to the law and transgression, it seems curiously modest in relation to the thought upon which it opens, which is a singularly far-reaching thought of being-with or without (*Mitsein*, Heidegger called it), developed with notions such as community, friendship, and fraternity. "*Le pas au-delà*," let us emphasize, *also* names the engagement of human relation that Blanchot thought from the ground of his "accompaniment"—in existence and writing—of Bataille and Levinas. The passage cited earlier (SNB 122/167) makes this point clearly enough, but it is underscored by the insistence of the motif of being-together throughout the volume as a whole. In a fundamental sense, *The Step Not Beyond* is about being-together—hence the searing poignancy of the late question: "Would I be with the one with whom I die?" (SNB 137/187). In brief, to think the singular event that is the coming to name of this modest phrase is also to think the sharing of death that Blanchot takes to be the (non)ground of the social relation. "*Le pas au-delà*" is a concept of relation at the limits of the social.

But if we cannot meaningfully define "*le pas au-delà*" (with the question "what is?"), and if what this name brings to language requires a *writing* for its thought, what might we hope to say of what it relates of being- (or better: dying-) with? Are we to entertain, here, a "literary" community (or literary communism)—and just how communal might such a thing be? Will this thought lend itself to a general articulation of some kind? The questions that seem to multiply with every step taken here derive, of course, from a fundamental assault on the gathering or assembling character of the philosophical concept. In the plural space of a language that breaks from the gathering *logos* and the grasp of the concept, categories such as singular, general, or universal must obviously be rethought. With regard to the human relation, we must think a community without common ground that remains beyond the reach of any discursive order of law or even, as we will see, any traditional notion of loyalty. And even the imperative character of this "must" must come into question for us if, as Blanchot suggests, the thought of the "*le pas au-delà*" follows and exceeds the *general* movement of experiences such as affliction, which *separates*, in its "ruined" sovereignty, from any social, historical or ethical cause (SNB 125/171). Quite apart from the difficulty of negotiating a space that is intermittently dense then rare, close then distended (too proximate or invasive in sections to favor passage to other sections, too fragmented to allow secure links), we face the difficulty of thinking in general terms a *plural* relation from mortal passages that are always singular—indeed we start (in the paragraph following the one cited before) from an experience of writing of which it is said that it is perhaps presumptuous or "too satisfying" to say that it holds "the possibility of a radical transformation, be it for *one alone*, that is to say, his suppression as a personal existence" (SNB 1–2/8)—the condition, perhaps, of Blanchot's reference, in *The Instant of My Death*, to what is called "my death."

The difficulty is poignantly exposed in an astonishing passage that furtively sketches one of the few distinct personages in *The Step Not Beyond* ("distinct" by the fact that traits of an actual visage are evoked; the rarity of the appearance makes the one other comparable instance—again, the sudden appearance of a girl—equally startling). The passage is lengthy but so forceful in its communication of aspects of the dilemma I have described that it must be cited in its entirety:

> ♦ He who, in the street, stops the unknown one with somber eyes and says to her: "*I'm afraid; would you accompany me for a moment?*" gives her the movement of fear as a companion forever. But he entrusts his thought to her, the safeguard of this imperiled thought, giving himself over to the unknown—though the unknown has a face, the face of an unknown girl—by an appeal that escapes not only what is fitting in relations, but even the human manner of relating relations, and is thus a mark of what one must call unreason. One must therefore pass by way of madness, here maintained within the limits of an initiative that is only hazardous, to make a step outside of madness, in the slipping that brushes the outside. Certainly, there is something unreasonable in forgetting—in not taking into account—that every human being is not immediately the *other* in whom, each time, trust might be placed, through a word (barely a word, a murmur difficult to hear) of one's thought, which is to say of one's madness. And that when the unknown one receives him in the simplest manner, taking gently by the hand he who has stopped her and bringing him through the night, as one brings a blind person across the street—that one can conclude nothing from such a movement of reception, from that improbable possibility opened between beings, opened by what could not be shared (the separation of "madness"), there is what makes reason vacillate anew, while giving it to retain, on the condition of concluding nothing from it (of not making sense of it), this shattering that does not belong to it.

Any conclusion, any interpretation, would be delirium, the temptation for thought of re-establishing a relation of equilibrium between itself and its Other. To say: this was a sign of Goodness, someone was for me the Good, is to deprive this human girl of herself, she who would probably have refused to be called good or be said to have done anything good, being well on this side of and well beyond any goodness. To say: this is how it would be in a perfect society, everyone openly receiving everyone without demanding anything, is to forget that madness or fear would be in some manner forbidden in this society, or placed in the charge of the community itself, without any particular person being able, other than by fault, to accept this sick particularity and give it a refuge. To say: he who confides himself absolutely finds already in the limitlessness of trust [*confidence*] a response to the entrapped speech, having carried his fear as far as friendship—fraternity without law—this is to make a law of what, having taken place only once and even, for that, taking place every time, announces itself as impossible, real in as much as impossible. He who has received this sign knows at once that not only is there no right in this, but that all those who, far from being received as he was, were rejected, sweep him henceforth away with them, with no recourse but the great river. How, then, can one pretend to acquit oneself of the "event" in speaking of luck or chance, a word immediately reduced to its indigency, especially when the other is *at stake* there? (SNB 60–61/86–87)

How do we think the import of an irreducibly singular event that refuses itself to any law? Obviously, it would be imprudent to take this narrated encounter as *exemplary* for the problem posed here, though it seems to offer the terms of the question, and does so in a near-timeless present. And we face the difficulty—as we do throughout the volume (and fragmentation infinitely compounds this problem)—that not all of these terms can be immediately explicated, starting with the very enunciation of the elemental phrase, "I'm afraid" (a phrase whose "relation" is not entirely human, as we will see later in *The Step Not Beyond*). The very simplicity of their evocation invites us to approach this narrative with an attention suited to an apologue or parable, though one that refuses itself as such.

The account is not without its precedent in Blanchot. It can be compared, for example, with other narrative events as spare as the one from "The Narrative Voice": "One makes a few steps in the street, eight or nine, then one falls" (IC 379/556). Or one might think of the emergence of the desert companion, "*il*" at the start of "Reflections on Hell" —an account that is especially pertinent for the present narrative in that it describes the tracing of the eternal relation Blanchot evokes at the outset of this narrative of encounter when he says that the address of the one who is afraid (an address issuing from the same infinite as that of the immediate proximity known in the desert) gives forever to the one who receives it "the movement of fear as companion."[7] The movement, "*il*," will remain—giving, as correlate of the relation to the desert, knowledge of what will be named "recourse to the great river." "*Il*"—this is already, in this case, the mark of a form of friendship that exceeds the always singular beings that know encounter.

We are told almost nothing of the "unknown girl with somber eyes." We know that she has a face (this distinguishes her significantly from others in *The Step Not Beyond* whose visage dazzles the one who seeks them, though it is not clear that the one who calls out immediately recognizes the visage). We know that this girl of somber eyes can somehow see in the night through which she guides the stranger, something like the *other* night out of which Orpheus sought to lead Eurydice, and that the modesty of her demeanor is such that she would "probably" refuse to accept the appellation "good" for herself or for her act. And, crucially, we know that she is *human*, a vital adjective offered almost clumsily to underscore for a third time in the narrative that the encounter occurs at the *limit* of human being and engages an *inhuman*, but is real only inasmuch as it occurs for an always singular human being whose capacity it exceeds. Hence the astonishing character of the last trait we have of this "human" girl with somber eyes: that she is somehow passible to words of fear that convey a thought that is skirting madness in the extravagance of the act of addressing her. Passible and hospitable: not simply to the fragile stranger whom she takes gently by the hand, but to the opening of his address and to the infinite it conveys—the abyss of a "madness" that cannot be shared.

Reason has "vacillated" in this exposure. Imperiled, it risks itself in the act of address, an overture that is properly *insensé* (not just beyond the bounds of propriety, but beyond the very bounds of human speech), and not just in substance (we will have to return to the status of the phrase "I am afraid") but in what it presumes of the other, who would have to be singularly passible to alterity—as this other improbably is—to receive this barely audible, barely intelligible address of an endangered, exposed thought. It then vacillates anew, we learn, in the impossibility of *concluding* from the staggering simplicity of the act of reception and the immensity of what opens between the two. It trembles as it is given to guard, in memory and from memory (the gathering into sense of memory), both the improbable possibility of the relation that opens between them and the interdiction of drawing meaning from this shattering disappropriation that comes to it.

For whom, to be precise, does reason vacillate? Undoubtedly, it vacillates for the subject of this experience—the one (*celui qui*) who has made the dangerous passage via madness, who has handed his thought to another like a precious object one passes over a stream before attempting the crossing, and who must now retain that to which it opened by this passage—not just "madness" itself, the unshareable of which is the immediate "cause" of this encounter, but the relation of hospitality, perhaps the friendship. Reason vacillates anew, it is said (but is this still for the "subject" of the event, or is it for the reasoning, narrating one—the one who lives after—who concludes, "one must surely") at the impact of the fact that "one" can conclude nothing from the event of the opening of such a relation. It is further given to retain this very movement of trembling or shaking which it cannot own, *on the condition* that it not resolve upon (turn into meaning) this very movement of thought. As though the dialectic that would be engaged by this movement in reason itself (a *real* step following the traversal of the night) were immediately prohibited, immediately refused to reason (it would forfeit what is not its own were it to conclude), leaving little more than a fold or ripple, the eternal vibration or oscillation of an inassimilable movement of being set underway (the "*Er*" of "*Erschutterung*"). Who is the subject? The one who has known this arrest of thought, and perhaps each one who will live with the (im)possibility of accommodating it.

It is a trembling reason that guards now against the temptation to indulge (this would be speculative delirium, another madness), in a *stabilizing* interpretation that would appeal to a notion of the good. Reason would purchase its stability, in such an act, at the expense of the very singularity of this finite being who would probably have protested (we are after the event) that she is well before and well beyond the good. Caution is given equally against a subsumption of her act in the positing of a sociopolitical ideal and against the ethical assumption that the "elevation" of fear in the absolute character of this act of *confiance* might meet in an equally unlimited confidence a sublimating response that liberates its stammering, "enclosed" words, an assumption that would illegitimately universalize what cannot be instituted as a law.[8] Again, the narrator guards the singular event for which there can be no concept. That the communication of fear, or a frightened thought, should attain the level of friendship in this improbable event of hospitable reception—such an event is unrepeatable as anything other than itself (though not quite an "itself"), each time it should occur. Unavailable to the self-presence of any reason and thus forever impossible, it is *real*.[9] For what remains of this occurrence, there can be no concept, only what the narrator terms a "sign"—a trace or index for a reason disappropriated of its hermeneutics and its right.

Who can receive what is communicated in this sign of friendship? Clearly, only one who has risked "confiding" himself absolutely. It remains a sign *of* the event, of the event as impossible (its very annunciation does not belong to any subject); it can therefore only be for the one who has been exposed to the real of this singular occurrence and who will know it, presumably, in its every return. It is also, for this one who has received it, a sign of exception, for it brings the immediate *general* knowledge of the fact that *there is no right*, here, in such a "case" ("*il n'y a aucun droit*"), and that, further, in every case where such fraternity without law was refused, where the supplication went unanswered, the one who approached the other in fear was lost. The knowledge of so much death is not abstract or somehow obscure—the one who received it is swept off henceforth by those lost, "with no recourse other than the great river." Could this, too, be a form of compassion with suffering humanity? Of what "recourse" is this apparent dissolution? Can there be some form of safeguarding here, in this memory, this forgetting?

How, too, does this knowledge immediately received from the sign of exception take form? How does the *announced* experience of the impossible (this too is a "concept of relation") *give* knowledge of all those refused? We know that the one who received this sign (who was received in hospitality) had in some manner placed himself at risk in taking the "hazardous initiative" of reaching out to the other and placing his imperiled thought in their hands. He had been in the position that the final sentence of the text tells us cannot be appropriately described with terms like "hazard" or even "event" inasmuch as *autrui* would be immortally imperiled there: *en jeu*. We know, further, that he addressed the other in fear, that he emerged from and traversed the other night of fear, communicating this movement (of fear) to the other. Could it be that the general condition, from which the subject of this encounter has known an exceptional delivery, is one of fear and that this fear has been *drawn out* in some manner in this encounter, so that relation with *all the others*—all those, so exposed, in fear—should also be given? It would be fatuous to say that the exception defines the rule here, but in this sign of exception, we appear to have a *communication* of the social relation by which a form of "recourse" is possible. It is hard to envision some form of salvation, but there is, perhaps, the opening of some responsive act, or the trace of its demand.

What language will be sufficient for this task? How could the one who must now attest or testify (to the impossible condition of their survival and the nature of their exception in relation to a more general abandonment) *acquit* themselves of what they have received in the sign of friendship? Clearly such testimony must offer more than fidelity to the event, because in what the one who will bear witness owes to the event, there will be not only the debt to all those lost before him. In the account there will always also remain responsibility to *autrui* (of whose survival one pretends to speak). The one who testifies thus faces the exigency of finding a language commensurate with the impossible real. This language must explicate—must seek to account, though terms such as "chance" or even "event" itself (given in the final sentence in quotation marks) remain so impoverished as to be almost flippant in relation to what must be thought. It must always also be responsible, in its testimony, for the fact that in such writing *autrui* is at stake. The writing, we could say, must somehow bear something like the sign of friendship. Anything less would risk repeating the refusal. The one who has survived bears the (impossible) responsibility of writing in such a manner that they would leave a place for *autrui*.

In the appearance of the term "acquittal," a problematic of guilt surfaces that requires of us more than what the final sentence offers in acknowledgement that a facile meditation on the problematic of writing will remain culpably insufficient as long as it remains in the order of the concept—playing chance against law or necessity, for example, with the inspiration of Mallarmé's reference to "this mad game of writing" and the example of "*Un coup de dès*" (there is a deftly stated warning here that the effort to bring the event to language in its exceptional character is no game, inasmuch as *autrui* is at stake). More is involved here than the guilt evoked in *The Instant of My Death*, to the extent that this latter guilt remains linked to an injustice. The guilt that emerges here and that casts its shadow over the writing of *The Step Not Beyond* is inherent to the finite transcendence—the always suspended transgression—of *le pas au-delà* itself. Only in the final pages, to which we will return much later, will the question of a possible "peace" emerge.

How, then, do we think the general import of the singular event? The last sentence of the passage we have been reading, with its implicit autocritique (*The Infinite Conversation* and *The Step Not Beyond* rely extensively on the thematic to which he alludes) says clearly enough that we must. Despite the prohibition of any conclusion, we cannot be satisfied with a language of the "chance" encounter when there is knowledge of so many lost. The stakes are too high for such a casual conceptual surrender. The one for whom this knowledge constitutes a debt must think the relation and write the relation in a manner that honors both the memory and the "improbable possibility." Bear witness and seek the possibility of a hospitable language. The exigency of writing, once again, is not a speculative construction—it proceeds from a general knowledge given in the real of the event whose resistance to reason will forever unsettle and haunt it. A language is thus *required*, and whether this required language remains attainable (theoretically, literarily) is the very question of *The Step Not Beyond*.

We will return shortly to the manner in which Blanchot seeks this language, but let us observe, first, that *The Step Not Beyond* will begin almost immediately with an evocation of the exigency of writing in the autobiographical account from which I have cited.[10] This account will then give way to an "anonymous" narrative line whose first topic is the protagonist's knowledge of "others" who share something comparable to his solitude. He knows that, like himself, they "frequent no one" (SNB 3/9) and that they are of an indeterminate number: *des gens*. Is this knowledge perhaps of the same character as that received by the narrator of the encounter we have read; does it come with the event of writing in such a way as to form part of its exigency? And might this knowledge be taken as at least part of what impels the long allegory of *The Step Not Beyond*—the extended conversation (strongly reminiscent of the conversation that opens *The Infinite Conversation*) that appears to present the "long path" undertaken by the one who wrote "*il—la mer*" as a search and preparation for those others? We would then have as the motivating event of the allegory both the "real" of the event (the event of having written something like "*il—la mer*," words bearing a "power" of tearing, destruction, or change, but from which no consequence or authorization can be drawn, even in view of the exigency from which they issue and that they draw forth) and the vague but insistent knowledge of others. In sum, the facticity of an existence fissured by the advent of writing and the relation it offers to others whose "real" absence demands the writing of this relation.

There is no reason for pressing this term "allegory," and it is used somewhat loosely here, albeit with the haunting precedent of Blanchot's account of Kafka's traversal of the desert of writing.[11] It might well help us, however, to define the role of the guiding narrative line and its relation to significant portions of the exposition that interrupt it (some of which are themselves narrative in character). The very first words of the text, we will recall, are an invitation: "Let us enter into this relation." This invitation, however, is as much a performative statement of engagement as the indication of a path.[12] Thus, the passage invited is undoubtedly *"le pas au-delà"*—but only as the movement of the text itself, which insistently theorizes in its opening section (after the autobiographical segment) the fictive relation to an *"il"* and then *sets this relation into play* in the narrative of a conversation. Recounting the disappearance of one of its interlocutors (let us recall: "if we were permitted, having disappeared from ourselves," SNB 1/8), this narrative effectively traces the relation to which the text invites us. It traces a *threshold* for the reception of those "others" that will haunt the narrative. "Let us enter into this relation": the passage will be interrupted in multiple ways; indeed, we could describe it as plural in character since it takes more than one enunciative mode and includes lengthy sections of theoretical and philosophical reflection. The text unfolds in a fragmented space and a disjunctive temporality. But the narrative line—the *fil conducteur*—will be sustained in this volume as an allegory of the relation between *je* (or *nous*) and *"il"*—or *"ils"*—that the text focuses upon so strongly in its opening pages.

I have alluded to Blanchot's evocation of this word *"il"* in my brief reference to the desert encounter presented in the opening passage of "Reflections on Hell," seeking to emphasize that the pronominal insistence of this term (one cannot avoid hypostatizing the term by reading in it a reference to "he" or "it") is displaced by Blanchot as he works to render it as an index or marker of relation. The pronominal "fixion" is only *displaced*—a "he" or an "it" will always haunt its appearance. But Blanchot will unwork the term in such a way as to give it all the weight of what it gives of relation (revealing in this manner what is undoubtedly one "origin" of the term in the syntagm *"il y a"*) and all the light redundancy of the pleonasm that indicates "little more" than the presence/absence of writing. *"Il"* will itself indicate *"le pas au-delà,"* inviting to its movement.

♦ *il*: at the edge of writing; transparency, as such, opaque; bearing what inscribes it, effacing it, effacing itself in the inscription, the effacement of the mark that marks it; neutral under the draw of the neutral to the point of seeming dangerously to fix it and, if we were capable of "following" it up to that edge where what writes itself has always already disappeared (tipped over, capsized) in the neutrality of writing, to seem to tempt us to have a relation to that which excludes itself from any relation and which nevertheless indicates itself as absolute only in the relative mode (of the relation itself, multiple).

Whether capitalized or small, in the position of the subject, in the state of a pleonasm, indicating some other or no other, or indicating nothing but its own indication, the he/it without identity; personal? impersonal? Not yet and always beyond [*pas encore et toujours au-delà*]; and not being someone or something, no more than it could have the magic of being or the fascination of non-being answering for it. For the moment, the only thing to say: he/it, a word too many, which by a ruse we place at the border of writing, or the relation of writing to writing, when writing indicates itself at its own border. (SNB 6/14)

The paragraphs that "explicate" the supplemental, even dispersed character of the word deserve lengthy treatment in themselves. Here, let us emphasize simply the role of "*il*" as a sign of relation (without relation)—a sign whose very redundancy as a "word too many" *communicates* what language gives of alterity (the topic of so many pages in *The Infinite Conversation*). We might call it a sign of writing, in this context, inasmuch as it marks the presence of the writing that haunts language. In the magnificent essay, "Literature and the Right to Death" (*La part du feu*, 1949), Blanchot described in an almost exhausting fashion the "communication" of the *il y a* via the ambiguous presence of language in its becoming-image. By 1973, this "communication" is attributed to the "self-indication" of writing under the draw of *le neutre* (with language "in general" now described as neuter).[13] Haunting the motif of writing are Heidegger's meditation on the tracing by which we can say of language, "*Es, das Wort, gibt,*" perhaps the *Relationsbegriffe* of Benjamin's own philosophy of language, and Mallarmé's poetic thought (particularly with the inflection given to it by Jacques Derrida in his stunning essay, "The Double Session").[14] But to assess the impact of the introduction of the problematic of writing in the decade or so preceding the publication of *The Step Not Beyond*, we must read it in conjunction with the developing thought of fragmentation and *le neutre*, a movement of philosophical and literary reflection that takes a very singular turn even as it retraces the passage to the outside that was already "*le pas au-delà*" in "Literature and the Right to Death." Again, this is not the occasion to trace these textual developments. The point is simply to note how Blanchot's many earlier formulations of the writer's effacement are now carried forward in the meditation on the act of writing and what it means for the "self" of the act to draw this "speech" into language. What is undertaken when the writing subject accepts to write "*il*"? "If I write *il*, denouncing it rather than indicating it, I know at least that, far from giving it a rank, a role or presence which would elevate it above anything that could designate it, it is I who, from this point, enters into the relation in which "I" accepts fixing itself in a fictional or functional identity, in order that the game of writing may be exercised" (SNB 4/11). A "fixing" of identity that is at the same time a wagering of identity on the part of a fractured self become token in a "simple change in the play of words":

> ◆ The relation of the self to the other, difficult to think (relation that *il* would "relate") because of the status of the other, sometimes and at the same time the other as term, sometimes and at the same time the other as relation without term, relay always to be relayed; then, by the change that it proposes to "me," the latter having thus to accept itself not only as hypothetical, even fictional, but as a canonic abbreviation, representing the law of the same, fractured in advance (thus once again—beneath the fallacious proposition of this broken, intimately wounded self—once again a living, that is to say, full, self).
> (SNB 6/14–15)

The language of chance and game barely mask the fact that "if I write *il*," I expose a fractured, fissured self (even as "I" come back). I write my death.

In *The Infinite Conversation*, the fragmented, dialogical sequence entitled simply "Parentheses" (redoubling, thereby, one of the longest sequences on "*le neutre*"—itself fragmented and dialogical[15]) *anticipates* this core problematic of *The Step Not Beyond* in a manner that deserves our attention again inasmuch as it hints at an answer to one of our guiding questions: how does the singular act of writing engage the relation of being- (dying-) with? It would seem worthwhile, therefore, to linger over this anticipatory exchange in which the exigency of writing is enunciated almost as an injunction once the supposition is offered that death is what might help us grasp the neutral character of the alterity brought to us by *autrui*.

"*Inscribe your death then*" (IC 311/457). These words of invitation and challenge follow the assertion that death can only be encountered by the self it obsesses (and thereby become "its" death) when the latter is reduced to no more than that "already broken," "fictive" partner that the Other "offers itself and receives as a gift" (IC 311/457). The exigency of writing thus comes as a kind of conclusion: "So you must then inscribe your death."

The meditation that follows is pertinent for our prior discussion regarding the language of the concept in that it emphasizes that such an inscription would have to occur in a region *separate* from the order of discourse, though it would not fail to "touch" and displace, while leaving "intact," the concepts of "truth," "unity," and "subject" presupposed in this discursive regime. A problematic of the scientificity of science opens here in which a "possibility of writing" allows us to entertain the thought of a science freed of the harness of an "an always prior unity of essence and meaning" (IC 311/458). Could such a concept of science also govern the thought of what pluralizes the space of discourse? A passage in *The Step Not Beyond* on the "science" of writing—a grammatology, let us say—is less sanguine,[16] though even the passage we are reading from *The Infinite Conversation* recognizes that science cannot give up its faith in "the identity and permanence of signs." This faith, exposed by literature as "ideological," would exclude it from any thought of the "provocation" of the neutral, the provocation of this "word too many" which, like "*il*," disperses and pluralizes itself. Thus, even the science of literature that has taken form under the name of theory cannot suffice for the "distance without concept" required for the inscription of death. Literature, in its turn, is not without its ideological weight, as we read, but it is only a literature (or some discursive form that would assume its exigencies) whose speech is destined to writing that can entertain what Blanchot names here the provocation of the neutral in the form of a "word too many" (*de trop*):

> The word too many: it would come from the Other without ever having been heard by myself [*Moi*]—nonetheless the sole auditor possible since it is meant for him; less to disperse or break him than to respond to the breaking or dispersal that the "I" conceals, making of itself a self by this movement of hiding that seems the beating of an empty heart. Where there is, or would be, a word too many, there is the offense and the revelation of death. (IC 312/458)

The neuter, the neuter: how strange this sounds for *me*.[17] It is an estranged, displaced self that receives that to which it is exposed in its own shattering or dispersal, a breaking from which it has turned in an occluding movement, an *eclipse*, that is something like the arrhythmic punctuation of its own dying. Denied (as audibly intelligible) to this self, but exposed in the space of this occluding turn—*there* where there is or would be a place for dying (*là où il y a ou il y aurait*)—the word too many would reveal the "offense" of death.

For the one who has sought "the distance without concept so that the death without truth should inscribe itself there," for this one who has become the fictive partner of the Other in the play of exposure and revelation, this injunction ("write your death") now becomes an invitation to a role *more necessary* than any founding or "centering" certainty. In the encounter with the young girl, no such necessity for the act could be ascribed (beyond what is necessary for the survival of *autrui*); but here, in the space of writing, a kind of *investiture* is proposed. Here are the final words of the "Parentheses":

> ±± *Will you, as a self, accept taking this self as problematic, as fictive, and nonetheless more necessary in this way than if you were able to close up around yourself like a circle sure of its center? Then, perhaps, in writing, you will accept as the secret of writing this premature yet already belated conclusion that is in accord with forgetting*: that others write in *my* place, this place without occupant that is my sole identity; this is what makes death for an instant joyful, aleatory. (IC 313/458)

Again, there is quite a bit more in the first question than an invitation. It seeks formal assent to commitment—a confirmation of engagement in a *fictive* movement (obviously, this is a curious fealty) wherein one both holds oneself as "problematic, fictive," and, *by thus writing*, disposed to receive *as* the secret of writing a conclusion that is both too early (there is no certainty here and it is lacking in mature responsibility) and already late (as though reason could not keep the pace with thought, or will have "slurred" in accord with a form of forgetting). The gift of this conclusion, given only in writing and as what writing has always concealed inasmuch as it occurs with the eclipse of the self (in that unoccupied place of its dying) comes to "make sense" of an affect, a movement of deliverance that will perhaps already have been known—at least from the time of that *instant toujours en instance*. It is not a statement that affirms something about the nature of writing so much as the concluding affirmation of lingering knowledge ("I don't know, but I sense that I am going to have known," SNB 112/153).

That the writing that occurs in "my" place (the site of "my" death, which I can never occupy[18]) should be the writing of others, this fact supposed and accepted is what can have made and can make death joyous, aleatory—like the toss of the dice (*alea*). Here chance is affirmed in a way that perhaps does not deny *autrui*. From here, one might perhaps write, having put oneself into play, and giving oneself over to repetition: "And when I die (perhaps any minute now) . . ."

So we have, here, the hint of at least a partial answer to the question of the possibility of a "responsible" discourse. That I should accept to prepare a place for the advent of the other, effectively writing "*il*" in response as I trace this site of my death—there is the act that releases the possibility of a joyous, aleatory affirmation of death as an exposure to the other whose number is always plural. Might such a writing be a step toward "acquitting" oneself of one's survival? Of the place one has taken—*my* place? And how might we understand this last phrase?

A beautiful fragment from the opening pages of *The Step Not Beyond* replays for us the scene of investiture we have read in *The Infinite Conversation*, signally its pertinence perhaps (by echo), but also hinting at the contingent character of the act of assumption or choice (what must be a self-choice—else this could never be "my" place). Almost immediately after the inception of the narrative line I have described, there are a series of references to the sounding of a word too many for one who finds it "almost easy" to live in its proximity:

> ♦ *It was almost easy for him, there where he lived, to live almost without signs, almost without self, as though at the edge of writing, close to this word, barely a word, rather a word too many and in this nothing but a word from which, one day in the past, gently welcomed, he had received the greeting that did not save, the summons that had awakened him.* (SNB 7/15)

This could be recounted, we are informed, especially if there were no one there to hear it: the advent of the word could be *told* if the proximity in which this self were living were without occupant. (Such a disappearance is precisely what the narrative will attempt.) Here, a strange sovereignty (an "excessive power . . . over himself, and, by way of him, over all things," SNB 7/15) comes with only the slightest restriction, obliging the interpellated one to a series of obsessive, almost ritual qualifications (the language of "almost," "perhaps," "hardly," "momentarily," "unless," and so forth) whose virtue he cannot claim to know. No, he did not know what they accorded him, the passage continues: "perhaps" (here, already, a suspensive citation) a *passage* of which he was not aware, "perhaps" a reserve, preserving him from the "decisive affirmation," so that he should still be there in order not to hear it. The affirmation of return—the affirmation of a decisive interruption? As though the "problematic" place of the self were perhaps not only necessary for the affirmation (joyous, aleatory), but possibly *incompossible* with it, forever denying the *knowledge* of this affirmation to any self. We will not cease to take the measure of this denial as we move forward. In brief, my place cannot become the site of enunciation of Eternal Return, or the return can only be announced there, but without me. But in the passage immediately following the one we have just commented, the advent of the "word too many" is recounted, for a third time, underscoring for us the profoundly *aleatory* character of the act of assumption:

> ♦ *As though there had sounded, in a muffled manner, that appeal, an appeal nevertheless joyous, the cry of children playing in the garden:* "Who is me today?" "Who will take the place of me?" *And the infinite, joyous response:* him, him, him. (SNB 7/16)

Is the "secret" of writing being accepted here? The passage suggests, in any case, that there is no authorization for the one who gently, almost indirectly, assumes this nomination; no right is assumed, no property or propriety secured, no pretention confirmed. There is simply the echo of a lightness in the act by which a self puts itself into play, like an echo from infancy that will eventually help the narrator "acquit" himself of the role he assumes.

My place, *my* death: an aleatory assumption undertaken by one who has known the exigency of writing. Summarizing the movement we have followed thus far, we see an "event" of an auto(bio)graphical character (an incipient writing of "*il*" in and by the words, "*il . . . la mer*," and the long path of writing that follows) *theorized* as the assumed becoming-fictive, problematic, of a fissured self, and then put into play, as on a chessboard, in a narrative involving relation to an other and to others. Accompanying, but also impelling this movement, is a question of community that will occupy long (fragmentary) passages of reflection on the passions of dying-with, their temporality, and their "subject."

And here again the question of method presents itself. How do we approach these passages without attempting to write the "theory" of *le pas au-delà* through their synthesis, and then, perhaps, applying the results to the guiding narrative line? How can we honor the juxtaposition of these modes of reflection with the narrative(s) while still pursuing a course of *reading* (which involves, if not method, at least some path: as indicated in the Greek *hodos*)? As it happens, a possible course is indicated by Blanchot himself in his later volume, *The Unavowable Community*, through multiple and insistent citations of *The Step Not Beyond*. Let us therefore attempt a detour in search of this path.

Perhaps Already a Thought of Community

As Jean-Luc Nancy notes in *La communauté affrontée*, a republication of the preface to the Italian translation of Blanchot's *The Unavowable Community*, Blanchot's response to Nancy's *The Inoperative Community* both *echoes* and *replies*; it even contains what appears to be a form of protest.[19] Nancy's brief essay devotes considerable space to his admission that he has never fully understood the nature of that protest, and his few suggestions regarding the message "intimated" to him by Blanchot do little to resolve the issue. It must be noted that he seems remarkably comfortable with his admission in that he openly acknowledges not having taken the time to review the texts.[20]

What prompted Blanchot's response? Beyond any divergence with respect to their reading of Bataille, Blanchot was undoubtedly disturbed by Nancy's failure to recognize the character and level of his engagement with the question of community (a word he had employed only with great care). Indeed, Nancy went so far as to assert in *The Unworking Community* that Blanchot had failed to grasp the import of his own appeal to the motif of communism and "was not truly able to communicate explicitly and thematically (even if "explicit" and "thematic" are only very fragile categories here), with a thinking of community."[21] In retrospect, it is an astonishing sentence that betrays a lack of awareness of Blanchot's extensive involvement with the question, and an insufficient recognition of why "thematic," "explicit," and even "communicate" were such problematic terms in Blanchot's case. For, even with quotation marks, they implicitly denied core elements of Blanchot's writing and commitments, including some of the most important literary and philosophical thinking about language in

France (arguably the most important preparation for the deconstructive thinking to which Nancy devoted himself). The gulf between the two authors was in fact profound, despite the points of proximity carefully noted by Blanchot in his response (and for reasons quite different from those alleged by Nancy). In some respects, Blanchot said almost everything on the first page of his book when he suggested that what had to be thought was a *failing* in language that words such as "communism" or "community" appear to bear in them. Despite, or perhaps because of, all his labor with the concept, Nancy had not sufficiently heeded the impropriety of the word.

Blanchot's response was indeed difficult, to be sure, but largely by reason of its indirectness. In returning to Bataille's struggle with the question of community, and in repeating in its manner the form of "contestation" that Bataille's text called for (thereby pointing to a form of community vis-à-vis not only Nancy and Bataille, but a host of others he draws into this exchange), it retraces an immensely complex history. But however allusive and indirect it might be, it is firm, both in its manner of reminding us of Blanchot's prior involvements with the topic and in its manner of bringing forward the requirement of thinking community at another level. It does this by effectively letting *The Step Not Beyond* speak as a meditation on community. Here, it is indeed quite direct, offering at least three explicit citations, together with other partial citations and indications. One might, in fact, read *The Unavowable Community* as a guide to important dimensions of *The Step Not Beyond*, and it is on this basis that I have paused to consider its orienting indications.

A passage containing two of these citations is quite astounding on close examination. It follows an account of Bataille's notion of a "principle of insufficiency" that defines the finitude of the human being and the exigency of a form of community that Blanchot compares to a "chain reaction" wherein the need for the other's contestation (and this is a need for the affirmation of finitude, not for its completion or complementation in some "sufficient" form) drives the singular being into a form of relation that could never become a communion (UC 7/17 and following). Such a movement *requires* the other, Blanchot insists, because the solitary being cannot bring itself radically into question without the other—and essentially without exposition to the other's dying (as Blanchot follows a more Levinasian slant, the requirement in question will be said to come from the other).

It is with regard to this motif of the death of the other that Blanchot draws forth the ground of his "community" with Bataille (which he elsewhere calls his *friendship*):

> What, then, brings me most radically into question? Not my relation to myself as finite or as the consciousness of being before death or for death, but my presence before another [*à autrui*] who absents himself by dying. To remain present in the proximity of another who by dying removes himself definitively, to take upon myself another's death as the only death that concerns me, this is what puts me beside myself, this is the only separation that can open me, in its very impossibility, to the Open of a community. (UC 9/21)

The reference to an "Open" is striking here, as is the subsequent appeal to a markedly Heideggerian formulation of finitude to which we will return. Yet the words that offer it in this passage are tenuous. What does it mean to hold oneself present in the proximity of *autrui* if the exposition in question is fundamentally disappropriating, even shattering? Blanchot continues by explicating this with a scene:

> The mute conversation which, holding the hand of "another who dies," "I" keep up with him, I don't keep up simply to help him die, but to *share* [*partager*] the solitude of the event which seems to be the possibility that is most his own and his unshareable possession in that it dispossesses him radically. (UC 9/21)

I hold myself present in speech and gesture, holding the other's hand (*main-tenant*), though "I" am displaced in this sharing with an other whose identity is even more unstable than my own: "*autrui* who dies." My address to this now fictive partner whose most "proper" possibility I reach out to share is silent, but the relation, as Blanchot underscores, is one in and of language, at the limits of language. Response is constructed in relation to a quite human need for aid (and to give aid), but what is calling radically delimits the construction. Blanchot stages the response for us with a citation from *The Step Not Beyond*.

> Yes, it's true (by what truth?), you're dying. Except that dying, you not only remove yourself, you are also still present, for here you accord me that dying like an accord that surpasses all suffering, and here I tremble softly in what tears, losing speech even as you do, dying with you without you, letting myself die in your place, receiving this gift beyond you and me." To which there is this answer: "In the illusion that makes you live while I am dying." To which there is this answer: "In the illusion that has you dying while you die" (*The Step Not Beyond*). (UC 9/21–22)

In mute conversation, generous dedication (to the other and to a gift beyond the self or the other) gives way to a bitter admission of the fictive dimension of any assumption of what happens in this relation. There is irreducible illusion in the manner in which the one lives with and by the other's death and constructs the other's dying (an event in excess of their physical perishing, but never entirely distinguishable from it) as "their" dying. There is no presence of and to the dying other in the now via what occurs in this dying, and no holding dying itself. The address to this other is humanly necessary, and there may be a truth cohabiting with its illusion, but the community to which it seeks to hold entails a more radical exposure.

Let us emphasize that Blanchot is not condemning this "fictive" construction of what is so humanly needed (we will see this point reaffirmed shortly).[22] But he is staging it for us as an answer to something that exceeds the hold of the self, and underscoring in this manner how exposure to the dying of the other brings "me," as well as "you" radically into question, indeed into an entirely different set of relations.

"There is what founds community," Blanchot continues ("*Voilà ce qui fonde la communauté*"—and let us not fail to keep in mind that this statement follows two lengthy citations of *The Step Not Beyond*). To what does he refer: the accord, the tearing, the comforting but illusory pretention to receive the other's gift in identification and substitution? The next, and rather formidable, sentence seems to answer without answering. "There could be no community were there not common to each of us the first and last event (birth, death) where the power to be (this event) ceases" (UC 9/22). Long paragraphs could be devoted to this sentence and its translation.[23] But in an attempt at paraphrase, let us render it by saying that what is in "common" is a *failing* in being that can never be an "event" or can only ever cease to be such for the subject of this passage whose being (which Heidegger defined as a being-able) lapses there. "Common" would be the exposure, the finitude of each being, which can never be subsumed *properly* as *its* finitude, and never constitute a substance for the "it" of the passage in which it is shared. Dispossession would be what is common—a "*défaillance*" that makes even the relation to birth a kind of failing.

A firm, and perhaps very important link to Heidegger is established here that can be somewhat surprising given the date of this text. Indeed, Blanchot appears to be pointing to those dimensions of Heidegger's account of the experience of human finitude (the finitude of the human *Dasein*), that allow us to grasp in what sense *Mitsein* must be understood as originarily constitutive for the *Dasein* (a reading that has profoundly deconstructive implications for Heidegger's political thinking of the 1930's, which Blanchot denounces subsequently in his volume). In *The Infinite Conversation*, Blanchot follows Levinas in ascribing to Heidegger the tendency to surrender ethics to ontology.[24] But Blanchot would have been especially sensitive to those pages in the existential analytic where the accounts of thrownness, anxiety, and guilt link the question of finitude to that of *Mitsein*, particularly inasmuch as these pages give us the "event" of birth as the experience of a kind of powerlessness.[25] And he may well have recognized that the Levinasian argument is not quite sufficient. When Blanchot implicitly cites Heidegger in this passage, in any case, he appears to acknowledge him as a crucial source for a thought of community. This is not to say that he stays within the disrupted circle of Heidegger's thought. The *exposure* implied by the common "failing" Blanchot describes will be carried into his thought of passivity and *le neutre*; only from there does the "failing" borne in terms such as community and communism come to language as the fragmented writing of community.

In fact, such a language begins to appear immediately after the sentence that calls up the reference to Heidegger. In view of the elliptical character of the exposition here, we do well to start from that point again:

> This is what founds community. There could be no community were there not common to each of us the first and last event (birth, death) where the power to be (this event) ceases. What does the community pretend to in its obstinacy in retaining of "you and me" only relations of asymmetry that suspend *tutoiement*? Why does the relation that is introduced with it displace authority, unity, interiority, by confronting them with the exigency of the outside which is its non-directive origin? (UC 9–10/22)

An immense jump is made between the second and third sentences, here, as the "cessation" in being marked by the nonevent of dying/birth presents itself as an interruption of speech that has claimed the relation of "you and I" (the phrase "*de toi et de moi*" has just been employed in the staging of the "illusory" sharing of death) in such a way as to expose its inherently dissymmetrical character and suspend the presumed familiarity. After the second sentence, one might have expected Blanchot to stress a movement that is developed at some length in *The Step Not Beyond*, wherein exposure to a "lapse" in the other exposes the self to an alterity "within." But immediately it is a question of language, and it becomes: who/what was speaking in that scene, that the asymmetry of the interlocutors should emerge in those last words? "*Toi*" and "*moi*," as we see now, were already becoming "*il*" for one another by the stubborn insistence of this other instance ("community"), despite the "obstinate" effort of one to maintain the semblance of an intimate relation.[26] (The phrasing is especially arresting here as Blanchot displaces the urgent effort of the one onto the insistence of community.) But why, Blanchot insists, does this movement disrupt or displace any subjective formation, exposing every self-authorizing identity (of the individual or the group) to the claim of the outside? This seemingly redundant question goes unanswered, but underscores again the insistence of a strange, unworking intention (the term was offered by Blanchot in his essay on Bataille[27]) to which a speaking is now attributed, should community *permit itself a form of avowal* by repeating "the discourse on dying":

> What does the community say if it permits itself to speak [*si elle se laisse aller à parler*] from its limits in repeating the discourse on dying: "One does not die alone, and if it is humanly so necessary to remain beside the one who dies [*le prochain de celui qui meurt*], this is, even in a ridiculous way, to share the roles and to hold back, to keep from slipping away, by the gentlest of interdictions, the one who, dying, comes up against the impossibility of dying in the present. Don't die *now*; let there be no now for dying. "Don't" [*Ne pas*], the ultimate word, the prohibition that becomes complaint, the stammering negative: "don't, you will die" (*The Step Not Beyond*). (UC 10/22)

We have initially the statement of a kind of law. The need to attend to the other is a necessary human response to what is as much an ethical exigency ("*on ne meurt pas seul*"— this is a firm, if colloquial, statement of ethical usage: one is not to die alone, that is, one must not let the other die alone) as an "ontological" condition (our solitary dying will in fact have never been ours alone). But Blanchot phrases this in a way that immediately displaces the human impetus. It is humanly necessary to be *le prochain* of the one dying because one must take on the vain, even derisory, task of *sharing the roles*. The phrasing does not quite suspend the human imperative, but links it to an enjoined function. Humanly, we must try to hold the other back; this, because we are *required* for the vain enunciation of the interdiction of dying.

The language of this passage is precarious and resists capture. On its face, it suggests that community speaks in the desperate appeal to the other. This is an appeal from a lapsing relation (a *living* relation, let us say at this point, that can only speak from a present) that in an effort to retain the other can only repeat in the form of a prohibition what is in fact the "truth" of the event, as *The Step Not Beyond* insistently underscores. For there is no present, no now, for the nonevent of slipping from being, for that *défaillance* for which the other seeks vainly to stand in. The present can no more hold or brook such a passing ("let there be no now for dying")—than can the one who slips and suffers what remains an immense failure, even if it is no more than a moment's (infinitely repeated) distraction (SNB 104/143). The true impossibility of sharing appears in the stammering negative that can only say its own desperate powerlessness (it speaks in this manner very much like "I cannot" in saying the exposure of language to its limits, though it also reveals its implication in a discursive order). This would hardly seem the voice of community Blanchot seeks to evoke, were it not for the fact that it also already speaks *for dying*. "*Il est interdit de mourir*," as we learn in *The Step Not Beyond*, is already the saying of dying itself.[28] The "ultimate word," "*ne pas*," is saying by and with its vain prohibition *le pas au-delà*.

Is this the last word of community?

The following paragraph goes on to underscore that this desperate injunction is not meant to hold onto a lasting ("non-mortal") *now* for a community that would somehow subsume the finitude of those who belong to it, or fall from it. It is, Blanchot says, almost exactly the contrary. It is thus already breaking from that "speech of temporal eternity saying now, now, now" that is refused by the protagonist of "The Infinite Conversation." Were the enunciation of the prohibition serving the law of discourse, it would deny its human impetus and foreclose the fact of the dying to which it answers, in either its "human" dimension or its "inhuman," neutral import. Blanchot is insisting here—at this stage of the discussion—that community serves the propagation of the *human* relation to the dying of the other, which entails exposure to an inhuman that no political order can honor (and let us once again recall the passage in which the young girl, insistently and almost awkwardly described as "human," helps the one who is afraid across the night, he who must then carry a burden in relation to all those lost). "The human" clearly marks a *limit* in this analysis vis-à-vis the claims of discourse; this is why Blanchot is careful to note that the human appeal could be mistaken for a vain attempt to hold the other present within the living relations of human community governed by the discursive law ("the one law," IC xxii/xxiv). At this "human" limit, the address to the other cannot do more or otherwise than stammer a desperate, broken prohibition. But Blanchot is asserting that community *opens* (which is also to say, communicates) at precisely this limit, where the human opens beyond itself. This is why it is constantly challenging the constitution of any self-authorizing formation (serving the rule of authority, unity, and identity) and exposing it to the claim of the outside.

The point follows immediately from the reading of the phrase offered earlier, namely, a reading informed by the late sections of *The Step Not Beyond*, where "*il est interdit de mourir*" circulates as the rumor of dying. The "ultimate" word speaks from the limit of human community as traditionally conceived (that space within which dying must retain a meaning); it echoes already with the word of a community ordered to the other. Blanchot, however, does not immediately take this tack. Instead, he pauses to offer a summary of the discussion thus far. Community, he states, does not tend towards a fusional communion and prohibits itself any productive end (in the production of some identity). Its end (Blanchot retains in displacing a language of purpose) is to propagate substitution.

> For what does it serve? For nothing, unless it is to make present service to the other even unto death, so that this other does not lose themselves there solitarily, but is filled in for, just as they bring to another that supplementing brought to them. Mortal substitution replaces communion. (UC 11/24)

The intimacy evoked in the scenes of dying we have been reading is again disturbed. The relation to the dying of the other is offered to us as a propagating call (in terms strongly evocative of the Levinasian notion of substitution). "Don't," the "ultimate word," is a word of exposure that calls the other in a serial movement to the service of *autrui*. Undoubtedly we are justified in saying that the serving one speaks already as *autrui* in this plaint, calling to the service of others by this supplication that says an exposure to the dying of the other. As Blanchot put it in a passage cited earlier: "To remain present in the proximity of another who by dying removes himself definitively . . . this is the only separation that can open me, in its very impossibility, to the Open of a community" (UC 9/21). But there is a singular ambiguity here that I want to take the risk of entertaining. Indeed, Blanchot's assertion is almost counterintuitive if we forget that what is being developed at this point is the propagation of the human relation to the dying of *autrui*. Community serves, he says, to *render present* the necessary service to *autrui* in such a manner that *autrui* should find themselves "supplemented" in their disrupted solitude *and aided thereby in bringing the same supplementation to another*. There may be a dissymmetrical exchange evoked here (the one who aids is in turn aided). But the dissymmetry must remain open, and if we recall the scene with the young girl and the one in fear, we glimpse another possible construction. Thus, if the one dying may be described as in some sense *in advance* of the other in their falling away (a narrative construction that we see in "The Infinite Conversation" or *The Step Not Beyond*), then we might also say that community propagates by a kind of precipitation: the one in advance is helped to serve another "ahead" of them. The chain, in this case, would form *ahead* through the service of a speech that falls always behind. This brings a second crucial point from the passage, namely that the *défaillance* in question must be distinguished from death in the "natural" sense; for, clearly, if the other is to take up the task enjoined, they must survive in some sense. Most references to death in the earlier parts of this text (by the force of the reference to Bataille) lend to an identification of death with mortal destruction. How could it be otherwise in light of the importance of *Acéphale* for this discussion? But the dying that precipitates community in fact marks the living presence of every other, as Blanchot insists near the end of the first section of the volume.[29] Thus, the two scenes of dying must not be taken immediately as "death scenes" (or we must hold open the possibility that they are not *just* that, even if they present themselves insistently that way) and the apparent intimacy of the scenes must be read, once again, from the "stubborn" manner in which community displaces the you and the I. Community, as the "rendering present" of the relation of responsibility to/for the other, is an exposition that calls to further exposition.

Exposition, however, is always to the exigency of the outside, and thus to the other speaking that was already echoing in "Don't." Blanchot thus introduces another step under the title of "Community and Writing":

> Community is not the site of Sovereignty. It is what exposes in exposing itself. It includes the *exteriority* of being that excludes it—an exteriority that thought does not master, even by giving it various names: death, the relation to the other, or speech when the latter is not enveloped in manners of speaking and hence does not permit any relation (of identity or alterity) with itself. Community, governing for each of us, for myself and for it, an outside itself (its absence) which is its destiny, gives rise to an unallotted, though necessarily

multiple speech in such a way that this speech cannot be discursively developed; always already lost, it is without use and without any work, and does not glorify itself in that loss. (UC 12/25)

Following Blanchot's powerful insistence on language here, we might summarize by saying that the speech of community *relays*; it relays a human exigency of attending to the other even as it relays a language of the "outside"—a neutral, fragmented language that resists any form of subsumption. "*Il*" speaks in community, governing "for me and for it" the effacement onto which it opens (as its "destiny") in an occurrence that is always singular even in its "common" appeal. *Where the gift of its "word too many" (always multiple) is brought to writing*, it might be claimed as the speech of "my" community (this could also be named the site of "my" death), but it is also the inscription of a radical opening, an open call to an other written in pure loss (that is, without any presumption of a possible return). This call, Blanchot suggests, might be understood as apocalyptic.

Thus we reach a last, astounding citation of *The Step Not Beyond*:

> Thus the sense that community, in its very failure, is linked to a certain kind of writing, a writing that has nothing else to seek than the last words: "Come, come you for whom injunction, prayer, waiting are unfitting." [*Ainsi il se pressent que la communauté, dans son échec même, a partie liée avec une certain sorte d'écriture, celle qui n'a rien d'autre à chercher que les mots derniers: Viens, viens, venez, vous ou toi auquel ne saurait convenir l'injonction, la prière, l'attente.*] (UC 12/26)

The very *ends* of the writing undertaken in a text such as *The Step Not Beyond* are indicated with this presentiment. The community whose condition and destiny are effacement is ultimately bound to a form of writing that draws out the speaking that is its dispossessing gift. No saying can *assume* this gift (and thereby speak for this community). It is a matter, rather, of writing (from) it, of receiving this anonymous, plural speech as a groundless opening, and finally, of joining it affirmatively. "*Viens*," or "*venez*," both calling upon and affirming this opening, are effectively *to* community itself, even as they open onto a saying of its possible advent.[30] Thus, in their messianic reach, we may hear in their address the hospitable marking of the place of the absent one who would announce this opening from the place of "*il*" (let us recall here Blanchot's response to Catherine David). But could this place ever be taken if it is indeed that of a neutral, plural speech? The last words *presume nothing*, merely offering themselves as a dispossessed, affirmative call to the other from a devastated (desert) site. Here is the joyous end of writing one's death, already, in its call, a saying of community.

We still have to follow the trajectory that leads to these words in *The Step Not Beyond*. Before leaving *The Unavowable Community*, however, we should observe that its preparation of a reading of the former text does not quite conclude with the last remarkable citation. For the argument that opens with the reference to writing in the section we have just read underscores the imperative at work in Blanchot's own efforts. The imperative of community, he suggests, *had to be written* in the postwar period.

Two important points now emerge from Blanchot's exposition of Bataille's engagement with the question of community and the requirement that emerged of *writing* what was sought in Acéphale. The first point is established when Blanchot develops the "unavowable" character of what was attempted in that last, and, for Bataille, most important attempt at an acephalic community. Blanchot notes initially that what prohibited the participants from speaking or writing about this project after its dissolution was not simply its infamous design, the envisaged sacrifice that violated the community's own renunciation of any project, any *work*. The true "secret" inhered in the dissolution to which it committed its *conjurés*. For the sacrifice was a form of self-abandon: "To bind oneself to Acéphale is to abandon oneself and give oneself: *to give oneself without return to an abandon without limit*" (UC 15/30). Giving even onto the nothing of their existence (that exposure or insufficiency "proper" to their being—their own dying, we might say), the participants gave themselves over to the time of a common effacement, the tracing of an absence that was the only secret of the undertaking (UC 15/31). The pages in which Blanchot develops these points are almost awkwardly drafted and uneven (as we see by a footnote that repeats part of the exposition). But in reiterating the point that this offering occurs in an unfettering of passions that is the condition of any truly acephalic community, Blanchot twice tells us that the "unavowable" of this community inheres in a structure of imminence and withdrawal ("imminence of a death closer than any proximity, prior withdrawal of what presented no withdrawal from it," UC 15/31) that provided a "presentiment" of a disaster that would transcend every form of transcendence. He thus firmly reiterates the point that time is the true "emotional element" of the passions released in this project:

The sole "emotional element" capable of being shared while escaping any allotment, remains the obsessive value of mortal imminence, that is to say, of time, which explodes existence and liberates it ecstatically from everything in it that would be *servile*. (UC 16/33)

What is especially worthy of note for us here is Blanchot's emphasis on the passions of finitude to which the participants would have abandoned themselves, for a very significant portion of *The Step Not Beyond* is devoted to an exposition not simply of dying, but also of the forms of shared ecstasis proper to affliction, fear, and anguish. At the horizon of each of these (though Blanchot exhausts this phenomenological term, as we have seen), is an experience of temporality in the form of eternal return, and an enigmatic opening of hope (from "imminence") and despair (from "withdrawal"). Again, if Blanchot is not purposefully pointing back to *The Step Not Beyond*, it is clear that it is shaping his exposition.

Imminence and withdrawal must be *drawn out* for the saying of "*Viens*," and this brings us to the second point Blanchot emphasizes in these pages. He had affirmed the imperative of writing in *The Infinite Conversation* in relation to Bataille. Here he has recourse to it in order to make the point that the imperative of community persisted for Bataille after the war and required its exposition in *The Inner Experience*. Bataille had to *contest himself* (or so we might understand Blanchot's reference to "self-reflection"[31]) in exposing the limits of an experience that could never be the experience of one alone, and was meaningless if it did not communicate itself as the untransmittable basis of communication itself, the abyssal ground of the *partage* or *Mit-teilung* of community. He sought to contest himself, and he sought the relay or chain reaction of contestation, thus a "prolongation" of the experience. This was not for the sake of its memorialization or rememoration, as a long paragraph insists.[32] It was for its propagation in the sole form of communication that remained fitting by reason of its own devotion to unworking: the literary. This is a claim that Blanchot does not hesitate to date as he (re)writes his own history before offering obscure testimony to a clandestine, "posthumous" community of readers from the time of the war.

> ♦ The absence of community puts an end to the hopes of groups; the absence of a work which, on the contrary, needs and presupposes works so as to let them write themselves under the pull of unworking, is the turning point which, corresponding to the devastation of the war, will close an era. (UC 20/38)

Let us forgo, on this occasion, the question of our own belonging to the epochal turn to which Blanchot refers.[33]

Once Blanchot has pushed the import of the Acéphale project to its limits and opened it onto the "disaster" it holds, he is prepared to name "the unavowable community," and he is apparently prepared to use the term "community" almost as an established concept. The phrase "inner experience," he tells us, says the contrary of what it appears to say in suggesting that the devastating movement of contestation comes from within the subject itself; this movement, he counters, "has as its more profound origin the relation with the other that is community itself, which would be nothing if it did not open the one who exposes himself to it to the infinity of alterity while deciding their inexorable finitude" (UC 16–17/33).

Yet, at this point in the exposition (or by the end of the first section of *The Unavowable Community*), there is still relatively little basis for distinguishing what is named "community" from what is also named "friendship" or, as in *The Step Not Beyond*, "fraternity." The discussion of what is exposed at that limit that is the *human* relation to *autrui* is immensely suggestive. But it is in fact hard to read "community" as much more than a kind of placeholder for a set of relations to which Blanchot, at this point, will only allude with reference to an experience of disaster in the disrupted temporality of return. Why the reticence?

Beyond any occasional considerations (which necessarily escape us, to some degree),[34] we must undoubtedly take the full measure—for Blanchot—of his suggestion that Bataille was driven to carry forward his preoccupation with community in *The Inner Experience* in part by reason of a collapse in his hope for groups. Had Blanchot not already identified in *The Step Not Beyond* the failure of political groups to overcome the pitfalls of authority and to embrace the uncanny alterity at the heart of community? The force of this statement is particularly striking in retrospect:

> ♦ The vain struggle for the anonymous. . . . We are not dupes of the present that would make us believe in some authority we would have or in an influence we would exercise, still less are we concerned with the past, still less are we presumptuous of a future. We expose to a harsh light the supposed impersonal responsibility of groups in which there is always asserted, either secretly or directly, the right of some to lead in aggrandizing their names with that of the group. The "cult of personality" does not begin with the person who places

himself above others to incarnate a historical truth. It begins with that truth itself, be it that of the party, the country, or the world, a truth always ready, once it immobilizes itself, to unify itself in a name, a person, a people, an epoch. How, then, does one arrive at that anonymity whose sole mode of approach is a *haunting*, an uncertain obsession that always dispossesses? (SNB 36/54)

If Bataille (in Blanchot's reading) had been driven to carry the imperative of community into writing, Blanchot surely experienced a comparable imperative in the postwar period (and particularly after 1968). This is not to say that he had come to dismiss the possibility of thinking forms of community beyond the literary direction in which he takes it, nor that he simply disqualified collective action for the sake of justice (on the contrary: he never disqualified this imperative). His own political passion probably never dissipated.[35] But it seems clear that he considered the experience of writing crucial to any approach to the "anonymous passion" (SNB 37/55) he saw at the heart of a politics of community. Hence the continuing wariness regarding the term (both of these last terms: politics, community), and the insistent reference back to *The Step Not Beyond*. At the end of the first section of *The Unavowable Community*, the thought of the anonymous relations to which Blanchot had already pointed has not fully emerged. The experience of the *passions* of community has yet to be developed, just as the exigency of *writing* community has yet to be engaged via the thought of the return (which the passage just cited continues on to describe as the condition for maintaining relation to the uncanny alterity in any relation of community). For these developments, we must effectively return to *The Step Not Beyond*.

But let us take the full measure of Blanchot's wariness and note the degree to which what he seeks in "community" delimits the claims of any political formation (delimiting thereby not just the temptations of "the groups," but the inevitable—inevitably ideological—political imperative the term "community" seems to bear), and even the order of the political itself. Community occurs at the limits of the political, but also breaches them in opening to an "infinity of alterity." Blanchot stages this breach for us in another "death scene" in *The Step Not Beyond* that presents all the elements of the relations we have considered thus far. Again, we must cite at length from a passage that takes its departure from a consideration of the transgressive character of dying ("what could never belong to a law,"

SNB 105/144) and its manner of confusing itself with death. It continues by considering what it means to attend this nonevent:

> Mortal indecision has no place, nor any mitigating status. Even when dying seems to fill a being to such a point that we call them, and not without discomfort, a dying one, we do not know, facing the indecisive strangeness, what becomes of we who are there, undone, beside this place where chance plays itself out, attending non-presence, touched in our most intimate fidelity: our relation, in ourselves, to a subject. And, in conformity with the customs of the day, we bustle about doing nothing, we help the living one, we help him to die. But we do not help dying: something happens there, in all absence, and by default, that is not accomplished, something that could be the "step/not beyond," does not belong to duration, repeats itself endlessly and separates we ourselves (witnesses of what escapes witnessing) from any appropriateness as from every relation with a Self, subject of a Law. And we can certainly understand and say that the silent speech, this infinite murmur, then also pronounces itself in us, that we die with the one who dies, just as they die in our place, in the place where we believed we sojourned—dying not because we lose a part of common life, but rather because it is a "dying," the intransitive loss, that we share with them, in a movement of pure passivity that the passion without tears claims sometimes to assume. This we can say, and no doubt rightly. Still, nothing is said if we do not force ourselves to think what even the evidence of agony does not reveal, the invisible rupture of prohibition, the transgression in which we feel we are accomplices, because it is also our own strangeness: something overwhelming, but also fundamentally shocking. In the narrow space where this is accomplished without being accomplished, there is no longer any law, nor society, nor alliance, nor union—and yet nothing free, nothing safe: only, beneath the appearance of a devastating violence and of a suffering that extinguishes itself, a secret that is not said, an unknown word that sweeps the silence away with it. (SNB 105–106/145–146)

There, already (1973), is the unavowable of community, in its most raw form. Prior to the last step of thought, there is sharing, there is substitution (again, an "inhospitable host" displaces us), there is accompaniment in a movement of pure passage that Blanchot names directly "*le pas au-delà*." In this shared passion, this movement of "pure passivity," there is already a displacement from the subjective relations governed by law or recognizable in any political formation. Thus the murmur that speaks here is itself unrecognizable in any symbolic order ("*What draws you among us.... Is it you, that plaint not yet heard?*" [IC xxii/xxv]). Yet this relation that we can "justly" claim—this still human relation—must be understood to harbor something more profoundly unsettling. It remains "illusory" if we do not force ourselves to make the next step and recognize, "beneath the appearance of devastating violence," something fundamentally unavowable—an unspeaking and unknown word that tears away the very silence. This too must be written, it would seem, if we are to approach the last words of community.

Can it be written, or does it perhaps exceed any relation whatsoever? It is quite striking that in the immediately succeeding fragment, Blanchot seems to back up from these last words to present in the form of a speaking what is said in that "silent word," that infinite murmur that is "also pronounced in us" before the shattering passage to what destroys this shared silence. There is relation, he seems to affirm in a remarkably indirect, and, by an astonishing alternation in tone, almost comforting manner:

> ♦ "*I don't know, but I know that I am going to have known*": thus dying speaks through the suffering silence of the dying one. (SNB 106/146)

These are words *of* dying-with—shared words that seem almost to speak on their own, as from an ungraspable memory, and speaking to a "certain" future from no self-sustained present. But comforting? Perhaps only the gathering of this motif in the latter sections of *The Step Not Beyond* permits us to use such an adjective. But a long meditation on a version of the phrase—a virtual explication of it—is particularly arresting by reason of its insistent care and the gentleness of its tonality. It is almost as though Blanchot wants to instruct us as to the nature of the attentiveness required by a literary language that is moving to self-effacement. He teaches us, in effect, to hear a dampened negation as he focuses on the evacuation of the self and of the present of its nonknowing (in this instance, the phrase bears a reference, in the present, to the future: *je ne sais pas, mais je pressens*) before drawing forth the irrevocable of a having known ("the completed absolute of knowing," SNB 113/155). "Having known," in this sentence, will have never coincided with a present and will have never been the possession of a self, but is in no way illusory:

> From the imminence of a future that I do not touch ("I sense that I am going . . ."), and without passing through any actuality, all has collapsed in the irrevocable of a *having known*. And "having known" is not a pretence, a mockery, the furrow of ignorance: having known is a redoubled knowledge,

the form of certitude. There would have been and there has been a kind of absolute knowledge which, without being, has always already disappeared through the lack of a subject, be it individual or universal, capable of bearing this knowledge in the present. (SNB 113–114/155–156)

The tone is oddly reassuring, once again, and the assertions have a peculiar force. But if this knowledge is forever denied to a subject, "be it individual or universal," in what manner might its trace haunt the one recalled to it by the "discourse" of dying? For whom would it insist? Has Blanchot taken back all he has given with this account of the eclipse of the knowing subject?

The Passions of Finitude: Le neutre

We broach now the question of the experience of finitude, given to us in a broad segment of *The Step Not Beyond* under the form of the question of the passions of being-with (or without), and the problem of their "subject." Three passions receive lengthy treatment, as we have noted: anguish, affliction, and fear. As passions of dying, they are not easily distinguished in a conceptual manner, though the first is demarcated insistently by the uncertainty in and onto which it opens, and even by the way it is defined *against* knowing. Indeed, we may have an instance of such a countermarking in the following arresting fragment:

♦ *Is it this, to die, is it this, fear?* Silent anguish, and this silence, like a cry without words; mute, although crying endlessly. (SNB 61/87)

Do we have in these anxious questions (to be repeated again in *The Step Not Beyond*), that which provoked the *"je ne sais pas"* of the discourse of dying? Would anguish, in its own certain uncertainty (SNB 62/88) and nonsurety as relation to the unknown, be the haunted difference from itself of the absolute knowledge to which that discourse spoke—the all-too-human relation to the unknown? Anguish ("anxiety" would appear to be an equally suitable translation) would be, in this case, a kind of always extant fault, a fissure in the peace communicated in the long passage on *"je ne sais pas,"* an always open (im)possibility in the finite knowledge of an absolute unknown. "No end, there where finitude reigns" (UC 20/38), Blanchot wrote in *The Unavowable Community*. The persistent questions, resonating against the silent cry of anguish, will remain without an answer other than anguish: "Once we have passed a certain threshold, always without our knowledge, though knowing it, in an uncertainty that is already its mark, everything belongs to anguish, including non-anguish, this is the trap" (SNB 62/88).

The topic of anguish undoubtedly merits an entire study. Its return in this text cannot be dissociated from its earlier appearances in Blanchot's work, notably in *Faux pas*, where it is said to open the sky.[36] Blanchot's relation to Bataille, explored in that earlier text, always overdetermines the word's use, as is visible notably in *The Unavowable Community*, and as was explicitly indicated in *The Infinite Conversation*. But there is indeed something raw about its ravaging return in *The Step Not Beyond* ("with something young about it that terrifies," SNB 65/92)—something that makes it indissociable, perhaps, from an equally terrifying return of madness to which Blanchot points in an anguished passage whose insistence forces the question of its possible autobiographical weight.[37] The return of anguish as it is described vividly in these pages by Blanchot is all-invasive and unbearable, inspiring a kind of horror that infects every act of speech and all silence, destroying with its arid force all standing meaning (the read or the written):

> ♦ Anguish makes reading forbidden (the words separated, something arid and devastating; no more text, each word useless, or else foundering in something that I do not know, drawing me into it with refusal, comprehension as an injustice). To write then, the effect of a negative hallucination, giving nothing to read, nothing to understand. (SNB 63/89)

Yet, in its *communication*, it remains a kind of knowledge of the unknown via the other.[38] A passage in the pages devoted to anguish captures beautifully the slippage described throughout *The Step Not Beyond* from a self—a writer, a philosopher—anguished at the falsity of the traps into which he is driven, no less than the reflection of the other in the mirror of words (a mirror that always also reflects the self and its investments in the glaring inadequacy of words and concepts), to an "I" displaced in the passion of relation to the other. It ends with the following:

> Anguish—this word that cannot be pronounced, that one would like to silence in crying out, with its impropriety, its philosophic and pathetic pretension; but, turned away from myself, "I" receive it from *autrui* as the unknown of all pain, the supplication of a powerless concern. (SNB 63/89)

In the space of the self's eclipse—which Blanchot also names here *solitude*—anguish becomes another form of relation to the other. It is always a *general* anguish:

> ♦ Knowing [*la connaissance*] brings anguish, and yet anguish does not depend on knowing. Anguish without knowing can indeed arise from another form of knowing; that which isolates it, that absolute solitude that comes from it and traces a circle around it, the loss of knowledge it brings with it and that does not diminish it—on the contrary, bringing always more anguish, the immobility to which it reduces one because it can only be suffered and never suffered enough in a passivity that cannot even promise us the inertia of a dead thing, the muteness that makes it silent even in words, everything that makes it escape and by which everything escapes; there is, starting from there, a line of demarcation—on one side no-one, on the other all the others, those who understand, care for, love and understand also that there is a line of demarcation, without their being themselves ever marked. Anguish robs and steals away. And yet anguish is in relation with all anguish; it is the anguish of all. (SNB 114/157)

The passage cited here follows a fragment in which Blanchot notes that awareness of what is "unbearable" in the world (torture, oppression, affliction, hunger, death camps) cannot, indeed, be fully borne: the one exposed to it risks collapse. Thus, it cannot become a knowledge "in general" (*la connaissance en général*); what this awareness would carry cannot be borne in knowing (*le savoir*) (SNB 114/156). We live therefore, between confusion and half-sleep. The menacing interruption of anguish thus comes as awakening to a form of "absolute" knowledge that requires, as we will continue to see, a passivity—a passion—that can never be sufficient (and is thus always guilty, as well as always false) to the "simplicity" (SNB 62/88), the savage innocence, of its unknown. This is an absolute, as we will see, that is also known in what Blanchot names "*malheur*."

But before turning to this second passion of being-with, let us continue with the theme of solitude, sounded in the passage cited earlier that identifies the "threshold" passed in anxiety as a line of demarcation that separates "no one" from "all the others," while asserting that this isolating anguish is nevertheless "the anguish of all." What isolates (in anguish), what leaves the one exposed to it separated from themselves and from the other, alone in the separate region of a failing, fragmented speech, petrified, also enjoins a task that is indistinguishable from a menace.

♦ Strange threats: *"I don't threaten you, I leave you in the neutrality of a life without threats, which doesn't even leave you a reason to live in order to defend yourself against the threatening anguish.—Then why this anguish that surpasses any threat?—Because I threaten you in others, in all that is other, an infinite field from which the anxiety that immobilizes you keeps you apart, reducing you to yourself alone, in the solitude of an anguish that encloses you by reason of the others.—The anxiety of all in me who disappears there.—Walled up in yourself by your anguished concern for others.—It is because the care has not used me sufficiently, has not brought forth that patience that would have made me pass beyond.—Don't hope you can use others to free yourself from yourself: you are condemned to yourself so that there should still be someone to receive others.—But I am nothing, nothing as a self.—Nothing, this is what is needed: bear the unbearable nothing.* (SNB 129–130/177)

Once again, this passage seems to call upon what precedes it across a space that remains unbridged (so often in this text, we are obliged to move *à reculons*). In that preceding fragment, Blanchot evokes something in speech that "withdraws" it from us and is perhaps more related to dying than living, leading us, in speaking of life, "to take our distance from hopes, fears, and living words, up to that limit that none of us can pass alive— except in speech" (SNB 129/176–177).[39] The limit is marked, then, by the "neutrality of a life without menaces," or, more precisely, by an anxious relation to alterity inasmuch as it involves something that does not concern any interests in one's life. Is the self thus called to impassibility? Were we to draw such a conclusion, we would foreclose the possibility of thinking response to the multifold exigencies of what Blanchot terms friendship or even community. The patience required of the anguished self (the task of bearing the "unbearable nothing") does not involve a mere "suffering" of the neutral, and it is certainly not a form of mortification (as might be understood from Bataille's admiring judgment regarding Blanchot's "death"); it remains an opening. As we follow the motif of "passion" in Blanchot, we must preserve (or allow) the conditions of response to a call to a *human* aid, as well as that excessively passive, patient turn into the double affirmation that speaks in *The Madness of the Day*. We must find in the estrangement of the relation to the other the release of another relation to life from that defined by will, interests, or a reason to live that would assert itself *despite* the knowledge of what is unbearable (suffering, oppression) or the frightening exposure that comes in affliction or anguish. We must hold open the possibility of thinking a veritable conversion in the relation to life and death that follows from engagement with *le neutre*. This is where the last steps are pointing. The hint that the "origin" of anguish may be exposure to *le neutre* itself gives a powerful suggestion that what is at stake in thinking the "passions of finitude" is an exposure of and to *le neutre* that is comparable to, though quite exceeds, the disclosure that Heidegger sought to think in his notion of *Stimmung*.

The anguish Blanchot is trying to think, again, does not take its origin from something that threatens "living" interests; it is not a matter of a mortal threat or a menace from some intraworldly source (or even that opening of being-in-the-world itself, from which *Angst* is said to derive in Heidegger's account). What is experienced as threatening (in anguish), what imperils thought, does not concern life; its relation to us is a neutral one. Anguish: the neutral. We can question about the neutral, one fragment says, by questioning it through anguish (SNB 69/97), which suffers no question (SNB 64/90).[40] Something like this appears to happen in the passage we are reading as one questions via anguish (or is questioned, via anguish—a plural, self-dividing anguish) regarding the anguished experience of finitude before the unknown of the neutral. The answer is devastating: You live your finitude (vis-à-vis an infinite other) in anguished isolation, enclosing yourself in care for the anguished other. Your claim to disappear in anxious care is in actuality a form of self-authorization from which no deliverance (by a worn endurance issuing in patience) can be expected. Do not expect to use others to free yourself from yourself. Self-relation must give way to a kind of assumed exposure that displaces the self while opening its place. You must become a null site, giving over to the nothing of the other.

There is the task: the enjoined relation to the other does not involve a dissolution of the self; rather, the self is condemned to itself (a remarkable phrase in this volume: but this is a self become other that could say "my anguish" in the way the writer might write "my death," and where the anguish in question marks an exposure) so that it may serve as host to the other. It must offer to the other a site defined by the nothing that falls to it—an "unbearable" that comes to it through the exposure of anguish when it slips into solitude and is no longer together with itself or with the other. The passion of affliction (*malheur*) brings the same task:

♦ *"You have only to receive the affliction of one alone, the one to whom you are closest, to take in all in just one."*—*"That doesn't calm me, and how would I dare say that I take in a single affliction wherein all affliction would be received, when I cannot even take in my own?"—"Receive the afflicted one in your affliction."* (SNB 118/161)

If the preceding passage on anguish still referred to a self, the pages on *malheur* adjacent to those on anguish late in the volume insistently displace this reference, as we see already in this movement whereby another protest of a self gives way to an injunction that gently bypasses the self (though there is still reference to a "you" in the informal second person; again, "your affliction" would be comparable to "your death"). Who receives? Clearly, we cannot think the "I" apart from the passion, apart from its displacement (*"pas"*) in this passion. And who addresses? A voice is given here once again to an infinite exigency, infinite in that no responsive bearing can ever be sufficient. As Blanchot states in his "Discourse on Patience" (which returns insistently to the condition of *malheur*), passivity, and the patience in which it must be borne, is never passive enough. In relation to the nonconcerning, every relation remains wanting. The exigent "other" voice that speaks here speaks from the relation between *il* and *I*.

"*Malheur*": the word does not pose special problems in itself (unlike *angoisse*, with its extensive philosophical baggage, forcing us to hesitate between terms such as dread, anguish, and anxiety). As in *The Infinite Conversation*, it seems aptly translated by "affliction." Here we must add a reference to misfortune, inasmuch as the term communicates with the motif of chance, and not without a connotation of some evil that befalls one, some form of fatality which "unhappiness" cannot quite approach. But *malheur* remains notably undefined in this text, and by reason of the force of its evocation in some passages, we are prompted to recognize in it Blanchot's later usage, where it is coupled with "disaster."[41] It comes as a kind of fate, Blanchot suggests in *The Step Not Beyond*, and though it can be experienced as nothing more exalted than a "discouraged fatigue," and expressed in nothing more than a plaintive incapacity, it reaches (as a significant passage on Freud explains) beyond one's *living* aspirations. *Malheur* does not develop in an "unhappy" consciousness suffering from some division or frustration in life's aspirations; like anxiety, it leads beyond the limits of life and inhabits words as something "more linked to dying" (SNB 129/176). Like anxiety, also, it is communicated—it comes from the other as virtually the *malheur* of all, even if it allows no communion. In this case in particular, and at least in one essential respect, the passion involved communicates with what Heidegger termed a "*Stimmung*": "♦ In accord with the affliction of all, the affliction that excludes all accord" (SNB 124/169).

Three passages, late in the volume, call especially for our attention here. We have already seen the conclusion of the first:

> ♦ If the self fails under the affliction of all, it risks being only the failing self, and extended by this affliction to the point of being the self of all, even as afflicted. But affliction does not authorize the self, the afflicted I, which leads one to think—only to think—that affliction has always undone the self, substituting for it the other relation, other and with the other, and that it nevertheless cuts it off as a punctual singularity in which it does not have the right to be self, be this a singular self: only possible to the point of being removed from whatever suffering there is in passivity, from the common feeling of suffering, and nevertheless called through this passivity that is not suffered, not authorized to suffer and as though exiled from suffering, to sustain the relation with the other who suffers.
>
> The "*pas*" of the completely passive—the "*pas au-delà*"?—is rather the folding back, unfolding itself, of a relation of strangeness that is neither suffered nor assumed. A transgressive passivity, a dying where nothing is suffered, nothing acted upon, which is unconcerning and takes name only through the abandonment of the dying of the other [*ne prend nom que par le délaissement du mourir d'autrui*]. (SNB 122/167)

As in the passage concerning the "threat" of anguish cited earlier, caution is given against a movement of *self*-authorization in the movement in question—a lapsing that becomes a self-expansion. But affliction, Blanchot affirms, does not authorize the self, *which leads to the thought* (thought's supposition—which, as we will see, leads to a presupposition of thought itself—would be opening from the ground of what is either a kind of interdiction or a *défaillance*, a failing support) that the self has always already been displaced in affliction. For its self-relation, there has been substituted relation with the other that reduces the self to a singular punctuality whose trait is a "passibility"—a passivity that *takes* in suffering (in its very opening or receptivity to the other) to the point of *separating* in and from this suffering and taking thereby the task of sustaining the relation to the suffering other.[42] Separation, we should underscore, is separation from the *common* feeling of suffering, and it is therefore tempting to assume that a step has been made here in relation to the notion of compassion with suffering humanity (unless, of course, the step has already been made).[43] The last section of the passage makes it clear that this would indeed be *le pas au-delà*, that the affliction in question is inseparable from a form of dying. It emphasizes, moreover, that the substitution we have seen is a movement (a passage in passivity—*pas*) that is not a fold of self-reflection, but nonetheless a folding in exposure that makes it possible for Blanchot to speak of *relation* to the other. This is a relation of speech; the punctual being is called to sustain relation in a movement wherein dying "takes" name in *le pas au-delà*.

The second passage entertains this as a relation of *thought*, which through its separating, transcending movement, interrupts the silencing force that comes over us in the word "*malheur.*" Blanchot proceeds here again by a kind of supposition and even presentiment (*pressentir*—again, the word used in the meditation on the phrase concerning knowing: "*je ne sais pas, mais je pressens*"), to evoke a passivity that would separate from a mere suffering of affliction and afford a response, to and for the affliction brought to it by the other, that would release a relation to it other than one governed by fatality. What is entertained here is not a freedom (thought is *more afflicted* by reason of the responsibility it engages), but something that transgresses the "somber sovereignty" of this force that claims to exceed any cause to which it might be accounted:

> ♦ Affliction: this word that befalls us without giving an explanation and without allowing us to respond to it: destiny without destiny. We can do nothing against affliction; so it speaks to us through its muteness. But, even if there is no action capable of effacing it, no gaze to fix it, are we not allowed to sense [*pressentir*] that there would be a passivity more passive than that by which we suffer it and from which it would be *given* to us to withdraw from it this trait of natural fatality—of a speech unpronounced but forever said—that it represents for us? *Perhaps* thought is, in its most passive passion, more afflicted than all affliction, being so for still being thought in the face of the affliction that reaches it in others; passivity that leaves a certain distance to respond to it, there where, pretending to escape any cause (social, historical, or ethical) or at least always to exceed it, it affirms itself in its somber sovereignty, in ruins. Yes, perhaps; only perhaps. (SNB 125/171)

The evocation of an almost actively oppressive dimension in affliction may well recall to us Blanchot's reading of Antelme's *L'espèce humaine*. Is Blanchot perhaps attempting to return to the structure of witness he explored in that essay (with implications for the thought of community and responsibility he is pursuing in this volume)? The echo is powerful, and following this connection with the earlier essay, we might be prompted to read in these lines a kind of deconstruction of the effect of fatality that is communicated in an affliction brought by a power that pretends to efface its human origins and its sociopolitical determinations.[44] No affliction is natural, Blanchot reminds us, and only the word can pretend to silence. In developing this latter point with reference to the earlier essay, one must recall its demonstration of the implication of murderous violence in a relation that exceeds its command (thematized in "The Indestructible" with the notion of the indestructible itself). Affliction manifests itself first in social conditions, as Blanchot emphasizes in both "The Indestructible" and "Reflections on Hell."[45] It also opens onto an infinite for precisely the fact that it involves a relation between human beings. In the passage we are reading from *The Step Not Beyond*, therefore, Blanchot entertains the possibility of thought's carrying the experience of affliction to its limits *from within*, opening it onto the infinite that haunts it (ultimately the neutral of the human relation to *autrui*) and thereby breaching the forbidding horizon—or lack of horizon—of this dark force that pretends to transcend its all-too-human origins. The "somber" sovereignty of affliction is thus exposed in its pretense, but precisely through a transgressive movement that would involve a passage "there": beyond any social, historical, or ethical cause. The transgressive interruption of this silencing force would thus open a relation to social, historical, or ethical "causes" that would be neither quite "free" nor "otherworldly," but *without ressentiment* and *without cause*.[46] Finite in its transcendence, but without a grounding or determining reason, such a thought would be "absolute" and in some sense released to respond affirmatively. We have still to define what it might mean to assume or affirm affliction; clearly it is not a matter of affirming the oppression at work in its social manifestations. It is a matter, rather, of affirming the infinite upon which affliction opens, thereby neutralizing affliction's own wounding, silencing force,[47] and in the same movement allowing an address to any social, historical, or ethical relation from what Blanchot called in his essay on Antelme, "the justice of a true *speech*" (IC 134/197). It is true that Blanchot does not easily use such a language in *The Step Not Beyond*, but in extrapolating from the passage under consideration, it seems entirely conceivable that we have a tentative thought of the relation to justice (from the nonground of the ethical relation) sought by Levinas.

It is worth underscoring here that the step from "The Indestructible," where we find the call for a subject who would receive the affliction of *autrui* ("subject," in turn, to an "intermediary" that would assume the dialectical struggle[48]), to the language of *The Step Not Beyond*, where we find the evocation of a thought that would perhaps assume the infinite of affliction from within, is considerable. Affliction was of course already "infinite" in the earlier text inasmuch as its experience entailed an opening onto the indestructible at the heart of the human relation. But in thinking affliction in the temporality of return and from his thought of passivity and *le neutre* (opening it in this way onto his thought of the disaster, as we see in "The Discourse on Patience"), Blanchot is able to introduce a new articulation of relation to the negative. We will see shortly how thought might be released to "disarm" the silencing character of affliction in a movement of double affirmation whose echo appears in the conclusion of our passage: "Yes, perhaps." No less significant is the development in Blanchot's thought of community, which can be glimpsed most immediately in the way the motif of "destruction" is taken over in "The Discourse on Patience" (and, reading back from this text, already in *The Step Not Beyond*). We find in that essay an astonishing reference with a furtive "we" to the presence/absence of "destroyed men" in the space of the outside. Its pertinence for *The Step Not Beyond* will only emerge as we enter the narrative line. But it is worth citing in anticipation these lines from the end of the passage on Bartleby:

> "I would prefer. . . ." Belongs to the infinite of patience, offering no hold to dialectical intervention: *we have fallen outside of being*, in the field of the outside where, immobile, and walking by an equal and slow step, the destroyed men come and go (my emphasis).[49]

Blanchot will never give up the double imperative of maintaining an ethico-political vigilance while answering another exigency, though his thought of community answers increasingly to the latter imperative.

But just two pages later, the distance a "punctual singularity" is called to sustain (perhaps as thought) seems almost to collapse. Relation with the other in affliction is named identification:

> ♦ Affliction: perhaps we would suffer it if it struck us alone; but always it reaches the other in us and, reaching us by others, it removes us even onto that most passive passion where our lost identity no longer allows us to suffer it, but

only to identify ourselves with it, which is always outside the identical, to carry ourselves, without identity and without the possibility of acting, toward the other who is always the afflicted, as the afflicted is always the other: a movement that does not reach its end, but which, like the "step/not beyond" of the completely passive to which we would respond in dying, gives itself as its own transgression; as though dying, outside of us, consecrated us to the other, even while losing us along the path and in holding us in this loss.

Affliction does not bear *itself* [*ne se supporte pas*]; it is in as much as it does not bear itself, in the neutral inequality where it lacks all support, just as it lacks the essence that would manifest it and make it be, that it demands to be *borne*, beyond what we suffer, by a transgressive passivity that is never our doing, and whatever we might do or not do, leaves us disarmed, absent from ourselves, in the seriousness of a lightness felt as frivolity, in the culpability of an innocence that accuses itself—sharpens itself, puts into question—because it is never "lived" as innocent enough. (How could it be lived, if it is not a matter here of the innocence of living, but of the innocence of dying?) (SNB 127/173-174).

The passage turns upon the question of the *subject* of affliction (its support in the sense of *hypokeimenon* or *subjectum*) and the identity of the one who would undergo this passion. In the displacement of the self by the affliction that touches the other in the self, passion becomes the passion of the other, or identification with the other's affliction (itself without identity). The movement is profoundly disappropriating, and yet it does not issue, in Blanchot's description, in the kind of dissolution that can occur in collective panic or comparable group phenomena. The latter are movements of dissolution where the self is carried away or along but in which there could never emerge the movement of thought that is required by the affliction that reaches us via the other (where thought is all the more afflicted for having to remain thought, in and before affliction). Here, identification transgresses itself in response to an infinite exigency that it draws out in its very exposure. It is thereby called to *bear* a groundless affliction, beyond suffering. Once again, what opens in this movement is perhaps to be called thought. But identification, here, remains identification with no *identity*, and we are given to think its movement only *with* that of others, by figure or simile ("*ainsi que le 'pas au-delà'*"; "*comme si mourir*"), the basis of comparison being the manner in which it *gives itself* as its own transgression and thus a *becoming other* that is held in its self-loss. What carries this disappropriating movement is perhaps still thought, but it is indeed a disaster for thought.

There is no subject of affliction, Blanchot emphasizes; it is essentially relational. No subject suffers it alone (it comes to us by way of the other, turning us to that afflicted other) and no subject or substance takes form in it. Its manifestation is without true property and permits no "proper" assumption. The light bearing that it demands by its very lack of substance can never be sure enough or pure enough—leaving us (and here is the lived experience for the self) in disarray and a sharpening guilt. We are reminded here that the passions of being- (dying-) with have their correlates in the affects of lived experience, which are perhaps never quite overcome or effaced. The point is driven home in a subsequent exchange between a plaintive self, anxious by reason of the unhappiness it adds to the world (afraid of rendering this "error" more general), and the exigency of what is perhaps *malheur*. It ends with the following injunction:

> *Be the lightness of dying, be nothing else for the other, even if this means "living" it in heaviness, seriousness, responsibility, sharp questioning, that is, in an afflicted incapacity for life for yourself.* (SNB 131/179)

The passage on "identification" we have just read gives ample warning with regard to any effort at synthesis at this point. But a cluster of shared terms may now allow us to describe what the thought of *le pas au-delà* brings to language with respect to the passions of being- (dying-) with. Clearly, this step is not so much taken as it *takes* in movements thought with a series of terms that includes passivity, passability, passing, passage, and passion itself, not to speak of the interdictions evoked by "*pas*" or their transgression (there is also "*trépassement*": passing away). We may note, too, that *le pas au-delà* is insistently attributed to the movement of dying-with, and that this latter passion (raised at one point to "the passion without tears," SNB 106/146) appears to mark each of those movements wherein a passivity transgresses itself in exposure. *Malheur* is thought with it, anguish is indissociable from it, and fragility "belongs" to it or is *of* it (SNB 123/169). But the common term here is in fact *le neutre*, which can never constitute a "common." Thus, Blanchot will describe the movement in which I give myself over to dying—neither suffering it nor assuming it, but *answering* for it (*répondre de*: here, again, is the task of what is perhaps thought)—as relation with the nonconcerning. Dying is in the neuter:

> ♦ Not "I die, this does not concern me," but "dying that does not concern me" puts me in play in all dying, through a relation that does not pass through me,

bringing me to respond—without responsibility—for this relation in the most passive passion (relation with the non-concerning) which I neither suffer nor assume. (SNB 123/168)[50]

And shortly before this, a long passage in which the near (but always self-preceding) affirmation of *le pas au-delà* comes to language:

> ♦ To *le neutre* would respond the fragility of what is already breaking: passion more passive than anything that would be passive, yes that has said yes before affirmation, as though the passage of dying had always already passed there, preceding consent. To *le neutre*—name without name—nothing responds, save the response that fails, that has always almost responded and failed in the response, never patient enough to "pass beyond," without this "step/not beyond" being accomplished. . . . Transgression is not a simple letting go: not that it decides and, reposing on nothing, would there exceed power, by chance and sovereignty, even onto the impossible. Transgression transgresses by passion, patience, and passivity, always transgressing the most passive of ourselves in that "dying in the lightness of dying" that escapes our presence and by which we would escape ourselves without being able to escape. Passivity, patience, passion which have renounced the disquiet of the negative, its impatient stirring, its nevertheless infinite errancy, and thus—thus!—would withdraw from *le neutre* that withdrawal in which its negative signalling still leaves it. (SNB 118–119/162–163)

I have elided Blanchot's critical remarks, in this passage, on the illusory ambition of the project of automatic writing (with its "mirage of passivity"). Transgression is not a simple "letting-go," he states, nor can there be anything like a "dictation," since the "dictated" will have always died away in a prior repetition. Saying is a resaying (*redite*), and what is said belongs to a fall or breaking of the self which can never be of the self's doing, never a present act and never instrumental, as is perhaps underscored with the disbelieving exclamation following "thus" at the end of the passage. [51] This is an acquiescence that forever anticipates its affirmation in a movement that has always already passed. Can we in fact speak of affirmation? The passage seems to suggest that the yes-saying is destined to repetition, perhaps in an affirmation of its return; we would thus have the incipient movement of the yes-saying from *The Madness of the Day*: *ce jour s'effaçant, je m'effacerai avec lui*. There is, in any case, a form of assumption (or a giving over to) of that to which the yes has acquiesced, and which, in fact, cannot be affirmed or negated, but which, in its releasing presence (when released from the negative) is given as what Blanchot might have called in an earlier period a nonpositive affirmation. This opening assumption, without cause, without ground, is not sovereign (in the residual sense of this term that haunted the project of Acéphale—the step toward the impossible is not a final act of power). Its saying takes form in renunciation, not simply of authority—this saying is in fact beyond any recusation— but of the negative itself, even onto the *malheur* or agitation of negation's bad infinite. Here, a transgressive passivity, carried by the lightness of dying, renounces or *lets go* of the trace of the negative in *le neutre*. How do we think this exposing release of the neutral, which is both exposure *of le neutre*—a strange, suspensive *Aufhebung* (a withdrawal of withdrawal)—and the release of a saying? This letting go is perforce of everything in an intentional relation that would reflect somehow the categories and procedures of reasoning that Blanchot reviews in his questioning expositions of the thought of *le neutre* (which never fail to problematize questioning itself), that seemingly tireless and ferociously abstracting movement of denying, removing, suspending and erasing that finally settles in the phrase examined and nearly emptied in repetition (as though it has been proffered by *le neutre* itself) in *The Step Not Beyond: ni l'un ni l'autre* (SNB 74-75/104-105).[52] There is little point in rehearsing all the negations and exclusions in this relentless effort to exhaust the hold of grammatical, logical, and epistemological categories confronted by *le neutre* and afflicted by it. The challenge Blanchot offers us is to ask what relationality lies "beyond" all the negative signaling that *le neutre* presents to a grasping reason, what strange presence of/to thought (foreign to any disclosure, but nonetheless releasing) is given in the distended space/time of fragmentation. "*Neutre*" is the passage by which "I" might affirm difference otherwise, *without* the negative, and without the need to negate the negative. But what releases in this passage?

Let us observe all of Blanchot's caution at this point. The lightness in which this step is borne must not be confused with freedom,[53] and we must therefore be wary of appealing to its connotation in a term such as "deliverance" (cf. SNB 132/180), even if the latter allows us to think a carrying and an exposure. There is a trace of releasement, to be sure, but dying is also light in the gratuitous loss to which it is committed (like that other "exteriority of being," or not being, speech: "*In pure loss, in pure loss*," SNB 132/180), in its irresponsibility, its inaccomplishment (a burden that can prove unbearable and drive the self to various acts of assumption) and in the terrifying "free fall" it represents. It is light (frivolous), despite the shocking character of what is exposed in it, its unavowable (SNB 106/146). That the transgression is "light" does not make it any less of a violation for the self that would face it or will have known it.

And yet, there is in this passage the release of another relation, no longer governed by withdrawal, for which an "I" answers (responsible in answering *for*), having acquiesced to "their" passing (their dying). Exposure to the presence of *le neutre*, as Blanchot entertains it here (an exposure *of* the neutral in its dissymmetrical field, which could never be present to consciousness), *impels* and *imparts*. Let us recall the "cold force" of its interruption (IC xxii/xxiv), the "other power" its effacing gift brings to language (IC 386/566). While its effects for the intentional will present themselves under the guise of neutralization, indifference, or paralysis, a radical exposure to the force of *le neutre* (an exposure that does not divert by or into negation) would involve something other than suspension, for there is both interruption and a delivering movement; *le neutre*, when engaged by the transgressive acquiescence envisioned here, brings an obscure impetus. All of this means that the relation drawn forth in this passage would not be one that is merely *suffered*, the burden would not be *ressenti*, however exhausting the lightness might become. Rather, the transgressive opening to *le neutre* would—perhaps—bring the passion in which it is carried to a speech that would deliver it from its mute inhibition, the indistinction of a fear submerged, a stricken anguish, or a shocked dying. The movement, again, would not be a mere neutralization of the somber affliction of these passions, not a suspension (even if the *Aufhebung* of *le neutre* might appear to be something like that *in itself*). Nor could it be called redemption. There is no simple transcendence and no definitive release *from*, but rather a releasing *in* (thought becomes more unfortunate in thus facing misfortune—but it also escapes its fatal, numbing character in speech). And by delivering these passions of finitude to a speech that responds for—can we say "hosts"?—the relation they carry (always also relation to *autrui*), this speech of immanent transcendence effectively becomes a form of *communication*. Anguish, as we have seen, is "the anguish of all"; similar phrases may be cited for fear and misfortune. Merely suffered, they engulf or submerge. *Autrui* is lost in them. But where these passions are borne in the affirmative saying of a dying-with, this relation can become what Blanchot named in *The Infinite Conversation* "a different relation." This is always a singular relation (opening in the singular instance of what is perhaps thought), but it is for the anguished, fearful, afflicted, perhaps loving other, and thus virtually for all in that it communicates what is "common" in this passion ("the affliction of *autrui* that is the affliction of all: the disaster"[54]). It is an opening for the other.

We must undoubtedly push further in an effort to think forms of experience of this singular relation that point to another thought of community, forms of experience that do not immediately communicate with the motif of writing and the practice of literature (which is not to deny links, particularly the thought of writing that Blanchot ties to repetition). The former may be as spare and elemental as encounter with the "unique whomever" (SNB 128/175). This is what Blanchot affirmed of relations with individuals in the streets and assemblies of the events of 1968—perhaps a minimal democratic condition. It is what he ascribed to gamblers (comparing them to the interlocutors in a conversation that proceeds by repetition in the brilliant concluding pages of his meditation on Bataille in *The Infinite Conversation*[55]). It may take the form of friendship, sexual relations, or a more collective form (as with the cortege of Charonne, taken up in the latter half of *The Unavowable Community*). In each of these cases a relation to the other passes by way of the absolute other, delivering to an anonymous relation (wherein no subjective unity or identity forms).

But *The Step Not Beyond*, as we have seen, seeks not only to explore the conditions of the event of communication in its long meditations on the passions of dying-with; it also seeks to think *and engage* the event. It seeks to enact a kind of open hospitality, a form of virtual accompaniment. Again, its wager is that the step of light transgression vis-à-vis *le neutre*, in a course of writing, renders death "joyous, aleatory," for the fact that the site traced in this movement opens to the "writing" of others. It should become a writing that is virtually for all:

> ♦ Effaced before being written. If the word trace can be admitted, it is as that index that would indicate as erased what was nevertheless never traced. All our writing—belonging to everyone and if ever it was a writing that was everyone's—would be like this: the concern for what was never written in the present, but in a past to come. (SNB 17/28)

The "care" in question—a concern for the nonconcerning —requires the inscription of a trace that can never be taken as signifying. What is brought to language in the passions of dying-with is not some unavowable signified. A different kind of opening/communication is required that is never subsumed in the order of meaning. Thus, while it may be said to occur in speech (and witness, again, the tremendous tributes paid by Blanchot to Bataille's speech), it is only available in its singular generality to reflective thought via the unworking of "a certain kind of writing," the long course of repetition wherein this language of another relation might begin (again) to (re)emerge.

> ♦ *And we do nothing but repeat. The nocturnal repetition, the repetition of the one who says: is it this, dying, is it this, fear?* (SNB 60/85)

We thus approach our third passion, which is distinguished among the passions treated in *The Step Not Beyond* for the fact that it appears within the guiding narrative—or, more precisely, as a component of its advance, as part of the initial tracing of its topography. The topos of fear is brought to language with the crossing of a threshold:

> ♦ *"I am afraid": so he would hear him say, hardly had he crossed the threshold; and what frightened was that calm word that seemed to use the "I" only to be afraid.* (SNB 11/21)

Let us reserve the question of the pronouns for the time being, except to remark that when fear speaks, or is brought to speech, as in this fragment, it has no subject of enunciation in any substantive sense. What speaks is a word that *uses* a "self" to carry fear into language. No self possesses this fear; it is the word that bears it (*"The calm word, carrying fear,"* SNB 13/23). It is a word "too many" that speaks in "fear." Let us therefore suppose that *"il"* would be the subject of enunciation of "I'm afraid"—an *"il"* that supports an "I."

There is a transgression in this usage that is perhaps as striking (frightening?) as what offends in the exposure to death. Of course, as one of the passions of dying-with, fear also borders on the *unavowable*. Where it is brought to language, something of the unavowable is spoken, perhaps witnessed. And, to be sure, we have seen a disappropriation of this kind in the passage from *The Infinite Conversation* that evokes the manifestation of the offense of death:

> The word too many: it would come from the Other without ever being heard by Me, nonetheless the sole auditor possible since it is destined for him (me), less to disperse or break him (me) than to respond to the breaking or

dispersal that the "I" conceals, making a self of itself in this movement of hiding that seems the beating of an empty heart. Where there is or would be a word too many, there is the offense and the revelation of death.
(IC 312–313/458)

Writing *fear*, *The Step Not Beyond* appears to open to that which the subject must turn away from, the fearful dispersion or breaking that is known in the temporality of return. One could undoubtedly say something comparable about the other passions treated thus far (including "fragility," of course).[56] But "I'm afraid" is the most ostensible instance of the provocation of the neutral to which Blanchot refers in defining the "word too many" (IC 313/458). Its provocation, as we will see, involves nothing less than an assault on the order of meaning itself. Its writing also mobilizes the exilic movement in the desert it helps create.

We still need to follow the narrative line to situate this topos within the space it helps define, but in the wake of our previous discussion, we should be prepared to engage the several pages primarily devoted to it. We recognize, first, the general schema of passion in the following passage:

♦ Fear, we call it mortal, though it hides the death toward which it draws us; but the fear exceeding the self in which it entrenches itself, absent from the one who carries it, as from the language that pronounces it, making us strangers to ourselves, is always the fear for *someone* who cannot be approached, and that death already turns aside from our help, though it is called for, awaited.
(SNB 58/83)

We find again an emphasis on the relational character of this passion, though the fear that touches me, or is communicated to me via *autrui* reaches beyond the other's dying. The scope of fear is not limited by death, and it would thus seem to extend unto the neutral of fragmentation ("*Fear, the fear that does not have death as its limit, be this the infinite death of* autrui; *nevertheless, I am afraid for the other who is afraid of dying, who will die without me, in the distancing from this self who would vainly replace their own,*" SNB 57–58/82). It reaches into what Blanchot terms with some frequency in *The Step Not Beyond* "the frighteningly ancient" and is thus relation with the "irrevocable" of an empty past (communicating, thereby, with the "madness" of a thought of the return). Unlimited in this way by the neutral, it is not fear for anything in one's life—it is radically *of* dying, and thus *of* what is experienced in that temporal slippage Blanchot thinks with the return. Unlimited, it is something like the element of the relation of dying-with: "♦ *Between them, fear, the fear shared in common, and, through fear, the abyss of fear over which they join without being able, dying, each of them, alone, of fear*" (SNB 48/70). Still, fear directs us to an other (*quelqu'un*) as disappropriated as "we ourselves" by what brings us to say "*I am afraid.*" The nonsubject of fear is comparable to the nonsubject of affliction. It is as though a singular *no one* were afraid: and afraid for a no one who is no more than "someone" who may or may not be able to say "I am afraid."

There is fear for the other in either case: fear for the one who does not know, who is not conscious of this preoccupying affect ("♦ *Someone who is afraid does not know it, does not call for help*"—"*But it is for that one that I am afraid, once and henceforth forever*" (SNB 58/83), and fear for the one who is open to the forgetting of fear ("♦ *Fear: as though he recalled this word that makes him forget everything,*" SNB 58/83). What calls for the response of fearing for is a shared fear that exceeds the self, the fear of a "community":

♦ *When he crossed through it, the city murmured in him constantly: I am afraid, be the witness of fear.* (SNB 57/82)

Thus, what was figured as the crossing of a threshold earlier is given here as passage in a city. And the crossing is itself given as relation, or gives relation, in this city of fear:

♦ *Fear, this is the gift they would give to us in the posthumous city: the possibility of being afraid for them: the fear given in the word fear; the fear not felt.* (SNB 58/83)

The question remains: What is the relation between those who inhabit this ruined space (and how does one "occupy" it)?[57] Does one inhabit it differently when one can say, with the other, "I am afraid"? Is the calm statement of fear a relation to the other that passes by what does not concern? Approaching a final calm, a voice in the penultimate fragment declares: "I no longer have . . . any thought that concerns" (SNB 137/187). Is this (also) a suspension of *fear for*?

We cannot approach this question without traversing the narrative (the city, the desert). But we must also attend to the question of language that surfaces with the enunciation of fear. For the saying (or writing) of this affect, which is identified as a core question in the sequence from *The Step Not Beyond* we have been reading ("We say pain, we say affliction. But fear?" SNB 58/83), obliges us to confront the force of this word "too many" which falls from language in the manner of "God," "madness," or even "*il.*" Like these others, "fear" communicates a "devastating" power of nondesignation that refers language back to itself, forcing a fragmenting rearticulation that cannot be suspended or salvaged in meaning (though this movement will always recur, via metaphor, for example, or in a concept such as "the death of God"). The presence of such a word fissures language, leaves it irremediably stricken (SNB 48/70). Here is the force of this dying that afflicts language in "fear":

> ♦ This fear of language, it was incumbent on him not to see in it anything but the possibility, always open, that some word [*un mot quelconque*] belonging to the series of words that are such only through their belonging to language, might turn back against this language to detach itself from it and lift itself above it in mastering it, perhaps shattering it, at least pretending to assign it a limit. Fear does not signify that language would be afraid, be this metaphorically, but fear is a piece of language, something language would have lost and that would render it entirely dependent on this dead part: entirely, that is to say, precisely by reconstituting itself without unity, piece by piece, as something other than an ensemble of significations. Certainly, metaphor will finally intervene to hold in suspense, by rendering inoffensive, the possibility of language's being other than a process of meaning. Through metaphor, the fear of language becomes the fear of speaking, or the fear which, being the essence of any speech, would render frightening any use of speech, as it would any silence. The fear of language: the fear that strikes language when it loses a word that is then *a surplus word, a word too many*: fear, God, madness. Or "*il,*" displaced from its rank and role of subject. (SNB 59/84–85)

Fear disintegrates, interrupts that referential expansion and gathering of language whereby it seeks an ever more inclusive whole of meaning. Here, a fragment would fall from its living unity, irremediably altering it. The movement is interpreted initially (but to whom does this interpretation fall exactly; and why does this interpretation appeal to a notion of sovereignty and/or transcendence—is a link made here to the sovereign pretention of "*malheur?*) as a turning upon and against language. As the passage moves into its second sentence, this movement is described as disruptive of any signification and presumably of any constitution of a "master signifier." Fear is identified here as a "dead" part of language whose loss fractures language, obliging language, by this death (is this the dying that speaks in language?) to reconstitute itself, piece by piece. Fear would fragment, and to bring it to language (to speech: "I am afraid") would be, presumably, to exacerbate this process or to mobilize it as the announcement of another language that would not thereby begin but would rebegin.[58] An *"il"* would be part of this movement, and perhaps a *"je,"* in relation with this *"il,"* would be the one to whom it falls to oversee this recurring possibility. But the *"il"* of this relation would displace this "I" from "its rank and role of subject." Metaphor, masking the lack of the proper, would vainly though inevitably carry "fear" back into language as properly *of* language, or restore to language its enunciating subject, be this as a frightened subject (the recurrence of the word "possibility" seems almost to suggest that metaphor would stand over against the *"il"* of fragmentation). In either case, this suspensive carrying over, here neutralizing or suspending the interruption of the neutral, would restore to language its integrity, offering it, perhaps, a surplus of fearful authority. But the fear of language cannot, finally, be so restored to meaning; the movement of metaphor only suspends and masks the event of interruption. "Fear," in this last phrase, is not a metaphor that restores a subject to language, any more than the transporting in "I am afraid" is metaphoric. The "phoronomy" of this fragmentary speaking (the speaking of the *pas* that carries to and for the other across the threshold or in traversing the city) does not surrender to the law of meaning.[59] Thus, with respect to "I am afraid," we can say little more than that it is of a *stricken* language, that its speaking is redoubtable for being devastatingly redundant in its communication of something which we can only metaphorically call "dead." For such a stricken language, we might again recall the ambiguity of the phrase Blanchot took from Hegel in "Literature and the Right to Death" ("the life that bears death and maintains itself in it").[60] But the metaphor of death seems to reach its limits here. Another relation inheres if we can say that fear is carried in language, or that there is some necessity of repeating the locution "I am afraid" for the fact that all language should be stricken with fear (a *panic* fear) by reason of this nonsignifying element that forces its fragmentation. What, then, is said in this *parole de fragment, "j'ai peur,"* this redundant word of a ruined city?

> ♦ *"It's true, I am afraid".—"You say it so calmly."—"Saying it, however, does not alleviate the fear: on the contrary, it is the word that henceforth frightens me; having said it does not allow me to say anything else."—"But 'I am afraid,' I as well: from the basis of this word that is so calm: like no one, as though no one were afraid."—"It is all language, from now on, that is afraid."* (SNB 59/84)

If the one *counters* the other in this repetitive exchange ("But 'I am afraid,' I as well"), might we suppose that the repeating rejoinder says more—or less—in its citation than what is said by the other who can only say "fear"? Is the second cautioning the other not to fall into the metaphor of fear, and, if so, what passage is named in the citation of a "neutral" fear? Are these words said lightly? Following this line of enquiry, we may perhaps suppose that the one who asserts the anonymity of "I am afraid" is gently *substituting* for the other, drawing them from their isolation, or drawing to another relation. We can assume, of course, that this light speaking of fear for the other, cognizant of a language stricken with fear, does not escape fear or overcome it—any more than the speech of the thought of affliction represents an escape from affliction. On the contrary, the saying of fear would expose further to fear by relaying and repeating the fragmentation of language. So while we may still recognize here the "deliverance" of an immanent transcendence (as we saw with affliction, where an afflicted thought answers for, carries for), we may perhaps also recognize in this speaking the relaying of *another language*, in which "fear" says relation to the dispersion of presence, to the neutral. Again, this would be the writing of a fragmentary speech, a *plural speech* like the one somewhat enigmatically evoked at the end of Blanchot's reflections on Bataille in *The Infinite Conversation*, where dialogue is described as a form of repetition where the "unlimited" is at play: "a relation that opens onto fear and yet to which speech, through its play, constantly engages us to respond: *"fear ... yes the fear, which only the unlimited in thought can reach"* (IC 215/319).[61] Here, of course, it is this very fear itself that is said and affirmed. But again, this is not the fear of a subject. It is a fear traversing language itself that is affirmed in a thought that exceeds any subjectivity.

How do we hold this passage from capture by metaphor, even while holding to the terrifying in this passage? Surely, we fail to receive this word too many, we fail the task of *fearing for* (a task of hospitality) if we render the fear of the neutral of dying itself neutral. The risk is there if repetition is taken as a kind of absolving reiteration (giving "fear" up to its inherent repeatability—stripping it of its subject and assigning it "merely" to language—would represent an acceleration of the "destitution" of fear). Such a "citational" emptying of "fear" in its inherent repeatability is surely there as a possibility. Yet there is, haunting even this repeatability, another mute (matted) saying (SNB 18/30) by which the other, of fear for example, would be said. The exigency speaking in such a repetition is perhaps what gives us to think what it would be to witness fear.

The passage with the young girl that follows immediately the two pages on which we have concentrated preserves fear from any "neutralization." It preserves its alterity, linking it intimately to madness. We cannot conclude from that passage whether fear is merely fear of madness (we know that harbor is sought for a thought in danger) or whether the madness in question might belong in some way to fear itself. Madness may be that to which fear exposes; unless the forgetting that fear brings with it is the balm (or the river). Blanchot gives us precious little to proceed with here beyond the apparent articulation of the exigency of undertaking the transgression of that limit (in and of language) that can never be defined before that passage and never by the language whose limit is so breached. The fear we are given to think here is the fear of *le pas au-delà*, *for* the other who is exposed to a dying. We will have known that in which we write and that for which we witness (fear), we will have written through its forgetting. This, too, would be part of writing one's death and receiving the other. It would be something like the condition of affirming effacement. Surely, it would be wrong to say that we will not know fear without this passage in writing. But it is difficult to see how we would otherwise escape the metaphor of fear, and no less difficult to see how this witnessing could take a general import.

This last point is brought home in Blanchot's references to the "frighteningly ancient," which cluster around the introduction of the motif of fear and relate to the experience (and knowledge) of the law of return. Fear, as we will see, is perhaps first to be thought from the Eternal Return. Fear is *of* the return.

A brief passage in a sequence of reflections linked to the name Nietzsche (the name will serve to designate a law that brings anonymity; SNB 22/34) provides this first step and immediately tells us that "the frighteningly ancient" is given in a time of repetition. Like "I am afraid," it is given in quotation marks that Blanchot will identify as marks of the irrevocable:

♦ If, in the "frighteningly ancient," nothing was ever present, and if, having barely occurred, the event should fall into it by the fragile, absolute fall, as the mark of irrevocability announces to us, this is because (whence our cold presentiment), the event that we believed we had lived, it too, was never with us or with anything at all in a relation of presence. (SNB 15/25)

The passage challenges our relation to temporal order in a radical manner. If the past is "frighteningly ancient" for the fact that it contains no past present, and if the past gives itself as irrevocable in an instantaneous fall of the event, *this is because*—and the conclusion is given in a cold presentment, in the shivering opening to what will be known in a future—what we had believed (for an indefinite time) we had lived (punctually) will in fact never have been in a relation of presence with us. No more than we were present to ourselves or to the other of this event. We will face in the future (as we know "now" by a presentiment that opens in the exposure) a mortifying evacuation of the present, rendering every event we thought we will have lived as always already of a past that never happened in any present. Fear, in short, takes its "origin" in exposure to nonpresence. From this menacing exposure that presents itself in a futural form, we know a *rewriting* of the (past) present; we open to what the mark of irrevocability announces: the effacing return of the "the frighteningly ancient."

A lengthier passage on the preceding page offers a "reflection" on this rewriting of the present. It is preceded with an assertion of knowledge that seems strangely premature, unless what is referred to is the knowledge that comes in a form of presentiment: what will be revealed as already having been known, by fear perhaps, in accordance with the law. (But would the presentiment itself not offer itself as always already known as it comes to be written?)

> ♦ *He knew it (in accordance, perhaps, with the law)*: the past is empty, and only the multiple play of mirroring, the illusion that there would be a present destined to pass and to hold itself in the past, would lead one to believe that the past was filled with events, a belief that would make it appear less unfriendly, less frightening; a past thus inhabited, be it by phantoms, would grant the right to live innocently (in the narrative mode, which, once, twice, as many times as a time can repeat itself, makes its evocation available) the very thing which nevertheless gives itself as forever revoked and, at the same time, irrevocable. About this, he reflected (but it's true, how to reflect on it?—reflecting it, restoring it to a certain flexibility?). Irrevocability would be the trait by which the void of the past marks, by giving them as impossible to relive and as thus already having been lived in an unsituatable present, the semblances of events that are there only to cover over the void, to give it enchantment while hiding it, while still announcing it through the mark of irreversibility. The irrevocable is thus by no means, or not only, the fact that what has taken place has taken

place forever: it is perhaps the means—strange, I admit—for the past to warn us (in sparing us) that it is empty and that the falling due—the infinite, fragile fall—that it designates, this infinitely deep pit into which events would fall, one by one, if there were any, signifies only the void of the pit, the depth of what is without bottom. It is irrevocable, indelible, yes: ineffaceable, but because nothing is inscribed there.

Irrevocability would be the sliding which, through vertigo, in an instant, at the very farthest from the present, in the absolute of the non-present, makes what "just came about" fall.

What has hardly just come about would slip and fall immediately (nothing more rapid) through irrevocability, into the "frighteningly ancient," there where nothing was ever present. Irrevocability would be, in this view, the sliding or the fragile fall that abolishes time in time, effaces the difference between the near and the far, the indices of reference, the measures called temporal (everything that makes contemporary) and buries everything in non-time, from which nothing could come back, less by lack of a return than because nothing falls there, except the illusion of falling there.
(SNB 13-14/23-24)

The knowledge of the simulacrum is devastating for the comfort that would be given by narrative—that innocent belief that makes the past *less frightening*. But it is a knowledge that the past's vacancy is remarked for us by the irrevocable character of these semblant events (that would have ceased in their power to *be* event). By this trait, as a reflective "I" notes (coming from nowhere in this passage, if not from the reflection of an "*il*"), the fall is made gentler for us—we are "spared." The past thus gives itself as void, as a bottomless depth in a fall that is irrevocable—yes!—but, as such, indelible and *for us* as trace of the void. The so-designated *échéance* (from *échoir* and with the hint of a fatality) would trace, in its irrevocability, the "absolute of the nonpresent." Is this a trace of the neutral? Blanchot calls it here the inscription of nothing, in an instant. "What has just come about" is thus perpetually refused (*re-tiré*—its trait is that *it cannot be recalled*), in an instant. The irrevocable, again, is in quotation marks, as if to remark the trace it takes of the neutral—as if to remark its *writing*.

How do we think the "vertigo," the radical turning about of this instant? It is as though the coming (of what has come from a future: *advenir*) is fatally diverted from the present, was forever suspended from the present of its arrival and yet remains, in the instant of its fall, for never being able to come back (to a present). Instantaneously, the barely new is frighteningly ancient. "*Ce qui vient à peine d'avoir lieu*"—Blanchot forces us to read this sudden passage in a suspended syntax wherein the coming is "*à peine d'avoir lieu*," cannot quite take a place. It remains at the farthest from the nonplace of the present, there, in a disrupted time, with the mark of the neutral.

In *The Writing of the Disaster*, Blanchot will call the *saying* of this disruption (by the trace of the irrevocable) the avowal of a *gift*: "effacement or destruction or gift that has always already avowed itself in the precession of a Saying outside any said, a speech of writing whereby the effacement, far from effacing itself in its turn perpetuates itself even onto the interruption that constitutes its mark."[62] So, while nothing of the event can be called back, or even return, as Blanchot says at the end of the passage, "the speech of writing" is already in itself return. I am thus called to assume the irrevocable in this forever interrupted present of the instant of return. This is the exigency of the return—the exigency of that law below, *là-bas* (SNB 14/25).

Are we following, now, a movement wherein the temporality of the nonevent takes a sign of exception—so that the forever "revoked" occurrence, forever destined to effacement, remains excepted from every past, present, or future (as articulated in a temporality grounded by the presence of a present) and, as such, also *unique* and always repeatable in its uniqueness? Let us note, without developing this point at length as yet, that throughout the passage on Eternal Return, Blanchot calls our attention to the play of "*sauf*" ("except," "save," or as an adjective, "safe"). Shortly after the passage we have been reading, Blanchot underscores that the exigency of return (*exigere*: to push out) would be the time of writing:

♦ The exigency of the return would therefore be the exigency of a time without present, time that would also be that of writing, future time, past time, which the radical disjunction (in the absence of any present) of the one and the other, be they the same, prevents us from identifying other than as the difference borne by repetition.

Between past, future, the greatest difference is given in that the one would repeat the other without the common measure of a present: as though between past and future there reigned the absence of present under the simplified form of forgetting.

What would return? Everything, *save* the present, the possibility of a presence. (SNB 16/27)

Turning this somewhat, we might ask: does the time of writing *except* in turn, in return, the present (of writing)—a present, without present, in which "I am afraid," the assumption of a "frighteningly ancient," would coexist with a "come"—presuming one should accede to such an affirmation? What would become of fear in this ec-static, messianic opening? The caution required by any reference to "salvation" (under the exigency of the law of return) obliges us to defer conclusion, but might we not consider naming the time of the affirmed *viens*, the time of the double affirmation, a time of exception?

Perhaps, we might respond, but only if we take the full immeasure of what it means to think/affirm the writing of the return. We must think *from* the writing of the return: the sign of exception that takes in the event with its fall from any present is "indelibly" a speech of writing.

> ♦ *In a certain way*, as soon as one approached the law of the return—the Eternal Return of the Same—through the movement that comes from it (this would be the time of writing if one did not have to say, also and first of all, that writing holds in it the demand of the return), this law—outside the law—would lead us to take on (to undergo by way of the most passive passivity, the step/not beyond) the temporality of time in such a way that this temporality, suspending, or making disappear, every present and all presence, would make disappear, or would suspend, the seat or the site of authority [*instance*] from which it is pronounced. (SNB 15/26)

It goes without saying that this thought is utterly ruinous for any effort to think the temporality of time as the horizon of Being. But Heidegger is not Blanchot's concern here. His focus is on the destruction wrought to the phrase "everything returns" which is stripped of the present in which it might be affirmed. Blanchot is waging Nietzsche against Hegel, the impossible affirmation of the return against the accomplishment of the logos that would say the "all" of the returning. On the one hand, Blanchot argues, as he did following Bataille and Nietzsche in *The Infinite Conversation*, the logos must be accomplished (or this accomplishment must be announced) for the possible advent of another modality of advent and affirmation. On the other, the affirmation of return forever ruins the present of "*tout revient*" and the present of its enunciation. The logos, so losing the presence of the present, would indeed be struck with fear (or the possibility of madness). Once again, only a writing could venture this step:

There, henceforth, for Nietzsche, is the exigency to be lived and thought. And writing alone can respond to such an exigency, on the condition that discourse, having accomplished itself as logos, withdraw from it every seat from which it might declare itself or sustain itself, and expose him to the menace, the vain prestige of what no one would henceforth dare to name: mad writing. (SNB 22/35)

"*Tout revient*"—its very affirmation strips the words of meaning, releasing "an extravagance of forms or relations that exclude one another" (SNB 22–23/35). Where would this leave us?

The question can provoke vertigo, but, in fact, writing "*everything returns*" from the ground of a fragmented logos (or simply affirming the return) is like writing "I am afraid" in the space of a stricken language: one says almost nothing (SNB 23/26). The first steps (the last steps) have barely been made at that limit that the thought of return transgresses: the limit of meaning from which terms like "mad," "God," "fear," or "*il*" return as words *too many* and as the first tokens of another language. The task has barely opened in its exigency: to write *without* the grounding present, to affirm relation to the future *save* for the present that holds all promise of "peace" hostage to its self-reference.

Toward Effacement

A bit more than halfway through *The Step Not Beyond*, we pass a point marked in the opening conversation of *The Infinite Conversation*. The other interlocutor has disappeared, and the discursive order to which the conversation belonged has been decisively disrupted, producing a change in the interlocutors' manner of speaking (the almost negligible matter of a lack of presence) and an overturning that leaves all intact. There is, however, a new element, or rather a new set of relations. For, "*they*" have now come:

> ♦ *Since their coming, nevertheless, the essential had been the astonishing character of everything, for if he had thought, generously and lucidly, that he was prepared to register an upheaval that would have found him ready to let himself be shaken from top to bottom, he perceived that for want of presence and with the exception of a change in the manner in which they would henceforth have to become accustomed to speak to one another, he could not decide what would make him fit to let himself be astonished in the*

> midst of all the unmodified things. It is true that this friend had disappeared. Since when, he could not say; they had been accustomed for such a long time to speak to one another from afar, from near, through the rumors of the city or else through the repetition of an ancient language, always ready to give them a place in its game. The fact that they saw one another, he realized, was only a derivative mode of their right to speak to one another, a right that was left to him to keep from letting be proscribed. They spoke, they saw one another; there was in this a sort of proper use of their constant cordiality, itself an expression, but to a much higher degree, of the relations each could not help having with all. Still, did he not have to recognize the exceptional character of relations that were not only amical, nor simply trusting, but on the contrary difficult, each time forbidden and almost private, even if it was convenient for him to present them as personal conversations, known and recognized in advance as such among so many others? (SNB 78/108–109)

What has happened *this* time?

Others have in fact been present to the conversation, this time, from the very beginning. The conversation turns upon them, and begins, as we have seen, with reference to them. A knowledge of their existence, we are told, given with knowledge itself (knowledge that is therefore "after knowledge," when knowledge has completed its project) gives the one we might name the protagonist the desire to seek them out, to encounter them, and the cautious awareness that they are several—an awareness that he protects from being too determinate with the simple designation "*des gens.*" This knowledge without a *determining* will is such that the protagonist recognizes that he may even know (*connaître*) those whom he seeks, but that such familiarity would not form the basis of the desired encounter, which will come not by necessity, nor, perhaps, by chance, but without design: "You will happen upon them" ("*Vous tomberez sur eux,*" SNB 3/10).

Who are they? Despite the narrative's own coyness, there is no reason to delay reviewing the scant hints offered to us by the conversation's interlocutors, who are devoted to *guarding* these others from the determination of the name or the attribute, preserving them from any descriptor. We know from the first exchange that the others are in some respects like the protagonist. They frequent no one (they have no habitual, ordinary relations), and are perhaps, therefore, pursuing relations—perhaps amongst themselves—like those he pursues with the other ("no one," SNB 3/10). We are told in a subsequent exchange (where their "topic" appears as one favored by the interlocutors as an eternal diversion, an innocent game), that the narrating interlocutor moves amongst them without being capable of encounter, or precision:

> ♦ *It was like an eternal subject of pleasantry, an innocent game: "You met them in the street?"—"Not exactly in the street: near the river, looking at the books, then going off or losing themselves in the crowd."—"It couldn't be otherwise; and rather young, no?"—"He had to stop at this word that involved, demanded, or promised too much; he did not concede it willingly until he let himself go ahead and answer: 'Yes, young, there is no other word; and yet, young without anything that made their age a moment of themselves or of youth a trait characterizing age. Young, but as in another time, thus not so young, as though youth rendered them very ancient or too new to be able to appear simply young.'"—"Since you observed them: did you have the time? was this possible? is this possible?"—"It wasn't, in fact, but nor was it to encounter them."*
>
> *It was true that, when he leaves him, following street after street, brilliant, animated streets, not servile, he sees no one, but this is only a consequence of what he calls his immortality and which he could more generously call the kindness of all, who let him pass in granting to him with their face—so beautiful are the faces, so beautiful they would be if he saw them—a light, the burst of a happiness, of a distress.* (SNB 8–9/17–18)

Young, of another time, discovered looking at books *near the river*. These passing others ("infinitely walking," SNB 39/57) appear to have a link to literature, if only as casual readers. And though the image is as dreamlike as it is typed (and thus as vague as the epithet "young"), it is surely not a big step to seek a link to a subsequent passage referring to the dispersed, plural character of those who bear the exigency of writing (at least as concerns the narrator's relations to others in the city):

> ♦ *As regards the exigency of writing, in the multiplicity in which it disseminates itself, there is nothing amicable or sacred; the events are useless, the days unsanctified, men, neither divine nor human. Those who carry this demand are transported by it and disappear in it: even if their name then serves to name it, they are neither important nor great. In their disparate plurality, and though belonging to the multiple, having only a multiple reality, they remain strangers, separate from one another, crossing without encountering one another; that is their solitude, a plurality that constitutes them neither on the basis of their own singularity nor in view of a superior unity.* (SNB 34/50–51)

But young? In what time, other than the time of writing—the time of return— could these anonymous writers so appear, taking (without taking—thus evading) the epithets meant to preserve their exposed innocence and their plurality?

> ♦ "We'll love them."—"We love them already."—"They don't know it."—"That's our good fortune."—"They know nothing of what we expect from them."—" They live in ignorance; this is what makes them so beautiful, so alive."—"They are frightening."— "We are frightening." They were young, beautiful, living; he accepted all these words, snares so innocent that even phantoms could not have let themselves be caught by them, knowing as well that quite different words could have been pronounced without attracting them the more or reaching them in that which preserved them. The only danger, a danger of innocence, came from this right to be several, right which, diverting them from being one or the other, risked delivering them gently to the call that they could only hear as several: together? "We will never see anything so beautiful."—"Is that the fitting term?"—"They will be too beautiful for one to perceive it."—"I don't believe they would like our arranging things in their place."—"This place that they don't occupy, happily." Happiness was there, in effect: a happiness that protected them from everything. "They will not know, they will be the most beautiful only together." (SNB 17–18/28–29)

How does "youth," here, communicate with what *The Writing of the Disaster* will give us to think under the name of infancy (a theme that appears in *The Step Not Beyond* with references to the cries of children and to their playspace)? Is this youth shared by those "young names" that will come to language in the interrupted conversation with the one who disappears?

These questions will have to be held in abeyance as we proceed. But in the spirit of frankness with which we have undertaken this section, let us hold open the possibility that the "others" in question at the start of the conversation are not immediately identifiable with those young names who join the interlocutors at the threshold of their conversation (though the invitation to them presupposes the arrival of the young names). Nor can we assume that they are identifiable with the one or ones to whom the invitation is proffered at the "apocalyptic" end of this long trajectory of writing. If *"viens"* is said with the effacement of the day to another advent, and from an opening onto an immemorial time (if it is said in response to the plural of that word to many, *"il"*), then it would be proffered to the opening of the relation that we might call "community" itself. Perhaps *"viens"* may be construed to be to the names themselves, if they mark the temporal opening of this advent—though the names, as we will see, are said in gratitude, whereas *"viens"* marks an assumption of what is thus gratefully received. But the "community" to be called would indeed hold those anonymous others for which this text has sought to trace a hospitable site. Anonymous, of an unlimited number, in a plural, neutral relation ("one only among others," SNB 128/175), these others would join, virtually, all those who carry fear, all those potentially not received in the manner of the scene with the young girl. The events of 1968 would have brought to Blanchot another glimpse of what he called for in his apocalyptic address: "*Viens, viens.*" The opening to which it calls is effectively that of the possibility of the meeting exemplified by the encounter with Foucault, where *l'un ou l'autre* were uniquely substitutable in a relation that exceeded any sociopolitical determinations while indicating the urgency of their just articulation.[63]

In asking "who" of those others, and even without seeking to establish identity, we precipitate a conclusion, a fragile fall that the text's narrative line (via the conversation) is devoted to preparing. Indeed, the relation between what is happening in the conversation and the relation sought with them is not sufficiently conceived if we understand the latter as simply a topic or design for the interlocutors' exchange. The relation to *them* is inextricable from the relation to the other interlocutor, as Blanchot is perhaps already indicating when he tells us near the outset, in his remarks on the *je/il* relation that "*il*" already holds in it a plurality (SNB 3/10). Only four pages later, the intrication of the narrated conversation and the desired relation to them is discreetly but insistently drawn across a series of fragments that we should now follow in their detail.

The first posits the relation to the other interlocutor in the terms of the fictively cast *je/il* relation. The model for the other of this conversation may well have been quite real (we will think immediately of Bataille, of course, but there may well have been more than one; in any case, an autobiographical strain probably continues in this text). But the friendship explored here is marked by an alterity that opens it to an almost infinite distension. Thus, the other interlocutor holds the place of an *other* who becomes *figure* in a space that will expand and then twist in an unrepresentable topology. Let us recall the "*il*" addressed by counterword in "The Infinite Conversation." The morphing figure of *The Step Not Beyond* seems to appear *there*, where the other interlocutor, "*vous*," enters into relation to an "*il*" (or becomes indistinguishable from "*il*") in a movement that will eventually draw "*je*" with it, even if the narrating instance holds its own position in order to support this other.

♦ He desired to say it to him: *this way of thinking about it in saying it—to whom?, or in saying he would say it—to whom?, even though he received this way of thinking or thought he received it from that point where it seemed to him he could fictively situate it, helped still to hold him back. For he had to be there, in this place where he was given a dwelling, like an assigned residence, so that the other should be over there, immobile, immovable, yet always hard to recognize, as though the right to identity had been refused to him at the same time it was granted to him.*

He desired to say it to him: *but how desire to speak, without the desire, and always in advance, destroying speech, even the most calm desire for the most calm speech. And still, he desired to say it, he would say it.* (SNB 9/18–19)

He *had* to be there. This is the necessity evoked in the "investiture" cited from *The Infinite Conversation* earlier—the fictive condition for the constitution of the site (the room, the dwelling) in which the *je/il* relation can unfold in its plurality and in which relation to an increasingly immobile other will unfold as a shared dying, or "reciprocal suicide," where "one would prolong his life so that the other could die there more softly" (SNB 52/75):

♦ *He realized that he had to bear the truth of a self (without changing it into anything other than the canonical abbreviation of a rule of identity) if he wanted to help him maintain himself in that transparency still never traversed and that allowed him to receive no other designation than the one that had been chosen as though in a game.* (SNB 19/31)

What is he driven to say to the other? As the conversation takes form, we will see a range of possible phrases emerge, though at this point in the conversation it becomes difficult to avoid the supposition that it has something to do with affirming the other's disappearance (which, as we have seen, is related to "their" coming). But here, near the outset, the words—speaking, desiring—are left only to be repeated as bearing the condition of encounter with the multiple others.

♦ *By what right, by what usurped power, had he planned [projeté] this encounter, and, in planning it, made it inevitable, or, on the contrary, impossible?* "It was only a thought."—"*Of course.*"—"But also a desire; something one could only think in desiring it."—"Without being able to think it, without being sure one desired it."—"Short of speaking of it, with the suspicion that speaking of it would be to speak of it prematurely, through an unfortunate indiscretion."—"Fortunate also; it was necessary."—"Was it necessary?"—"We'll know later."—"We will know too late."

> To speak, to desire, to encounter: he realized that, playing with these three words (and thereby introducing the missing fourth, the game of the lack), he could not produce one before, or rather than, the other two, unless playing it first did not in any way give it a primary role, not even that of a card sacrificed with a view to a strategy. . . . This remains true, nevertheless: he had to encounter them (in one way or another, it hardly matters) for speaking about them to be possible; he had to encounter them in order to desire to encounter them (or sense that he could have desired this), and it was necessary, in order for him to encounter them (even if he never encountered them) that desire prepare him for it and speech dispose him to it, by the space that each of these hold and without whose void the encounter would fill itself, accomplish itself, in the manner of an historical event. (SNB 9–10/19–20)

Conversation and narrative mix, as we see, with theoretical speculation as the passage moves from italics to roman type. After the preceding description of the fictive constitution of the relation to the other, we might expect a comparable "projection." But "projection," here, comes to take a fairly precise hermeneutic meaning once the speculative play with the destructive card game has concluded. The description of a hermeneutic circle has only one complicating condition: "that desire prepare him for it and speech dispose him to it, by the space that each of these hold. . . ." The theoretical statement thus returns, by echo, to the previous passage on the constitution of the fictive space in which "he would tell it to him" (following the schema of *je/il*). Is the last line not evoking the need for the space of the conversation, the space opened by the speech of writing?

Then the following intricating passages:

> ♦ *In the cold happiness of his memory, as though the memory were of all, and the forgetting of no one.* (SNB 10/20)

> ♦ *Had he then forgotten it, the encounter always to come that nevertheless had always already taken place, in an eternal past, eternally without present? How could he have come to the instant of a presence if time's—their time's—detour was to deprive them of any relation to a present? A strict law, the highest of laws, and such that, being itself submitted to it, it could not find the moment in which to apply itself, and in applying itself, affirm itself. With one exception? Was not this exception, precisely and insidiously offered, a temptation destined to tempt the law, as the thought that he would come, be it with these three words, to the end of this very thought?* (SNB 10–11/20)

The word "encounter" (*rencontre*, which could also be rendered as "meeting") is usually reserved, throughout these pages, for the relation to "them." Thus, the first line of the second passage seems to draw us back to the theoretical statement that preceded it (the statement articulating encounter, desire, and speech). Memory and forgetting, however, name the "conditions" by which the two interlocutors remain *there* for one another, and it is only from the alternating beat of these conditions, as we will see, that relation to the young names and "them" becomes possible. The second sentence of this passage may well evoke time itself, or the time of the interlocutors (a subsequent statement offers a strong echo in support of this), but the pronoun "*il*" could refer to either of the interlocutors, or, just as probably, to the *past* that is eternally without present. In the latter case, we would understand this sentence as saying that the event by which encounter with the others would come to "the instant of a presence" would require the impossible conjunction of this eternal past with a present forever denied to the interlocutors. Such a conjunction would seemingly be prohibited by the law of the return, which is strictly denied any such instant for its own enunciation (the dilemma we encountered with the phrase "*tout revient*"). But an exception is entertained as a tempting, transgressive promise to the law itself in the form of a thought that would *think through* the four terms that have governed the sequence of fragments we have been reading (desire, speech, encounter, and thought itself, which strikingly disappeared in the articulation of the hermeneutic circle). Such an occurrence, it is suggested, would bring the affirmation of the return to language, conjugating, in their difference, past and future. Precisely such a conjugation appears to be named in the final sequence of the text.

It is still too early to address what is happening in that last, plural union. The exercise of reading the last sequence of dense fragments from the opening section of the volume, however, gives us at least a glimpse of the intricate course of the narrative line. The conversation, we discover, is not just about relation to the others; it is also *for* relation to them. And while the relation between the two interlocutors holds its own exigencies, the meeting that unfolds there only becomes the (possible) accompaniment evoked at the end by virtue of the coming for which this conversation prepares. The protagonist goes to the conversation to find the distance required for the plural relation with those others who, like him, are ceaselessly in transit, essentially nomad. The one needs the relation of friendship with the other to enter relation with the others, though this need must perhaps be thought as originating in the relation of friendship itself. Friendship entails aid to the other, but it is also opening to an outside, which is here the plural community of the outside. Reciprocally, it is also in and through community that friendship accomplishes the effacement that is "proper" to it and to which it gives itself over as to a kind of law: "*Tout doit s'effacer.*"[64]

Or so a simple formulation of the narrative might go. Let us return to the point from which we started, though let us preface this reentry into the narrative with Blanchot's carefully worded warning about the nature of the space we seek to enter, which he designates in a fragment on fragmentation with the terms "complementary," "secondary," or "supplementary" with respect to the "primary" it would shatter.

> But if to write is to dis-pose marks of singularity (fragments) from which routes can indicate themselves without reuniting or joining the marks together, but as their separating—a separating of space of which we know only the gap: the gap, without knowing from what it separates—there is always a risk that reading, instead of animating the multiplicity of transversal routes, reconstitutes a new totality from them, or worse, seeks in the world of presence and of sense to what reality or thing to be completed correspond the voids of this space that offers itself as complementary, but complementary of nothing. (SNB 51/74)

In attending to the intricacies of this series of fragments, we have timidly pursued an aspect of what Blanchot calls for here. The challenge augments as the space of the interlocution unfolds or distends in relation to the figure of the other in the room (a relation that is doubly, but dissymmetrically, articulated, we might presume, since the relations between interlocutors must be thought from both sides: there are *two* others in the room).

> ♦ *Both of them knowing that the other was going to die, everything was enlarged through a generosity of space. Nocturnal provocation, when waiting up is no longer preoccupied with time.* (SNB 49/71)

But let us take this cue to enter the narration, for a "nocturnal provocation" will come in the narrative we are reading with memory. After a description of the conversation as "exceptional"—meaning, in this case, not only "reserved," in the sense of "personal" (between friends, confiding), but also private to a degree that is *forbidden*, perhaps not only by philosophy, but by the law—the narrator refers to what has driven him to these exchanges.

> *But what was his part, what fell to him outside his role, which was, moreover, interchangeable, in exchanges that were never imposed upon him except through the haunting of memories over which he had so little control that he came to believe they did not belong to him, a memory, rather, of nobody? He remembered, no doubt, memory so ancient of a Thing that could not be called present, nor to come, only less ancient than the memory by which he felt struck—struck gently, almost affectionately, in the way that at night, in the night, timid words traverse sleep: sudden, nevertheless.*
> (SNB 78–79/110)

The phrasing of this passage is so delicate and obscure that it will allow little more than questions. Is this "Thing," which will shortly be said to remember them ("he affirmed anew his accord: they are coming, not without adding: the Thing remembers us," SNB 81/113), converging here with knowledge ("*je sais que j'aurai su*—the motif is recalled on the preceding page; SNB 80/112)? And would this be as subject or as object? The memory, and memories, are (or will be) *his*, undoubtedly, but "he" is given here as "il" ("*Il se souvenait, sans doute*") and the memory/memories bear a neutral trait,[65] as does even that memory that comes to strike him. Thus, it is fundamentally unclear whose memory (and of what thought, of what Thing) brings what we will shortly see described as returning words, "blind words" of fearful reach and consequence.[66] The provocation is brought, in any case, by *something like* the sudden words that traverse sleep, and their manner of striking him ("gently," "affectionately," perhaps "intimately," to recall Blanchot's words on "the intimacy of thought" [IC 213/316]) is, in turn, *somehow comparable* to a somnolent experience he has when entering the room, which is perceived as suddenly immense, its void ("*l'infime interstice*") accentuated. The insistence on figuration indicates that we are clearly in the space of the imaginary. The "generosity" of this space, we read, could accommodate the entire city:

> *And it was of sleeping that he had to think when, paying him the customary visit, he could not but notice the suddenly immense room, surrounded by books as if to accentuate the emptiness of the space, where it seemed that the whole city, had it wished to, could have spread itself out, with the great central river and the immobile residents of its banks, a disturbance of perspective that was corrected by the slightness of the person seated very far away in a corner on a chair, quite old, in the manner of a reminiscence rather than a memory, diminished, as might be someone who had waited too long, without one knowing to what expectation he hoped still to respond.*
> (SNB 79/110)

The entire city, with its river and those who dwell on its banks, immobile. Space, as we will come to discover, has now begun to fold into space inasmuch as the course of the conversation will shortly give us the two interlocutors themselves as immobile occupants of the riverside. But let us hold off commenting the intriguing theme of Blanchot's river and note simply the return of the indistinct figure of the other—fictively projected in the scene we read earlier, and progressively disappearing, *together with the narrator*. We encounter this figural diminishment already some pages before the passage we have been reading:

> ♦ *It is like a figure he doesn't see, that is missing because it is there, having all the traits of a figure that would not figure itself, and with which the incessant lack of relation, without presence, without absence, is the sign of a common solitude. He names it, although he knows that it has no name, even in his language, this beating of a hesitant heart. Neither of them lives, life passes between them, leaving them on the edge of space.*
>
> *Out of words, in the midst of words.* (SNB 63/90)

It is as though "progress" in the conversation implies, at least at this stage, an ever more radical figural capture or torsion that effaces the traits of the other (introducing, accordingly, the recurring question of recognition) and displacing both of the figures in both space and time—displacing them so radically, in fact, that both space and time suffer a radical indefinition. In the "nocturnal provocation" by which the "edges" of space begin to be drawn (with "life" flowing between), the other will be given as reduced ("*exigue*"), as something less than a memory in the time of return. The narrative passage that follows the one we are reading evokes the shared task of holding the other in memory, and then gives the figural play almost as a figural destruction reminiscent of the work of Francis Bacon (SNB 81/112–113).[67] From the void of this imagined, dreamlike space, and in the extremity of the wait (and hope) it communicates, this disfiguration suffices to reawaken the ancient fear.

The time of this fear "provoked by nothing" is no less distended than the space of its emergence. For how long had he prepared to advance when his progress is halted with a formality that recalls the "rules" of the exchange (borders or handholds before the abyss of fear to which the imaginary suspension has opened). These words from the other prompt an acknowledgement that he is late—late not in relation to the meeting time, but in relation to his memory. His memory, or what it brings, has preceded him here.

> *"Still, lagging behind my memory: as though in following the eternal straight roads, I was suddenly forced to confront, alone and suddenly, though as I had always feared, the risky words we had intentionally pronounced in* their *regard: dangerous words, words of one blind"*—*"Words of one who is blind: this is precisely what is needed; but have we not agreed to meet the risk, together?"*—*"Yes, together, but the risk also threatens us there."*—*"Have you thought that the risk might begin by refusing to leave us together to say it?"*—*"The risk proposed to us by such words, such voices without regard, is too great for us to have been able to formulate it with the same words."* (SNB 79/110–111)

Once again, he is in the street (among them?) when he is brought up before words that he and his friend had pronounced in their regard (*à* leur *propos*). Words spoken for them (a substitution is hinted at by the emphasized pronoun; but we must also note the strange redundancy of the formulation: "*paroles . . . à* leur *propos*—which suggest that words have been spoken for—or at least with regard to—their words) now suddenly confront him, alone, and with his solitude. The event that preoccupies the interlocutors is evidently one of language. Indeed, it is a kind of speech event that has implicated the narrators themselves, bringing back to them the danger they had recognized in their act of calling to the others in such a way that they could respond *together*. In this case, the danger appears to be one of separation, and it menaces in an impending act of speaking that will recall to us the circumstances of the rupture of "The Infinite Conversation."

"*Paroles d'aveugle.*" There are few passages in T*he Step Not Beyond* quite as elusive as this one (and let us pass over the risks for the commentator here; for the rarity of the space, and meaning, can prompt laughter). Have these words been *prophetic* in their manner of bringing back (to no present) the risk they carried, despite their apparent innocence ("traps so innocent," SNB 17/29) and their lightness ("*voix sans regard*," SNB 111: unconcerned, unseeing). *Sans regard*—yes, this is what is required in this space where speaking is not seeing (in the light of representation, against the horizon of a consciousness present to itself). And we have heard the protagonist's relation to *them* described as "blind" inasmuch as they let him pass in offering, in their visage, "a light, the burst of a happiness, a distress." They were words of a still "nascent" relation. But why are other words required for the risk (of being together) these words carry?

An apparent answer is given with an abrupt transition to the question of what has happened (presumably in the street). Again we find the intrication sketched before, where the daring thought and the encounter with *them* (a thought whose formulation is destined to tempt the law itself) is bound to what is envisioned with *him* (if one may so name the disfiguring imaging to which the narrating "I" gives himself over). What was confronted in the street if not the disappearance of this other that is implicated by the constitution of a relation to them? And had it not already been enunciated? But the danger to which he/they have exposed themselves with those blind words spoken in the name of others (a more severe translation, now, of what is said in "*à leur propos*") is something for which neither seems quite prepared.

Why the apprehension in this saying of what has been implied by this project? Unless there is no preparation (beyond a cold presentiment) for the separation and effacement that now begin to *take* in the space of the conversation that is becoming the space/time of the return. The narrator's words, indirect before the statement to which he was exhorted, thus remain tentative and require a cautious accommodation ("as a simple moment of their language," SNB 81/115) even as the figural deconstitution of the other progresses and a new field of relations opens. We should recall again, here, the words about narrative fragmentation cited earlier, particularly as we witness an apparent continuation of the conversation in a space that has transformed abruptly and dramatically.

> *That this friend had disappeared, borne, carried off by the great wave of his perpetual memory, did not prevent this same one, with his customary benevolence, from answering for the disappearance himself, both as though nothing had happened and as though it had obliged him to draw out, in his presence, all the consequences of his unfortunate avowal. The consequence developed slowly, but also immediately, with the suddenness of an unforeseeable resolution. Whereas it seemed to him that from now on he would have to make an effort to rejoin him, this other maintaining himself in the fiction of a distancing for which his person, even as present, would bear the intensity, even as an immutably diminished being, he saw him, behind his table, seated comfortably and sumptuously, a majestic personage who received him with his customary benevolence, though this time a little frozen with immobility.* (SNB 82/114)

Once again, what *happens* in the conversations between the two friends most immediately is the articulation of a word, a phrase (as in the "The Infinite Conversation"). At this juncture, it is the enunciation of an "unfortunate avowal" (a phrase that might prompt some reflection); we will see momentarily the consequences for speech. But the latter are given initially in the figure and in an alteration in its resolution (the term speaks to us of decision; indeed, an earlier sentence referred to a branching of decisions implied by the affirmation—but does it not first evoke a displacement of focus in this case?). The one who was said to have disappeared now assumes a presence "qualified as majestic." This latter phrase, emphasizing the adjectival play, reminds us that we are in a literary space *of words* (a comment on the insistence of the word "disappear" does the same thing). The definition of this space has shifted, almost "relaxed" in some sense, and the other is given more immediately, in a more imposing presence (if a little fixed by immobility). A brief fragment had underscored the becoming-image of the other in the distress in which he received the affirmation of his disappearance (♦ *"But what shadow of a presence would I have had I not at every moment already disappeared?"* A strange emptiness, the lack of a response; SNB 80/111). The following fragment (the one prior to the one describing the transformation of the image we are reading) underscores his figural redoubling, though his figuration, here, seems to imply a kind of ruining usage and abandonment (*"like a figure that space, having played with it so much, would have had to abandon on the shore,"* SNB 81/113). But here, the displacement "by infinite degrees" produces, in the near dissolution of space—with only a river between them—an imposing presence, which is itself acknowledged as "another way of failing apart from space" (SNB 82/111). Even his words—and this is "the most extraordinary"—seem to become images of themselves, hollowing out a gulf of insignificance between him and the other as they grow awkward, impeded (stricken by an *"embarras de parole"*). The narrator is taken aback by the transformations to which he attends, unsure how to proceed. But the faltering that afflicts the other's words is assumed by this other with a sovereign (if somewhat stammering) ease that is said to be the equivalent of the narrator's own disarray and perhaps his own *embarras de parole*:

> *Impeded speech that found its equivalent in silent, inexorable ease, leaving place only for the continuous murmur of the river crossing the room between the immutable hills. Ease as of a thing already written and nevertheless always still to be written and always not writing itself. "So there you are, in your turn, sovereign over speech."—"For the benefit of age." According to his conviction, the monumental character that was suddenly visible, that of a dead sovereignty, that of a name sovereignly alive, vicissitudes that drew them towards one another in a deep past, placing them on*

the plateaux of a powerful scale, was also destined to materialize, by contrast, what lightness there would be in this coming that no one had any intention—or perhaps only episodically—of marking in the present by saying (in the sustained murmur of a fluvial speech): they're coming, they're arriving—for speech rebounded, as from edge to edge, from past to past. Which did not prevent them, in their elegant timidity, freer every day, from denying us our own discourse about them in reducing us to this solemn, venerable manifestation. (SNB 82–83/115)

A river appears again, audible, this time, in contrast with the silent sovereignty of the other's figural presence. Does it join the same waters of his disappearance, the great flow of his perpetual memory? And is the *parole fluviale* that says *their* coming not of the same source? The alternation of memory and forgetting—are these not the vicissitudes that attracted the two interlocutors toward one another in a profound past and which are now shared like the flow of the stream between them that marks their common disappearance? This *parole fluviale* cascades now from edge to edge (though "edges" are already morphing, here, into thresholds and window sills) as an eternal past comes to language in the time of return.

The narrator, ever anxiously reflective (and again, as always, there is something lightly comical here), interprets their monumentalization in a play of contrast. Their monumental stature will have served to mark the lightness of *their* coming and is even an effect of this relation. For it appears that the discretion of the speakers (they seek to avoid the present in this annunciation of their coming) remains an obstacle—as long as their discourse takes this form, they do not come. They are denied the coming, or they are denied the passions expressed in relation to them by the very manner in which they have been reduced—in waiting, in fear—to these solemn, venerable manifestations.

What are we to make of the monumentality of these last men, colossi on the borders of a stream of relations they cannot quite enjoy? How do we understand the immobility that overcomes their solemn presence?

The play of figuration is again maddeningly allusive, but let us note at least that the two interlocutors seem to have approached the stature of the dead in the space of their exchange. They have the magnified presence of "public" death, which Blanchot attributes at one moment to an accomplished theoretical stature.[68] Is there a subtle self-reflection (on Blanchot's part) in the reference to a sovereignly living name—or even that of a dead sovereignty? In any case, this exchange, across space, from bank to bank, is also bringing to language the other dying that Blanchot figures in this text as disappearance in the time of the return. Blanchot had envisioned something very close to this scenario (including the reference to a river) in the great text on friendship that closes *L'amitié*. A common strangeness makes it impossible to speak *of* the other (friend), Blanchot writes, explaining the immense discretion of this memorial text for Georges Bataille. He then evokes an "interval" between two who have been bound by relation to the unknown, a "pure interval" measuring the interruption of being that prohibits all thematizing or objectifying relations: "We must renounce knowing those to whom something essential binds us."[69] Hence the discretion of friendship itself, into which a relation to death has always entered:

> *It is true that this discretion becomes, at a certain moment, the fissure of death. I could well imagine that in a sense nothing has changed: in this "secret" between us that is capable of finding a place in the continuity of discourse without interrupting it, there was already, from that time when we were in one another's presence, that imminent, though tacit, presence of the final discretion, and it is from this discretion that the friendly words affirmed calmly their precaution. Words from one shore to the other shore, a word responding to someone who speaks from the other edge and that seeks to accomplish, already in our life, the immeasure of the movement of dying.*

Are the two "last men" of *The Step Not Beyond* not themselves such limit-figures, speaking from one bank of the river to the other—sovereign names bringing a history to its end, but at the same time, and in this very immobilization, remarking another relation—bringing another affirmation to speech? Their stature, in other words, is the play of this limit. They stand in isolation against the very murmur that flows from them, and while their imposing majesty is perhaps an effect of the timidity of those whose arrival they announce, the immobility is itself progressive or dynamic; we might say that it even condenses in fear, maintaining the two in a relation of speech that moves from immobility to immobility.

> ♦ *Immobile before this immobile friend, though he is never enough so. Hence the feeling of a menace, and fear—the fear that nothing provokes; one of the two moves, this is not quite life; one goes to get up perhaps, it will be night, the other continues to mount guard with his vacillating words.* (SNB 91/126)

> ♦ *"We speak, we speak, two immobile men whom immobility would maintain facing one another, the only ones to speak, the last to speak"—"Do you mean that we speak from now on because our words would be disconnected, without effect, a stammering*

from the depths of the ages?"—"Stay calm, look how I'm calm."—"You are not calm, you are afraid as I'm afraid, the fear makes us majestic, solemn."—"Solemn, majestic." (SNB 91–92/127)

The two are stricken with fear. To bring the affirmation (of return) to language is to disinhabit the present in a neutral relation that permits no initiative (we can never be immobile, perhaps discreet, enough). But the two are also joined in fear and this relation has been drawn out as a greeting and a waiting: "♦ *Immobile, stricken with dignity as one would be stricken by death, leaning slowly toward one another, as one inclines to greet another (greeting thought), we awaited our common fall*" (SNB 84/117).

We are almost, with these words, at the point identified in the last pages. And if we once again link the last sentence to the fragment that precedes it ("♦ *Entwined, separated, witnesses without attestation, coming toward us, coming also toward one another, in the detour of time that they were called upon to make turn*" SNB 84/117), we glimpse the limit at which the impossibility of a "common" fall appears—a fall for which, as the very next fragment tells us, almost nothing (or, more precisely, a nothing) is required ("♦ *That this was impossible did not prevent that a mere nothing would have sufficed for it to come about—but precisely a mere nothing*" SNB 84/117). Here is the penultimate fragment of the narrative, anticipated by the fragment we have just read:

> ♦ *Coming toward us, as they came toward one another, through that plurality that unified them without manifesting unity: their young return.*
>
> *He thought, saving the we, as he believed he saved thought by identifying it with the fragile fall, that their young return would permit him, even while ceasing to be together (for a long time, he had no longer heard anything, even by echo, that might have passed for an acceptance, a confirmation, of the daily appointment), to fall into community. Fragile fall—common fall; words always bordering one another.*
>
> *And he knew, thanks to the too ancient knowledge, effaced by the ages, that the young names, naming twice, an infinity of times, one in the past, the other in the future, that which is found only not yet there [en deçà], that which is found only beyond, named hope, disappointment. Hand in hand, from threshold to threshold, like immortals, one of whom was dying, the other saying: "Would I be with the one with whom I die?"* (SNB 136–137/186–187)

There again, it seems, is the attempted thought: the thought of the saving exception ("saving"—but is this not pure loss?) and passage into community.

Again, relation to them presupposes *his* disappearance. But it is also the saying of a different form of accompaniment involving at least four terms (or two terms multiplied). *Their* young return, as we see, becomes the condition of "community" (a common fall), and their young names have come to *name*: "one in the past, one in the future . . . hope, disappointment" (SNB 137/187). The next fragment (which is the last, and in some respects, concluding exchange in the narrative line) tells us that *these* (hope and disappointment) are what the other has allowed to speak in the silent murmur of his fluvial speech—even as he, presumably the benevolent interlocutor, has remained unable (as we learn shortly before; SNB 134/183) either to pronounce or to silence the two names that have excepted themselves from language, having passed through it and exposing themselves to the arid wind of the city of fear.

What has been brought to speech here, in the manner of response to a gift? *The Step Not Beyond* is strewn with hints to which we must return. But we should also recall, and perhaps first of all, the powerful meditation on hope that is offered by Blanchot in *The Infinite Conversation*, in his essay, "The Great Refusal."[70] There, and from the basis of a reflection on Yves Bonnefoy's *L'improbable*, Blanchot attempts to name a hope without hope "that poetry (writing) must teach us to reaffirm" (IC 34/47). We have already turned to this essay to indicate the "impossible" in suffering and the desire that is relation to it. The "hope" that Blanchot seeks to evoke is to be thought from the same relation, as Blanchot suggests with a return to words from Hölderlin that Heidegger designated as his *inaugural* poetic words ("But now day breaks") and in which Blanchot finds an "ecstatic" passage from an interrupted statement of a glimpsed coming ("I waited and I saw it come") to a present whose "nuance" (a nuance of affirmation) bears "our entire poetic destiny" (IC 39/55): "the Holy be my word." Once again, Blanchot traverses a temporal passage Heidegger also sought to disclose, following in perfect accompaniment, but in a way that will finally suspend the Heideggerian trajectory. The poetic space, he continues, is that of a desire he does not hesitate to qualify as "strictly mad" (IC 40/56).

There is a hope, Blanchot writes, that passes by way of the idea—a hope that projects from its present a futural presence (this is "chimerical, fatal"; IC 40/57). Then there is a hope that *recaptures* relation when relation is lost in the temporal order of the possible. This hope renounces and yet reaffirms itself in its own effacement, *surviving* in relation to the impossible.

This is the hope that speaks in the utterly outlandish presumption of inviting/accepting the other (here, in Hölderlin's poetry, the sacred) into one's speech.

Blanchot's call in *The Step Not Beyond* will be more bereft, more neutral, when he writes, at the end of his "trajectory of writing": "*Viens . . .*" But these words from after the disaster bear no less aptly the epithet "apocalyptic." They are words of hope and desire (perhaps of gratitude, and not without fear) that speak from the gift of effacement known in the time of return.

But if the future (never to be present) is not more than the prophecy of an empty past, and if the past that has never occurred in any present is destined only to a phantasmatic return (forever repeating itself in its *non-lieu*); if the one is forever riven from the other for want of a present that would conjugate them, "communicating" only via an infinite rupture that is for the self of this experience an unsituatable, uncrossable line, nevertheless demanding its crossing. . . .What hope? What hope for an "irrevocable" past (always *en deça*) and what hope for a future (an "*au-delà*") barred from any present, the two forever sundered? What transgression of this strict law could still be held out—what exception, by thought, could offer itself?

That the "subject" of the return is called to exception, or tempted by an impossible passage is nevertheless part of the exigency of this strictest law. The exigency is borne in the writing by which the effacement of the event leaves a trace of hope:

♦ For having always missed the present, the event had always disappeared without leaving any trace other than that of a hope for the past, to the point of making the future the prophecy of an empty past. (SNB 12/23)

But it would also appear that there could be no futural turn were exposition to the irrevocable event not already assent, were the writing of the return not already implicating the subject's transgressive acquiescence. We have seen precisely such an implication in Blanchot's description of relation to the neutral (SNB 118/162), a description that is entirely pertinent inasmuch as the assent to dying described there must be thought in the time of the return. "Writing the event," we might say, is to take the trace of hope, and the relation of hope and disappointment is an already transgressive movement that *The Step Not Beyond* seeks to bring to language. *Le pas* au-delà (the hope); *le* pas *au-delà* (*the disappointment*). But this relation must be articulated in a manner that exceeds its apparently fortuitous statement of transgression and law, for transgression and law must themselves be rethought.

The task is attempted in a second naming of hope and disappointment:

♦ *The hope of transgressing the law was tied to the disappointment which, in this very movement of transgression, led him to pose an equal law, though of a higher power, which he then had to transgress anew, without any hope of succeeding except by posing anew an always higher law, which made of this infinite passage from the law to its transgression and from this transgression to another law the sole infraction that sustained the eternity of his desire.* (SNB 23–24/37)

The passage lends itself to two interpretations that may be essentially linked. On the one hand, the "law" named here appears to be that from which *exception* is sought (the law of the "cosmic order"—the logos). Exception, in its turn, would engage the time of the return (itself governed by another "law" that fails to *stand* as law) we have just been entertaining. The movement between these laws may remind us of the assertion that the affirmation of the return can only happen once the completion of the logos has occurred. In this interpretation, the transgression named in the preceding passage would be understood initially as a transgression of order, and the recurrence that is named there could perhaps be described with a theory of sets, *except* insofar as the infinite passage itself comes to appear under the guise of *another* law and as a transgression sustaining the eternity of a desire.

But the description of the movement of transgression in this passage is also complemented in *The Step Not Beyond* by a series of descriptions of this play of opening and prohibition indicated by *il*: "(*il*) *l'ouverture interdite*" (SNB 20/32).[71] To follow "*il*" ("if we were capable of following it up to that edge," SNB 6/14) is to transgress, or seek to transgress, the discursive order, but to engage this movement is to enter a serial play of another relation to law, or another movement of arrested steps:

♦ *Was there still an obstacle he could not get past to reach the immense uncertain space, or did this obscure and devastated space (serial desert) constitute the only impediment, the final obstacle?* (SNB 33/50)

The movement evoked here seems finally most pertinent to the description of an alternating passage between hope and disappointment, even as it conforms to the first interpretation. Both accounts, in any case, end in the same evocation of *another* form of passage from the one governing transgression of the discursive order. This other form of transgression is given to us in a subsequent passage on grace and chance.

Grace and chance are themselves figured here as transgressive forms of exception. The reasoning is playful and sometimes fiercely difficult as Blanchot contrasts the relation of the law to its subject with that of grace. The law, in its coldness, is "despite you" (*malgré toi*); grace, in the form of a sovereign gift, is "without you" (*sans toi*). Chance allies these two relations by "freeing, in its '*tutoiement*' for anonymity" (SNB 25–26/39–40). Luck, synonymous with chance, implies a relation whereby the law finds itself "interdicted," though the scandal is only apparent in that the law then cedes to a higher law that encompasses the alterity that has provoked its resurgence. The recurrence described in the passage on hope and transgression is thus envisioned again in a way that seems to underscore the alteration that overtakes this recurrent movement:

> Chance—or the luck, or the grace that places the law in parentheses, in accordance with the time outside of time—is thus reintroduced under the jurisdiction of another law, until, in its turn, this latter—then, in its turn. . . . It remains to be determined in what relation, if it is neither lawful nor fortuitous, the movement would be that would always pose, starting from transgression, an *other* law, as it would pose transgression in starting from the law and as its other; a movement of alterity, without law, without chance, a movement that we do not at all name through the negative of these words. (SNB 26/40)

Has Blanchot now named the neutral of a movement between law and transgression that would allow us to think the affirmation of transgression/transcendence in a nonnegative manner? The next paragraph appears to point precisely to this possibility:

> "Luck is mine" [*j'ai de la chance*]. A formula as strong as it is brazen, since luck dispossesses and disappropriates. Which would come down to saying, oh player who pretends to speak in the name of the game: I possess what dispossesses, being the relation of dispossession. Which comes down to saying that there is no luck for luck, and to saying that the only luck would be in this anonymous relation that could not itself be called luck, or only that luck that does not fall [to someone: *qui n'échoit pas*], with which the neutral would be at play in letting itself play in it. (SNB 26–27/41)[72]

There then follows a paragraph that calls into question the appeal to either "transcendence" or "transgression" for a passage in thought at what we must also hesitate to call a "limit." The former terms remain too close to a theological determination, while the latter still alludes to what would remain "sacred, both in the thought of the limit and in that demarcation, impossible to think, which would be introduced in every thought by the crossing of the limit never and always accomplished" (SNB 27/41). The neutral and the *pas* that would engage it must be held from any thought of the sacred or any theological determination.

"Threshold," as we have seen, is perhaps the name that must be employed here, barring any too rapid appeal to the metaphor of death for this spatiotemporal demarcation at the limit of space and time where the neutral comes into play, or comes, like a messenger, in a word too many. Like the young names, who come to the site of the conversation from threshold to threshold.

Could the recurrence of their approach in the alternating time of the narrative (the time of memory, the time of forgetting), a movement sustaining an "eternity" of desire, constitute that limit at which a fragile fall would occur— that prohibited border of a time outside time from which a *viens* could be affirmed (not as a horizon, but as something more like a sustaining opening)? We would be thinking, in this case, the time of exception in which the return itself would be affirmed.

Let us read from the beginning once more (SNB 1/8):

"*If it were given to us*" (*s'il nous était permis*): We can understand this now as the interregnum of chance: the time of exception. "*Having disappeared from ourselves*": both interlocutors have effectively disappeared once their sovereignty appears and they enter the time of return in the saying of the now cascading relation. They have also disappeared from the "us" of being-together (*ensemble*), though they are (or are to be?) "*saved*" in another *we* of a plural community.

Again, "*if we were permitted to write.*" What grace or fortune is named here if not that granted (in the manner of a gift) by the young names themselves who are brought to the site of the conversation almost as messengers?

> ♦ *The ancient fear, the aging of the ancient fear. "Are you afraid?—Anciently afraid." We were thus, under the guarantee of the young names, the innumerable occupants of fear in the deserted city: hiding fear, hiding ourselves from fear."* (SNB 134/182)

The young names offer an enigmatic guarantee; they bring, effectively, a *droit de cité* in the deserted city of fear. We have noted the dynamic of fear, and it is now time (indeed, we can now cite in a pertinent manner a sentence that appears in the conversation but without markers attributing it to a speaker: "the time is coming when the time will come"; SNB 77/107) to follow the last steps in the figuration of this unfrequented, *desert* space.

The names have been brought to language (to the "threshold") in the "fluvial speech" of the interlocutors, their "thin murmur." The other's speech, we are told, has now taken on a neutral character (the words are precisely articulated, but without correspondence to any "particular" word, it remains a stream of sound) that the narrating interlocutor—it is apparently him, but the pronouns are here indeterminate—is tempted to take as a "long animal sobbing" (SNB 85/118). But he must also recognize that he is called to rescue here a "triumphal affirmation." "They are coming!"—coupled, perhaps, with the "*je m'efface*" that is the aleatory condition of this joyous triumph. But would we not then understand the others that come to write in this place—or their writing itself— as "hope" and "disappointment"? Are these not what the other gratefully brings to language as guarantors of an anonymous plurality?

There also occurs, at this juncture, a most enigmatic crossing of the guiding narrative line with another narrative we have entertained (or so it would appear). The time/space of the young names—alighting now almost as birds (we might think again of Francis Bacon)—somehow intersects with that of a young girl who bears a trait similar to that of the one who helped the fearful one across the night.

> ♦ While they settled on the threshold, far away, yet perhaps already leaning over us and watching us as though we were a single thing, he sees, falling over the face of the young girl, as the night falls, the dark hair that completely hides it [*les cheveux sombres qui le cachent tout à fait*]. (SNB 91/126)

The falling of her hair over her face, which also hides *him* (the pronoun is ambiguous: it could refer to her face, *son visage*, or to him, *lui*), is the sole event (unfolding with the uncertain duration of nightfall) at this point of intersection. Imagining that a lock of hair has fallen from a lowered head, we might ask whether he is somehow in her presence in a space of reading, or in a space of something like sleep. How does his or her screening—his or her disappearance from view—relate, in the time of return, to the effacements of the conversation? The subsequent and juxtaposed fragments sharpen this question inasmuch as it becomes clear that the topology of the room utterly disrupts the constitution of a common space of encounter.

> ♦ On the threshold, coming from the outside perhaps, the two young names, like two figures of which we would be unable to affirm whether they are, behind the window, within, or without, for no one, save these two who expect everything from us, could say where we are. (SNB 100/138)

The threshold to which the young names come cannot be identified as either inside or outside, at least in relation to the interlocutors, whose location can be given only by those who come, in their *expectation* (hope, disappointment). They are not, to put this in the simplest terms, occupying the same space as that of the hosts.

We confront here what is surely an unanswerable question. Could everything have been turning in relation to the encounter with the young girl with somber eyes, an event that has returned here in a kind of flashback (the intensity of this momentary apparition suggests the term)? Could this sudden intervention of an apparently "real" relation reveal what is the true kernel of the narrative? Of course, we started from the supposition that the narrative was a kind of allegory of an attempt at an answerable, hospitable writing—a writing that would acquit itself of what was given in the narrative event of encounter with the young girl. But this return of the event (in what we might take to be its subsequent unfolding) points to a more complex relation between this event and the narrative line than anything the term allegory would allow. Blanchot, as we have seen, spoke of complementary or supplementary spaces, evoking a multiplicity of relations that cannot be subsumed in a single narrative space. Surely, we would fail to take the immeasure of the fragmentation of this text if we insist on locating the point or points where it is pinned to the real and thus *organize* the narrative around it. Why would the instance of a real encounter be any more orienting than the plural opening of that *vide d'univers* (SNB 20/32) that also marks itself in the "*il*" of their encounter (giving her the movement of fear; SNB 60/86). That opening of language, at the limit of language, that opening that bears with it the exigency of writing, infinitely exceeds its real circumstances. The real kernel, if we must have one, surely lies in that multiple opening, and it is from the fragmenting of that opening that the "supplementary," intersecting relation of narrative lines must be thought.

Convoking the "*il*" of encounter, we will be reminded again of the desert encounter of "Reflections on Hell" (a passage to which we will return). And, indeed, the posthumous city of fear shares the growing aridity of this space; the wind of rumor that blows through it suggests that it is always more deserted (SNB 134/182 and 134/183): *the desert grows*. It is the space of a vast dormitory or shelter—or a cemetery (a space for those *dying* in a form of homelessness):

> *All around, there were men apparently asleep, lying right on the ground, with covers thrown over them in the way one throws earth onto an embankment, and these innumerable little knolls, thoughts of the crumbled city, amassed evenly until they became the naked floor of the room.* (SNB 112/153)

Let us observe that there is no river in this space swept by the arid wind of anonymous rumor; the wind itself, become a "rumor of froth," has become that flowing of what Blanchot once prominently named "the eternal outside" (SL 83/98). There are the young names, and there is fear. Hope and disappointment, sustaining desire, and the gift of fear, to which the itinerant interlocutor is called as witness.

The narrative space, here, is so rare, so empty, that any account will be mercilessly exposed to the echo of its vanity. Its element, as we have seen, is fear, whose effects give us the images of the deserted, desiccated city, a space evacuated of any present and almost any life beyond those "innumerable occupants of fear" (SNB 134/182) who figure as "innumerable monticles, thoughts of the crumbled city" (SNB 112/153). The devastation is comparable to that of the deserted space that Blanchot evoked in *The Book to Come* in his evocation of the site of prophetic speech.[73] Are the vast number of these dormant, displaced others—these *destroyed men*[74]—those who are *at stake* in the effort to trace the threshold of relation that will be called, in the last pages of this text, "community"? The harsh, primal character of the image powerfully recalls the scene cited earlier from Paul Celan's "Conversation in the Mountains," and we might well entertain a strong link (regardless of any intertextual references) in that a figure of a relation to time comes to transmute, in Celan's text, the speaker's relation to those others lying about him in the empty site of what is perhaps a concentration camp.

For the lack of figuration of "the ancient fear" beyond those effects of devastation in the city that require "the illusion of a tomb" must be understood against the insistence of figuration in the appearance of the young names who offer, in the naming, figures of time. However, let us move slowly here and note, first, the forceful denial of any figure for fear, which appears as we approach the end of the text:

> ♦ *It wouldn't matter if you were to say: I don't believe in fear; that too ancient fear, without idolatry, without figure and without faith, the beyond of fear that is affirmed in no beyond, would still push you through the narrow, eternal streets,* without a goal, toward *the daily appointment, that which does not propose itself to you as an end; whence the fact that, even in reaching it every day, you are never there.* "Because I reach it in flight, fleeing it endlessly."
>
> "*You respect fear.—Perhaps; but it does not respect me, it has no regard.*" The most grave of idolatries: to have regard for that which is without regard. (SNB 134/183)

Sans égards, or without concern: fear is an affect without subject that is irreducibly *of* the neutral. Where fear opens, and in what it brings to language, there is nothing attested:

> ♦ The Neutral, the gentle interdiction of dying, there where, from threshold to threshold, eye without regard, silence carries us into the proximity of the distant. A speaking still to be said beyond the living and the dead, *bearing witness for the absence of attestation.* (SNB 76/107)[75]

What, then, of the young names and the other figures who appear under the draw of fear—pushed toward the narrator by fear or offered to him in "the mystery of the illusion," tempting him, it seems, with the idea of a spatial embellishment of their advance? [76] Is there a writing "under the secret of the ancient fear" ("*sous le secret*" suggests a pull or a draw) that allows what grants in fear but does not succumb to this capture? What would it mean to be a witness to fear without idolatry? Is the "illusion of a tomb" in the desert city no less necessary than the figuration offered by Kafka in his own traversal of the desert, as Blanchot gives it to us in *The Literary Space*?[77]

Let us underscore again that the narrator has come to the conversation in fear (hence never quite there, even if always punctual) with the apprehensive knowledge that *their* coming implied his friend's disappearance. He has *returned* in the conversation (in the dynamic of the return itself, in immobilization—seized by memories, driven by fear) to the event of their calling, "fulfilling" thereby the exigency of writing, which comes late in the text as the prayer of the city just cited: "Be the witness of fear." He has written his own disappearance in this trajectory, bringing to the figure, at the threshold of the conversation (neither inside nor outside) those "witnesses without attestation" that are called to *turn* the time in its very detour. These witnesses, in fact, name the time, as we have seen in the penultimate passage of the narration, where the names join the "we" whom the narrator would save in community.

> *And he knew, thanks to the too ancient knowledge, effaced by the ages, that the young names, naming twice, an infinity of times, one in the past, the other in the future, what is found only not yet there, what is found only beyond, named hope, disappointment.* (SNB 137/187)

Though they are yet unattested (witnesses themselves without witness), the narrator seems to *recognize* the names from the ground of his "too ancient knowledge" ("I will have known": can we understand this now as happening at the turning of time, i.e., when they return?). He recognizes them as a newly returning time—new *figures* of the return, or new figures of the returning of what is found only *en deçà*, what is found only *au-delà*. They effectively *give time, bring about time*, to what will have never taken place and will never take place outside the pure passage of this juncture. This would appear to be the temporal condition, the opening for receiving those who have been figured playfully as "the beautiful" without idolatry (i.e., as anonymous). This is a projection of the relation to the other that is not without fear, but *without regard for fear*, drawing from the neutral of this relation the possibility of an affirmation of this time.

Fear is never overcome, but this does not prohibit the concluding naming of an impossible peace and even an apparently peaceful acquiescence. The anguished, menaced one who was invited to bear nothing—"him, or a man like him" (IC xviii/xviii)— is now invited to accept what cannot be desired and what cannot be promised. Hope and disappointment are expressed in a grateful silence that is without combative exchange:

> ♦ "Be at peace with yourself" [*Sois en paix avec toi-meme*].—There is no one in me to whom I might say *tu*.—Be at peace.—Peace, that war merely appeased.—Be at peace, without peace without war, outside any page to write, any pact to sign, any text and any country.—The outside does not promise peace.—Be, without

your knowing, at peace with yourself, in the beyond of peace you could never attain.—What you promise, I do not desire.—Receive without desire the promise I do not make to you."

Outside any mercenary speech, the silence without refusal gives thanks. (SNB 136/185)

This peaceful accession is then *apparently* figured in an event that rejoins the narrative line:

> ♦ *There had been a kind of event: the unforeseeable without plaint, evading attention. Yes, this is what it was about; what was it about? As though death, fully achieved, had left all intact, except all [quitte seulement de tout], acquitted of that dying for which had persisted, amicably, the speech maintained in silence. Thus, the false appearances seemed to have left him [l'avoir quitté]; and this, this discharging [quittance] of regret and the secret, a movement of immobility, far from the true and from appearance, apart from play and openness, definitive slowness, repose without the promise of leisure, with the tranquillity that cannot be eluded: gift of serenity in the face henceforth entirely visible, escaping the evasive.*
>
> *Shadow of time, of once, receive their figures. Respond no longer to one who would want to hold memory, captive.* (SNB 136/185–186)

What peace is this? The repeated "*quitte*" evokes, by etymology, a tranquility that follows upon the becoming-immobile of the interlocutor who passes before his narrating partner. We have followed this passage by which a monumental apparition (evocative of the "great dead") briefly figures in the movement of immobility named here, and it would appear that this passage has now achieved that point where dying itself is brought to a lasting calm. On the page before the one we are reading, we see "survival" defined in what are perhaps resonant terms,[78] and in the penultimate paragraph of the narrative, this motif of a calm dying will be underscored. Accomplished death—the accomplished death of the last man—has left everything intact, but *without* the totality (accomplished by negation). The line of the present (in relation to which the whole is gathered) has been passed, but *without transgression*. Or the transgression has somehow been neutralized or transmuted; death itself is acquitted of the prohibited dying.

These are extraordinary words, and their stated implication ("thus, the false appearances *seemed* to have left him") is no less astounding. Is the appearance indeed illusory, a mere seeming? Two preceding passages that underscore the nonrelation of dying to being (dying must not be understood from a reference to *being*-dead), or life, would appear to suggest precisely this.

> Dying does not localize itself in an event, nor does it last in the manner of a temporal becoming: dying does not last, does not end, and, prolonging itself in death, tears this away from the state of a thing in which it would like to find peace. It is dying, the error of a dying without completion, that renders the dead one suspect and death unverifiable, withdrawing from it in advance the benefit of the *event*. (SNB 93/129)

The "error" of dying would seem to unsettle forever the repose of death, even "accomplished" death, and its character of simulacrum would seem to oblige us to take on fully the emphasized "seemed" that appears in the passage we are reading. As we read in a passage near the one we have just seen:

> ♦ Dying, in this sense, does not have the crushing solidity of non-being, the irrevocability of what has come about, of being in the past. It is nothing more than a simulacrum, something that renders seeming [*fait semblant*: "pretends"] and only seems to efface itself in effacing us. The "seeming" [*le faire-semblant*], the disintegration of dying [*l'effritement du mourir*], is that which, at each instant outside the instant, makes us slip, in parallel with the sinuous line of life, along a perversely straight path. (SNB 94/130)

How could the step of transgression in dying—the step beyond—ever be free of death's error? Even if "we" know effacement in this step, it would seem that the haunting simulacrum (ever returning) will make every figure of this passage "semblant," as Blanchot firmly underscores. (And as for any "homecoming" in this passage, let us note again the crumbling [*l'effritement*] of the desiccated soil.)

The astounding nature of the description of the event offered in this passage near the end of the narrative is further visible if we contrast it with almost any other description of moments where death and dying have somehow coalesced, or where the one is brought to appear in the other. Seeking to maintain the contrast, we would have to conclude that the serene visage is not to be confused with that of the being claimed in public exposition (SNB 100/138, the theme of the claim of society appears throughout this section), or with that final sovereignty that death ("*cette grande fallacieuse*," SNB 102/141) confers on the exposed corpse (which, "in truth," is also exposed to the outside). Clearly, it is not to be confused with those more disturbing apparitions in which the obscene slips into view in some conflation of death and dying—apparitions, as in the death camps, whose importance for this text must not be underestimated.[79] And, obviously, the serene, open visage is not to be confused with that "mask of infidelity" that we take on inevitably by reason of the fact that our dying is never "natural" and never something of which we can be absolved, in view of the *défaillance* that occurs there:

> Obscure centre of fallacious relations. We do not die offending, any more than we are guilty in writing; nevertheless, there is a rupture there that the term "finitude" illuminates poorly and of which the religious myths make us overly conscious. Dying is a "law of nature," and yet we are not natural in dying. We cannot do otherwise, and this necessity about which we are sure without believing in it (always surprised, in the final moment, by the unbelievable) puts the mask of infidelity, eyes closed, on each of our faces: we abandon ourselves, abandon those to whom we should not be absent, we abandon "life," and that by a sort of distraction, as though we could have avoided the inevitable had we been more attentive. But it is surely more than a betrayal: it is a false betrayal. Everything is falsified when dying comes into play. (SNB 104/143)

The writing of this frozen, forever inscribed infidelity, is no less vain.

And yet, as we read in a passage from the same sequence of fragments concerning the appearance of death—and yet:

> The very last moment, this shivering of a heart that no longer beats to life.
>
> The very last moment: little matter that in writing this word, we should feel all the deceit there is in writing it, even if we add that it does not belong to moments, that it is therefore not the very last—and yet (must we then thank you for this "yet," the supplementary word that nothing follows this time, save—save this pure gratitude?) (SNB 101/139–140)

Once again we find a gratitude in the space of the last moment, here for another "*signe hors signe*" (SNB 7/16) and giving way—since nothing follows, despite the question regarding an obligation—to the silence of a pure gratitude. We have read hope and disappointment into the silence of grateful acquiescence to unpromised peace. Moving to the next fragment, might we read into the serenity of the open face also the grateful assumption of acquittal? Might acquittal be part of that grace that releases hope and disappointment?

"Acquitted of that dying." Again, it is an astounding sentence that appears to name the interruption of that incessant, mocking voice in us that says the transgression of dying: "'It is forbidden to die' [*Il est interdit de mourir*], we hear this in ourselves constantly, not as the call of an obligation to life, but as the very voice of dying, breaking the interdiction" (SNB 96/133). A sovereign grace has somehow intervened (let us not overlook the insistence of the second person), or transgression is without fault for being *otherwise*—in which case there is perhaps acquittal because the prohibition of dying only holds in relation to a present. A long citation is required here:

> "As though dying allowed us in some sense to *live* in the eternal detour of a past and the eternal detour of a future that no present would unify."—"To die is without declension."—"This inert infinitive, agitated by an infinite neutrality that could not coincide with itself, infinitive without present."—"Hence one might affirm: it is prohibited to die *in the present*."—"Which also means: the present does not die, and there is no present for dying. It is the present that would in some way pronounce the prohibition."—"While the transgression of dying, which has always already broken with present time, and in the inaccomplishment always proper to it, comes to substitute for the trinitarian duration unified by the predominance of the present, the time of difference in which this will always take place because this has always already happened: dying, returning."—"The interdiction remains intact [*sauve*]: in the present, one does not die."—"It remains intact." But, in as much as it is the present that pronounces it, and in as much as transgression in-accomplishes itself in a future-past time, removed from any affirmation of presence, the transgression has also always already withdrawn from the prohibition the present time of its pronouncement—has prevented it or prohibited it in dislocating it."—"There would be "affirmed," then, a time without present, according to the exigency of the return."—"This is why the transgression itself is not accomplished." (SNB 107–108/147–148)

In the affirmed time of the return, in which, as we have seen, the "movement of immobility" takes form, the relation to dying would take the *neutral* form of a passivity that has transgressed itself. As we have read: "Passivity, patience, passion" (SNB 119/163). Would this passage not suspend, with the present itself, both the prohibition and the infraction, even onto that gentle interdiction of dying where silence carries us? With it, would go, of course, the perfidy of the simulacrum. And does the openness of the visage (its nonevasiveness) not finally derive from a suspension of the neutral's withdrawal, or from what the neutral perhaps grants in this passage (hence the gratitude)? *Only in the affirmed time of the return could resentment toward the past be so overcome.*

None of this is without fear or distress ("Both in distress," SNB 136/186). But the death/dying we have just followed prepares us to recognize that another modality of relation, in which dying *lasts* in the figure of a young return, allows the poignant question of accompaniment. Let us not call this a "present," but the *main-tenant* of this passage is powerfully advanced.

> *Hand in hand, from threshold to threshold, like immortals, one of whom was dying, the other saying:* "would I be with whom I die?" (SNB 137/187)

It is not a "present," but there is nevertheless a bridging of past and future as a calm dying passes the threshold under the guise of "that calm of life for which our hearts beat" (SNB 137/187). The impassible limit that effaces (falling from the present, we are effaced) is itself effaced in the instant of affirmation. But "affirmation," given only in quotation marks (SNB 107–108/147–148), must be understood with the nuance of gratitude and in the neutral: in the letting-go of a fragile fall and without the reserve of anxious memory. Nor is it quite clear that the "we," or thought, can be saved here, except as a "common fall." It is not clear, in fact, that the question of accompaniment can finally be answered.

For the final exchange gives effacement, "self"-effacement, as separation:

> ♦ *"Why do you no longer say anything?—"Have I ever said anything?"—"You let speak, without anything being said, in the manner of a thanks, the hope, the disappointment, that carry all saying."*
>
> *"Why do you no longer say anything?"—"It is good to be able still to repeat this question in a low voice, lower each time: a clear, neutral, impeded voice."—"I no longer have, even in the form of this last question, a thought that concerns you."— "It is good to renounce holding us together in the discernment of a thought."—"Why give back to me what I can no longer give, under the illusion that it is good?"— "It is good."*
>
> *He was so calm in dying that he seemed, before dying, already dead; then, after and forever, still living, in that calm of life for which our hearts beat—thus having effaced the limit, at that instant when it is the limit that effaces.*
>
> *(In the night that is coming, may those who have been united and who efface themselves not feel this effacement as a wound they would be inflicting on one another.)* (SNB 137/187)

There is no sure way to attribute these statements, despite what offer themselves as recognizable markers. Following those markers (the impeded voice, for example), and the general tenor of their conversation (which would imply that the narrator first asks why the other is no longer saying anything and that the repetition of the question is by the other), we may follow the exchange in such as way as to understand the benediction of the disappearance of concern as words of the narrating interlocutor. (Is this benediction "praise of the near to the far"? SNB 135/185.) The words thus have an interesting effect on what appears to be the narrator's previous effort to save their relation (the *nous*, but understood outside any "together"). I cannot give you this regard, even under the form of a renunciation, he is told: why return what I have not been able to give under the illusion that this incapacity is something good? In relation to which the narrator *separates*, with a pure assertion—*without cause*—that is perhaps a pure gift, but indistinguishable from the stubbornness of a wounded assertion.

Comparable effects follow if we attribute the words in an inverse manner, though the benediction would apply to a *défaillance* that verges on failure, even if renunciation of a "holding together" was in fact already implied in the identification of thought with a fragile fall ("He thought . . . that their young return would permit him, even while ceasing to be together") that would take the form of a community. Could it have been the calm other who gives this benediction? Could the benediction have brought the calm[80]? In the fragmented space of these last moments, nothing finally justifies the attributions. We cannot even pretend to assign the dying with any certainty. And what would justify the assumption that the conversation follows a steady alternation? The interlocutors are speaking *sur l'arête— ligne d'instabilité— de la parole* (SNB 135/184), where union and separation are themselves indistinguishable.

Separation, however, seems to take the last word. Once again: "*In the night that comes, may those who have been united and who efface themselves not feel this effacement as a wound they would be inflicting on one another.*" This last line of the narrative repeats the sentence from which we have begun: "*Ce jour s'effaçant, je m'effacerai,* but with the warning that this "act" of effacement, which has just been blessed, should not be taken as an act committed by one against another. As though peace, in these last steps, must still be urged, as though the experience of the common fall, a separating community, can never be wholly preserved from the returning resentments of the self. Did we perhaps already witness, in the apparent irritation of the dispute regarding the return of what has not been given, a trace of what will inevitably recur?

In any case, Blanchot is clearly telling us that the peace, the calm attained by at least one in relation to another, is forever vulnerable.

But what of *them*? What of the girl with somber eyes? The text ends with a *divided* scene of dying whose apparently intimate character remains radically open. There is almost no trace of those *others* to which the interlocutors referred playfully and insistently at the start of the conversation, and no concluding reference to those to whom the "apocalyptic" invitation was issued. The interlocutors are *"mort mourant,"* side by side (though *côte à côte* could conceivably return us to the image of riverbanks). However, they fall in separate modalities. For the one in advance, there is (apparently) a calm passage. For the other, accession to the time of the return with the arrival of the young names brings the thought of a fall *in community* that would be permitted to *him* (*"leur jeune retour lui permettrait"*). Would this be community with the other, with the others? (They would be "words always bordering one another"—but here again, a reference to a *"côte"*: *se côtoyant*. Is this what has become of *fréquenter*?). The question then becomes one of accompaniment as the young names come to name, joining hands. The passage suggests strongly (though a reader may be inclined to resist such a literal rendering) that the names themselves are the immortals in question—a turn that suggests that they have somehow come to occupy the place of the interlocutors, or, more precisely, that if the interlocutors speak as "immortals," it is *from* and *as* this coming to name of hope and disappointment which has been allowed in the silent gratitude said by at least one of the speakers. The "four" terms would be two to the extent that the interlocutors achieve the supposed community.

But what accompaniment is said in *"serai-je avec qui je meurs"*? Is this the saying of hope, or is this the saying of a surprise, and perhaps, in this, even melancholy (hence a form of *déception*)?[81] There could be hopeful surprise in the sense that the proximity of the other could be taken as the sign of the event of dying. ("Does the proximity of this other mean that I am dying?") Indeed, though the question must bear in part on the identity of the other ("Is this the one?"—but nothing limits this to *one*), the poignancy of the question emerges even more powerfully from the doubt/surprise bearing on *"je meurs,"* since this is, in a very strict respect, an impossible enunciation—nothing one could ever pronounce in the present of the event. To rephrase again: "Is this common fall now my dying?" (*"Est-ce cela la peur, est-ce cela mourir?"*) As a such a saying, it could be a turn in "the discourse of dying" (thus joining, in its indecision, *"je ne sais pas"*), and as such it could possibly open beyond the "intimacy" of that scene and follow upon the invitation issued just before the sequence describing the calm of the last steps—that "apocalyptic" end of "a certain trajectory of writing." It could be *announcing* an advent (but only in its question, in all uncertainty).

And what of *déception*, which is given in the English translation as "deception?" The term surely must first be heard as "disappointment" (here and largely throughout), but we cannot exclude the possibility of a breach of illusion of some kind. And there remains the melancholy of a discovery of the self at this point of passing. For the strange syntax of the phrase brings the question to bear as much upon the "I" as upon the ambiguous other (at a syntactical limit, we can even hear a suggestion that the "I" itself is occupying this place of the proximate other). Are the *"je"* of *"serais-je"* and *"je meurs"* the same? Perhaps this is the closest one can come to the saying of one's dying. Could there in fact be community without the remarking / effacing of this affirming instance—without something like this dying question of the self (that "self" being the enigmatic one who could write "my death")? Hope and disappointment could conjoin precisely in that the "messianic" advent (of community) can never be known by the "I"—except, perhaps, at the point of its passing or effacement, which may also be given to us in that repetition of *"je."* Ultimately nothing limits the "who" of this phrase and the question of identity that echoes in what is perhaps the surprise of recognition, perhaps a form of discovery. Nothing contains its anonymity. At the threshold, or in the cascade of thresholds, *outside* the space of the conversation ("for a long time"), the intimate question may have an endless substitutability. It remains open—even onto *"il."*

The reader tempted by the thought of closing the hermeneutic circle or even a stability of reference in these last paragraphs is ultimately denied. Even the peace attained at this apparent limit remains extremely precarious. Yet the grace of this ending is undeniable, however much it frustrates. One could even say that it is ever more graceful, the more it frustrates. Of course, it is possible to read these last passages as the coy deconstruction of a denied promise. But we fail, then, to reach the dispossessed anonymity that is affirmed. *Seule demeure l'affirmation nomade.* The immense achievement of *The Step Not Beyond* inheres in its generation of that impossible affirmation and the invitation it affords—an opening of pure hospitality; nothing more, finally, than the writing of what the fearful one received from the young girl.

It is always possible to offer a speculative reconstruction. I noted earlier, for example, that the encounter with the young girl could perhaps be read as the kernel of the fragmented narrative, which remains secondary, supplementary, or complementary in relation to the "real" event. The narrative line would thus turn on the axis of relation sought to "all those others" brought to the knowledge of the narrator through that encounter. Returning to the conversation—which is to say, *writing* the conversation—the narrator would have been seeking the time (outside time) and the distance (a nonspatial proximity) that form the threshold of this relation, the site from which the invitation issues. The narrator would thus have been writing his disappearance, his "death," *via the neutral* (its word too many) of his relation to the other interlocutor. His effacement, with that of his partner, would allow the others to write in this place to which come the young names.

But again, this organization of the narrative would appear to force a schematic unity that is ultimately foreign to the mobile character of the anonymous relations we have identified. The relations of intersection and repetition (those repetitions given to us by and with the word "fear," for example—the link between the scenes with the young girl and the narrative line turns on this word) do not require a logical articulation. Indeed, the "indifference" of these relations to one another (if we may so name the effect of the neutral on their articulation) seems to require an active assumption of a textual topology that utterly defies the spatiotemporal saturation provided by the imperative of narrative order. The text ends with a foregrounding of the divided scene of dying and strangely leaves aside those others that preoccupied the interlocutors (their last traces seem to come in the descriptions of the city of fear and perhaps in the "apocalyptic" address). A classical—cathartic—conclusion (resolving the issue of fear) would have required some resolution of the relation to those others. The text is in fact offering only the site of the relation and the call.

The site is radically *evacuated*, and the call is without determination. The text simply emphasizes the strictly finite character of the act from which it would issue—its intensely human conditions. It is a call from *one alone, in friendship, in community*. Which is to say, in the interrupted, last steps of a mobile relation.

FINAL NOTE

Through the Double Imperative

For one who has accompanied the movements to which the last pages of *The Step Not Beyond* attest, there can be few grounds for a conclusion: repetition, perhaps, but surely no conclusion. Could one possibly add a final word to the "last words" of this writing or the benediction of the last exchange? Should the site of those disappearing not be marked by silence once it has been limned, at least until a new writing begins?

The present study began, however, from a question that this closing note of reserve should not leave unaddressed. I recall that Blanchot's gesture of coupling his essay on Robert Antelme's *L'espèce humaine* with his essay "Being Jewish" had the possible effect of bringing into question the affirmative statement of this latter essay. Jewish thought, he told us, teaches that speech opens a relation of hospitality toward the other that does not reduce their otherness to a common measure. Being Jewish offers a relation, from an exilic movement, that does not contain (violently) within the horizon of

Being: "In this sense, speaking is the promised land where exile is fulfilled in sojourn, since it is not a matter of being at home there, but always Outside, in a movement where the Foreign offers itself, yet without renunciation" (IC 128/187). But "*L'espèce humaine*" placed the indestructible of this relation with the infinite under the shadow of a mortal menace that was said to be inseparable from the very exposure achieved in speech. Where the speech of the other human being (the human in their otherness: *autrui*) is brought to presence, violence awaits or has already summoned. Its advent is perhaps not inevitable (at least in the murderous forms evoked in this essay), but this is a most tenuous "perhaps," since a form of violence inheres as a possibility in language itself: a negating power that is not only inseparable from the hospitable word, but perhaps also irremediably so. We will remember that Blanchot's statement in "Reflexions on Hell" devoted to Camus's meditation on the revolutionary's "I cannot" and to the gaze of Orpheus (as it takes form in and from his song) is powerfully insistent in that regard. The exposure of the other, we read there, occurs *with* an imminent violence. *The Instant of My Death* offered Blanchot's own testimony regarding the exposure of death by death. Could we think this exposure differently, or inhabit it differently?

The readings of "The Infinite Conversation" and *The Step Not Beyond* undertaken here have brought an answer that might be restated as follows: there is a writing that does not just hold death in abeyance through so many nights; here, exposure occurs in a turn that opens upon the infinite of the desert that is given in that exposure. In this advance, the desert (*midbar*) of separation opens to the speaking of the other relation; the desert itself becomes the site of a threshold for this speaking (*dibur*).[1]

Had Blanchot not pointed to something like this from the very opening of "Reflections on Hell" with his evocation of a movement in which the desert "becomes friend"? The contrast offered with the subsequent reflections on Sisyphus and "the man of revolt" remains largely latent in the essay, but by retracing its terms now, it may be possible to underscore once more the significance of the turn just evoked. Let us recall again this opening, which is a bit more enigmatic than it might first appear.

> One can reflect on this situation. It can happen that someone is very close to us, not close: the walls have fallen. Sometimes still very close, but without relation: the walls have fallen, those that separate, and also those that serve to transmit

Through the Double Imperative 227

signals, the language of prisons. Then one must again raise a wall, ask for a little indifference, that calm distance by which lives find equilibrium. A naïve desire that takes form after having already been realized. But from such an astonishing approach, one retains the impression that there was a brief moment of luck; a moment bound not to the favour of the look that may have been exchanged, but to something like a movement that would have preceded us both, just before our encounter. At this instant it seems that *he* was truly our companion in an infinite and infinitely deserted space where, by a marvelous chance, he had suddenly appeared at our side; so it was and so it was going to be, inexplicable, certain, and marvelous. But who was *he*? Only the desert, perhaps? The desert become our companion? Marvelous, this remains marvellously desolate, and then the companion has once again disappeared—there is nothing but desert. But in its harsh truth and arid presence it is suddenly close to us, familiar, a friend. A proximity that at the same time says to us: "*the desert is growing.*" (IC 171/256)[2]

The walls have fallen and suddenly *one is there* in an unmediated proximity. But this nearness without relation also seems marked by a chance event that has prepared the meeting (the stuttering of the second and third sentences appears to say this fold, and perhaps take into their folding the formation of a desire for mediation). The accompaniment that occurs here, for one and perhaps for the other, thus engages *il*, and as this last companion recedes (was *he/it* ever there?), a familiar proximity, a form of friendship with the desert itself is given to what is effectively a solitude, for one or more. The advent of *il*, that "relaying" trace of alterity, thus gives the space from which "it" comes and onto which it opens as one of a possible speech or writing. Nihilism thereby shows another face.

Nietzsche's phrase "the desert grows" is given at least another valence (±), or *turned*, in this preface to an examination of Camus's confrontation with nihilism in the figure of Sisyphus and in the figure of revolt he seeks to couple to the Sisyphean affirmation for a thought of its overcoming.[3] The reading is generous, but it is also forceful. We see this from the outset, as Blanchot opens Camus's reflection on suffering to its limitless "truth," which is to withdraw from the one who undergoes it the space they require to suffer it and the promise of that little time that would hold it within the realm of the possible. A suffering that exposes to the impossible thereby joins abjection, affliction, oppression, misery, and then hunger, sickness, and fear as experiences that render the individual an empty neutrality. Thus while the experience may be lived in a particular, individual manner, it belongs already to the anonymous relations of multitudes ("It seems that an infinite in number is the truth of this other form of affliction," IC 173/258). The experience of this neutral of suffering opens to an unbinding collectivity without count, an "equality" of "infinite dissemblance" that escapes any political determination (be this in the determining initiative of a collective revolt).

Despite the glimpse it offers of this desolate site of affliction, Camus had sought in the experience of Sisyphus ("a man who still works, but uselessly; deprived of the work of time, but not freed from the absence of time, he is given over by this absence to the measurelessness of an eternal rebeginning," IC 175/261–262) an incipient affirmation that gives way to the "no" of the one who revolts. Camus's Sisyphus is thus very close to Marx's proletarian, Blanchot observes (and perhaps even closer, we would have to add, to that experience from which "refusal" takes its origin, in Blanchot's account). For Blanchot, however, the endless return of Sisyphus could never be articulated with the revolt of the slave because it offers no ground; Sisyphus's rock figures an exposure to the outside that disrupts his relation to himself. There is an affirmation in the passion of Sisyphus, but this is the effect of a no that is powerless to negate, a no that cannot begin but can only rebegin, a no in which speaks a yes of dissimulation. Camus's claim that the absurdity of this trial might vanish with its own affirmation and thus give way to a movement of revolt risks becoming a mask in which nihilism dissimulates and propagates itself all the more effectively. Even more grave, Blanchot adds, it risks masking that access a confrontation with nihilism might give to "a dimension of ourselves no longer measured by force [*puissance*]" (IC 178/266).

I pass over crucial pages in which Blanchot documents the manner in which Camus skirts an issue that Hegel seizes in passing (by a jump) from the yes/no of the absurd into the progression of the dialectic. He is deeply respectful of Camus's wariness of the forms of violence that attend the employment of the negative. But is there a path other than that of the Hegelian (Marxian) solution that Blanchot acknowledges as perhaps the only way of acceding to a possible world (IC 181/271)? Are we not obliged to negate the haunting "error" of Sisyphus, even if the conceptual means for drawing this experience into the grasp of the negative remain elusive? Was that not, in fact, the solution Blanchot himself had identified as necessary in seeking the path from a just speech into a just political order in the context of the camps?[4]

We have already considered at length the exposition that follows as Blanchot finds in Camus's reflections on those he named "the Just" (derided by others as "nihilists") evidence of a speaking that would expose without negating the naked presence of the human other. Like the speech (the song) of Orpheus, the "I cannot" of Kaliayev draws forth that extreme and irreducible limit of human nakedness and powerlessness that marks the other face of what is named in nihilism. In so doing, it gives the "secret" of language in the form of a self-deferral (destined to become in Blanchot's thinking a time that effaces time) and marks the limit of the negative. But, as we have reiterated in returning to this essay, this exposure is destined, as it is in the case of Orpheus, to a violent end. The negative was always waiting. Does that same end await the companion in the desert? Will the cause of justice in a "possible" world always exact some such sacrifice? And must the "double" solution to which Blanchot gave a provisional and uneasy assent in seeking to meet both the exigencies of social justice and that more obscure exigency drawn forth in literary writing take the same fatal turn?[5]

"Reflections on Hell" does not permit this last set of conclusions. The violence of the negative may form a kind of horizon in this text, but its movement of reflection repeatedly turns to a space not defined by that horizon. There is little ground for concluding from its pages that surrender to the Hegelian solution is inevitable. On the contrary (but without countering), it gestures insistently toward the other experience of the desert even as it explores the ambiguities of the desert meeting. Perhaps the furtive companion was something more than a mirage, but does not fascination hold dangers as great as those of a delusional errancy in that vacant space? Undoubtedly it does, but the latter question will carry Blanchot into the topic of desire in the last pages of his essay, and thus to another articulation of "the exigency of another relation" in the most extreme void of the other night (IC 192/287). The essay thus reiterates, from beginning to end, the call for that other turning that we have attempted to follow under the rubric of "*le pas au-delà*" and that "The Infinite Conversation" had figured under the name of writing.

Have we regressed in thus returning to an essay that appears only to gesture repeatedly toward a messianic end as it deconstructs solutions to the question of nihilism and advances into an abyssal space (of desire)? "Reflections on Hell" offers something more, however, than a seductive promise. Read in the light of *The Unavowable Community* and *The Step Not*

Beyond, it can be seen to be opening to a thought of community that reveals the necessarily provisional and insufficient character of the double imperative Blanchot described to Bataille and articulated in *The Infinite Conversation* in terms of two "irreconcilable" movements (IC 65/92): "*to name* the possible, *to respond* to the impossible." To glimpse this insufficiency, one need only weigh the question Blanchot poses to dialectic in this essay and then consider the question of the orientation of this dual imperative: *for whom* must one speak, and *from where*?[6] Was Blanchot's commitment to social justice not essentially directed toward those suffering oppression under the forms enumerated in this essay: affliction, fear, and so forth (even as it was articulated, on occasion, in quite formal language, as in the thought of the right to dissidence)? Was he not seeking to speak ultimately for those vulnerable others who will at some point be cast as *abject* by a political order that must deny them on the grounds of its definition of what counts as political subjectivity—for those in our societies who inhabit the realm of Sisyphus if only by their condemnation to an infinite of labor that found a grim, ultimate figure of its absurdity in the murderous labor of the death camps? "A region announced by extreme suffering, extreme affliction, the desolation of shadows, a region approached, in life, by all those who, having lost the world, move about *between* being and nothingness; a swarming mass of inexistence, proliferation without reality, the vermin of nihilism: ourselves" (IC 179/268). The last statement, concluding in an astonishing first person, does not grant the grounds of a comfortable solidarity to those of "us" who have not known the real oppression most of these terms connote (not to speak of the extremity of the conditions in the camps). It suggests, instead, that "we" have almost inevitably failed to recognize the nature of the prisons we inhabit within the walls to which the essay refers, and that if we should happen to confront this slavery and open to the truth that speaks from in and beyond it (that is, from the neutral known in our own exposure to the slavery of others), we might glimpse and begin to *think and bring to speech* the exigency of another community in the very abyss of that "community without community" onto which suffering opens at its limits.

The vocation of the (committed) writer, Blanchot wrote to Catherine David, is itself a double one. It entails, first (in the order of Blanchot's phrasing), "saving the place of the one who will come"—a task that is in turn double since it involves both the contestation of any usurping authority (thus criticism and refusal) and the effort of holding open the indefinite, multiple place of *il*. We need not retrace the latter movement, which belongs to *The Step Not Beyond* as a whole. The writer's vocation then includes—but would this not be first?—the obligation of maintaining "the immemorial memory that we were slaves, that even liberated we remain and will remain slaves as long as others remain so, that there is thus no freedom (to put it too simply) except for others and through others." Again, critique in some measure, and a call for a universal freedom that implies the imperative of a political solution or solutions of a general reach directed against oppression. This statement is not made from a place of freedom, however, or a given knowledge of what freedom might be (however "free" we might take ourselves to be). Freedom, we read, is *for the other* and *through the other*. Thus, a political stance cannot involve speaking "for" the other except insofar as this "for" denotes, originally, an absolute ethical priority accorded to the other and a "responsibility for" that takes its meaning from substitution in the sense Blanchot drew from Levinas. And who would this other be if not, each time, the singular, and with them, the infinite number submerged in fear, affliction, and fatigue—among whom the ones who seek this stance must always learn again to count themselves (hence the imperative of an immemorial memory). Only from here, which is to say, from the exposure known in this shared relation, would the didactic stance (and statements of general import) gain its truth. Again, there is freedom only with and through the other.[7] Freedom must be thought from relation, and its condition is a hospitable opening that *The Step Not Beyond* figured for us from the ground of the encounter of the young girl with the one afraid in the street. Does the imperative of the didactic relation, which Blanchot affirms immediately after his statement about the ethical ground of freedom, not therefore cede in priority to the task of *learning to speak*? Must the imperative of the teaching relation, as regards both ethics and politics themselves, not take form in, and end in, an act of hospitality? Is this not what Blanchot attempted to give us in *The Step Not Beyond* from the encounter in the streets to the saying of *"viens"*? The *vocation* of the committed writer must be defined by a call that occurs in relation to the other.

To this side hospitality, to the other, solidarity.[8] As we have seen, Blanchot recognized fully the pressures that force the writer into a didactic position. These have their origin in nothing other than the necessity of representation in the established (or to be established) public space—the requirement of naming political injustice and identifying the conditions for its overcoming. Thus the need for rigorous, insistent exposition, and often struggle. However ferocious his assault on representation in seeking to "affirm the rupture" in May and thereafter, it seems evident that Blanchot retained the imperative of naming the possible for the sake of general conditions of justice. But the cause(s) of justice for the oppressed inevitably drove him past the terms of the double imperative he articulated in his letter to Bataille because he clearly recognized that no modern political reason directed to emancipation (at least as defined in the political thought of modernity) could address the question *"for whom?"* from any ground other than that of the metaphysics of subjectivity. The experience of *all of us*, he saw, will at some point exceed and fall from the dialectical account, and this account can only foreclose the neutral to which affliction (or fear, or anguish, or the like) opens. The dialectic, perhaps any effort to say the whole (to recall Blanchot's phrase from his notes for *The International Journal*, for which see the following appendix), will block the affirmative turn that Blanchot sought to think and say. Blanchot would have recognized in the founding principles of human rights the same limitations. No struggle for equality can give this term its *human* meaning without recalling in some manner the fundamental inequality (and an exposure to something beyond the human) that lies at the heart of what Blanchot can only hesitantly name the ethical relation (IC 63/89), just as no true speech can occur that does not recall the irreducible separation that renders speech possible. The task, therefore, must be to retain, in speech, a fidelity to the abyssal ground of human relations, despite the danger. Returning to the scene in the desert, Blanchot asks whether it would not be entirely reasonable to interrupt the encounter with the stranger and raise a wall in accordance with the second dimension of the double imperative (the necessity of mediation for a possible communication, if only to preserve the meaning of this experience). But then he turns again to the other dimension of that imperative, suggesting that its "meaning" cannot rest within meaning and requires the risk of another turn:

> There is perhaps no experience more dangerous, more doubtful, but also, perhaps, more essential; for what it suggests to us is that the proximity and force of communication depend—to a certain extent, but to what extent?—upon the absence of relation. What it also suggests is that one be—to a certain extent, but this is precisely an extent without measure—faithful to this absence

of relation and faithful also to the risk one runs in rejecting all relation. As though, finally, this fidelity—a fidelity where faithfulness is not possible—this risk, this migration without rest across the space of the desert and the dispersion of hell could also bloom in the intimacy of communication. (IC 176/263–264)

Clearly, it cannot suffice to assert that every naming in the order of the possible must remember the response to the impossible that certain forms of writing seek to prevent us from forgetting. It cannot suffice to say that this commitment to the possible must not foreclose the emergence of other relations (another community, if you will, that involves an altogether different affirmation of freedom). For every saying in the order of the possible will perforce forget, and however much it attempts to remark its forgetting, it will never accede to that profound forgetting from which affirmation comes. We are therefore enjoined to think solidarity with and from hospitality in order to redefine freedom from an immanent relation to those experiences of affliction (each of which open at some point onto "dying") from which none of us are free. Writing will take its place here, and part of its imperative will be to hold open what is exposed in this relation, to shield from the violence of the possible itself for the sake of another relation.

This perhaps too simply stated turning of the double imperative, whereby we urge an attempt to name the possible from response to the impossible and seek social justice from the nonground of another community, may appear to hold political response forever hostage to an impossible engagement of the impossible. But while the necessary orientation is clear, it cannot be a matter of a simple inversion of standard priorities (which dictate securing justice first and then attending to those dimensions of experience that might be seen as exceeding the political domain itself). A more supple vigilance is obviously required, a constant turning between solidarity and hospitality in various modalities of urgency and patience. Nor is peace in any way guaranteed. If we take into account Blanchot's insistent reference to the notion of refusal, we recognize that response to affliction will of necessity take a very hard form in some circumstances (one that is itself sometimes without ground in the perspective of political reason).

Refusal takes its origin, we remember, in the near-silent speaking of the weak or vulnerable; it comes from beyond the established categories of political subjectivity. This also means that it is not finally separable from the affirmative turn we have sought to follow, as we saw in "The Infinite

Conversation" and *The Madness of the Day*. Thus, in the sphere of ethico-political relations, the double imperative is in fact displaced, without being eliminated, by this other that is at the very heart of Blanchot's thought: refusal/affirmation. At the same time, Blanchot establishes a clear imperative from the ground of the notion that all extreme suffering is shared (be this in a solitary manner). Such suffering, such *dying*, leads, as the essay on Camus tells us, into an experience of nihilism confronted by the greatest number, and from which modern political solutions can only turn, thus comforting nihilism itself. Blanchot would have us recognize (and here again we see the need for the didactic function) that the abject, fearful, anguished other is in fact already in us. Thus we start from a political imperative that Blanchot might have found in Leviticus: allow strangeness to be native to you.[9] Here, a possible community sets at its ground conditions of peace that forever require the thought and practice of what Blanchot termed writing, itself violent in relation to law ("every law, and also its own," IC xii/viii), but also harboring the promised relation in the benevolence of a step made as though it were the last one.

APPENDIX

Blanchot in *The International Review*

The circumstances surrounding the attempted creation and eventual abandonment of *The International Review*, as it came to be called, are now well established. For a period of several years in the early 1960s, a number of prominent intellectuals from Europe and North America pursued actively the project of simultaneous publication in at least three languages (French, German, and Italian) of a literary journal of a radically innovative form. Commitments at an organizational level came from individuals such as Hans Magnus Enzensberger, Leszek Kolakowski, Dionys Mascolo, Maurice Blanchot, Louis-René des Forêts, Uwe Johnson, Elio Vittorini, and Francesco Lionetti, and throughout the relevant documents we find mention of associations involving figures such as Michel Leiris, Roland Barthes, Pier Paolo Pasolini, Italo Calvino, Alberto Moravia, Ingeborg Bachmann, Martin Walser, Günter Grass, Carlos Fuentes, and Iris Murdoch. The projected scale of participation was immense, and the documents speak consistently to the awareness that what was sought was an entirely new form of literary intervention in the public world.

The essential facts regarding the participation of Maurice Blanchot in this venture are also established, and I will pause over them only to note that this ambitious international project gripped Blanchot's attention at a moment that very soon followed his public reentry into the French political world in response to Charles de Gaulle's seizure of power in May 1958. Having participated in the drafting of the *Déclaration du droit à l'insubordination* (to which he offered the title and the crucial notion of a *right* to insubordination in the course of an intense effort at joint writing), and having faced the juridical pressure that ensued, Blanchot concluded that French intellectuals were traversing a critical juncture that required new forms of commitment and collective action. Thus, in addition to the powerful brief statement published in October 1958 in the second issue of *Le 14 juillet*, "*Le refus*,"[1] we have a letter to Sartre applauding his intention of transforming the format of *Les temps modernes* in response to the new political and intellectual configuration.

Blanchot's letter to Sartre has been appropriately cited as a crucial document for understanding his thinking in this important moment of renewed political intervention. It does more, in fact, than applaud Sartre's recognition of the importance of literature for this political moment and his acknowledgment of "the new relations involving political responsibility and literary responsibility, as manifested by the *Déclaration*" (L 219). It calls upon Sartre to respond to what Blanchot describes as the emergence of a new consciousness of the role of intellectuals. The *Déclaration*, Blanchot writes, recalling Sartre's own reaction, had brought to the fore a historical and sociopolitical exigency that revealed in the action of its signatories a new "power of decision" to which they were summoned to respond (L 218). In the same movement, their acts had revealed, through the "impersonal force" of the *Déclaration*, a new form of collective being; the *Déclaration* figured for them "an anonymous community of names" (L 218). Sartre was now invited to embrace the change that was occurring and to help mark it for the intellectual world as a public event by joining a new project that would be committed to a practice of 'total critique':

> I believe . . . that a review of *total critique*, critique in which literature would be grasped in its proper meaning (also with the help of texts), where scientific discoveries, often very poorly set forth, would be subject to the trial of a general

critique, where all the structures of our world, all the forms of existence in this world would come into a single movement of examination, research, and contestation—a review, therefore, where the word "critique" would also recover its sense, which is to be global, would have today, precisely today, an importance and a force of action that would be very great. (L 220)

When Blanchot concludes his letter to Sartre by evoking the shared presentiment of an approaching crisis "that will only render more manifest the critical situation that is our own" (and dwarf many of its aspects; L 220), we have all the elements of the thinking that will justify the step toward the project of *The International Review*.

When the step is made, however, Blanchot gives his name to something more than we might have anticipated. He dramatically redefines the character of the event to which he has invited Sartre to respond, and he rethinks the nature of a collective response. He tells us, more precisely, *how* a new thought of literary responsibility in an international context will be elaborated. The coherence of this thinking—at least a crucial line of it—is arresting, and if I should succeed in drawing it forth in these few pages, it may catch the reader's attention forcefully enough to prompt the question as to whether this text holds some form of summons for contemporary thought.

It is evident that the step to which I have alluded comes via Blanchot's association with Dionys Mascolo, the editor of *Le 14 juillet*. Blanchot's response to Mascolo's initiative in this last venture could not have been more absolute: "I want to express my accord. I refuse all of the past and I accept nothing of the present."[2] A bridge is made here with Blanchot's thought of refusal, but the accord also involved an assent that carried Blanchot into a dialogue concerning the new international initiative. Whether it is in fact Mascolo who prompts in Blanchot this attention to the international character of the crisis he had evoked in his letter to Sartre, or whether the exchange was more complex (the internal working papers devoted to the project of the review attributed to Mascolo and Blanchot, respectively, are very similar, and we must not forget the other associates in this collective project), it is clear that Blanchot's political understanding is at least momentarily *seized* by this motif. The strength of Blanchot's recognition of the urgency of an international perspective is given immediately in the opening paragraph of his reflections on the meaning and projected form of the review as he defines the "gravity" of the project at hand. Citing the motif of a "change in times" that he also developed in dialogical form in a brief text of 1960,[3] Blanchot "ontologizes," we might say, the *sense* of urgency he evokes in his letter to Sartre: "We are all aware that we are approaching an extreme movement in these times, what I would call a change of times" (PW 56/179).[4] He then declares that this sense of crisis does not relate solely to the French context, or to that of any other particular site, but rather derives from the fact that all problems are now of an international order, and every international problem is now "insoluble." Thus, to the argument of Blanchot's dialogical essay "On a Change of Epoch," which addressed the meaning of the global sway of a new order of *Technik*, Blanchot brings an overlying development that brings an essential and dangerous ambiguity to every situation. The essay on the "Change of Epoch" had in fact touched on the presence of the nuclear menace and situated it within the enumeration of the fundamental symptoms of a change in times; but the new statements allude to a different understanding of this menace in the context of the Cold War and seem to give a more determining character to factors such as the unstable stricture of "nuclear deterrence." Little analysis is offered of the governing "state of tension," but it is difficult to read the statement that this state of affairs excludes any traditional idea of peace and cannot be resolved by a "good old, classical war" (PW 56/179) without bringing to bear a thought of the question of nuclear terror.

The latter theme will not be further developed in Blanchot's working papers for the *Review* (though we find another reference to it in the closing notes via a question regarding its bearing on a "change in meaning in the notion of violence"; PW 65/190–191). The emphasis shifts, rather, to the implications of the fundamental assertion that the *Review* must "be ceaselessly focused on its own gravity" (PW 56/179) by responding to the enigma of a change in times. Blanchot starts, here, with a striking statement: "The project is essentially collective, as it is so on an international scale" (PW 56/180). The phrasing is muted enough to forestall a question about the adequacy of the explanation that follows it (to which I will return). When it is paired with an equally challenging sentence that occurs after a subsequent treatment of the imperative of discussion and dialogue for a collective venture of this kind, it becomes clear that Blanchot is genuinely confronting the implications of his assertion that the extremity of the moment requires a particular form of collective response. The sentence to which I have referred opens the second paragraph of the second part of Blanchot's reflections on the exigencies defining the project and the form of response that must be sought:

> For the current project for a review, such a necessity [of discussion and dialogue] is even more imposing; as an international review, it must be so in an essential manner; not only multinational, nor universal in the sense of an abstract universality, maintaining only a vague and empty identity based on the problems addressed, but a placing in common of literary, philosophical, political and social problems as they are posed according to the determination of each language and within each national context. (PW 57–58/181)

In brief, and to repeat, we are told that the project is *essentially* collective because it is collective on an international scale and that the project can only be essentially international if it achieves a genuinely international form of collectivity. An impatient reader could assume, from this nearly tautological formulation, that Blanchot is simply adapting his thinking to the circumstances of the project and that a rather banal necessity dictates this focus on collective interaction. But Blanchot has in fact fundamentally recast his commitment to collectivity as it is stated in the letter to Sartre. He has done this under the pressure of his claim, dramatically stated in the concluding paragraph of the first section, that what is at stake in this project is "the search for truth, or a certain just demand, perhaps a demand for justice, for which the literary affirmation, by its interest in the centre, by its unique relation to language, is essential" (PW 57/180–181). Any effort to articulate the truth (or justice) of this extreme moment will bring forth a new meaning of collectivity inasmuch as a just response cannot be thought either merely locally or through some universalizing formulation.

The question of the review's collective functioning is indissociable from the question of its form and must therefore be pursued farther if we are to grasp the meaning of Blanchot's statement that this review might be said to be essentially in search of its form (PW 63/188). I hinted earlier that Blanchot's initial explanation of the meaning of a collective organization did not seem to meet the strength of his appeal to it. The explanation reads as follows: "This means, not that we seek a thought that would be common to all, to all the participants, but that through a placing in common of our efforts, our questions, and our resources, above all through an internal movement carrying us beyond our own thought, we might bring forth new possibilities" (PW 56/180). Such an argument is already implicit in the letter to Sartre: a collective undertaking will carry individuals beyond their solitary trajectories and into a space of exchange where a movement that is not proper to any individual claims their thinking. But what does a "placing in common" (the phase appears twice) imply in the international context Blanchot evokes? How will a collegial structure or a multiplication of discussions and exchanges further this movement? If the task is to exceed a genial sharing of perspectives (serving a form of cultural pluralism), and to avoid an abstract consensus or universalism, if the collective is to become truly genetic, to use Kolakowski's term,[5] then a more concrete form of exchange must be achieved.

Blanchot's initial statements about the collective structure of the review thus seem insufficient. However, the course of his reflection points to a movement at the core of this venture that would realize the concreteness he demands when he evokes terms such as "truth" or "justice." We already catch a glimpse of what is involved when Blanchot refers early in his papers to the manner in which literary, philosophical, political and social issues must be placed in common from the grounds of the way they are posed according to "the determination of each language" (PW 58/181). To take the meaning of these words forward, we need to pause over Blanchot's comments on the scope of this endeavor and the place of literature.

We have seen that the endeavor is conceived as *international*—a description that may be said to have a potentially global extension even if the collectivity devoted to it remains merely European in its constitution. Every problem or question, Blanchot tells us, has an international determination; this is one defining trait of the "change in times" that must be thought. But the ambition of the review, in Blanchot's understanding, reaches beyond the aim of capturing this international determination of every sociopolitical issue; it seeks to think every question or problem from the perspective of the *whole* and with an attention to what *exceeds* the whole:

> There are very few things that should interest us in this review, or in other words we should not give the impression that we are interested in and curious about everything. Or rather, we should be interested only in the whole, there where the whole is at stake, and always regain this interest in and passion for the whole; then, we must ask ourselves if the essential interest does not also lead to that which is outside the whole. (PW 57/180)

These words will be developed in subsequent pages in terms of a divergence between a horizon of questioning that is embraced by dialectic (conceived in a sense that is essentially determined by the Marxian legacy, but also surpasses it) and an "exigency" of literature and art that carries us beyond this horizon. Readers of Blanchot will be familiar with this divergence between the order of the possible covered by dialectical reasoning and the order of literary experience, a "fundamental" order of research engaging a "power without power" that is "perhaps not subsumed by possibility" (PW 58/182). They will also be familiar with Blanchot's insistence that both orders must be affirmed in what they entail of an irreducible responsibility:

> There seems to result from this an irreducible difference and even a discordance between a political responsibility that is at once global and concrete, accepting Marxism as nature and dialectic as a method of truth, and literary responsibility, a responsibility that is a response to an exigency that can only take form in and through literature.
>
> This discordance need not be reduced from the outset. It is a given; it exists as a problem, not a frivolous problem, but one to be borne with difficulty, all the more difficult in that each of the discordant terms engages us absolutely and in that their dissonance, in a sense, engages us as well. (PW 59/183)

These last words form point 5 of part II of Blanchot's working reflections. Point 6 affirms quite simply that there exist "elements of a solution" that the review will have to explore.

The solution Blanchot will explore in the subsequent pages of his reflection will not take a form that might in any way be described as a surreptitious return of dialectic. It also gives the notion of a "placing in common" of problems, questions and approaches a radical twist since it defines both the space of this juxtaposition and the nature of the dialogical interchange in which it might unfold or which might result from it in ways that deny any simple conceptual or affective accord. The notion by which Blanchot explores this solution, the notion of the *fragment*, will set the question of the review's collective and international character on an original path.

The appearance of the motif of fragmentary writing first appears via a proposition that the review's central undertaking (something that would constitute its spine or guiding "element": its *fil conducteur*) would consist of parallel chronicles, one a reflection of the "intellectual course of things," established by contributions from each editorial group and focusing essentially on literary events (taking this phrase in a broad sense), the second more dialogical and critical, unfolding the political situation and "general movement of the world" (PW 60/184). The proposal suits brilliantly Blanchot's dedication to the question of a change in times, though we cannot presume that it is properly Blanchot's. Nor can we assume that the description of the serial structure of the chronicle, or the appeal to the "short form" in music (PW 61/186) are really to be attributed specifically to Blanchot. The appeal to the fragmentary dimension of these very contemporary forms, however, points us toward a distinctly Blanchotian space that Blanchot himself will explore increasingly in the coming decades.

I do not want to suggest that Blanchot's motif of the fragment effectively overwhelms the proposals for the envisioned chronicle addressed to the *"cours des choses."* An intriguing suggestion for the constitution of a kind of counterhistory through a juxtaposition of soberly edited items of information ("the elements of a true and more secret history" [PW 62/186]) should be noted in this regard. But the meaning and purpose of the chronicle, as stated by Blanchot, would seem only to be served, in the strongest sense, by the notion of the fragment that Blanchot advances in these pages, for only the fragment achieves the address to "the whole" and "what is beyond the whole" in a way that meets the literary responsibility Blanchot seeks to articulate in and through the review.

> The purpose of the review is to try to prepare a new possibility, one that would permit the writer to *say* the "world" and everything that takes place in the world, but as a writer and in the perspective proper to the writer, with the responsibility that comes solely from the writer's truth: thus, a form of responsibility that is totally different (though no less essential) from that which brutally characterized relations between literature and public life from 1945 on, known under the simplistic name of "Sartrean commitment." (PW 60/185)

Blanchot's manner of evoking the possibility that the review is to prepare indicates strongly that the term "world" has taken a Heideggerian inflection and points to a totality of experience that can only be given as a "totality" by a literary engagement with language that involves something of the order of what Heidegger termed the "essence" of language. "Totality" is a precarious word here, for it must accommodate not only what Blanchot designates in the opening paragraph of his reflections as an "insoluble" state of affairs (as determined by international tensions), but even a form of experience that involves what Blanchot will call, in his definition of the fragment, an essential discontinuity (PW 61/186).[6] I will turn shortly to a powerful example of the kind of discontinuity Blanchot seeks to think. I want first to emphasize Blanchot's attention to the way this "saying" of the world in a change in times must entail a particular engagement with language as such (to use Benjamin's term), or the "being" of language, and thus its "original power" or "power without power" to proffer something like "world."[7]

Blanchot's reference to the question of language is relatively discreet, but it is insistent, and it surfaces fairly dramatically when Blanchot turns to the problem of translation and declares that the translator will be, in a certain sense, "the true writer of the review" (PW 62/187). This declaration is predicated upon an understanding of translation as an "original" form of literary activity that Blanchot illustrates with a powerful evocation of Hölderlin's translations of *Oedipus* and *Antigone* (PW 62/187). The latter discussion, strongly reminiscent of Benjamin in respect to the question of the difference between languages, clearly signals at what level the question of language is being engaged in this essay. The translator's intervention in language must touch upon the essence of any individual language. All literary "saying" must be thought at this level.

It is not insignificant that the most extended discussion of the fragment—a discussion that reaches the same rhetorical pitch as the preceding one on translation—appears immediately after the points made about the "difference between languages" (a difference that includes a *historial* dimension: "the languages are never contemporaneous" [PW 62/187]) and the subsequent remarks on the extremity of "the example of Hölderlin" [PW 62/187]). The understanding of the problem of translation points to an always fragmentary saying of being. This is clearly a critical issue for an international undertaking that seeks a "placing in common" of sociopolitical or ethico-political issues and seeks responses ("to say the world") with a global reach. "How is one to maintain this difference of historical level in a translation?" Blanchot asks (PW 62/187). Then there is the problem of dialects—a problem "never adequately resolved" (PW 62/187) and differently pressing for each of the languages involved in the undertaking. A traditional understanding of the task of translation, even a relatively sophisticated one, would not indicate here an insurmountable problem. Blanchot's reference to the fragment serves to draw out the issue as one with radical implications for this collective project. Clearly, Blanchot wants to link the question of the difference of languages to the topic he broaches under the phrase "essential discontinuity" in his enumeration of the different ways in which one might grasp the fragment.

But a very significant step is made when he moves to define this notion of discontinuity, for he appears to open the notion of "saying the world" to dimensions of experience that would unsettle even what he has evoked thus far with respect to the question of translation. Thus, he speaks of a literature of the fragment that is "situated outside the whole, either because it supposes that the whole is already realized (all literature is the literature of the end of time) or because next to forms of language in which the whole is constructed and speaks—the speech of knowledge, work, and salvation—it senses an entirely different speech that frees thought from being merely a thought with unity in view, demanding, in other words, an essential discontinuity" (PW 63/188).[8] This statement does not indicate that he has left behind the question of the difference of languages (the saying of this difference would already lead into the space he evokes); but it does seem to point at the same time toward his understanding of the *il y a*—and here we would meet Levinas—or his later thought of *le neutre*.

To use a Blanchotian abbreviation, we could say that this "step" will have all the distended complexity of Blanchot's *"pas au-delà"* and leads to the heart of the question Blanchot seeks to address when he remarks on the divergence between literary and political responsibility. Can a "saying of the world" include the writing of the neutral or the *il y a* and achieve a form of ethico-political responsibility? With Levinas, but also moving beyond him with this thought of literature and language, Blanchot clearly thinks it can. An *integral* response to the discontinuities of factical existence in the world is possible by way of the fragment, presuming that an "integral" meaning is grasped in its becoming. In brief, Blanchot wants to affirm the essential finitude of every act of "saying the world" and is thereby led to understand the elaboration of the review's chronicle as an arrangement, perhaps a *relay* of singular events of writing. Collective work at an international level must be thought from the grounds of this structure of fragmentary communication.

It is time to focus a bit more precisely on this question of the fragment, and for this purpose I would like to turn from the "working pages" I have been commenting to a brief text by Blanchot—a fragment—prepared for *The International Review*: his stunning meditation on "Berlin" (PW 73–75).

This is a text that says very precisely what it means to live an insoluble problem, and is no less precise about what it means to try to say this. We find here, in fact, an explicit discussion of the fragment.

The text reads initially as an enumeration of the levels—political, socioeconomic, "metaphysical," existential, linguistic—at which we might understand the problem of "division." Punctuated with an insistent "this is not all," the writing is intense and jagged, leaving its shifts of perspective without mediation:

> Berlin is not only Berlin, but the symbol of the division of the world. . . . That is not all. Berlin is not a symbol, it is a real city where human dramas are lived that other large cities cannot know: here the division should be called a tearing (PW 73).

Blanchot offers no resolution of perspectives as he moves between the declaration that Berlin is "for all" (any thinking human being, as he says at a later point; PW 73) the problem of division, and evocations of the singularity of the experience of dwelling in this place (for each of its citizens) that offers no possibility of dwelling. Blanchot's emphasis, however, does not fall simply on discontinuity; it falls, rather, on the *indivisible* character of this problem of division. No individual aspect of Berlin can be rendered truthfully in isolation, he suggests. Thus, while no full mediation of perspectives is possible, "Berlin" demands in thought and in writing a "complete" formulation. The problem of division presented by Berlin must be rendered, each time there is an effort to render it, in its totality. This can be done only fragmentarily:

> In other words, every time we evoke a problem of this kind—there are others, after all—we should remind ourselves that to speak of it in a just manner, we must also let the abrupt wanting of our words and our thoughts speak, we must let speak the impossibility of speaking of it in a supposedly exhaustive manner.[9]

The *situation* that is Berlin, an irreducibly existential situation or site of "world" that surrenders to no transcendental perspective, demands, each time, and powerfully, an effort to say the *indivisible* of this worldly situation. Thus, it demands a form of speech or writing that testifies to this exigency as it remarks its own inability to meet it—a writing that must convey both the intransigence of this demand (the imperative of saying the totality of the experience that is Berlin) and the *impossible* of this demand. The "divisions" of Berlin cannot be finally subsumed in any dialectical account; they are irreducible inasmuch as they are traversed by fundamental discontinuities of language and a human experience that Blanchot describes as an irremediable tearing.

The only possibility of saying this world inheres in a saying that communicates its own finitude and thus *relays* the impossible exigency to which it answers, offering meaning in and as an irreducible becoming. Fragmentary writing would relay "the affirmation that meaning, the meaning as integral, could never be immediately in us and in what we write, but is still to come, and that, questioning meaning, we grasp it only as becoming and what will come of the question" (PW 74).

The brief account I have given of this fragmentary writing should be extended into a discussion of Blanchot's struggle with the question of dialectic. The motif of "division" in the text on Berlin signals this problem clearly enough, as does a striking reflection on the problem of *abstraction* presented by a wall that sought to establish, along an oscillating line of enigmatic passage and exchange, a visible and tangible division (PW 74).[10] An immense question of a philosophical-historical order opens here that vastly exceeds the space of the present essay. How do we assess Blanchot's retention of the language of dialectic in this moment of return to a form of writerly political activism, and how do we think it together with the muted references to Heidegger's thought of language and *Technik* and with what Heidegger offers to Blanchot regarding the necessity of fragmentary writing and the place of art for the question of truth (offered by Heidegger in response to Hegel)? I will pause here over merely one point: Blanchot's insistence in this moment that the "truest" or most "just" political intervention is a *literary* intervention that will guide a necessary reflection. It is striking, in the pages I have commented here, how insistently Blanchot suggests that literature must constitute the first step in the search for a "solution" to the problem of the discordance that inheres between political responsibility and literary responsibility. It is no less striking how insistently the motif of the *question* is itself submitted to pressure as Blanchot undertakes the search for a suitable form for the review (PW 64/188–189). The radical character of Blanchot's efforts on behalf of this review lies here, I believe: in this intransigent commitment to the search for a way of "saying" the world that escapes the abstraction of political or "sociological" representation.

I will not attempt to explore the grounds for the failure of this collective venture, for they too require a broad and detailed historical analysis.

It would be necessary to explore the way in the which the German and Italian committees found themselves unable to embrace the French proposals for a "placing in common" by reason of their understanding of the very singularity of their respective situations and intellectual tasks. The divisions between intellectual groups in their national situations proved considerably more recalcitrant than Blanchot had anticipated, and for reasons that cannot be reduced to issues of personality or contingent attitudes. The German committee, in particular, understood the task before them in ways that eventually ruled out any joint address to sociopolitical issues; they saw no grounds for conceiving contemporary divisions or discontinuities as *shared* and ended by seeking contractual conditions for collaborative arrangements. The Italians, for their part, were less distant, but still wary of French mysticism. *Plus ça change*, one is tempted to say. The radical character of the question of situational difference (a genuine challenge to the fragmentary "solution" proposed by Blanchot) seems to have given way to quarrels shaped by national prejudice.

Have global movements (realignments of economic and political power, but also shifts in communicative structure and possibilities) changed these conditions, or pointed to a new necessity of something like collective response on an international level? A cautious answer in the affirmative seems possible, though it is not at all clear that an urgent need for such a response has quite emerged in intellectual circles (nor can we expect this need to emerge as long as the meaning of a *political* intervention on the part of intellectuals remains at once so diffuse and so narrow). What is urgently required, however, is a reflection on the possibilities of drawing forth such a sense of urgency. How do we prepare the grounds for understanding the "power of decision" Blanchot glimpsed in the acts of the 121 signatories of the *Déclaration*? Does this task not entail an exploration of the conditions for *saying*, concretely, the abstraction, but also the opaque facticity of our contemporary world(s)? The hold of the grand theoretical narratives that prevailed in the last quarter of the last century has considerably weakened, and intellectuals, in significant quarters of the West, at least, have found themselves stripped of that symbolic authority that informed the "power" to which Blanchot referred in his letter to Sartre. But the international movement Blanchot sought to institutionalize with his efforts for *The International Review* did not presuppose broad affiliation (at least in numbers), and it did not seek to achieve a theoretical hegemony of any kind.

It presupposed simply the power (without power) of literature and fragmentary writing in general to relay an exigency: the demand, emerging from a sense of ethico-political urgency (sensed with various degrees of lucidity and indissociable from experiences of pain, anxiety, and various forms of existential destitution stemming from the abstraction of the modern world) that intellectuals find ways to think and say their time.

The project failed, I emphasize, and this failure should pose real questions for Blanchot's founding assumptions, including both his faith in the possibility of a dialectical elaboration—however *limited*—of the divisions defining the international context, and his understanding of the relationality that would be brought to language by an international response that would be elaborated through a work of translation. I believe it would be a mistake to write off this failure as somehow inevitable for such a "literary" venture (an attitude that could well be prompted by a remark such as Blanchot's own regarding the utopic character of this project and the necessity of embracing failure utopically). Such an assumption falls critically short of the notion of literature Blanchot sought to evoke. The project for *The International Review*, as Blanchot conceived it, may not have left an "historic index" that might claim the present.[11] But its ambition of *saying* the "world" articulates a need that emerges ever more strongly as the abstraction of most contemporary theory comes into view—and this at a time when an inchoate sense of global change in our sociopolitical world is almost as visceral as the awareness of the new temperatures assailing our bodies.

NOTES

INTRODUCTION

1. The response was published in *Le Nouvel Observateur* in a special issue entitled "Literature" (May 1981). David had asked: "(1) Can a writer today still believe in the virtues of committed [*engagé*] literature? (2) What is the best that this genre has produced, in your opinion? (3) Would you be prepared, under certain circumstances, to write in the service of a cause? If so, which one?" Cited by Zakir Paul in *Maurice Blanchot, Political Writings, 1953–1993* (New York: Fordham University Press, 2010), 193.

2. Ibid., 117–118.

3. Maurice Blanchot, *The Step Not Beyond*, trans. Lycette Nelson (Albany: SUNY Press, 1986), 1/7. (Here and throughout these notes, see the list of abbreviations for the French original, indicated by the second number.)

4. The Jewish ceremony of Pesach urges all Jews to recall their past slavery in Egypt; it effectively calls for a rememoration of the Exodus. I do not doubt that Blanchot was acutely sensitive to this notion.

5. "Peace, peace far and near" ("*Paix, paix au lointain et au proche*") is the title of a contribution to an exhibition catalogue, *De la Bible à nos jours: 3000 ans d'art* (Paris: Société des Artistes Indépendants, 1985). It was published one year after *The Unavowable Community* (Barrytown, N.Y.: Station Hill Press, 1985), and thus it offers some insight into what Blanchot was seeking to bring to articulation in that volume, as I will try to suggest in Chapter 6.

"Near" and "far" are fairly unstable terms in Blanchot's text (they redouble and redefine themselves constantly). But I hear in "near" (and thus also in "far") both *le prochain* (hence *autrui*) and those "third parties" who are near us, though at a distance defined by social mediations; I hear in "far" (and thus "near") both the infinite of the forever inaccessible (the presence of *autrui*) and the imperative of serving *all*.

6. I refer here to Heidegger's response to Jünger, originally entitled "*Über die Linie*," a phrase that undoubtedly remained with Blanchot, who discussed Heidegger's argument with reference to this motif in *The Infinite Conversation*, trans. Susan Hanson (Minneapolis: University of Minnesota Press, 1993), 150/225–227).

7. Lycette Nelson discusses the challenges presented to the translator by the phrase "*le pas au-delà*" in the introduction to her translation of *The Step Not Beyond*, noting that its meaning is radically ambiguous, since "*pas*" can mean either "step" or "not," thereby giving, literally, "the step beyond" or "the not beyond." Prohibition and transgression, as well as a confounding of transcendence and immanence (which produces a very radical understanding of the structure of "finite transcendence"), are said in the same phrase. Blanchot's textual deployment of the phrase renders its signifying play even more disruptive, particularly as one reads it in relation to the many occurrences of "*pas*" in Blanchot's writings.

8. I will translate this term with both "the neutral" and "the neuter," depending on context, and with a preference for the latter whenever it is thought in relation to language. Both terms are in fact required in many instances, and I will sometimes revert simply to the French.

9. Blanchot, *The Infinite Conversation*, xxiii/xxvi.

10. Maurice Blanchot, *The Madness of the Day*, trans. Lydia Davis (Barrytown, N.Y.: Station Hill Press, 1981), 6.

11. And, fortunately, they continue to inspire critical attention. See, for example, Mark Hewson, *Blanchot and Literary Criticism* (London: Routledge, 2009).

12. There is an important exception to this statement: Leslie Hill's *Maurice Blanchot and Fragmentary Writing* (New York: Continuum, 2012), which contains a significant chapter on *The Step Not Beyond* and which reached completion at almost exactly the same time as this volume. This is a most impressive piece of work with which I am in profound agreement. Hill brings forth powerfully, through impeccable scholarship and brilliant reading, the meaning of Blanchot's coupling of "the neuter the fragmentary." Though our readings of *The Step Not Beyond* follow different paths, their profound affinity surfaces, I believe, in relation to our respective approaches to Blanchot's political thought. Because this manuscript reached me at such a late date (in relation to my own project), I have refrained from taking up its contributions, though I have introduced into this book a few relevant notes.

Let me add that in the spring of 2009, at the University of Aberdeen, I had the great pleasure of hosting a workshop on *The Step Not Beyond* that featured Leslie Hill, Michael Holland, Kai Gohara, and Ian MacClaughlan. The rich discussions on this occasion further strengthened my sense that a sustained reading of *The Step Not Beyond* would be a worthy undertaking.

Derrida's essay, "Pas," first appeared in *Gramma* 3/4, (1976): 111–215; it was subsequently collected in *Parages* (Paris: Galilée, 1986 and 2003) and translated, by John P. Leavey, in *Parages* (Stanford, Calif.: Stanford University Press, 2011).

13. I refer to a statement from the preparatory papers for the establishment of *The International Review*, to which I return in the Appendix.

14. I echo the title of a recent, posthumous publication of a book on Blanchot by Philippe Lacoue-Labarthe, *Agonie terminée, agonie interminable: Sur Maurice Blanchot*, ed. Aristide Bianchi and Leonid Karlamov (Paris: Éditions Galilée, 2011). In this text, as in what I take to be his most important engagement with Blanchot, *Phrase* (Paris: Christian Bourgois, 2000), Lacoue-Labarthe inclines strongly to tones of affliction, but in both cases Lacoue-Labarthe acknowledges the affirmative movement in Blanchot's thought in a manner that appropriately echoes Bataille.

15. I have quoted in this sentence from the "Note" to *The Infinite Conversation*, to which I gave considerable attention in my foreword to *The Station Hill Blanchot Reader*, ed. George Quasha and Charles Stein (Barrytown, N.Y.: Station Hill Press, 1999), xv–xxv. It continues in the following paragraph in the following terms: "Writing, the exigency of writing: no longer the writing that has always (through a necessity in no way avoidable) been in the service of the speech or thought that is called idealist (that is to say, moralizing), but rather the writing that through its own slowly liberated force (the aleatory force of absence) seems to devote itself solely to itself as something that remains without identity, and little by little brings forth possibilities that are entirely other: an anonymous, distracted, deferred and dispersed way of being in relation, by which everything is brought into question—and first of all the idea of God, of the Self, of the Subject, then of Truth and the One, then finally the idea of the Book and the Work."

16. Other "first steps" include chapters on Blanchot's essay "Literature and the Right to Death" (in which I also discuss Derrida's "*Pas*") and on Blanchot's *Death Sentence* in my book *Language and Relation* (Stanford, Calif.: Stanford University Press, 1996), 227–272. Chapter 3, on *The Madness of the Day*, also had a predecessor in a contribution to a collection recently edited by Kevin Hart, *Clandestine Encounters* (Notre Dame, Ind.: University of Notre Dame Press, 2010): "Writing and Sovereignty: *La folie du jour*," 178–195, and the reading of "The Infinite Conversation" was prepared by a briefer engagement with the text in "Un simple changement," *Blanchot dans son siècle*, ed. Monique Antelme et al. (Lyon: Parangon, 2009), 228–236, that was itself preceded by a presentation and translation of the text in *Enclitic* 3, no. 1 (1979): 48–81.

17. I attempt to elaborate this point most particularly in an essay on Gérard Granel ("A Politics of Thought: Gérard Granel's *De l'université*"); indeed,

I republished this essay in a mode of autocritique, seeking to bring forward the imperative of a more affirmative thought. See *The Claim of Language: A Case for the Humanities* (University of Minnesota Press, 2004), 3–22.

18. Blanchot, *The Madness of the Day*, 18.

19. Blanchot, *The Step Not Beyond*, 33/49.

20. This statement is contained in *Maurice Blanchot: Passion politique*, ed. Jean-Luc Nancy (Paris: Galilée, 2011), 61.

21. For the emergence of the motif and practice of contestation, see the excellent contributions of Michael Holland ("An Event without Witness: Contestation between Blanchot and Bataille") and Kevin Hart, "The Counter-spiritual Life" in *The Power of Contestation*, ed. Kevin Hart and Geoffrey H. Hartman (Baltimore: Johns Hopkins University Press, 2004), 27–45, 156–178.

22. For an autobiographical statement regarding Blanchot's relation to Judaism, see, for example, "Do Not Forget," *Maurice Blanchot, Political Writings 1953–1993*, 125–129. We read there the following statement:

> I will not enter any further into these biographical detours, whose memory is nonetheless very present to me. It was obviously the Nazi persecution (it was carried out from the beginning, contrary to what some philosophy professors would have us believe, in order to persuade us that in 1933, when Heidegger adhered to it, National Socialism was still a respectable doctrine that did not merit condemnation) that made us feel that the Jews were our brothers and that Judaism was more than a culture and even more than a religion, but rather the foundation of our relations with others. (125)

The latter point will be developed in "The Indestructible," as I will observe in a reading of that text. It is not clear that Blanchot is claiming the date in parentheses for the advent of the sentiments he goes on to describe; he may well be, and this is a substantial challenge to those who seek to establish a contrary stance. Once again, Blanchot himself offers a brief account of his prewar commitments that includes pertinent self-critical remarks in the letter published in *Maurice Blanchot: Passion Politique*. We find there an account of the relation between the literary commitments and what he terms his "conversion" that supports the formulaic one I have offered. Here is his statement of the disjunction to which I referred:

> I have left aside what had been my true life during this time (no doubt since 1930), which is to say writing, the movement of writing, its obscure search, its essentially nocturnal adventure (all the more so as, like Kafka, I had only the night left to me for writing). In this sense, I was exposed to a veritable dichotomy: the writing of the day in the service of this or that individual (don't forget that I also wrote at that time for a distinguished archaeologist who

needed writing assistance) and the writing of the night that rendered me foreign to every exigency other than itself, all the while changing my identity or orienting it toward an ungraspable and anguishing unknown. If there was a fault on my part, it lies undoubtedly in this division. But at the same time it hastened a kind of conversion in me by opening me to waiting and to the comprehension of the overwhelming changes that were being prepared. I would not say that there is a writing of the right and a writing of the left: that would be an absurd simplification and beside the point. But just as one finds in Mallarmé an implicit political exigency that underlies his poetic exigency (Alain Badiou frequently alludes to this), the one who binds himself to writing must deprive himself of all the assurances provided by a preestablished political thought. (61)

Jean-Luc Nancy asserts that we must question the division he establishes here. I believe it is perhaps more urgent to explore what he means by the fault he committed in sustaining it.

As for the remorse to which I refer, a turn of phrase later in "Do Not Forget" (in the course of substantial remarks on Heidegger) also offers something of a hint: "This interruption—which for Heidegger was the promise of a Germany as heir to Greek excellence and, in this capacity, as the nation called upon to enlighten the world by dominating it, whatever the price may have been—was also for us and above all for the Jews the interregnum when all rights, all recourse ceased, when friendship became uncertain and the silence of the highest spiritual authorities left us without guarantee, not only threatened but anxious about not responding as one should to the silent call of others" (127).

23. Blanchot suggests this explicitly in strongly Levinasian phrasing in the concluding words from "Peace, peace far and near," to which I have already alluded. They suggest the "messianic" link between justice and ethics that I take to be Blanchot's true "cause" in his late thought: "Messianic *impatience* is perhaps the danger of dangers. Ethics is linked to a teaching of patience within urgency itself, for the address of the other does not leave any time and demands a response from me that exceeds me, that withdraws me from myself and, in this withdrawal, opens me to something greater than myself and than any self." Blanchot then continues in the next paragraph: "Justice demands and calls for ever more justice: in me, outside of me, and in justice itself, thus also in the knowledge and exercise of justice. All of which presupposes what we could call the tragic imbroglio of *the other* and others, hence the intervention of the social and political, under the guarantee of the law, in the service of all that is far (first of all) and all that is near—the redoubling of the word *peace* may come from here, so that this last word may be deepened as an echo of itself in an incomparable repetition" (165–166).

1. TOWARD THE QUESTION OF PEACE

1. See *Totality and Infinity*, trans. Alphonso Lingis (Pittsburgh: Duquesne University Press, 1961), 104.

2. In the opening pages of "The Temptation of Temptation," in *Nine Talmudic Readings*, trans. Annette Aronowicz (Bloomington: Indiana University Press, 1990), Levinas addresses the question of the philosophical status of his reading of the Tractate:

> Finally, in my commentary, the word "God" will occur rarely. It expresses a notion religiously of utmost clarity but philosophically most obscure. This notion could become clearer for philosophers on the basis of the human ethical situations the Talmudic texts describe. The reverse procedure would no doubt be more edifying and more pious but it would no longer be philosophical at all. Theosophy is the very negation of philosophy. We have no right to start from a pretentious familiarity with the "psychology" of God and with his "behavior" in order to understand these texts, in which we see traces of the difficult paths which lead to the comprehension of the Divine, coming to light, if one may express it thus, only at the crossroads of human journeyings, where these very journeyings call to or announce the divine. (32)

While much of Levinas's commentary in this essay moves by way of a theological language (and I should note that it does not entail a discussion of the Sabbath itself), he also seeks the more difficult paths to which he refers here. My own reference to a "form of life" is prompted by an insistently philosophical account of "being Jewish" in the essay by Maurice Blanchot that I will address in my next chapter.

3. The context of the address is touched upon in Jill Robbins's brief but precise reading of it in "Circumcising Confession: Derrida, Autobiography, Judaism." This essay is collected in *Jacques Derrida: Critical Thought*, ed. Ian Maclachlan (Hampshire: Ashgate, 2004), 126–145.

4. I do not know how familiar Levinas might have been with this work, but the link between the texts is intriguing and well grounded in the knowledge Benjamin and Levinas shared of early twentieth-century Jewish speculative thought. Elsewhere I offer a reading of Benjamin's volume that is pertinent to this topic regarding the infinite character of the temptation of knowledge. See Christopher Fynsk, *Language and Relation* (Stanford, Calif.: Stanford University Press, 1996), 190–210.

5. For the mention of a "*weak* messianic power" and the role of theology, see Benjamin's "Theses on the Philosophy of History," in *Illuminations*, ed. Hannah Arendt (New York: Schocken, 1968), 253–254. The reference to the dialectician who realizes his properly *critical* role appears in Konvolut N of the

Arcades Project. See *Benjamin: Philosophy, Aesthetics, History*, ed. Gary Smith (Chicago: University of Chicago Press, 1989), 59.

6. In Levinas's French: "Nous allons faire *afin de com-prendre*."

7. "But if time is to show the ambiguity of being and the otherwise than being, its temporalization is to be conceived not as essence, but as saying" (OB 9/23).

8. I refer to Agamben's discussion in *Remnants of Auschwitz: The Witness and the Archive*, trans. Daniel Heller-Roazen (New York: Zone Books, 2002).

9. "Or is not the ego ... a solidarity that begins by bearing witness of itself to the other? Is it not then first of all a communicating of communication, a sign of the giving of signs, and not a transmission of something in an opening?" (OB 119/189).

10. "This is the pre-reflexive iteration in saying of this very saying, a statement of the 'here I am' which is identified with nothing but the very voice that states and delivers itself, the voice that signifies" (OB 143/224).

11. It has frequently been said in recent years that testimony can only be *of its own impossibility*; it can only say its own inability to say that to which it testifies. One could translate Levinas in these terms since the trace marks the subject's exposure to an "infinite" that exceeds its capacity and the order of possibility. But Levinas's effort to think the glorification of the infinite in saying obliges us to try to move beyond a formulation that remains perhaps too much in the order of the "said" and does not entertain sufficiently how language might convey the "*fact*" of the experience of diachrony.

12. I presume that Levinas would be uncomfortable with this formulation, since he does not want to surrender the face to phenomenology; clearly, he does not want it to be taken as an image (it is "inconvertible into forms," he says; OB 90/145). But, later in his exposition, he will state clearly that the face is both visible and invisible. On this point, see the section entitled "From the Saying to the Said, or the Wisdom of Desire" (OB 153–161/239–253). Of course, the very status of the term "metaphor" here is quite problematic, since any attribution of traits is occurring in a general movement of saying "*l'un pour l'autre*." Moreover, we need to address the very complex question of the relation between saying and appearing in this figural movement.

13. I allude, here, to an image that appears in Paul Celan's remarkable prose poem "Conversation in the Mountains," in *Paul Celan: Collected Prose*, trans. Rosmarie Waldrop (Riverdale-on-Hudson, N.Y.: Sheep Meadow Press, 1986), 17–23. It arises in a recollection of the death camps that I think might be described as "primal":

> 'I lay on the stones, back then, you know, on the stone tiles; and next to me the others who were like me, the others who were different and yet like me, my cousins. They lay there sleeping, sleeping and not sleeping, dreaming and not

dreaming, and they did not love me, and I did not love them because I was one, and who wants to love One when there are many, even more than those lying near me, and who wants to be able to love all, and I don't hide it from you, I did not love them who could not love me, I loved the candle which burned in the left corner. I loved it because it burned down, not because *it* burned down, because *it* was *his* candle, the candle he had lit, our mother's father, because on that evening there had begun a day, a particular day: the seventh, the seventh to be followed by the first, the seventh and not the last cousin, I did not love *it*, I loved its burning down and, you know, I haven't loved anything since.

'No. Nothing. Or maybe whatever burned down like that candle on that day.

I have undertaken a reading of this poem in a paper as yet unpublished entitled "The Love of Time." Of course, Levinas would understand acquiescence to a given (sanctified) time and the transformative power of the saying of this relation from the relation to the other. But as the saying of this "primal scene" occurs in conversation with another, there is greater proximity between these two texts than might at first appear.

14. An important part of my meditation on the meaning of "sabbatical acquiescence" is informed by a famous tale recounted by Abraham Joshua Heschel in his book *The Sabbath* (New York: Farrar Straus & Giroux, 1951). It is a tale about Rabbi Simeon ben Yohai and the way he is brought to accept the earthly world through harsh divine guidance. The tale concludes with Rabbi Simeon's discovery of the meaning of this acceptance through an encounter with an old man bearing two bunches of myrtle in honor of the Sabbath. I cite this tale in *The Claim of Language* (Minneapolis: University of Minnesota Press, 2004), 85 n. 30.

15. "But if time is to show the ambiguity of being and the otherwise than being, its temporalization is to be conceived not as essence, but as saying. Essence fills the said, or the epos, of the saying; but the saying, in its power of equivocation, that is, in the enigma whose secret it keeps, escapes the epos of essence that includes it and signifies beyond in a signification that hesitates between this beyond and the return to the epos of essence" (OB 10/23).

16. One could trace the history of Derrida's attention to this problem through the entirety of his long engagement with the text of Levinas. I cannot pause here over this immense conversation, but I would like to point to one particularly interesting discussion in Derrida's *Adieu* (Paris: Galilée, 1997). Late in his discussion, Derrida links the problem of justice as a "non-dialectisable contradiction" to the topic of the revelation at Sinai and his earlier discussion in this volume of a question that appears in one of Levinas's "Talmudic readings": "*A recognition of the Torah before Sinai?*" (203). The topic of such a "recognition"

before the event of revelation would seem to lead us back to the problematic addressed by Levinas in "The Temptation of Temptation." It leads Derrida to the question of a "structural messianicity": "Not an a-historical messianicity, but one that would be proper to a historicity without a particular, empirically determinable, incarnation" (119–121).

17. "It will be possible to show that there is a question of the said and being only because saying or responsibility require justice" (OB 45/77). In a more expansive statement:

> The way of thinking proposed here does not fail to recognize being or treat it, ridiculously and pretentiously, with disdain, as the fall from a higher order or Disorder. But it is on the basis of proximity that being takes on its just meaning. In the indirect ways of illeity, in the anarchical provocation that ordains me to the other, the path is imposed that leads to thematization and to an act of consciousness. The act of consciousness is motivated by the presence of a third party alongside the neighbour approached. A third party is also approached, and the relationship between the neighbour and the third party cannot be indifferent to me when I approach. There must be a justice between incomparables. There must, therefore, be a comparison between incomparables and a synopsis, a placing together and contemporaneousness; there must be thematization, thought, history, and writing. But being must be understood on the basis of *being's other*. (OB 16/33)

18. John Llewelyn gives, nevertheless, a very sound and suggestive account of the structure of saying and the presence of the third party in his essay, "Levinas and Language," in *The Cambridge Companion to Levinas*, ed. Simon Critchley and Robert Bernasconi (Cambridge: Cambridge University Press, 2002), 119–138.

19. First of all and constantly: "Justice is impossible without the one who renders it finding himself in proximity.... Nothing is outside the control of the responsibility of the one for the other (OB 159/248).

20. I noted previously that the face escapes any phenomenological constitution and is also visible. The point is emphasized when Levinas writes:

> It is not that the entry of a third party would be an empirical fact, and that my responsibility for the other finds itself constrained to a calculus by the "force of things." In the proximity of the other, all the others than the other obsess me, and already this obsession cries out for justice, demands measure and knowing, is consciousness. The face obsesses and shows itself, between transcendence and visibility/invisibility.... The neighbour that obsesses me is already a face, both comparable and incomparable, a unique face and in relationship with faces, visible precisely in the concern for justice. (OB 158/246).

21. It is important to note that Levinas's formulations do not always lend to this interpretation. Consider, for example, the following challenging sentences:

> Consciousness is born as the presence of a third party. It is in the measure that it proceeds from this presence that it is still disinterestedness. It is the entry of the third party, a permanent entry, into the intimacy of the face to face. The concern for justice, for the thematizing, kerygmatic discourse bearing on the said—from the depths of saying without the said, the saying as contact—is the spirit of society. And it is because the third party does not come empirically to trouble proximity, because the face is both the neighbor and the face of faces, visage and visible, that the bond between the order of being and proximity is unexceptionable. Order, appearing, phenomenality, being are produced in signification, in proximity, starting with the third party. The apparition of a third party is the very origin of appearing, that is, the very origin of an origin. (OB 160/249)

The interpretation I am offering places a stronger emphasis on the constitutive character of the substitutive act of saying than does this description of the place of the third party and the "unexceptionable" link between saying and the said, or between the face as trace and as phenomenal presence. I do not mean to suggest that the encounter with the other does not already involve relation to the other of the other, but I want to suggest that the relations of commensurability that enable something like justice must be thought from the subject's act of saying the world to the other (a motif to which I will return shortly).

22. "An order common to the interlocutors is established by the positive act of the one *giving* the world, his possession, to the other, or by the positive act of the one justifying himself in his freedom before the other, that is, by apology. Apology does not blindly affirm the self, but already appeals to the Other. It is the primordial phenomenon of reason, in its insurmountable bipolarity" (TI 252/282). I am inclined to see a comparable formulation in one of Levinas's "thesis" statements from *Otherwise Than Being*: "The overemphasis of openness is responsibility for the other to the point of substitution, where the *for-the-other* proper to unveiling, to monstration to the other, turns into the *for-the-other* proper to responsibility. This is the thesis of the present work" (OB 119/189). This statement separates two moments in the saying of responsibility in a manner that seems inconsistent with other formulations, but it is not unfaithful to the argument if we understand that the "Here I am" of prophetic witness is already taken in the movement of responsibility.

23. Put too briefly, Levinas thinks subjectivity more insistently from and in the relation of obligation in *Otherwise than Being*, and always in response

and conversion. "The subject . . . is diachrony," as he puts it at one point (OB 57/96); it is born with the ruin of the subject of representation. *Totality and Infinity*, on the other hand, describes a subject in possession of a world and the economic relations in which it is produced that is compelled to give itself to the other in the traumatism of encounter. The theme of *jouissance* appears in both texts (in both cases it is a matter of giving the bread that satisfies one's hunger, and giving oneself in this act), though in the later volume it is stressed in the context of the bodily dimension of the relation of diachrony. In the earlier text, the separateness of the subject enjoying its world is stressed. But because saying always contains a reference to being and the said, it is impossible to maintain fast distinctions between the arguments. As I have tried to suggest, the need to account for the possibility of justice obliges us to return to the earlier volume.

24. In *Being and Time* (trans. John Macquarrie and Edward Robinson [New York: Harper & Row, 1962]), paragraph 18 (devoted to "Involvement and Significance"—in brief, the signifying structure of the Dasein's *pragmatic* relations), Heidegger writes the following:

> In the *act of the understanding*, which we shall analyse more thoroughly later (Compare Section 31), the relations indicated above must have been previously disclosed; the act of understanding holds them in this disclosedness. It holds itself in them with familiarity; and in so doing, it holds them *before* itself, for it is in these that its assignment operates. The understanding lets itself make assignments both in these relationships and of them. The relational character which these relationships of assigning possess, we take as one of *signifying*. In its familiarity with these relationships, Dasein "signifies" to itself; in a primordial manner it gives itself both its Being and its potentiality-for-Being as something which it is to understand with regard to its Being-in-the-world. . . . These relationships are bound up with one another as a primordial totality; they are what they are as this signifying in which Dasein gives itself beforehand its Being-in-the-world as something to be understood. The relational totality of this signifying we call *"significance."* This makes up the structure of the world— the structure of that wherein Dasein as such already is. (*Being and Time*, 120)

We find a number of statements in the late 1920s and early 1930s comparable to this one that indicate that world is something the Dasein *gives itself to signify*. This "saying of world" (the phrase is not Heidegger's) actually makes possible the project of fundamental ontology, as we learn in the early methodological statements of *Being and Time* (see paragraph 7, 61–62, in which Heidegger speaks of the phenomenology of the Dasein as a "hermeneutics," in "the primordial signification of this word").

We would have to develop at some length how this act of signifying may be thought in relation to Heidegger's notion of *Mitsein*, and, from there, how a substantial connection could be drawn between this thought of language and Levinas's notion of "saying the world" to the other. Unfortunately, this analysis would take us too far afield on this occasion, even though I believe it may be essential to a full understanding of Levinas's propositions. Let me say simply, at this point, that the argument I am pursuing in this essay regarding the possibility of justice, as Levinas understands it, takes seriously Levinas's many assertions that the trace of the passing of the Infinite in the face of the other must be *drawn out* in the saying of responsibility. The trace does not appear outside the responsive saying that would also bring to it the possibility of becoming a reference to the third party and articulating this reference within the commensurable relations of justice. For the movement from the ethical relation to the political one, or one of justice, Heidegger's understanding of the articulating character of responsive speaking is invaluable.

Let me add that I do not intend to pull Levinas back to Heidegger with these references in any manner. I would argue that the reading of the texts I am suggesting would have a transformative effect on both of them.

25. I recognize that I am using the word "conversion" somewhat freely here. But I do so in reference to that act of adherence Levinas describes in "The Temptation of Temptation," and with the thought that the people of Israel essentially "converted" at Sinai. I will have to return to this topic on another occasion, in answer to the inestimable generosity of Rabbi Andy Bachman.

26. "In this overflowing of sense by nonsense, the sensibility, the self, marks itself, in its bottomless passivity, only as pure sensible point, as dis-interestedness, or subversion of essence" (OB 164/255).

2. "THE INDESTRUCTIBLE"

1. I refer here to the opening statements of the preface to Emmanuel Levinas's *Totality and Infinity*, trans. Alfonso Lingis (Pittsburgh: Duquesne University Press, 1969), 21–30.

2. I cite here the final explication of a phrase that appears more frequently and concisely as, "Man is the indestructible that can be destroyed" (see IC 130/192).

3. Robert Antelme, *L'espèce humaine* (Paris: Gallimard, 1957). For additional commentary on Robert Antelme's work, see Martin Crowley, *Robert Antelme* (Oxford: Legenda, 2003).

4. Levinas, *Totality and Infinity*, 23.

5. The motif appears in *The Infinite Conversation*, but it also appears again in strong terms in the late essay "Discours sur la patience (en marge des livres d'Emmanuel Levinas)," *Le nouveau commerce* 30–31: 33.

6. "This is a speech, assuredly, of which we are not directly aware and, it must be said again, a speech that is infinitely hazardous, for it is encompassed by terror. Radical violence is its fringe and its halo; it is one with the obscurity of the night, with the emptiness of the abyss, and so doubtful, so dangerous, that this question incessantly returns: why the exigency of such a language? What do we have to do with it?" (IC 187).

7. In *Infant Figures* (Stanford, Calif.: Stanford University Press, 2000), where I have previously turned to the last two citations from Blanchot, I try to develop the possibility that the self-annunciation of thought according to "another measure" might take the form of (or proceed from) an acquiescence, a kind of affirmation or assent. The central dialogue of the volume is directed toward this notion.

8. One must consider here a tortuous footnote that concludes Blanchot's essay and in which he asserts that "the question expressed by the words "being Jewish" and the question of the State of Israel cannot be identified, even if they modify one another" (IC 447 n. 4/190–191). While recognizing the necessity of political response to the afflictions suffered by the Jewish people, particularly after the Shoah, Blanchot does not consider the state form a sufficient response to the question of being Jewish, which he terms "universal." The concluding sentence is particularly interesting in that it urges reserve before philosophy's temptation to try to hold its own with political powers in deciding on the meaning and future of the "truth" offered by Judaism:

> I would be tempted to conclude by saying that in the society that is being tried in Palestine—a society caught up in struggle, under threat, and threatened by nothing less grave than the necessity of this struggle for "safeguarding" (as is also the case in societies that have issued from Marxism or have been liberated from colonial bondage)—it is philosophy itself that is being dangerously measured against power inasmuch as this society, like the others, will have to determine the meaning and the future of "nomadic truth" in the face of the state. (IC 448/191)

The point would seem to be here, once again, that "being Jewish" cannot be commensurate with the order of "powers" or any political program.

9. For a rich and deeply informed perspective on this question, one should consider Kevin Hart's *The Dark Gaze: Maurice Blanchot and the Sacred* (Chicago: University of Chicago Press, 2004); see, in particular, 177–181, among many other important passages.

10. Giorgio Agamben, *Remnants of Auschwitz: The Witness and the Archive*, trans. Daniel Heller-Roazen (New York: Zone Books, 2002). While this book clearly owes a great deal to Blanchot's meditations on the Shoah, its one reference

to them consists in a charge that Blanchot "misunderstands" his own words in "The Indestructible" (135). There is little point in dwelling on the merits of this curious and rather murky claim. It seems, simply, that Blanchot's meditation on the inhabitants of the camps is insufficiently radical for Agamben in that it does not meet his understanding of the experience (beyond experience) for which he finds an exemplary figure in the "Muselmann." Blanchot's meditation on the exposure of *autrui* (which Agamben never really confronts) would fail to capture the Muselmann's "inhuman" state and does not measure up to Agamben's effort to push the categories of ethics into the "gray zone" described by Primo Levi (an effort that should recall to us the work of Lawrence Langer, who is not cited by Agamben). Beyond the fact that Agamben is hardly consistent in evoking this abyss (how could he write, for example, that the Muselmann, who touches inhumanity in suffering the impossible, "has much to say but cannot speak" [120]), a confrontation between these texts would have to take up their discursive structures. One can certainly find points in Blanchot's work where a pleasure in speculative paroxysm seems to overcome him, but one also finds a crucial sobriety. These words, for example, after a return to the motif of need in *The Writing of the Disaster*: "But the danger (here) of words in their theoretical insignificance is perhaps that they claim to evoke the annihilation where all sinks always, without hearing the 'be silent!' addressed to those who have known only partially, or from a distance, the interruption of history. And yet to watch and to wake, to keep the ceaseless vigil over the immeasurable absence is necessary, for what took up again from this end (Israel, all of us) is marked by this end, from which we cannot come to the end of waking again" (WD 84). Or these words after commentary on the fact that musical concerts were organized in the camps that momentarily effaced the distance between executioners and victims (like the soccer games that so offend Agamben): "There is a limit where the practice of any art becomes an affront. Let us not forget this" (WD 83). While there are many arresting and haunting formulations in Agamben's book that honor Blanchot's imperative ("nevertheless, one must . . ."), it remains hard for me to grasp how Agamben can give himself over so freely to theoretical and speculative analogies in such a context, or write a sentence like this one: "Let us then formulate the thesis that summarizes the lesson of Auschwitz" (133). Further, it would seem to me that rhetoric is one of those "arts" where cognizance of the limit to which Blanchot points is critical.

11. Sarah Kofman, *Smothered Words*, trans. Madeleine Dobie (Evanston, Ill.: Northwestern University Press, 1998), 70.

12. Ibid., 71–72.

13. Blanchot refers here to "a denial so absolute, it is true, that it does not cease to *reaffirm* the relation with the infinite that being-Jewish implies" (IC 129/189).

14. As we proceed, this assertion will come to require qualification. The event of exposure will increasingly be thought as the opening of a plural speech, "simple," and plural. This speech will remain, nonetheless, always shadowed.

15. The question is not meant to be "rhetorical," but if the answer proves negative, it must be followed by this other one: must the Jews somehow be consigned to bearing witness to this impossibility?

16. I refer here to the phrase, "Whoever sees God is in danger of dying" (IC 129/189).

3. BEYOND REFUSAL: *THE MADNESS OF THE DAY*

1. I allude to "recitation" in this paragraph because I first learned of *The Madness of the Day* by hearing it read aloud by Jacques Derrida at the time of its publication in a small seminar, an experience I cannot fail to record in gratitude. Derrida was surely answering the imperatives I have noted in that he returned to the text on numerous occasions in print. See *Parages* (Paris: Galilée, 1986). My reference to Kafka's sentence in this paragraph alludes, of course, to the stunning pages of Blanchot's "Literature and the Right to Death," where we read perhaps the most developed statement available on the question of "literariness" as it was engaged by Blanchot.

2. The joyful vision to which I have referred is one in which a man steps back from the threshold of a door (after having first passed through) to allow a woman with a baby carriage to enter before him. She, the baby carriage, and the man then disappear into what he will call the "orifice" of a house and the "dark beginning" of a courtyard. The excitement that this vision brings will occasion what can only be described as an immense erection. The incident of near-blinding then follows immediately after the narrator's assertion that he had no enemies and that, unmolested, he would sometimes experience, as a vast "solitude" opened in his head, the "disappearance" and reappearance of "the entire world" (MD 11). (Thus we learn that he had already known some form of "effacement" of the day when someone crushed glass over his eyes, though here the coming and going of the world is strongly reminiscent of movements described in *Thomas the Obscure*. The word "solitude" also stands out here, since this word is so insistently applied by Blanchot to the condition of writing.)

We should note, too, how apocalypse supplants apocalypse in this fatal conjunction of a vision and the violent interruption of vision. Here is the narrator's description of an ordering of events whose rigor one is prompted to call *tragic*, and all the more so as our hero has more than one trait of an Oedipus: "This brief scene excited me to the point of delirium. I was undoubtedly not able to explain it to myself fully and yet I was sure of it, that I had seized the moment when the day, having stumbled against a real event would begin hurrying to its end. Here it comes, I said to myself, the end is coming, something is happening, the end is beginning, I was seized by joy" (MD 11). Following the tragic reference, we might say that we *start* in *The Madness of the Day* with a hero on the way to Colonus. I develop the references to Oedipus in "Sovereign Writing," *Clandestine Encounters*, ed. Kevin Hart (Notre Dame, Ind.: University of Notre Dame Press, 2010), 184–185.

Can we, in any case, read the narrator's affirmation of "immense pleasure" at the start of the narrative (not to mention an apparent shift in his relation to the norms of sexual difference) without hearing in it a trace of this "primal" experience? At the same time, can one *think* the return of this joy from its interruption if the fragmentation of this narrative prohibits any "logical" account? The evident limits of any theoretical account oblige us to take recourse to the language of psychoanalysis with only the greatest caution. The narrative's warning in this respect is absolute (for the literary theorist inevitably meets the refusal experienced by the doctors). We are thus confronted with the dilemma of thinking an impossible affirmation of return.

3. PF 316/46. But see also "Discourse on Patience," where Blanchot provides a rare self-explication: "(Whoever sees God dies: this is because "dying" is a manner of seeing the invisible, a manner of saying the unsayable—the indiscretion in which God, become in some sense and necessarily a god without truth (if not a false god), would be given over to passivity)" (36).

4. The following paragraph in Blanchot's text will explain that "a child is being killed" is an *impossible* statement. When and where it would be enunciated (as unpronounceable), Blanchot writes, we would be drawn outside consciousness and unconsciousness: "other than ourselves and in a relation of impossibility with the other" (WD 72/117). My reference to the theoretical character of the statement from the preceding paragraph is meant to underscore the gap between the saying or figuration of the passing that occurs in effacement, and any account of that passing.

5. "Delimit" is a difficult word here: can one delimit without negating? The key point here would lie in differentiating (no less challenging a word) the transgressions pursued with the law, themselves sometimes of a repetitive and affirmative character in relation to the "disaster" of the near-blinding, and the affirmation of the start of the narrative. I pursue this point in "Sovereign Writing" with reference to a passage in *The Infinite Conversation* that invites us to push past a Bataillian configuration.

6. See Christophe Bident, *Maurice Blanchot: Partenaire invisible* (Seyssel: Champ Vallon, 1998), 60–64; see also Laurent Jenny, *Je suis la revolution* (Paris: Éditions Bélin, 2008), 109–136.

7. The oft-cited sentence that announces this affiliation is itself worthy of note. Mascolo cited it as follows: "I want you to know that I am in agreement with you. I refuse all the past and accept nothing of the present" (BR 107).

8. These texts are presented in *Maurice Blanchot: Political Writings*, trans. Zakir Paul (New York: Fordham University Press, 2010), 15–35. The response to Madeleine Chapsal was first published in English in Michael Holland's important collection *The Blanchot Reader* (Oxford: Blackwell, 1995), 196–199.

9. *L'amitié* (Paris: Gallimard, 1971), 131. Etienne Balibar offers a superb analysis of Blanchot's rigorous understanding of the "right" to insubordination in his essay "Blanchot l'insoumis," in *Blanchot dans son siècle* (Lyon: Parangon, 2009), 289-314. This analysis, which treats of a "'foundation without foundation' of the law, to which bear witness the necessity of insubordination or civil disobedience" (295), supports the suggestion I want to make in this essay that the act of refusal marks the limit of the political order. The event that is *"le pas au-delà,"* as I will try to suggest below, is a passage and a turn at that limit that exceeds the political relation.

10. "To make speak, and through torture, is to attempt to master infinite distance by reducing expression to this language of power through which the one who speaks would once again lay himself open to force's hold; and the one who is being tortured refuses to speak in order not to enter through the extorted words into this game of opposing violence, but also, at the same time, in order to preserve the true speech that he very well knows is at this instant merged with his silent presence—which is the very presence of *autrui* in himself" (IC 132). The reference to a refusal of this kind recurs in these pages. Compare also, in the same volume (IC 62/88), Blanchot's reference to the refusal that occurs when one speaks at the level of weakness and destitution.

I would add that refusal, when it issues in violence (Blanchot also recognizes this possibility; see WD 121/186), can be said, in some cases, to bear what William Haver has described as an "ontological priority" vis-à-vis any political order (or order of reasons); again, because it issues from a "very poor beginning" that ultimately has its source outside law. See "The Ontological Priority of Violence: On Several Really Smart Things About Violence in Jean Genet's Works," published in the e-journal *polylog*.

11. IC 17–19/21–24.

12. I have written (non)power in light of a text from this moment that affirms a power of refusal (PW 80), whereas the passage I have just cited and will explore below declares that the refusal in question "is not a power." I have argued in *Language and Relation* that Blanchot implicitly diagnoses such ambiguity in "Literature and Right to Death."

13. "The book has not disappeared, it must be recognized. However, let us observe that everything in the history of our culture and in history itself that has constantly destined writing not for the book, but for the absence of the book, has constantly anticipated, and at the same time prepared for, this upheaval" (BR 204).

14. The words are not without echo in relation to Blanchot's articulation of "Being Jewish." See the section "Communism without a Heritage" in "Disorderly Words" (BR 202–204).

15. As I noted in my introduction, Gérard Granel gave a playful and utterly uncompromising one in *De l'université*. As it happens, this text, and a significant number of other statements devoted to the Heidegger's political thought throughout Granel's impressive body of work, remained too Heideggerian, too much the work of a disciple, for Blanchot (PW 129).

16. I refer, of course, to *Le ressassement éternel* and to its presentation in *Après coup* (Paris: Minuit, 1983). For commentary on this topic and a reading of the text, see "The Glory and the Abyss" by Vivian Liska and Arthur Cools in *Clandestine Encounters*, 32–60.

17. The statement to Bataille echoes a formula found in *The Infinite Conversation* (to *name* the possible, to *respond* to the impossible; IC 65/92; see especially 68–69/48), though in terms that are more overtly related to the issue of politics:

> For my part, I can see, for some time at least I've seen better, the double movement to which I must always answer; both of them necessary, and nevertheless irreconcilable. The one (to express myself in an extremely crude and simplifying manner) is the passion, the realization, and the speech of the whole in dialectical completion; the other is essentially non-dialectical, not at all concerned with unity, and does not lean toward power (toward the possible). To this double movement there answers a double language, and, for all language, a double gravity: the one unfolds in a speech of confrontation, opposition, and negation in order to reduce everything opposed and in order that truth should in the end be affirmed in its totality as a silent equality (the exigency of thought is borne along this way). But the other is a speech that speaks before everything, and outside everything, a speech that is always initial, without concordance, without confrontation, and ready to receive the unknown, the foreign (the poetic exigency passes this way). The one *names* the possible and wills the possible. The other *responds* to the impossible. Between these two movements, both necessary and incompatible, there is a constant tension that is often very difficult to bear and, in truth, unsustainable. But one cannot renounce, in a choice of sides, either the one or the other, nor the research without measure that is demanded of men by the necessity in them [*qu'exige des hommes leur nécessité*] and the necessity of uniting the incompatible.

See *Georges Bataille: Choix de Lettres, 1917–1962* (Paris: Gallimard, 1997), 595–596. (*Il faut, besoin, nécessité, exigence*—the terms belong to a language shared with Bataille that demand to be thought together on another occasion;

I would also note that the reference to "thought" in this instance seems rather limiting—it should perhaps be reserved for what takes form in confrontation with the double necessity.) As for the articulation of this dual imperative in *The International Journal*, see the Appendix.

18. *L'amitié*, 326: "Everything we say tends only to veil the one affirmation: that everything must be effaced and that we can remain faithful only by watching over this movement that effaces itself, to which something in us that rejects all memory already belongs."

4. A SIMPLE CHANGE IN THE PLAY OF WORDS: *THE INFINITE CONVERSATION*

1. With the discreet reference to "The Infinite Conversation," I have restored to the text the title it bore when it was first published in *La Nouvelle Revue Française* 159 (1966): 389–401. In *The Infinite Conversation*, it bears no title. In fact, it is not mentioned in the table of contents and thus has no more status as an "included" item than the "Note," or the epigraphs from Nietzsche, Mallarmé, and Blanchot himself (the latter epigraph also reappearing, by an added twist, in "The Infinite Conversation" itself).

2. See, for example, Blanchot's essay, "Thought and the Exigency of Discontinuity" (IC 3–10/1–11).

3. I am drawing again (nostalgically!) from a preface to a translation of this dialogue I proposed in *Enclitic* 3, no. 1 (1979): 48–81. For a more informative and elaborate discussion of the strange position of the opening dialogue as a whole, see Leslie Hill's "Weary Words: *L'entretien infini*," in *Clandestine Encounters*, ed. Kevin Hart (Notre Dame, Ind.: University of Notre Dame Press, 2010), 282–303.

4. I use the latter term in the sense given to it in *The Infinite Conversation* in the important "Note" that opens the volume (it goes without mention in the book's table of contents).

5. Christophe Bident takes this up in *Maurice Blanchot: Partenaire invisible* (Seyssel: Éditions Champ Vallon, 1998), 167–180. The reader might also consult the admirable book by Patrick ffrench, *After Bataille: Sacrifice, Exposure, Community* (London: Legenda, 2007).

6. "I think that the work of an accompanying discourse—a work that should lean toward modesty—might limit itself to proposing a point from which one would better hear what only a reading can bring forth. This point, moreover, may vary. Let us seek a way to place ourselves so that the limit experience, which Georges Bataille called the 'interior experience,' whose affirmation draws his own search to its greatest point of gravity, will not simply offer itself as a strange phenomenon, as the singularity of an extraordinary mind, but keep for us its power to question" (IC 203/302).

7. To quote again from the commentary on the death of the *infans* in *The Writing of the Disaster*: "'The ever-suspended question: having died of this 'ability to die' which gives him joy and devastation, did he survive—or rather, what does to survive mean then, if not to live through acquiescence to the refusal, through the desiccation of emotion, withdrawn from any interest in oneself, dis-interested, thinned out to a state of utter calmness, expecting nothing?'—consequently, waiting and watching [*attendant et veillant*], because suddenly wakened and, knowing this full well henceforth, never wakeful enough" (WD 116/179).

8. The text twice refers to attempts at reflection, as we will see. In one instance, reflection is inhibited by forgetting; in the other, it is presented as a simulacrum.

9. In a passage of the first section of *The Infinite Conversation*, Blanchot takes up the question of whether the term *autrui* can suffice for the relations at stake between one and the other (since the one must also be other for the other). He continues as follows: "For the moment, we shall have to make two remarks, and say first of all that this redoubling of irreciprocity—the reversal that makes me apparently the other of the other—cannot, at the level at which we are situating our analysis, be taken over by the dialectic, for it does not tend to re-establish any equality whatsoever; on the contrary, it signifies a double dissymmetry, a double discontinuity, as though the empty space between the one and the other were not homogeneous but polarized, as though this space constituted a non-isomorphic field bearing a double distortion, at once infinitely negative and infinitely positive, and such that one should call it neutral if it is well understood that the neutral does not annul, does not neutralize this double-signed infinity, but bears it in the way of an enigma" (IC 71/101). It is noteworthy (though this point will only take on significance in our reading of *The Step Not Beyond*) that Blanchot continues by addressing the question of community: "What of the human 'community' when it must respond to this relation of strangeness between man and man—a relation without common measure, an exorbitant relation—that the experience of language leads one to sense?" (IC 71/101).

10. This need for the other will only be pronounced later in the dialogue: "*When you are there and we speak, I become aware that when you are not there I am implicated in a speech that could be entirely exterior to me.*"—"*And you would like to say it to me in order not to be implicated in it alone.*"—"*But I am not alone in it: in a certain way, I am not in it*" (IC xix/xix).

11. The French gives "*C'est pour quoi . . .*" (IC xv/xv).

12. Let me acknowledge that I am holding back commentary on "*le neutre*" because I want to allow the term to accrue meaning (and its lack thereof) through the movement of the conversation. Clearly, the host's dying is in the neuter/the neutral and exposes to it. (Once again, I will translate the term with both "the neutral" and "the neuter.")

The Infinite Conversation contains numerous valuable pages of reflection on *le neutre*, particularly in the context of a discussion of the poetry of René Char. There, its full, "neutralizing" import for a thought of Being emerges, as does its manner of haunting language. We might also turn to Blanchot's reflections on "the narrative voice" in this same volume. The following, for example: "The narrative voice bears *le neutre*. It bears *le neutre* insofar as: (1) To speak in the neuter is to speak at a distance, holding this distance in reserve without *mediation* and without *community*, and even undergoing the infinite distancing of distance—its irreciprocity, its irrectitude or dissymmetry: for *le neutre* is precisely the greatest distance governed by dissymmetry and without one or another of its terms being privileged (*le neutre* cannot be neutralized). (2) Neuter speech does not reveal, it does not conceal. This does not mean that it signifies nothing (by claiming to abdicate sense in the form of non-sense); it means that *le neutre* does not signify in the same way as the visible-invisible does, but rather opens another power in language, one that is alien to the power of illuminating (or obscuring), of comprehension (or misapprehension) (IC 386/566).

13. The distinction is ultimately quite tenuous, however; for there is also no ground for distinguishing between reflection and a simulation of reflection.

14. Blanchot's description of the "becoming-image" of language in "Two Versions of the Imaginary" (SL 254–263/245–259) would be pertinent to what happens to language in the space of fragmentation. In *The Infinite Conversation*, Blanchot also refers to a "simulation" in literary writing attributable to *le neutre*: "*Neutral would be the literary act that belongs neither to affirmation nor to negation and (at a first stage) frees meaning as a phantom, a haunting, a simulacrum of meaning*" (IC 304/448).

15. In *The Writing of the Disaster*, we read the following: "We constantly *need* to say (to think): something (quite important) happened to me there. By which we mean at the same time: this could not possibly belong to the order of things that happen, or to the order of the important, but is rather what exports and deports. Repetition" (WD 20/9).

16. "Let us suppose an interruption that would in some sense be absolute and absolutely neutral; let us conceive of it as being no longer within the sphere of language, but exterior and anterior to all speech and to all silence; let us call it the ultimate, the hyperbolical. Would we have attained with it the rupture that would deliver us, even if hyperbolically, not only from all reason (this would be little), but from all unreason, that is, from the reason that madness remains? Or would we not be obliged to ask ourselves whether from out of such an interruption—barbarity itself—there would not come an exigency to which it would still be necessary to respond by speaking? And would we not even have to ask whether speech (writing) does not always mean attempting to involve the outside of any language in language itself, that is to say, speaking within this Outside, speaking according to the measure of the 'outside,' which, being in all

speech, may very well also risk turning speech back into what is excluded from all speaking? To write: to trace a circle in the interior of which would come to be inscribed the outside of every circle" (IC 78–79/111–112).

17. See Hill, "Weary Words," 282–303.

18. Here, in *The Infinite Conversation*, emphasis is placed on the way fatigue has a kind of *supplemental* relation to life— the two are indissociable (but let us call this a "failing" supplement, even if the promise of its overcoming offers reason to go on living):

"Friendship is given only to life itself. —But it is a question of my life, which I do not distinguish from weariness, the difference being that weariness constantly goes beyond the limits of life" (IC xx/xxi). In evoking a relation to what does not concern the interests of life, I am introducing an accent from *The Step Not Beyond*.

19. *Le Petit Robert* notes that "*la loi d'airan*" was the name given by Lasalle to the law of capital that reduces the worker's salary to the vital minimum.

20. "*Everything begins for him—and at this moment everything seemed to have come to an end—with an event from which he cannot free himself*" (IC xviii/xviii–xix).

5. COMPASSION FOR SUFFERING HUMANITY: *THE INSTANT OF MY DEATH*

1. The autobiographical dimension of this text is attested to by a letter Blanchot wrote to Jacques Derrida, dated July 20, 1994, to which Derrida refers in *Demeure* (Paris: Galilée, 1998), the essay that accompanied the publication of Blanchot's text (IMD 52/64). In that letter, Blanchot suggests that the incident recounted in *The Instant of My Death* (where he had "the good fortune [*bonheur*] of almost being shot") had effectively happened to Blanchot fifty years earlier. Derrida draws from this evidence to offer a lengthy critical and philosophical essay on testimony that follows Blanchot's narrative line by line. The essay is presented together with a translation of *The Instant of My Death* in a double volume: *Demeure*, trans. Elizabeth Rottenberg (Stanford, Calif.: Stanford University Press, 2000).

2. For this experience of finitude, we should recall the statement from the "primal scene" of *The Writing of the Disaster*: "Nothing is what there is, and first of all, nothing beyond" (WD 72/117).

3. I am thus taking a fairly focused approach to the text. For other readings, in addition to that of Derrida, see, for example, Thomas S. Davis, "Neutral War," in *Clandestine Encounters*, ed. Kevin Hart (Notre Dame, Ind.: University of Notre Dame Press, 2010), 304–326, and Philippe Lacoue-Labarthe, "The Contestation of Death," trans. Philip Anderson, in *The Power of Contestation* (Baltimore: Johns Hopkins University Press, 2004), 141–155. The essay by Lacoue-Labarthe contains a quite powerful paragraph arguing that Blanchot's narrative is to be read in relation to a veritable civil war in France and thus "the

long ideological and political struggle that has divided the French intelligentsia since the thirties." He continues as follows: "That is why, moreover, *L'instant de ma mort* can also be read as the "story" of a deliverance and a redemption—or a defense. Death is *contested* there, the "almost-deceased" in Blanchot, in other words the "always-already-deceased" in him (the other "he" is), is summoned as the witness of a conversion, or of a radical break—and suddenly, as if miraculously, freed of death and of the *mortiferous*. In the name of another politics, without injustice or anything unjustifiable, whose sole object will be to loosen the grip of the political and whose fleeting upsurge will be recognized by Blanchot in May 1968. In other words, in the name of a *survival* which is perhaps nothing other, nothing more in any case, than existence" (*The Power of Contestation*, 52). I believe that Lacoue-Labarthe is making a vital point in this last sentence, though I am not sure I can grasp the meaning of the phrase "sole object" in relation to the advent of "another politics," and I believe that the question of "existence" has to be opened onto that of being-with. I do recognize with pleasure, however, a question we shared in the early 1980s regarding the limits of the political relation. I regret very much that Lacoue-Labarthe did not have the opportunity to address openly and in detail the terms of that "long ideological and political struggle" (a dense reference to the most immediate chapter of that struggle relating to Blanchot is contained in a long parenthesis that closes the paragraph from which I have cited). This would have been a major contribution to the history of modern French thought.

4. This is an interesting revision of the statement in *The Madness of the Day* (I refer back to Chapter 3) to the effect that the guns failed to go off "for no reason." The comment appears to be linked to the reference to a general madness in the world in that moment.

5. Obviously, we cannot know how far this guilt extended; we cannot exclude the possibility that the guilt felt here with regard to a privilege defining his social distinction was overdetermined with other burdens.

6. It should not be necessary (though I am afraid it is, so easily can one be misunderstood in this context) to say that this does not mean that the "facts" and the set of political questions with which Derrida sought to negotiate in his commentary are in any sense negligible. But, as I sought to explain in my introduction, my approach to Blanchot in this volume concentrates on a movement at the limits of the political that transcends many of the terms of the debate that surrounded Blanchot's political interventions as it was structured in the early 1990s. I am seeking to understand where and how the question of the political—or the ethico-political—is reopened in Blanchot's work during the war and in the postwar period.

7. We should note that Blanchot is quite careful with the notion of "testimony," though always recognizing the vital importance of a singular

speech—always marked by fiction—that brings to language what remains to "us." I recall here Blanchot's qualified use of the term in his pages on Robert Antelme's *L'espèce humaine*, starting from the first sentence: "for this book is not only a testimony regarding society in the camps, it leads us to an essential reflection" (IC 130/191). Later in this text, the qualification of the term "testimony" is more pronounced, as Blanchot brings forth the essential, namely Antelme's impossible effort to give its due, its "right," to that "true" speech that, "in truth," is heard by no one: "It is not, as I have said, not simply testimony regarding the reality of a camp; nor is it a historical reporting or an autobiographical narrative. It is clear that for Robert Antelme, and very surely for many others, it is a question not of telling one's story, of testifying, but essentially of *speaking*" (IC 134/198). It is true that when Blanchot meditates on Celan's phrase "there is no witness for the witness," he is touching upon this last problematic of speaking. And there is no question that he is preoccupied with questions of veracity and the relation between "the essential" and the empirical, as we will see in the discussion of Hegel. One might also recall, in this context, *Death Sentence*, a text that is quite precisely dated (if not always "accurately"), but that bears the following words from its concluding pages: "But I must say that for me it seems it did happen that way, setting aside the question of dates, since everything could have happened at a much earlier time. But the truth is not contained in these facts. I can imagine suppressing these particular ones. But if they did not happen, others happen in their place, and answering the summons of the all powerful affirmation which is united with me, they take on the same meaning and the story is the same" (SHBR, 186). It seems unlikely that Blanchot gave himself over to quite this degree of freedom in *The Instant of My Death*, even if the misdating of Hegel's encounter with Napoleon seems willful. But we should be careful to observe the essential but ultimately untenable distinction that Blanchot tries to make in the essay on Antelme.

8. Ecstasis, release, compassion, survival in another space and time, a secret: all traits that suggest we have to do with another form of "primal scene" in *The Instant of My Death*. However, Blanchot's respectful reticence before the language of psychoanalysis (the title of the scene in *The Writing of the Disaster* is accompanied by a question mark) should give pause before any attempt at a theoretical generalization from the basis of these shared traits.

9. The assertion behind this surmise is made quite strongly again in Blanchot's essay on Bataille in *The Infinite Conversation* (IC 207/307–308); every lived event in the world of the possible is shadowed by an experience of the impossible.

10. This crucial point is also made at length in the essay, "Reflections on Hell," where Blanchot links suffering to other forms of affliction and misery,

noting that the "truth" of the extreme or irremediable suffering he describes in "The Great Refusal" shows in affliction (*malheur*) or hunger when it is understood in its general character (carrying the singular into the anonymous experience of "the greatest number").

> There is said to be community in affliction, but there is a point at which what is suffered in common neither brings together nor isolates, only repeating the movement of an affliction that is anonymous, neither belonging to you nor making you belong to a common hope or to a common despair. One speaks of an equality in affliction, but this is an infinite dissimilarity, an oscillation without any level, an equality without anything being equal. And it is not certain that in order to approach such a situation we must turn to the vast, overwhelming upheavals produced in our time. There is a weariness from which there is no rest; it consists in no longer being able to interrupt what one is doing, in working always more, and, in sum, for the common good; one can no longer be weary, separate oneself from one's fatigue in order to dominate it, put it down and find rest. So it is with misery: affliction. (IC 173/258)

The reference to fatigue as a social phenomenon in this passage is especially interesting, since it would ultimately communicate with the fatigue of writing the neutral.

11. I attempted to point to such an echo in *Infant Figures* (Stanford, Calif.: Stanford University Press, 2000; see "Antigone's Friendship," 131–143), though with reference not to this particular text, but to *The Unavowable Community*. The understanding of *philia* involved here leads past Blanchot's reference to the classical notion in his discussion of Foucault in *Michel Foucault tel que je l'imagine* (Montpellier: Éditions Fata Morgana, 1986), 63–64.

6. THE STEP NOT BEYOND

1. The sentence that follows the words from which we have begun reads: "I know, I imagine, that this unanalysable sentiment changed what existence remained to him" (ID 9/17).

2. We might add that Heidegger would have given "being underway"—but here it is important to recall another word of warning from a fragment later in the volume, for which I will draw on the Heideggerian locution: "Speech is always the speech of authority (to speak is always to speak according to the authority of speech). But there is no sceptre for the one who writes, even disguised as a beggar's stick: nothing to lean on and no being underway [*cheminement*]" (SNB 46/67).

3. Hill comments on seven explicit references in the volume in *Maurice Blanchot and Fragmentary Writing* (London: Continuum, 2012).

4. "The "*pas*" of the completely passive—the "step/not beyond"?—is rather the refolding, unfolding itself, of a relation of strangeness that is neither suffered nor assumed. Transgressive passivity, dying in which nothing is suffered, nothing set into action, which is unconcerning and takes name only through the abandonment of the dying of *autrui*" (SNB 122/167).

5. The reader familiar with Derrida's "*Pas*" (in *Parages*, trans. John P. Leavey [Stanford, Calif.: Stanford University Press, 2011], 11–101) will recognize the abyss that lies beneath the issues that I have briefly touched upon here. "*Pas*" (Derrida's essay) does more than demonstrate what "*pas*" does to the question "what is . . ." (and the thought of Being itself); it releases "*pas*" to its disseminative potential, both as it traverses syntactic and semantic orders, and in the way it opens onto what Derrida calls in this essay "another scene" of writing. Derrida's "conversation" poses an immense methodological challenge to any reading of Blanchot's oeuvre, let alone a text such as *The Step Not Beyond*. In strict terms, it suspends the possibility of any founded method for reading this body of works, exposing every interpretative path to the possibility of an infinite detour. At the same time, it brings home the necessity of following the way "*pas*" is brought to language (as a disruption of language) in each of its occurrences.

The Step Not Beyond has its own singularity—or singularities—in this respect. Derrida's essay engages certain fragments of this text quite powerfully, so powerfully that one might wonder at points how to advance after it in anything but a repetitive or explicative mode. A reading of the text would profit enormously from a development of some of Derrida's insights in relation to those fragments (even at the risk—and adventure— of entering that infinite process of reading and rereading to which Derrida points). But there are significant sections of this text that seem to require a different form of attention (particularly those elements of it that answer to what Christophe Bident identified as its ethico-political orientation). I might add that I was intrigued to discover that "conversation" (as I attempted it in *Infant Figures* in relation to Blanchot) was not the required mode for this reading, on this occasion.

Let me emphasize that I believe the special importance of "*Pas*" inheres in the manner in which Derrida adheres to the necessity of thinking *à partir de* ("in the departure of," let us say) the disruption named with "*pas*." This textual accompaniment, in conversation, guides his approach to the many topics he takes up in this essay, including that of the writing/enunciation of "*viens*," to which we will return (I discuss the relation of "*pas*" and "*viens*" in *Language and Relation* [Stanford, Calif.: Stanford University Press, 1996], 240–242). Again, Derrida's essay is invaluable for the manner in which it draws us constantly back into the linguistic movements (and transgression of every linguistic "order") of Blanchot's texts and their implication for dialectic and any thought of the event.

Notes to pages 128–36   275

6. Compare *The Step Not Beyond* (41/60), where "importance" is distinguished from what "imports"—a movement of carrying that Blanchot will distinguish in this volume from the assumption of responsibility or any weightiness.

7. This opening passage from "Reflections on Hell" evokes the sudden collapse of every separating barrier between two beings, and then continues as follows:

> One retains the impression that there was a brief moment of luck; a moment bound not to the favour of the look that may have been exchanged, but to something like a movement that would have preceded us both, just before our encounter. At this instant it seems that *he* was truly our companion in an infinite and infinitely deserted space where, by a marvellous chance, he had suddenly appeared at our side; so it was and so it was going to be, inexplicable, certain, and marvellous. But who/what was *he*? Only the desert, perhaps? The desert become our companion? Marvellous, this remains, marvellously desolate, and then the companion has once again disappeared—there is nothing but desert. But in its harsh truth and arid presence it is suddenly close to us, familiar, a friend. A proximity that at the same time says to us: "*the desert is growing.*" (IC 171/256)

8. This is, once again, a "fraternity without law." Jacques Derrida will multiply questions regarding Blanchot's appeal to fraternity in *Politiques de l'amitié* (Paris: Galilée, 1994), though the strangeness of Blanchot's usage in this case prompts reserve on Derrida's part.

9. This is a notably rare term in Blanchot, to my recollection. One will recall, however, the event in *The Madness of the Day* (again involving an encounter with a woman in a street), which the narrator insists is "real." The latter event, wherein a woman enters a revolving door with a carriage, may well be linked, in turn (but now we enter the "*pas*" of a becoming-figural), to the passage in *Celui qui ne m'accompagnait pas* in which a figure disappears in ascending a turning staircase: "Among all the impressions that struck me, I believe the strongest was this one: that never had the evidence of reality been as pressing as in this sliding toward disappearance; in this movement something was released that was an allusion to an event, to its intimacy, as though, for this figure, disappearing was her most human truth, and also the closest to me" (SHBR 290/65).

10. This exigency is underscored twice in the opening pages: "It is certainly satisfying (too satisfying) to think that, by the mere fact that something like "*il—la mer*" is written, with the exigency that results from these words and from which they also result, that somewhere the possibility of a radical transformation is inscribed, be it for one alone, that is to say, his suppression as a personal existence. . . . Do not draw any consequences from these words written one day

(which were, or could have been at the same time, and just as well, other words), nor even from the exigency of writing, supposing you were indeed charged with it, as you persuade yourself and sometimes dissuade yourself" (SNB 1–2/8). On the event of writing, one might also recall the sentences from the start of the conversation that opens *The Infinite Conversation*: "From the instant that this word—a word, a phrase—slipped between them, something changed, a history ended" (IC xiv/xii).

11. We will return to Blanchot's insistence on the figure of the desert in his commentary on Kafka in *The Literary Space*. Here, let me merely point to a later statement in this essay that arrives after Blanchot introduces the topic of the image and idolatry: "To what extent was Kafka aware of the analogy between this move outside truth and the movement by which the work tends toward its origin—toward that center which is the only place the work can be achieved, in the search for which it is realized and which, once reached, makes the work impossible? To what extent did he connect the ordeal of his heroes with the way in which he himself, through art, was trying to make his way toward the work and, through the work, toward something true?" (SL 81/94). This precedent, I should note, does not conflict with the "analogy" I drew in describing the narrative line of "The Infinite Conversation" as a "being underway to language." For Blanchot, the latter would always be a "being underway toward writing" and the "truth" of the exilic relation he finds therein.

12. In *Maurice Blanchot and Fragmentary Writing*, Leslie Hill provides a marvelous reading of this opening sentence of *The Step Not Beyond* (it is the only fragment not preceded by a diamond). The sentence suspends at the threshold it marks, even as it invites. To his compelling exploration of its possibilities and temporal structure, I would only add a reference back to Levinas's characterization of the temporality of the promise or prayer. It is from such an understanding of the sentence's resonance (its remarking of what has already opened as to come) that I hear a hospitable invitation that will be echoed in the closing page of the volume.

13. This motif (that the presence of language—"*that there is language*"—is neutral) is persistent and vitally important for Blanchot's thought of *le neutre*. We meet it in the lengthy fragment on *le neutre* in *The Step Not Beyond* when Blanchot remarks that its presence in language via the grammatical category may prompt us to forget that it is borne by all language: "As though language 'in general' were neuter, since all the forms and possibilities of affirmation unfold there, on a neuter basis [*sur fond de neutre*]. The neuter is thus implicated in the functioning of all language" (SNB 73/103). A subsequent fragment offers the following: "The power to name the neuter was, as always, the power not to name it, to dedicate to it, from closer and closer, all language, all that is visible and all that is invisible of language, and yet to withdraw language from

it, precisely through that giving that reduced the neuter to being nothing but the recipient of its own message" (SNB 83/115). Hence the always insufficient task of "indicating" the neuter through a remarking of the writing at the limit of language and the "relay" of "*il.*" The literary task enjoined by *le neutre* also appears in *The Writing of the Disaster* in a passage on Wittgenstein, who despaired, as we know, of presenting the fact of language (the condition of any "ethical" language): "the neutral is thus in relation with the infiniteness of language, which no totality can ever close and which is affirmed—if ever it is—outside of the affirmation and of the negation that established knowledge and usage make familiar to us. Whence the obligation not to speak *on* language without bearing in mind that one is confining oneself to the limitation of a particular body of knowledge, but rather to speak *on the basis of* language [*à partir du langage*], which is precisely not a basis, except inasmuch as it is the unspeakable demand which nevertheless is that of speaking" (WD 133/202).

14. Jacques Derrida, *Dissemination*, trans. Barbara Johnson (Cambridge, Mass.: Harvard University Press, 1984). The topic of Blanchot's relation to Mallarmé is of tremendous importance in itself, as goes almost without saying. But the pertinence of this relation to *The Step Not Beyond* is given special relief if one considers it in the light of Derrida's masterful engagement with the question of mimesis in "The Double Session." In this perspective, the question I raised earlier regarding simulation and feigning takes on special poignancy and the stakes of the question regarding being- (dying-) with appear more clearly. Let me offer a far too summary and allusive response to the question that presents itself here by restating a point I have tried to emphasize, namely that the exilic movement I try to follow in this study proceeds *from* an event of interruption. One might very well say something comparable for the experimentation undertaken by Mallarmé, but his "*hymen*" unfolds without a definitive breach of (what Blanchot figures as) the glass. In Blanchot's case, the self-indication of writing at the edge of language (Derrida's presence here is unmistakable; SNB 6/14) is a repeated exposure of language's exposure to an outside (the "hyperbolic" interruption described in *The Infinite Conversation*). This transgressive retracing of the threshold has a fragmenting force. The engagement of the return, as we will see, gives us perhaps a "false appearance of the present" (Blanchot even cites the phrase; SNB 12/22), but the one who asks "would I be with whom I die?" is not, I want to suggest, a "solitary captive of the threshold." Not only is the transgression *shared* as the opening of a community, but this community is also radically open. Of course *Le pas au delà* (I cite the title in French to underscore the syntagm) brings the question back to us each time the movement it names appears; moreover, there is no proving an opening onto the event. But there is something like a compelling exigency and an impelling passage.

15. These pages form the focus of a careful and searching master's thesis by Burhanuddin Baki for the Centre for Modern Thought at the University of Aberdeen that I hope will reach timely publication. *The Step Not Beyond* makes an insistent appeal to the thought of *le neutre*, but gives it sustained focus on only one occasion: a long fragment that takes its departure from the appearance of *le neutre* in Greek thought and language and concludes with a meditation on the writing that "neutralizes" Being (SNB 72–76/101–107). The fragment merits long scrutiny (another thesis), but does not, perhaps, quite suffice for the appeal made to the notion throughout the volume. In this respect, one sees to what extent *The Step Not Beyond* proceeds from Blanchot's earlier writing, particularly *The Infinite Conversation*. A study that undertakes to draw forth the thought of *le neutre* from Blanchot's later work must document the way it develops the notion of the *il y a* (let us call this development a further disruption of ontology, but with the recognition that the thinking involved here moves at the level of Heidegger's thought of Being and *Ereignis*), while extending the meditation on the way this alterity marks and is marked in language. It will not suffice, however, to say that the thought of "*le neutre*" translates Blanchot's earlier appeal to the *il y a*, unless we take "translation" in a very active sense. The mobilization of this word allows an extensive reengagement with the question of the negative and the "meaning of meaning," to which "Literature and the Right to Death" was devoted, and a radical development of the thought of relationality that is obliged by the notion of fragmentation (involving dissymmetry, discontinuity, the curvature of space, and so on, terms that offer a singular challenge to mathematical thought, as Baki has demonstrated). Its challenge to grammar (and that "God" to which we have been beholden "up to now" by our faith in it) is particularly powerful. From the thought of *le neutre* Blanchot is prompted to ask whether this last "now," as named by Nietzsche, marks a threshold: "Are we to conclude from this qualification that we are at a turning point—a turning of necessity where, in place of our language and by the play of its difference, up to now folded back into the simplicity of sight and equalized in the light of a signification, another sort of exteriorization would come forward [*se dégagerait*], and such that, in this hiatus opened in it, in the disjunction that is its site, there would cease to live these guests who are unwonted because habitual, unreassuring because too sure, masked but endlessly exchanging their masks: divinity in the form of logos, nihilism in the guise of reason?" (IC 166/249).

For other discussions of "*le neutre*," one might consult Christophe Bident's richly suggestive essay, "The Movements of the Neuter." One might also consult Marlene Zarader's *L'être et le neutre: à partir de Maurice Blanchot* (Paris: Verdier, 2001), though this study strikes me as particularly problematic by reason of its refusal to entertain Blanchot's literary thought (and practice) in its resolutely philosophical analysis of the term, and its failure to engage the question of language at the level to which it is carried by Blanchot's text.

16. These words appear in an important passage on the topic of anonymity and the demand of writing. Asking where one might locate this exigency (in the biography of the writer, in the work?), Blanchot turns to the question of a science: Might this exigency be carried in "a more general knowledge, the knowledge proper to the necessity of marks, of inscriptions, of gestures, even of traces, knowledge by which it would end up judging scientific ideology or pronouncing on the ability of the sciences to attain a certain scientificity?" "In doing this," he continues, "it risks immersing itself in an ill-defined problematic that eternal metaphysics has no difficulty welcoming by introducing it into the hope of its books. What, then, is to be done with this movement that does not recognize itself in anything it does not contest? Perhaps maintain it as an exigency always previously exhausted, that is, as non-living repetition, forgetting that there is no time for writing, if writing has always preceded itself in the form of a rewriting" (SNB 34/51). Derrida, of course, recognized the limits of any grammatology, but also remained tempted, for some time at least, by a "more powerful" science informed by a thought of the trace.

17. This is the epigraph to *The Infinite Conversation*. The line also appears in the first section of the volume (IC 71/102).

18. "♦ Fragility that is not that of life, fragility not of that which breaks itself apart, but of the breaking apart, that "I" cannot reach, even in the collapse of the self that gives up and gives its place up to the other" (SNB 120/163).

19. Jean-Luc Nancy, *La communauté affrontée* (Paris: Galilée, 2001), 38: "But I was also struck by the fact that Blanchot's response was all at once an echo, a resonance and a reply, a reservation, even, in some respects, a reproach."

20. "I decided to write these lines without returning to the texts, leaving space to memory which alone can give again the movement followed at the time and imprinted in me: to reread would make me rewrite history" (*La communauté affrontée*, 34). These are astonishing words that were perhaps only offered to excuse haste (the history in question, after all, is rather banal; its understanding is possibly another matter). There is also some humor in his gesture of citing from memory (without returning to correct) the passage I have commented from IC 313/448 in "Fin du colloque," in *Maurice Blanchot: Récits critiques* (Tours: Farrago, 2003), 628. A more serious gesture of neglect occurs in *Maurice Blanchot: Passion politique*. There, Nancy defers judgment about the letter he offers to the public (14–15), but then goes on to draw from it for statements on *The Unavowable Community* that link the thought of community presented there to the commitments of the 1930s (18, 30–33).

This is an obscure and increasingly violent gesture as it unfolds. The proposed reading of *The Unavowable Community* represents a veritable misconstruction in its attribution to the text of a notion of "communion." Moreover, Nancy seems to assume that Blanchot had not addressed the question of community in the manner of the last volume since the period of the 1930s, and that he implicitly returned to positions held at that time, but guarded in the interim. Again, one might be tempted to understand these ill-founded remarks as signs of a continuing neglect in relation to the text. But neglect has in fact passed into active suppression in this case. Not only are Blanchot's insistent and explicit remarks on communion in *The Unavowable Community* disregarded; Nancy's proposal effectively elides vast portions of his work (do I dare say "unworking"?) in the period of the war and thereafter. Most pertinently, it elides all of the work that follows what Blanchot terms his "conversion" in the passage from the letter cited (I note again that the term is used to describe the passage beyond the "split" in Blanchot's writing existence: the writing of the day, and the writing of the night—any religious connotation remains still distant), and first of all everything from *The Infinite Conversation* and *The Step Not Beyond* bearing on community and the relation to *autrui*.

Nancy then goes on to complete his reflections by questioning the character of the "conversion" itself, an operation that begins with an expression of doubt as to whether there was any thinking in this movement at all (!) and another deferral of judgment (and responsibility): "But what we will have to learn how to assess later, when the true fundamental work will be possible..." This, unfortunately, is not the last of it. Nancy goes on to impute implicitly to Blanchot a "hatred for the Jews" that he could not have avoided because he was "Catholic not only by childhood and education, but by soul and constitution [!]" (37) and therefore swept up in a larger movement. If any "conversion" is to be recognized, Nancy argues, it belongs to Blanchot's generation as a whole and can finally be inscribed within Christianity (38–39). Blanchot, again, had not used the word in the sense Nancy takes it here, and he certainly never claimed a conversion to Judaism in any strict sense, though he claimed to have opened very early to the recognition of the meaning of the persecution of the Jews. Nancy thus allows himself a very free use of a word Blanchot would never have advanced lightly. In short, Blanchot, not to mention the Jewish thought to which he turned in humility, merited more respect, particularly after the care he showed in his response to Nancy.

All of this is, of course, very saddening, and I am especially saddened to have to raise a voice of protest in regard to this crude, almost incomprehensible operation carried out by an old friend. Let me simply leave a few words to Blanchot. The first are from the first paragraph of the very letter Nancy has published: "Neither the analysis nor the critical judgment of Todorov touch me. For the judgment judges him as well. And whether or not I should belong to the past is truly without importance. *'Tout s'efface, tout doit s'effacer'*" (47).

A longer citation is from "Peace, peace near and far" —a passage in which Blanchot takes up the challenge to "all established language" by the questions posed to thought by Judaism (published just one year after *The Unavowable Community*):

> It does not suffice to put philosophy into question; one must awaken a question of meaning in it that it has not known how to bear, in spite of the effort of so many exceptional thinkers.... How can the Infinite—which is not a pure and simple beyond, nor a definitively superlative supereminence, but a "growing surplus of Infinity"—expose itself to the constraint of finitude without breaching it through a dangerously communion-like experience that will exclude or dissolve the sacred value of separation? In our time, we need a thinker who is extraordinary (I mean this in the literal sense, not as an indication of praise) to teach us once again that the meaning of the beyond and of transcendence may find a place in *ethics*, which would not merely be a forgotten or neglected discipline but would impose a philosophical reversal upon us, an upheaval of all our theoretical and practical assumptions (even if these are not scorned, but put back in their place). (164)

21. Jean-Luc Nancy, *The Inoperative Community* (Minneapolis: University of Minnesota Press, 1991), 7. Lars Iyer focuses on this sentence in a veritable rebuke to Nancy in *Blanchot's Communism* (New York: Palgrave Macmillan, 2004).

22. This point emerges clearly in *The Step Not Beyond* (105–106/146) in another presentation of the sharing of dying to which I will turn later. It stresses the *transgressive* character of the sharing involved inasmuch as it entails exposure to an unavowable in community.

23. "*Il ne saurait y avoir de communauté si n'était commun l'événement premier et dernier qui en chacun cesse de pouvoir l'être.*" I have opted for a more awkward phrasing over Pierre Joris's more elegant one: "There could not be a sharing of community without the sharing of that first and last event which in everyone ceases to be able to be just that (birth, death)," which is strong by reason of the recognition that the failing *to be* (given an almost transitive form in the French) bears on the event itself. For a being defined by its ability to be (*Sein-können*), these fundamental existential moments (birth, death) mark a *lapsing*—a common exposure—that opens the groundless relation of community.

24. In the essay "Knowledge of the Unknown," Blanchot writes, "For Heidegger, being-with is taken up only in relation with Being and inasmuch as it bears, in its manner, the question of Being" (IC 52/74). The point, we should note, is not denied by Heidegger: indeed, he makes it explicitly in one of his essays on language. I comment on this point in *Language and Relation*, 83.

25. This is a line that I had pursued in my early work on Heidegger, presented in "The Self and Its Witness," *Boundary* 2 10, no. 3 (1982): 185–208, and

subsequently in *Heidegger: Thought and Historicity* (Ithaca, N.Y.: Cornell University Press, 1986). I might note that I have always assumed that this reading was indirectly made possible by Blanchot's discussion of the ethical relation in *The Infinite Conversation* (notwithstanding the statement I cited by Blanchot in the previous note). Derrida's evocation of "the community of the question" in the opening paragraphs of "Violence and Metaphysics" (on Levinas) then prompted me to link the question of *Mitsein* to the problem of community as it figures in the *"re-trait"* of the political that I followed in Derrida's text for the colloquium on the work of Jacques Derrida at Cérisy la Salle in 1980 (in *Les fins de l'homme: A partir du travail; de Jacques Derrida*, ed. Philippe Lacoue-Labarthe and Jean-Luc Nancy [Paris: Galilée, 1981], 487–493). One will understand that it is intriguing to me that the question of *Mitsein* should return in Blanchot's text in this manner in 1984.

26. "♦ *Between you and me, it is like between something that is more than you and something that is less than me: him and him*" (SNB 128/175).

27. Another instance appears in the following passage from the essay "Interruption," in which Blanchot addresses the radical interruption between beings who are other for one another: "Now, what is in play and demands relation is everything that separates me from the other, that is to say the other insofar as I am infinitely separated from him—a separation, fissure, or interval that leaves him infinitely outside me, but also claims [*prétend*] to found my relation with him upon this very interruption that is an *interruption of being*" (IC 77/109).

28. The sentence is thus radically unstable. It says the "real" state of affairs as it enunciates the human care for the other; but it is also already community's interruption of that sharing the one seeks in aiding the other. Blanchot ascribes a phrase like this to dying quite insistently in *The Step Not Beyond*. For example: "'Dying is prohibited,' we hear this constantly in ourselves, not as an obliging call to life, but as the very voice of dying, each time breaking the interdiction (as happens all too clearly to one who in taking their own life dies prohibited)" (SNB 96/133). The status of *"il est interdit de mourir"* is thus comparable to that of *"on tue un enfant"*—impossible for the conscious, caring subject. Blanchot's accounts of this impossibility in the latter part of *The Step Not Beyond* are especially challenging. But one might say at least that it is impossible because dying does not belong to the space of the law (the sentence is thus "unpromulgatable"). Should it be brought to appear in death, it may suffer exclusion, as occurs in some societies (this is the point with which the passage cited opens and with which it concludes when it evokes the shocking character of the event of dying), but it does not fall under the jurisdiction of the law ("Transgression belongs neither to the day nor to the night. Never does it encounter the law, which is

nevertheless everywhere," SNB 107/147). Thus, "Don't" appears only to open onto this *énoncé*, echoing what speaks always in us.

29. In my foreword to Maurice Blanchot, *The Station Hill Blanchot Reader* (Barrytown, N.Y.: Station Hill Press, 1998), I noted that one could not cite the following passage frequently enough: "Now, 'the basis of communication' is not necessarily speech, or even the silence that is its foundation and punctuation, but the exposure to death, no longer my own exposure, but someone else's, whose living and closest presence is already the eternal and unbearable absence, an absence that the travail of deepest mourning does not diminish. And it is in life itself that that absence of someone else has to be met. It is with that absence—its uncanny presence, always under the prior threat of a disappearance—that friendship is brought into play and lost at each moment, a relation without relation or without relation other than the incommensurable" (UC 25/46).

30. As in "The Infinite Conversation," there is address to the other, the silent partner for whom a place had been left at the table (the place of the "thought" that waited in conversation, as conceived by Bataille). This is the one to whom a neutral, but defiant, plaint was addressed ("This concerns neither the one nor the other"); the same position is marked by the one who is addressed under the guise of the circle. The conversation, as we have seen, traced the passage from a will to interruption into an affirmative, resolute conversation. Here, the address to the other is transmuted into an invitation that is apocalyptic in tenor, as Blanchot underscores with a footnote to Derrida's essay in *Les fins de l'homme*, "D'un ton apocalyptique adopté naguère en philosophie," reinforcing the point by welcoming Derrida's interpretation of this very sentence as it appeared in *Le pas au-delà* (UC 57/26). It may thus be paired with the line from *The Madness of the Day*: "*Ce jour s'effaçant.*" To whom is this welcome uttered if not to the one (or ones) whose place is to announce the coming of a just community, or whose coming would constitute such an annunciation?

What is one to make of this new summoning of the end of the day, with its messianic appeal? It appears to bring the "messianic" into the time of community as a possibility inherent in its writing, remarking its possibility almost as a structural trait. One could thus read in this gesture a deconstruction of a theological reference (and how else could such a reference cohabit with a thought of *le neutre*?). But perhaps we bring the appeal to deconstruction a bit too early in this manner, foreclosing a strain in this thinking that is less easily theorized. The event is so furtive, however, as to make conclusions extremely difficult, and answers are not much easier within our more immediate context. Are these, in effect, the last words of *The Step Not Beyond*; do they perhaps speak from beyond the temporal threshold that we will see traced in this text? In *Death Sentence*,

Blanchot gave such a saying to the narrating voice in the magnificent concluding passage. In *The Step Not Beyond*, the sentence in question, "*Viens, viens,*" cannot easily be attributed to the protagonists. It speaks at the very limit of the most extreme opening: "Would I be with the one with whom I die?" Of course, the latter part of the narrated conversation begins from a statement of the fact of "their" coming. But perhaps the event of their coming (in no past present) is precisely what can be announced only in a futural opening that is at the very limit of this writing.

31. "In a way, the instability of the illumination needed to expose itself to others even before being transmitted, not in order to attain in them a certain objective reality (which would have denatured it immediately), but in order to reflect itself therein by sharing itself and letting itself be contested (i.e., enunciated differently, or even denounced in accordance with the objection it carried in itself)" (UC 17/34). To restate the imperative a bit more directly in relation to the passage from Acéphale to *The Inner Experience*: the thought needed contestation in order to be taken to its limits through an ever more severe challenge to thematic content and the illusory temptation, for example, of a shared work of death. The project, in its own self-recusion, demanded a rearticulating repetition and even denunciation. Community remained, in this respect, an unmet exigency, and will always remain so.

32. "One can write that word (ecstasy) only by putting it carefully between quotation marks.... Its decisive trait is that the one who experiences it is no longer there when he experiences it, is thus no longer there to experience it. The same person (but he is no longer the same) may believe that he recaptures it in the past as one does a memory: I remember, I recall to mind, I talk or I write in a rapture that overflows and unsettles the very possibility of remembering. All mystics, the most rigorous, the most sober (and first of all Saint John of the Cross), have known that that remembrance, considered as personal, could only be doubtful, and belonging to memory, took rank among that which demanded escape from it: extra-temporal memory or remembrance of a past which has never been lived in the present (and thus a stranger to all *Erlebnis*)" (UC 19/37). These words have an important bearing on the "testimony" of a text such as *The Instant of My Death*, and perhaps bear upon any recollection involving the exigencies of community: hence the unending imperative of reading and writing, rereading and rewriting where the question of community is involved.

33. I am not at all sure that this is a question that can be appropriately answered, though it is difficult not to recognize grounds for discouragement. It seems most appropriate to embrace Blanchot's own stance in going from "from discouragement to discouragement," while noting Blanchot's evocation of the "ideal" community of readers in his subsequent section, "The Literary

Community." This recollection might speak to those committed to the ephemeral communities of thought or literary and artistic practice that limn the event, blessed with infantile enthusiasm: "There it is: something had taken place which, for a few moments and even through the misunderstandings peculiar to singular existences, allowed one to recognize the possibility of a community established previously though at the same time already posthumous: nothing of it would remain, which saddened the heart while also exalting it, like the very ordeal of effacement writing demands" (UC 21/40).

34. I refer here to issues such as Blanchot's health. It also appears that Blanchot was using the publication to sketch a thought, rather than develop it (the sketch serving to point, in part, to what had already been developed).

35. Nancy focuses on this motif in the letter of 1984, and it undoubtedly shapes the ad hominem character of his remarks. (The difference between Blanchot's individual investments and what he sought to develop in a reflection on the passions of being-with is one of the places where one can locate the thought Nancy is unsure of finding). Let me also recall again Blanchot's remarks on the writer's "revolutionary" impetus in "Literature and the Right to Death." As I suggested in *Language and Relation* (229), it might well be that Blanchot is implicitly situating his earlier political passions in the imaginary investment in the negative that he attributes to Sade. As I noted on that occasion, this leads to something far more unsettling than a "national aestheticism."

36. See *Faux Pas*, trans. Charlotte Mandell (Stanford, Calif.: Stanford University Press, 2001), 1–16.

37. "♦ *One can write it once, live it once; just as, in extremity, and by inadvertence, one might in a unique way touch madness—but what happens when it returns a second time?*" Blanchot continues with the dilemma faced by one who is without recourse in this return: "*What is left? Once again the extreme possibility, that possibility offered by madness for one to defend oneself against it and on which it has placed its mark—a forbidden possibility? certainly, but is not madness which was no less forbidden, also there, without right, not freeing from all legitimacy, but condemning every life, every death to a* supplementary *illegitimacy?*" (SNB 103/142). Could this be the anguished underside of Blanchot's meditations on the "error" of suicide?

38. I borrow a title and the movement it describes from an essay in *The Infinite Conversation*. These are pages that begin with reference to the topic of fear ("fear: anguish," IC 49/70), indicating from the outset a reference to Bataille. Here, the question concerns the experience of fear and the possibility of a thinking relation to it. Can the philosopher think fear and remain a philosopher? Can we conceive of a thought that is afraid? The question is easily posed in theoretical terms, but forbidding when grasped in its full existential import. The text then moves into a consideration of relation to the unknown

brought to us by *autrui*, and thus the first treatment of Levinas in *The Infinite Conversation*.

39. Compare the opening paragraph of "The Narrative Voice (the "he," the neutral)" (IC 379/556).

40. This is not to say that questioning about *le neutre* is otherwise impossible, though there is surely some irony in the phrase with which Blanchot introduces his long meditation on the topic in *The Step Not Beyond*: "We can always ask ourselves about *le neutre*"—the irony inhering in the fact that *le neutre* cannot be the object of a question, or will always suffer (neutrally) a questioning that it exceeds (SNB 69/97).

41. Such a usage is visible, for example, in the "Discourse on Patience." My reference to a later usage (thus pointing to the thought of disaster) should be qualified, though, and may be misleading. A letter to Bataille dated August 8 (probably from 1960) speaks quite directly to his physical condition with the following words: "It has seemed to me for a long time that the nervous difficulties from which you are suffering—to speak in the terms of medical objectivity—are nothing but your way of living authentically this truth, holding yourself at the level of the impersonal affliction that is the world in its depths." The letter continues with words on the motif of hope to which I will return, and then adds in its final paragraph: "Forgive me for these words, they are written from the thought borne by your letter and in order to tell you how close it is to me. That something one might call affliction, but that one must also leave without a name, could, in a certain manner, be common to us—this is mysterious, perhaps misleading, perhaps unsayably true." *Choix de lettres*, 1917–1962, ed. Michel Surya (Paris: Gallimard, 1997), 591–592. I would note also the multiple references to *malheur* in the second section of *Death Sentence*, where it is used to describe the disastrous relation to the other from which issues the doubly affirmed "*viens*." I attend to the appearance of the word at some length in *Language and Relation*, 245–271.

42. Passing by the Scots (!) *tane* (OS *tacan*, etc.), I would want to link this term "take" to the series explored by Blanchot that includes maintain and sustain.

43. The "Discourse on Patience" distinguishes passivity from suffering quite markedly in words that constitute almost a self-critique. "Once, I appealed to suffering. . . . But the word 'suffering' is far too equivocal" (DP 25). In the succeeding lines, Blanchot goes on to discuss the shortcomings of the word "passivity" itself, dissociating it so severely from anything we might associate with the word that it is left almost vacant. There is a transgressive step in passivity ("the step of the entirely passive") that removes it from the registers of a subject's action or suffering. "Separation," of course, bears a strong Levinasian connotation; indeed, the "Discourse on Patience" is especially valuable for highlighting the Levinasian dimension of Blanchot's thought of this period.

44. Let us recall these words from "The Indestructible": "What force [*puissance*] would want is to leave the limits of force: elevate itself to the dimension of the faceless gods, speak as fate and still dominate as men. With an unfaltering instinct, Antelme holds himself at a distance from all natural things.... This is what bears meditation: when through oppression and terror man falls as though outside himself, there where he loses all perspective, every point of reference, and every difference and is thus handed over to a time without respite that he endures as the perpetuity of an indifferent present, he has one last possibility. At this moment when he becomes the unknown and the foreign, when, that is, he becomes a fate for himself, his last recourse is to know that he has been struck not by the elements, but by men, and to give the name man to everything that assails him" (IC 131/194).

45. Moving from a discussion of individual suffering to forms of collective experience, Blanchot evokes an anonymous affliction: "One speaks of equality in affliction, but this is an infinite dissimilarity, an oscillation without any level, an equality without anything being equal. And it is not certain that in order to approach such a situation, we must turn to the vast, overwhelming upheavals produced in our time. There is a weariness from which there is no rest which consists in the fact that one can no longer interrupt what one is doing, working always more, and, in sum, for a general well-being" (IC 173/258).

46. *Without ressentiment*: I evoke a Nietzschean motif here with an eye to his meditations on cruelty and his thought of an affirmation beyond ressentiment, developed very effectively by Gilles Deleuze in *Nietzsche and Philosophy*, trans. Hugh Tomlinson (New York: Columbia University Press, 1962). The thought of a transgressive movement from within is also developed by Deleuze, though I would also point to important statements by Lacan and Lyotard on the topic of *humour*. (Lacan's remarks on a way of living in a capitalist structure are especially pertinent here: see the opening pages of *The Four Fundamental Concepts of Psychoanalysis*, volume 11 of *The Seminar of Jacques Lacan*, ed. Jacques-Alain Miller, trans. Alan Sheridan [New York: Norton, 1978].) Of course, the question of Blanchot's presence in these texts must also be pursued if we are to undertake a comparative analysis. *Without cause* comes, of course, from *King Lear*, where it is doubly affirmed by Cordelia in a crushing sentence drawn from the depths of relation to another's affliction and from love (which might well lead us back to Blanchot's own evocation of love in *The Step Not Beyond*, though it remains so furtive as to resist development).

47. To be precise, this "disarming" is like the removal of a dart: "*retirer ce trait*," Blanchot writes. The word that comes from the other afflicts the body of the one who responds.

48. "When my relation with myself makes me the absolutely Other whose presence puts the power of the Powerful radically into question, this movement

still signifies only the failure of power—not 'my' victory, still less 'my' salvation. For such a movement to begin truly to be affirmed, there must be restored—beyond this self that I have ceased to be, and within the anonymous community—the instance of a Self-Subject: no longer as a dominating and oppressing power drawn up against the other that is '*autrui*,' but as what can receive the unknown and the foreign, receive them in the justice of a true *speech*. Moreover, on the basis of this attention to affliction without which all relation falls back into the night, another possibility must intervene: the possibility that a Self outside me become not only conscious of the affliction as though this Self were in my place, but become responsible for it by recognizing in it an injustice committed against everyone—that is, it must find in this injustice the point of departure for a *common demand*" (IC 134/197). The interlocutor in this conversation goes on to speak of this last subject as the representative of a class structure and evokes the imperative of dialectical struggle.

49. "Discourse on Patience," 28.

50. The subsequent passage underscores the notion of answering for: "♦ To answer for that which escapes responsibility" [*Répondre de ce qui échappe à la responsabilité*] (SNB 123/168).

51. The passage succeeding the one we are reading underscores the incapacity of intention as regards the transgression in question:

> ♦ *If it sufficed for him to be fragile, patient, passive: if fear (the fear provoked by nothing), the ancient fear that reigns over the city, pushing the figures before it, and which passes in him like the past of his fear, the fear he does not feel, sufficed to render him still more fragile, well beyond the consciousness of fragility in which he still holds himself back; but just as the phrase, in interrupting itself, gives him only the interruption of a phrase that does not reach its end, fragile patience, in the same way, within the horizon of fear that besieges it, testifies only to a resort to fragility, even there where it maddens thought by making it fragile, unconsidered.*
> (SNB 119/163)

A subsequent passage then gives us the profoundly aleatory nature of the fall:

> ♦ *He had lost, before having attained it, that share of impassibility that would have allowed him not to be unhappy with himself, in order not to increase the general unhappiness: having fallen suddenly, by an unforeseeable fall, fortuitous and fragile, below impassibility, without ever being sure of being at one's most passive, and perhaps because there could never be a present passivity—in the present, in any present whatsoever.* (SNB 131/179)

52. It may well be that Blanchot's reference to the "negative signaling" of "*le neutre*" refers to what the word itself offers by etymology: "*ni l'un ni l'autre.*"

But if my suggestion (that this negative signaling is manifested in every respect in which *le neutre* retreats from categories of reason and grammar), then we may surmise that Blanchot is inviting us to move past the long and quite abstract expositions of the meaning of the term.

53. Denouncing the illusion (impossible to escape) of dying freely: "Thus the thought: to die freely, not in accordance with our freedom, but by passivity, abandon (an extremely passive attention), in accord with the freedom of dying. Yet dying is not only before any power, the impossible in relation to us, what we cannot assume freely nor suffer by constraint: dying, in the absence of a present, in the lack of traces it leaves, is too light for dying, for constituting a dying" (SNB 125/170).

54. "Discours sur la patience," 35.

55. "The non-familiar intimacy of thought between two men speaking who are bound by the essential establishes a distance and a proximity beyond measure. As exists perhaps between two gamblers. A non-personal intimacy from which the particularities of each person cannot be entirely excluded but which, in principle, does not take them into account. Indeed, each player may bring his particular existence into play, but as a player he is without particularity, introduced by the game into anonymity and reduced to the abstract truth of the infinite risk that takes away from him all determined social reality: without history, without anecdote, himself an unknown through this relation with the unknown wherein he affirms himself, and each time asking (as though it were an implicit rule) that all that is known of him be forgotten, or at least not brought into the game" (IC 217/322). Blanchot goes on to evoke the possibility of such relations "being endured over a lifetime."

56. See SNB 65/92: "A word chosen by anguish."

57. One is tempted to pause here and consider the enormity of what is proposed to thought in this passage. It is easy enough, of course, to conceive of a community of fear (using a sense of the term "community" that is profoundly foreign to the one sought by Blanchot). Let us merely recall Hobbes's account of the role of fear for the constitution of the modern political subject (recalling the work of Roberto Esposito) and the mobilization of fear in contemporary Western democracies. I will remain, on this occasion, within the relatively spare terms of *The Step Not Beyond*, for the questions there are already formidable. I will be taking the larger questions up in a separate project.

58. Of the word "God," Blanchot writes in the next passage: "And yet, like fear, like madness, it disappears, be this as the messenger of another language for which such a disappearance could not take the place of a beginning" (SNB 60/85).

59. "Phoronomy" is a term used by Derrida in "*Pas*" to stress that the "spaces" of Blanchot's fiction (the hotel rooms, for example, or the rooms of the conversations we have read) must be thought *from* the movement of "*pas*."

60. Blanchot, SHBR, 383.

61. "Rather than dialogue, we should name it plural speech. Plural speech, inasmuch as in its simplicity it is the search for an affirmation that, though escaping all negation, neither unifies nor allows itself to be unified, always referring to a difference always more tempted to defer. This is a speech that is essentially non-dialectical; it says the absolutely other that can never be reduced to the same or take a place in the whole. . . . Hence, it seems to me, the interlocutors' strange situation: they are bound by the essential yet they are not together since, properly speaking, where they are no whole is possible. . . . Being the bearers of a speech that speaks in view of this unique affirmation that exceeds all unity, they do not oppose one another, nor are they in any way distinguishable as to what they have to say; and yet the redoubling of affirmation, its reflection, differentiates this affirmation always more profoundly. . . . Hence an understanding that, growing unceasingly more profound, is nonetheless without accord, founded upon a hiatus that must not allow itself to be filled or even denounced" (IC 215/319–320). I have cited at length, but in fact the entire concluding section of Blanchot's essay on Bataille is pertinent to the passage we are reading from *The Step Not Beyond* by reason of its insistence on repetition over a dialectically organized exchange. It approaches its conclusion with the words, "I will not push further our understanding of such an intense proposition," having compared such speaking (as we saw) to a game of dice. *The Step Not Beyond* would appear to be moving at the extreme point reached in this meditation.

62. *The Writing of the Disaster*, 116/179.

63. *Michel Foucault as I Imagine Him*, in *Foucault/Blanchot*, trans. Jeffrey Mehlman and Brian Massumi (Zone, New York, 1987), 63–64.

64. The phrase appears in Blanchot's important essay on friendship in the volume by that name (*Friendship*, trans. Elizabeth Rottenberg [Stanford, Calif.: Stanford University Press, 1997] 289; *L'amitié* [Paris: Gallimard, 1971], 326), and again in *The Step Not Beyond* (53/76). For the question of need, which could well bear extensive treatment (communicating, as it does, with Heidegger's notion of usage, *der Brauch*, though opening the latter to the question of *Mitsein*), we might cite two important fragments: "♦ *The desire to encounter them was as familiar to him as the silence of snow on the rooftops. But, by himself, he could not keep the desire alive*" (SNB 20/33); "♦ *What frightened us was that they had such a need of us, need of our ignorance, our disappearance, our ardent complicity, that of a dead thing signaling to them and attracting them*" (SNB 84/116). As we have seen, Blanchot's discussion of "the principle of insufficiency" in *The Unavowable Community* points firmly to the need in question. Contestation requires the other and opens onto community.

65. A long passage on *le neutre* in *The Step Not Beyond* appearing only ten pages before might well be pertinent here: "*Le neutre*, in the singular, names

something that escapes nomination, but without a lot of noise, without even the noisy bustle of the enigma. We call it, modestly, inconsiderately, the thing. The thing: because, from all evidence, things belong to another order and because things are what are most familiar to us, making us live in an environment of things, yet without their being transparent. . . . The thing, like *il*, like *le neutre* or the outside, indicates a plurality that has the trait of singularizing itself and the fault of appearing to repose in the indeterminate. That the Thing should have a relation to *le Neutre* . . ." (SNB 73/102). I hesitate to expound at greater length on this motif, given how furtive it is in the text and how many references crowd to mind (I think immediately of Heidegger and Lacan). Clearly, however, it preoccupied Jacques Derrida, who entitled three years of his seminar for Yale with this term (in "*Pas*," we read of the attempt to "approach the coming of a *viens* that is a narrative: there is the impossible, the unpresentable obscenity that will no longer let us go, like the Thing which, as he says somewhere, 'remembers us'" (*Parages*, 74).

66. One may well recall here the "knocking" that Lacan attributes to comparable words (the insistence of a comparable "real"?) in his analysis of Freud's presentation of the dream of the burning child in his *Four Fundamental Concepts of Psychoanalysis*. I take this up in *Infant Figures*, (Stanford, Calif.: Stanford University Press, 2000), 105.

67. The connection seems particularly compelling in that Bacon's canvases frequently contain a haunting presence that hovers or alights near the principle figure. A figure of a pope at the Aberdeen Art Museum (to take a local example among many) shows an undefined presence on the edge of a kind of balustrade before the seated figure.

68. "♦ If, by a reduction or a preliminary dissidence, we could separate death and dying, speech and writing, we would obtain, be this at great expense and great pains, a kind of theoretical calm, a theoretical happiness, that calm and happiness that we accord, in the depths of their happy tomb, to the great dead—the dead are always momentarily great—who are also, and par excellence, the imposing figures or the supporting pillars of theory" (SNB 92/127). This passage continues in its second paragraph with a reference to speech's capacity for an artful weakness: "all the more itself the more it impedes itself, held back to the point of stammering. . . . In this way, one would say, still living and even failing in order to be as close as possible to life, which never shines more brilliantly than at the moment of losing itself" (SNB 92–93/128). The pairing of majesty with stammering mirrors in an obscure manner the fate of the figure we are following in the narrative.

69. *Friendship*, 291/329.

70. What I will draw from this essay might also be read in relation to the words on hope that Blanchot addressed to Bataille in the letter cited earlier. Here are Blanchot's words: "I believe that we know it: that things at bottom

offer no escape—I see nothing that would turn me aside from saying this with you. I would only add that this "without exit" [*sans issue*] can only be affirmed in and through the necessity of always seeking an escape, though the inexorable decision of never renouncing the effort to find one. These last days, I have been remembering Robert Antelme's book (the narrative of his time in concentration) and I recalled, almost with fright, the kind of hope that never ceased to accompany him in the absolute absence of hope, and that rendered sacred, for him and for his companions, the last human needs: a hope that appears to me as terrible, perhaps atrocious, a hope that is nonetheless without hope." This motif returns in a letter written a year and a half later to Bataille: "René Char has written me a very somber letter, evoking the universal disaster. It is true, but what is terrible is not the failure [*défaillance*], it is the hope that nevertheless keeps us standing. I would add that friendship is the truth of the disaster" (*Choix de lettres*, 595).

Char's correspondence with Blanchot, as Leslie Hill reminds us (*Maurice Blanchot and Fragmentary Writing*, 23), also provides the source for an important reference to the motif of disappointment, which appears at the end of "The Fragment Word," in *The Infinite Conversation:* "Thus, through fragmentary writing, the return of the hesperic accord is announced. It is a time of decline, but a decline of ascendancy, pure detour in its strangeness: that which, making it possible to go from disappointment to disappointment [*de déception en déception*] leads from courage to courage" (IC 307–310/455). "Courage," as we see, could be another "young name."

71. "(*il*) the barred opening: this was what was indicated by this name that was barely a word and that designated it/him so eminently in designating no one and what is more by an indirect indication that seemed nevertheless to relate more and more indirectly to this precise, determinate-indeterminate point, the void of a universe" (SNB 20/32).

Compare this passage, two pages earlier: "♦ A word twice word, that is to say, mute; this word softly lightened by what strikes it with mutism would be a word too many that would not resound. (*il*) has that mattness, even though one might represent it, alternatively, and with equal awkwardness, either as a massive door, shut off by the bolts that close it, and that anyone at all could get around in order to reach the infinite space to which it opens access while simulating its prohibition, or as who knows what transparency, what void of the universe where everything—and every word—could disappear, if the transparency were not the most impassible of crossings" (SNB 18–19/30).

72. We return, of course, to the question of the game and the "intense proposition" with which Blanchot concluded his meditation on Bataille.

73. "When speech becomes prophetic, it is not the future that is given, it is the present that is taken away, and with it any possibility of a firm, stable, and

lasting presence. Even the eternal City and the indestructible Temple are suddenly—incredibly—destroyed. It is once again like the desert, and speech also is desert-like, this voice that needs the desert to cry out and that endlessly awakens in us the terror, understanding, and memory of the desert." (*The Book to Come*, trans. Charlotte Mandell [Stanford, Calif.: Stanford University Press, 2003], 79; *Le livre à venir* [Paris: Gallimard, 1959], 117–118). The evocations of the desert—the outside—in this text are particularly powerful.

74. The phrase is drawn from "Discours sur la patience," where it figures twice. I have already cited the conclusion of the passage on Bartleby, where these men are described as "immobile, walking with an equal and slow step." It recurs in a fragment in which "the interruption of the incessant" in fragmentary writing opens a space where living/dying is confused with the disaster of a time without present that is borne in waiting: "Hence the fact that the destroyed men (destroyed without destruction) are as though without appearance, invisible even when one sees them; if they speak it is by the voice of others, a voice always other that in some sense accuses them, brings them into question, obliging them to answer for a silent affliction that they bear without consciousness" (34).

75. Note that a figure for fear would not be the same thing as this powerful image of what effectively prohibits any *Bild* in that pure relation to the neutral that is fear. A figure for fear would be something of the order of an "*eidolon*," the possible object of an idolatry. (Is there, in the "interdiction of dying," also a *Bildverbot?*)

76. ♦ *"Don't forget that we are not to do anything to make them come." – "And nothing that would make them not come."—"Not seek them."—"Not flee them."— "That is too symmetrical: you can, without searching for them, without fleeing them, still direct your will so that the chances of encounter are not of your making: avoid them so that the inevitable remains obscure."—"There is not a will more general than my will that should make me worry about substituting myself for it; it is like a necessity, attracting or repelling, but always attracting and whose draw I would be given to recognize, without my own doing and even without waiting."—"An attraction by which, holding us in the mystery of the illusion, we also think we can recognize them, name them, keep them at a distance under the brilliance of the name, and thus, embellishing it, facilitate the approach."—Always close, too close for them to be near us."—"And nevertheless separated solely by the movement of their coming."—"They are coming."— "They are not coming"* (SNB 111/152–153).

77. The passages Blanchot devotes to Kafka's errancy in the desert (on "the other shore") and to his effort to approach its "truth" are surely a crucial precedent for the appearance of the image of the desert in *The Step Not Beyond*. See, in particular, SL 70–71/78–80. Also pertinent are the reflections on idolatry: 80–83/93–98.

78. "♦ To survive: not to live, or, not living, to maintain oneself, without life, in a state of pure supplement, a movement of supplementation in relation to life, but rather to arrest dying, an arrest that does not arrest, making it, on the contrary, *last*. "*Speak on the edge* [l'arrête]—*the line of instability—of speech*." *As though he* [il] *attended the exhaustion of dying: as though night, having started too early, at the earliest time of day, doubted it would ever reach night*" (SNB 135/184). For the extreme instability of these words, "*arrêt*," "*arrêter*," and "*arête*," see the accompanying note by Lycette Nelson (SNB 139).

79. On the death camps, see SNB 96–97/133; on suicide, SNB 98/135; on sickness or old age, SNB 98/136; For a comparison with the obscenity of sexuality, see SNB 99/137.

80. Though the reference would seem at best faint here, it might be noted that the prayer of benediction, drawn from Numbers 6:24–26 concludes: "May Yahweh lift his face onto you and give you peace."

81. "♦ *He caught himself—a melancholic surprise—hoping, fearing: at the limit of these two words*" (SNB 18/29).

FINAL NOTE: THROUGH THE DOUBLE IMPERATIVE

1. David Patterson, in *Hebrew Language and Jewish Thought* (London: Routledge Curzon, 2005), 70, is especially eager to find an opposition within a word that brings together "desert" and "speech" (the "speaking being" is *medaber*). Blanchot, from the ground of his meditation on the prophetic word, and with the notion of "going out" he draws from Levinas, moves toward a far more profound understanding of the relation given by the Hebrew language.

2. The appearance of this passage in "Reflections on Hell" is all the more complex for the fact that it is citing and developing lines from *Le dernier homme* (Paris: Gallimard, 1957), 28. I will have to return to this instance of citation on another occasion.

3. "*Le désert croît*" is the phrase used in the French translation by Aloys Becker and Gérard Granel (Paris: Presses Universitaires de France, 1973), 46–47. It is likely, however, that Blanchot was using the German original, which gives *Verwüstung* (a motif pursued by Leslie Hill in *Maurice Blanchot and Fragmentary Writing* [London: Continuum, 2012], 37–50).

4. Of course, I do not question his appeal to the necessity of acting in relation to a "common demand"; the difficulty comes in the words of the interlocutor, who refers to "class consciousness, for example" (IC 134/197).

The passage on Hegel in "Reflections on Hell" is worth citing again in its entirety, particularly in light of the connection that appears with the later discussion in *The Writing of the Disaster*, where Blanchot takes up the theme of the "impossible necessary death" (shortly before the treatment of the death of the *infans*; WD 67/111). The passage begins by evoking the wall of China ("a defense against the desert"), and then reiterating that "it is not Camus, but Marx . . . it is not Camus but Lenin" who see in the man stripped by oppression of resistance to oppression a kind of dead weight. He continues:

> And Hegel, in his turn, cannot, without a leap that remains the enigma of enigmas, pass from the primordial Yes/No—from the movement that we have called "error," a movement of infinite migration where one is no more than errant—to the force of mediation and the progression of the so-called real dialectic (supposing, in Hegel's case, that it is real, and not marked by a double idealism that is at the same time speculative and empiricist). These are, perhaps—but not everything has been said when the word "dialectic" is pronounced—the conditions without which there would be no world, and that the one struggling to make the world possible cannot lose sight of. In a certain sense, then, Sisyphus must be killed; he is that part of us we must deny if we want to begin, become at least slaves, engage in revolt. Killing, here, would be the means of ceasing to kill, the means of opening a path to a world in which, if one does not escape death, one endeavours at least to submit it to a measure whose lack one rejects, arrests, and condemns. But the problem remains: how can one make disappear what has disappearance as its essence? (IC 181/271)

The last question is the one Blanchot explored in relation to the theme of the death of the *infans*.

5. I recall my earlier discussion of the double solution as it is articulated by Blanchot in his letter to Bataille (see Chapter 3, note 17).

6. The essay in *The Infinite Conversation* from which I have quoted appears to end with this point. Having evoked the theme of responding to the impossible, we read the following: "This response, this speech that begins by responding and that in this beginning says over again the question that comes to it from the Unknown and the Stranger—here is what lies at the basis of the responsibility that is subsequently expressed in the hard language of exigency: one must speak" (IC 65/92–93).

7. This would appear to be the ground of the friendship claimed posthumously with Foucault: "Friendship was perhaps promised to Foucault as a posthumous gift, beyond passions, beyond problems of thought, beyond the dangers of life that he experienced more for others than for himself." In *Foucault/Blanchot*, trans. Jeffrey Mehlman (New York: Zone Books, 1990), 109; *Michel Foucault tel que je l'imagine* (Montpellier: Fata Morgana, 1986), 64.

8. I adapt from memory a phrase from Edmund Jabès.

9. I draw, here, from the chapter title of a manuscript by Edith Doron, "Of Things and Thresholds: Exilic Education, Hospitality and the Practice of

Community in the Children's Museum." My understanding of hospitality has been profoundly shaped by the important work underway in this and subsequent work by her.

APPENDIX: BLANCHOT IN *THE INTERNATIONAL REVIEW*

1. This stunning essay is collected in *L'Amitié* (Paris: Gallimard, 1971), 130–131 and available in *Political Writings*, trans. Zakir Paul (New York: Fordham University Press, 2010), 7.

2. Cited in *Blanchot: Partenaire invisible* (Seyssel: Champ Vallon, 1998), 378.

3. IC 264–271/394–404; the essay is also available in *The Blanchot Reader*, ed. Michael Holland (Oxford: Blackwell, 1995), 134–181.

4. I will return to the place of Heidegger's thinking in these reflections as I proceed, but I would note that this motif of a "change of times" bears a strong Heideggerian inflection, particularly as Blanchot evokes the nature of the obscure awareness of this turning. It is interesting to note, however, how circumspect Blanchot is in citing Heidegger at this juncture, and how sharp his criticism has become: "Certainly, technics is dangerous, but less dangerous than 'the genius of place.' There is perhaps something to be said against the paganism in which anti-Christianity seeks to shelter itself—Heideggerian paganism, the poetic paganism of rootedness. Truth is nomad" (PW 64/189).

5. Cited by Anna Panicali, *Lignes* 11 (Paris: Lignes, 2005), 168.

6. I would prefer "whole" to "totality," here, were it not for Blanchot's attempt to distinguish "the whole" and "what is beyond the whole." I am reminded in this instance of lines from Gérard Granel's *De l'université* (Mauzevin: Trans-Europ-Repress, 1982), 65: "The world is certainly an existential for Dasein, and certainly a figure of the whole for it, but it is not Dasein's object: it is its pragma. The genre of the whole involved here is comparable only to that which forms for each individual that inevitably missed totality they call their "life," and to whose lack they must try to be adequate." I want to suggest that it is a comparable notion of the whole (or totality) that Blanchot evokes in speaking of "saying the world," inasmuch as the latter phrase must embrace more than the totality of "everything that takes place in the world." There is no doubt that Blanchot seeks a very "worldly" form of literary saying; there is a strong ethico-political inflection to this meditation. The literary responsibility Blanchot seeks to articulate, however, involves more than a *representation* of intraworldly matters and touches on "the worldhood of the world," as Heidegger would put it.

My reference to Heidegger may seem heavy-handed in this context. However, Blanchot's initial statement concerning the task of the review, with its allusion to a "change in times" that requires both historical and "historial" levels of reflection, already strongly prepares this reference. I would add that I do not mean to contain Blanchot with this reference; Blanchot's notion of "essential discontinuity" points toward dimensions of experience that exceed what Heidegger entertained, even with his notion of "disorder" (*Unfug*).

7. I pursue this issue as it appears in Heidegger, Benjamin, and Blanchot in *Language and Relation* (Stanford, Calif.: Stanford University Press, 1996), and in the first chapter of the present volume with respect to the problem of the relation between ethical saying and justice in Levinas's thought. *Totality and Infinity* was originally published with Martinus Nijhoff in 1961. I do not want to argue for an immediate connection between Blanchot's understanding of the writer's act of "saying the world" and Levinas's understanding of a commensurate act of saying in the ethical relation. It seems clear that Blanchot is using the term "world" in a manner that bears a stronger sociopolitical inflection. I am struck, though, by the strength of the phrase in Blanchot's thinking for the *Review* and cannot help but wonder at the temporal coincidence. Along the same lines, I cannot help but wonder whether Blanchot's recourse to the notion of "justice" in his working papers is in some way shaped by Levinas's own usage of the term in this period. Unfortunately, Blanchot gives no definition of either "truth" or "justice" in these papers, beyond a vague allusion to dialectical truth and an insistence that the writer's saying must be *concrete*.

8. The lines that continue this citation suggest just how radical Blanchot's thinking of fragmentation is becoming: "In this sense, all literature is a fragment, whether brief or infinite, on the condition that it designate a space of language where each moment takes on its meaning and its function by making all others indeterminate or else (this is the other side) where some affirmation that is not reducible to any unifying process is at work" (PW 63/188).

9. This assertion is illustrated with remarks on the writings of Uwe Johnson, literary works that communicate the very impossibility of saying the divisions they must embody. The "strangeness" of Berlin is rendered in "the very hiatus he had to maintain, with a somber and unrelenting rigour, between reality and the literary grasp of the meaning of that reality" (PW 75).

10. The only footnote in Blanchot's text reads as follows: "The wall pretended to substitute the sociological truth of the situation, the factual state, for the more profound truth of this situation, which one might call, with considerable simplification, dialectical" (PW 75). The body of the text goes on to state that the importance and "scandal" of the wall in its "concrete oppression" inheres in its abstraction and in the way it reminds us that abstraction does not derive from a faulty way of thinking or an impoverished use of language, but is rather "our world, the one in which we live and in which we think on a daily basis."

11. From Benjamin's Konvolut N of the Arcades Project (cited and discussed in *Language and Relation*, 213).

INDEX

Abraham, 42
Adorno, Theodor, 66
Agamben, Giorgio, 25, 46, 255n, 261n, 262n
Antelme, Robert, 9, 35, 38, 46–54, 67, 73, 115, 167, 168, 225, 260n, 272n, 291n

Bachman, Rabbi Andy, 260n
Bachmann, Ingeborg, 235
Bacon, Francis, 197, 209, 291n
Badiou, Alain, 253n
Baki, Burhanuddin, 278n
Balibar, Etienne, 265n
Barthes, Roland, 5, 235
Bartleby, 70, 71, 169, 291n
Bataille, Georges, 3, 5, 8, 12, 65, 73, 78–80, 83, 85, 129, 144, 145, 146, 149, 152, 154–57, 161, 163, 176, 181, 186, 202, 230, 232, 251n, 264n, 266n, 267n, 272n, 285n, 286n, 291n, 295n
Benjamin, Walter, 18, 21, 70, 128, 138, 243, 254n, 297n
Bident, Christophe, 11, 264n, 267n, 274n, 278n
Bonnefoy, Yves, 204
Buber, Martin, 22

Calvino, Italo, 235
Camus, Albert, 37, 89, 113, 226, 227–29, 234, 295n
Celan, Paul, 27, 211, 255n, 272n
Chapsal, Madeleine, 66, 265n
Char, René, 269n
Cools, Arthur, 266n
Crowley, Martin, 260n

David, Catherine, 1, 4, 7, 69, 153, 230, 249n
Davis, Thomas S., 270n
de Gaulle, Charles, 67, 68, 236
de Man, Paul, 5
Deleuze, Gilles, 5, 287n
Derrida, Jacques, 5, 6, 26, 28, 29, 89, 111–13, 119, 138, 251n, 254n, 256n, 257n, 263n, 270n, 271n, 275n, 277n, 278n, 282n, 283n, 289n
des Forêts, Louis-René, 235
Descartes, René, 61
Doron, Edith, 295n

Enzensberger, Hans Magnus, 235
Esposito, Roberto, 289n
Eurydice, 37, 114, 132

ffrench, Patrick, 267n
Foucault, Michel, 5, 6, 191, 273n, 290n, 295n
Freud, Sigmund, 128, 165, 291n
Fuentes, Carlos, 235

Genet, Jean, 265n
Goethe, Johann Wolfgang von, 119
Gohara, Kai, 250n
Granel, Gérard, 9, 84, 251n, 266n, 296n
Grass, Günter, 235

Hanson, Susan, 48
Hart, Kevin, 251n, 252n, 261n
Haver, William, 265n
Hegel, Georg Wilhelm Friedrich, 37, 42, 112, 119, 128, 180, 186, 228, 272n, 294n, 295n
Heidegger, Martin, 3, 5, 8, 25, 36, 38, 41, 68, 70, 84, 85, 92, 107, 116, 128, 138, 146, 147, 148, 164, 166, 186, 204, 242, 246, 250n, 252n, 253n, 259n, 260n, 266n, 273n, 278n, 281n, 290n, 291n, 296n
Heschel, Abraham Joshua, 256n
Hewson, Mark, 250n
Hill, Leslie, 11, 102, 126, 250n, 270n, 273n, 276n, 294n
Hobbes, Thomas, 289n
Hölderlin, Friedrich, 74, 115, 117, 119, 204, 243
Holland, Michael, 11, 250n, 252n, 265n

Iyer, Lars, 281n

Jabès, Edmund, 295n
Jacob, 22, 42, 44
Jenny, Laurent, 264n

Job, 23
Johnson, Uwe, 235, 297n
Joris, Pierre, 281n
Jünger, Ernst, 250n

Kafka, Franz, 59, 137, 212, 252n, 263n, 276n, 291n
Kaliayev, Ivan, 37, 229
Kofman, Sarah, 49, 262n
Kojève, Alexandre, 5
Kolakowski, Leszek, 235, 240

Lacan, Jacques, 5, 6, 287n, 291n
Lacoue-Labarthe, Philippe, 251n, 270–71n
Langer, Lawrence, 262n
Lassalle, Ferdinand, 270n
Leiris, Michel, 235
Lenin, Vladimir Ilyich, 295n
Levi, Primo, 262n
Levinas, Emmanuel, 4, 9, 12, 17–33, 34, 35, 36, 40, 41, 43, 46, 50, 54, 79, 84, 127, 129, 145, 148, 151, 168, 234, 244, 253n, 254n, 255n, 256n, 257n, 258n, 260n, 276n, 282n, 286n, 294n, 297n
Lionetti, Francesco, 235
Liska, Vivian, 266n
Llewelyn, John, 257n
Lyotard, Jean-François, 9, 287n

MacClaughlan, Ian, 250n
Mallarmé, Stéphane, 135, 138, 253n, 267n, 277n
Malraux, André, 120
Marx, Karl, 228, 241, 295n
Mascolo, Dionys, 66, 235, 237, 264n
Moravia, Alberto, 235
Murdoch, Iris, 235

Nancy, Jean-Luc, 144–45, 253n, 279–80n, 281n, 285n
Napoleon, 272n
Nelson, Lycette, 126, 249n, 250n, 294n
Nietzsche, Friedrich Wilhelm, 4, 5, 182, 186, 187, 227, 267n, 278n, 287n

Oedipus, 69, 74, 263n, 264n
Orpheus, 37, 114, 132, 226, 229

Panicali, Anna, 296n
Pasolini, Pier Paolo, 235
Pasternak, Boris, 40, 41
Patterson, David, 294n

Riemann, Georg Friedrich Bernhard, 98, 107
Robbins, Jill, 254n
Rosenzweig, Franz, 44

Sade, Donatian Alphonse François de, 285n
Saint John of the Cross, 284n
Sartre, Jean-Paul, 1, 39, 66, 93, 236, 237, 238, 239, 240, 247
Sisyphus, 226, 227, 230
Sophocles, 119

Todorov, Tzvetan, 280n

Vittorini, Elio, 235

Walser, Martin, 235
Wittgenstein, Ludwig, 277n

Zakir, Paul, 249n
Zarader, Marlène, 278n
Zummer, Tom, ix

www.ingramcontent.com/pod-product-compliance
Lightning Source LLC
Chambersburg PA
CBHW031235290426
44109CB00012B/298